SLEEPY PRINCESS
IN THE DEMON CASTLE

♦ ♦ ♦ ♦ ♦ ♦

D1290099

4

Story & Art by
KAGIJI KUMANOMATA

NIGHTS

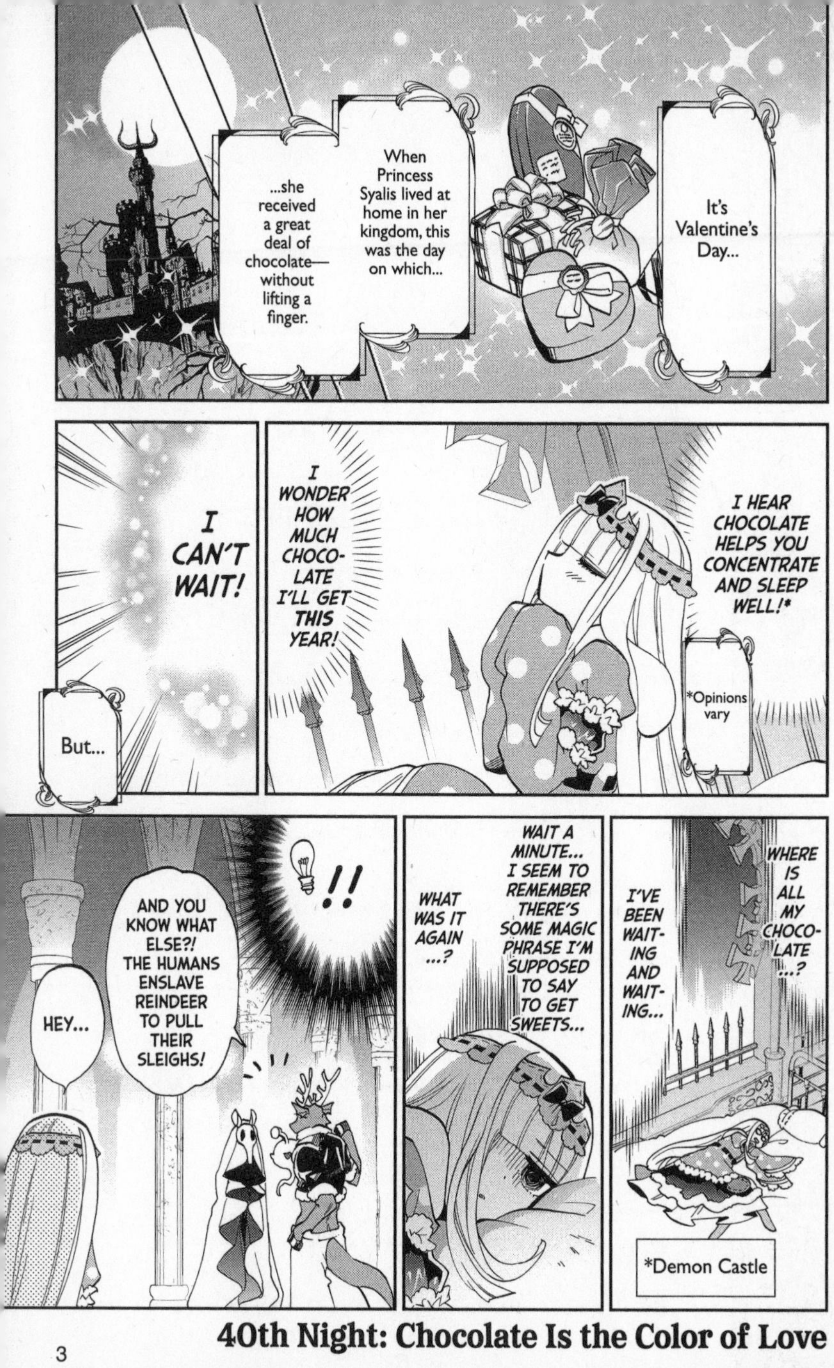
It's Valentine's Day...
When Princess Syalis lived at home in her kingdom, this was the day on which...
...she received a great deal of chocolate—without lifting a finger.
I HEAR CHOCOLATE HELPS YOU CONCENTRATE AND SLEEP WELL!*
*Opinions vary
I WONDER HOW MUCH CHOCOLATE I'LL GET THIS YEAR!
I CAN'T WAIT!
But...
WHERE IS ALL MY CHOCOLATE ...?
I'VE BEEN WAITING AND WAITING...
*Demon Castle
WAIT A MINUTE... I SEEM TO REMEMBER THERE'S SOME MAGIC PHRASE I'M SUPPOSED TO SAY TO GET SWEETS...
WHAT WAS IT AGAIN ...?
!!
AND YOU KNOW WHAT ELSE?! THE HUMANS ENSLAVE REINDEER TO PULL THEIR SLEIGHS!
HEY...

40th Night: Chocolate Is the Color of Love

40th Night: Chocolate Is the Color of Love

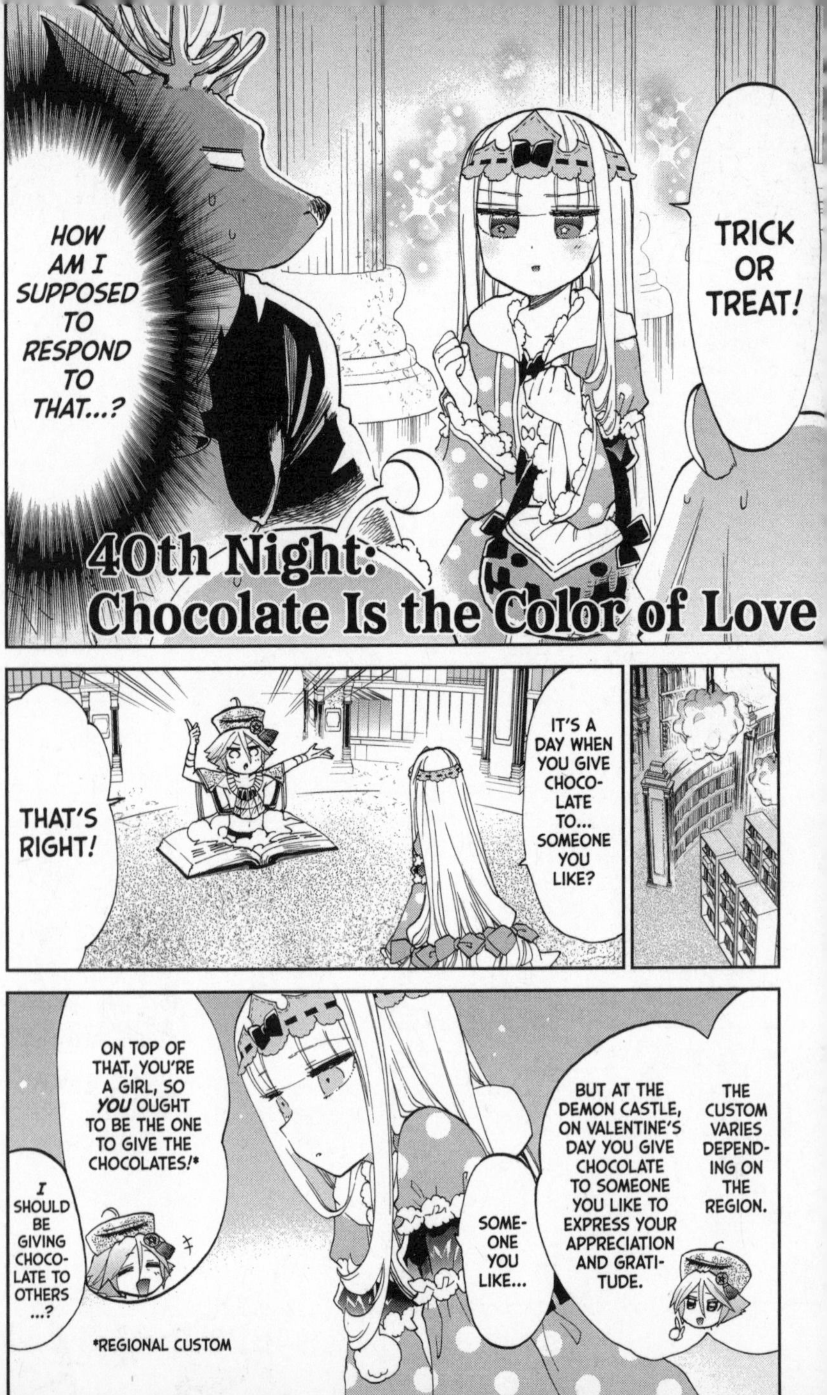
TRICK OR TREAT!
HOW AM I SUPPOSED TO RESPOND TO THAT...?
40th Night: Chocolate Is the Color of Love
IT'S A DAY WHEN YOU GIVE CHOCO-LATE TO... SOMEONE YOU LIKE?
THAT'S RIGHT!
THE CUSTOM VARIES DEPEND-ING ON THE REGION.
BUT AT THE DEMON CASTLE, ON VALENTINE'S DAY YOU GIVE CHOCOLATE TO SOMEONE YOU LIKE TO EXPRESS YOUR APPRECIATION AND GRATI-TUDE.
SOME-ONE YOU LIKE...
ON TOP OF THAT, YOU'RE A GIRL, SO *YOU* OUGHT TO BE THE ONE TO GIVE THE CHOCOLATES!*
I SHOULD BE GIVING CHOCO-LATE TO OTHERS ...?
*REGIONAL CUSTOM

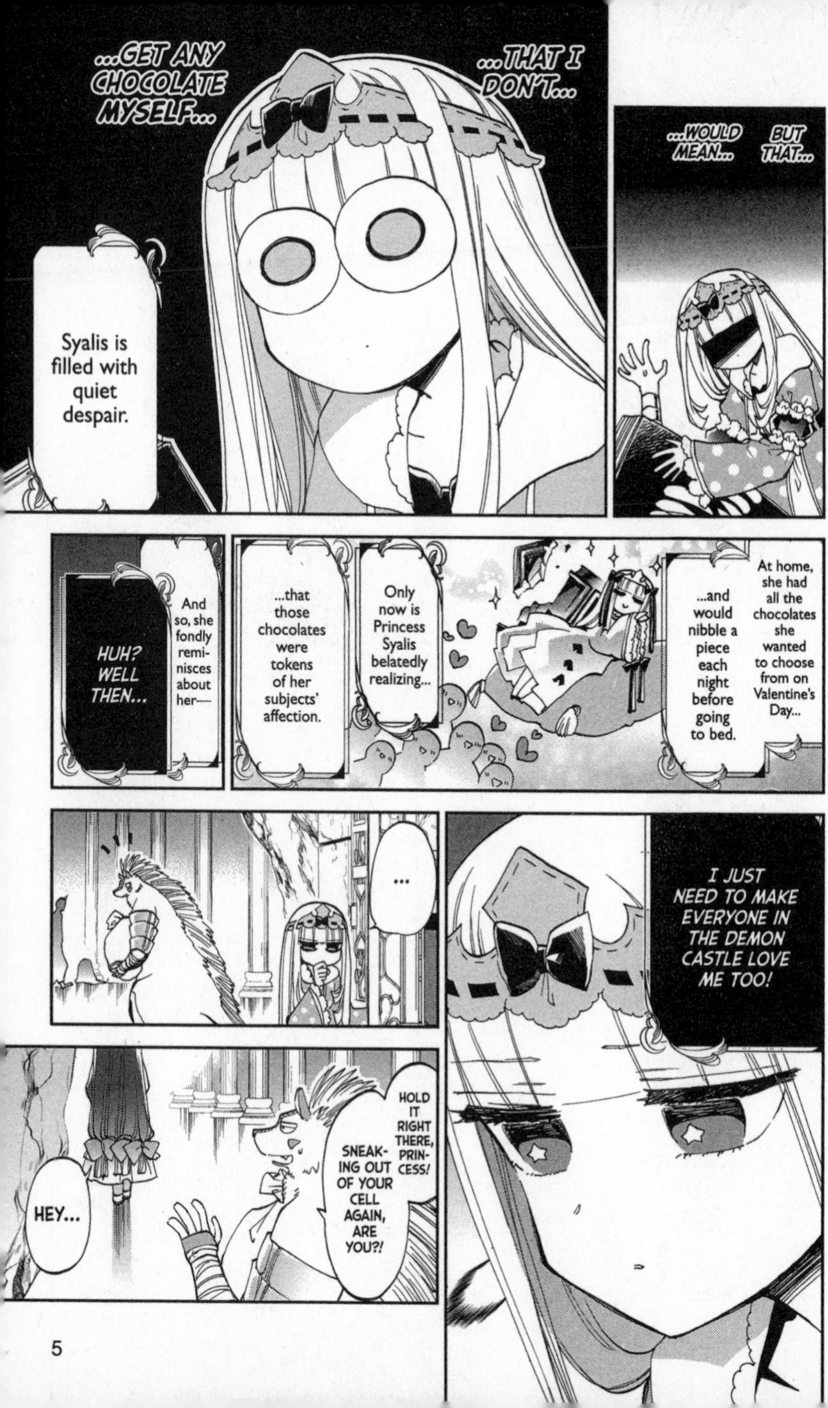
BUT THAT...
...WOULD MEAN...
...THAT I DON'T...
...GET ANY CHOCOLATE MYSELF...
Syalis is filled with quiet despair.
At home, she had all the chocolates she wanted to choose from on Valentine's Day...
...and would nibble a piece each night before going to bed.
Only now is Princess Syalis belatedly realizing...
...that those chocolates were tokens of her subjects' affection.
And so, she fondly reminisces about her—
HUH? WELL THEN...
I JUST NEED TO MAKE EVERYONE IN THE DEMON CASTLE LOVE ME TOO!
...
HOLD IT RIGHT THERE, PRINCESS!
SNEAKING OUT OF YOUR CELL AGAIN, ARE YOU?!
HEY...

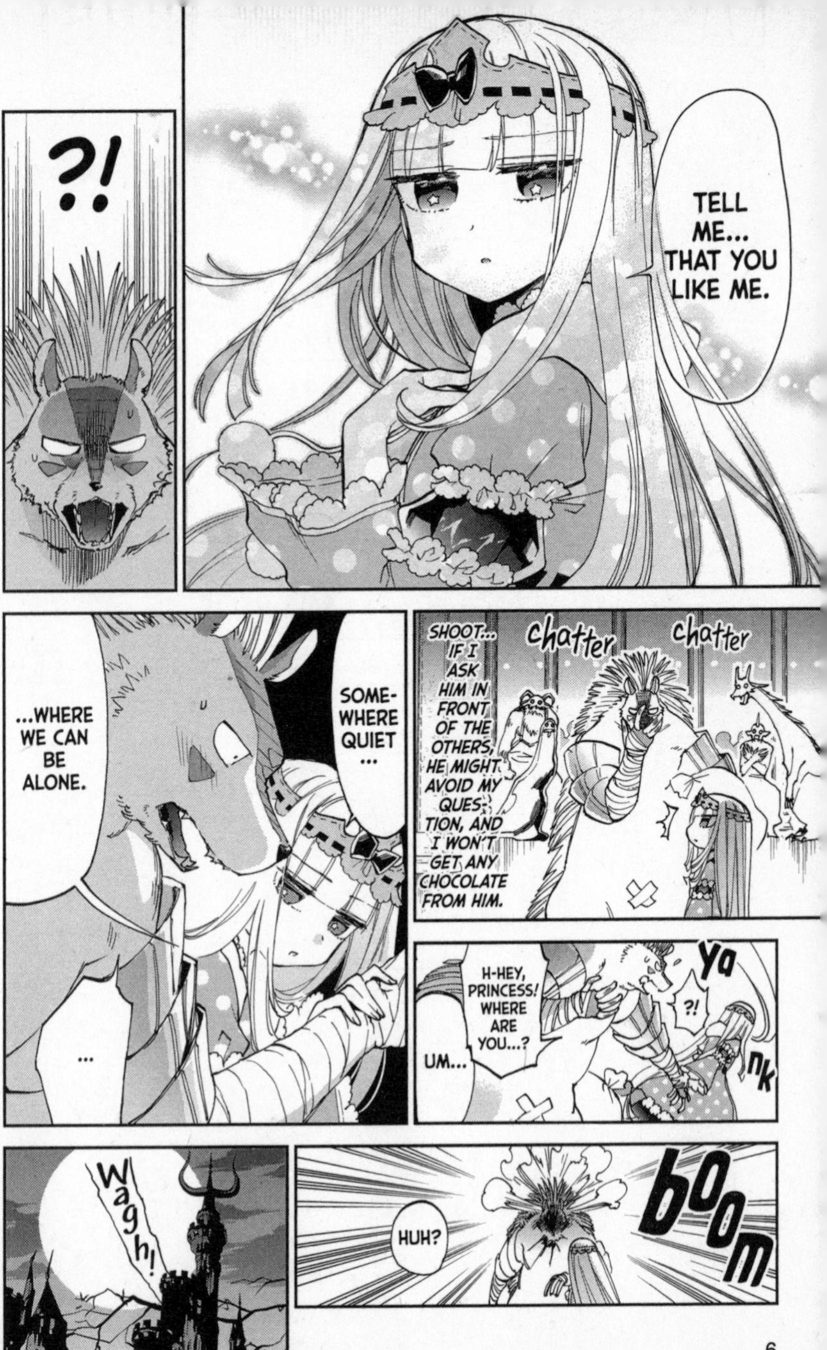
TELL ME... THAT YOU LIKE ME.
?!
chatter
chatter
SHOOT... IF I ASK HIM IN FRONT OF THE OTHERS, HE MIGHT AVOID MY QUES-TION, AND I WON'T GET ANY CHOCOLATE FROM HIM.
ya
?!
H-HEY, PRINCESS! WHERE ARE YOU...?
nk
UM...
SOME-WHERE QUIET...
...WHERE WE CAN BE ALONE.
...
boom
HUH?
Wagh!

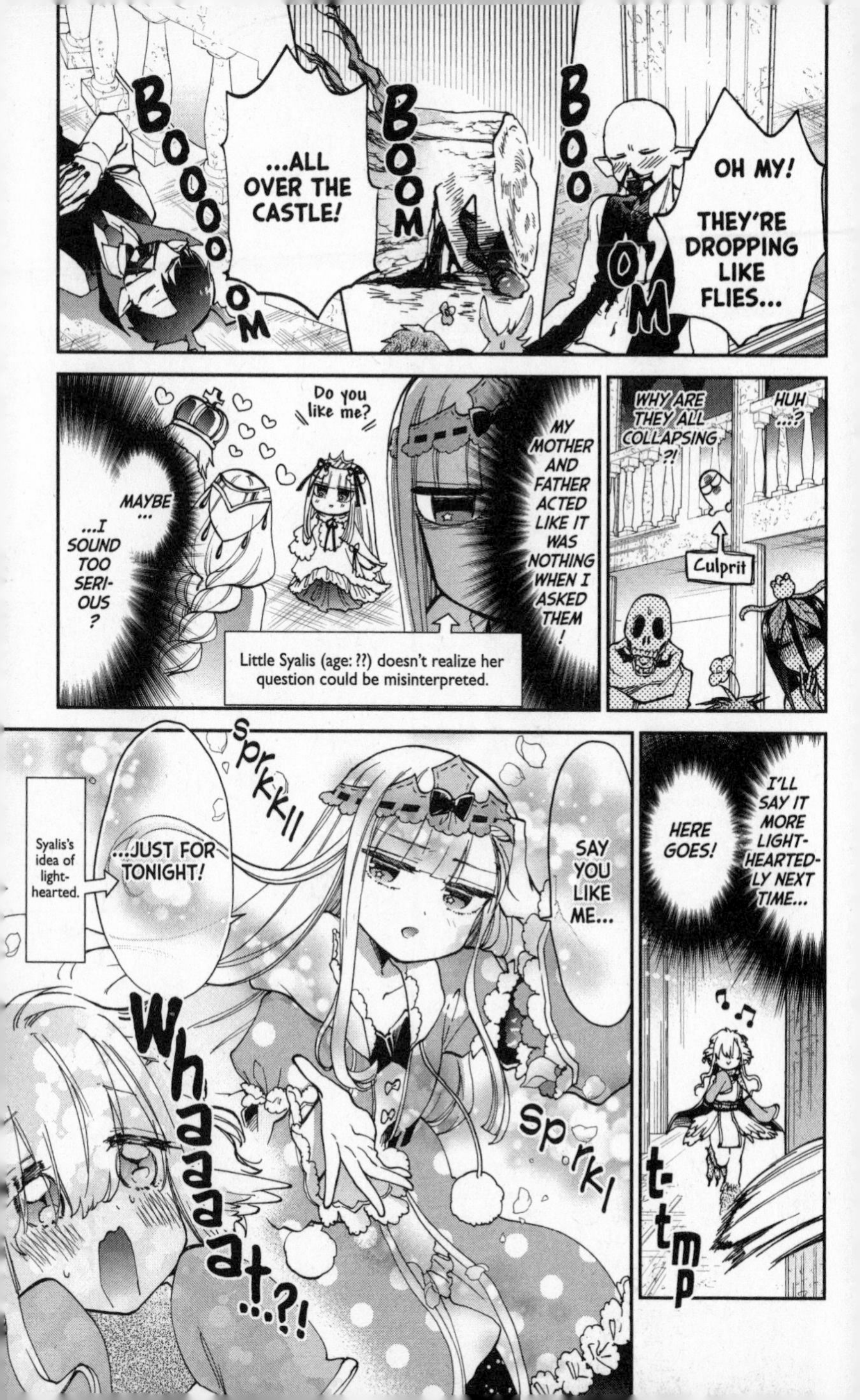
OH MY!
THEY'RE DROPPING LIKE FLIES...
BOOOM
BOOM
...ALL OVER THE CASTLE!
BOOOOOOM
HUH...?
WHY ARE THEY ALL COLLAPSING?!
Culprit
MY MOTHER AND FATHER ACTED LIKE IT WAS NOTHING WHEN I ASKED THEM!
Do you like me?
MAYBE...
...I SOUND TOO SERI-OUS?
Little Syalis (age: ??) doesn't realize her question could be misinterpreted.
I'LL SAY IT MORE LIGHT-HEARTED-LY NEXT TIME...
HERE GOES!
t-tmp
sprkkll
SAY YOU LIKE ME...
...JUST FOR TONIGHT!
Syalis's idea of light-hearted.
sprkl
Whaaaat..?!

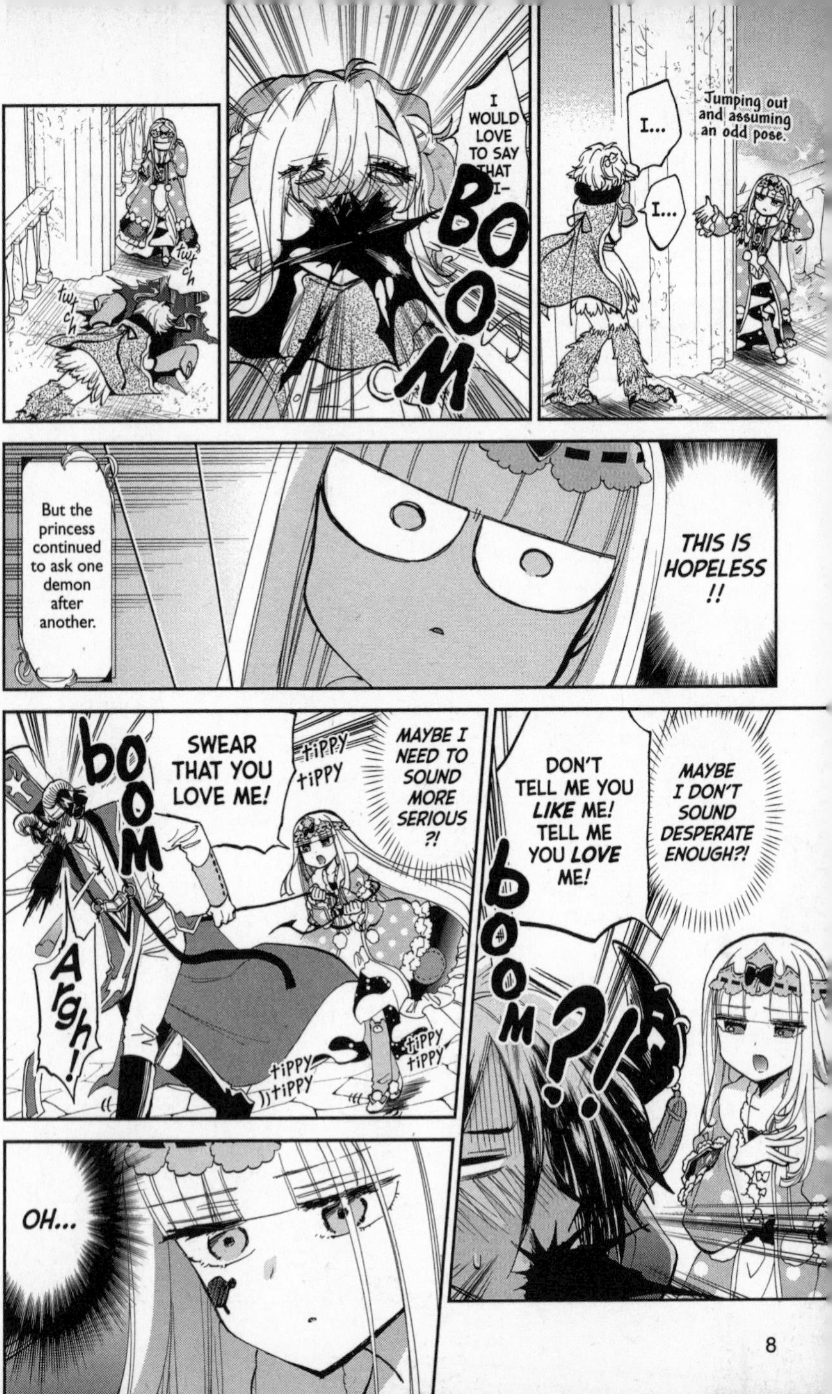
Jumping out and assuming an odd pose.
I...
I...
I WOULD LOVE TO SAY THAT I—
BOOM
twitch
twitch
THIS IS HOPELESS!!
But the princess continued to ask one demon after another.
MAYBE I DON'T SOUND DESPERATE ENOUGH?!
DON'T TELL ME YOU LIKE ME! TELL ME YOU LOVE ME!
boooom
?!
MAYBE I NEED TO SOUND MORE SERIOUS?!
tippy tippy
SWEAR THAT YOU LOVE ME!
bOOM
Argh!
tippy tippy
tippy tippy
OH...

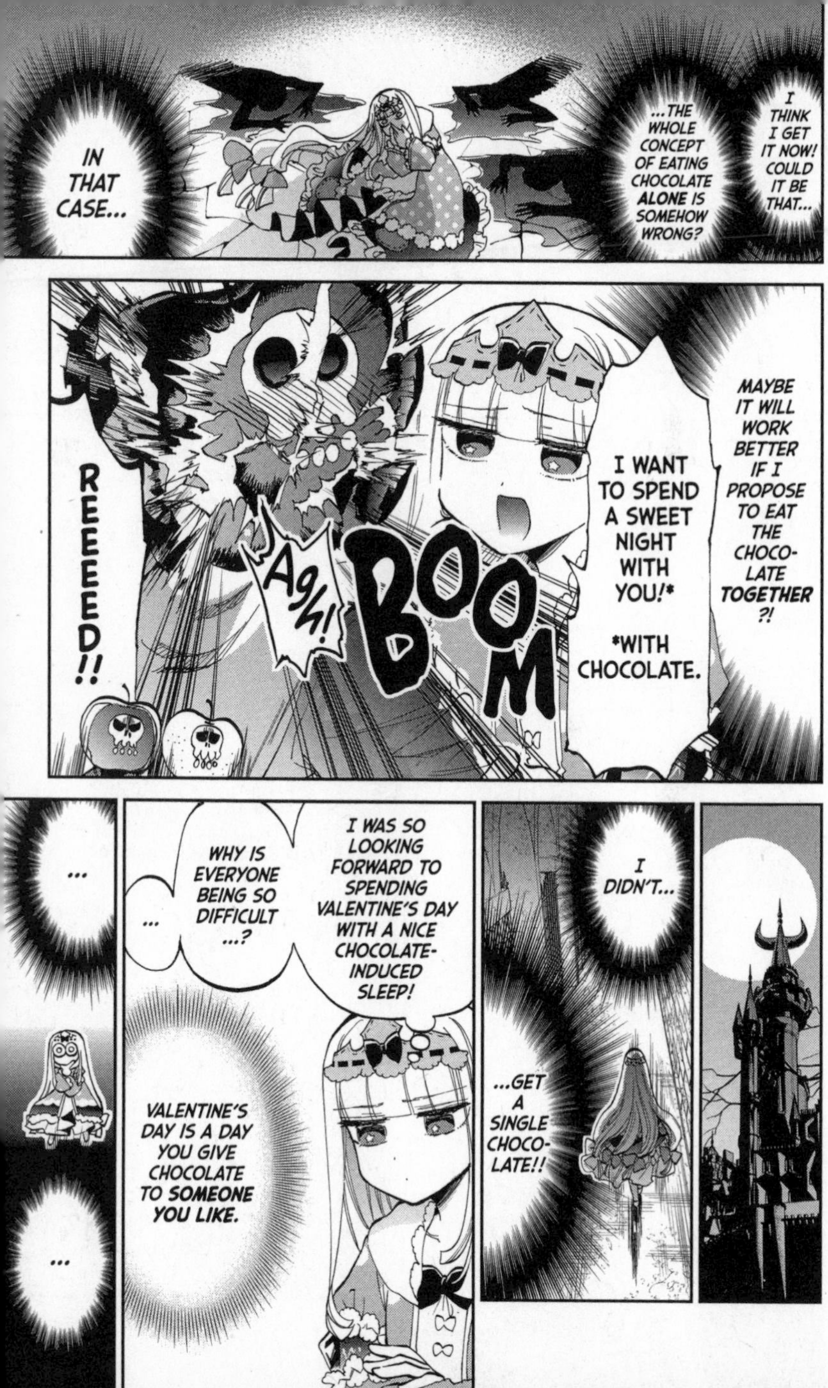

I THINK I GET IT NOW! COULD IT BE THAT...
...THE WHOLE CONCEPT OF EATING CHOCOLATE **ALONE** IS SOMEHOW WRONG?
IN THAT CASE...
MAYBE IT WILL WORK BETTER IF I PROPOSE TO EAT THE CHOCOLATE **TOGETHER**?!
I WANT TO SPEND A SWEET NIGHT WITH YOU!*
*WITH CHOCOLATE.
BOOM
Agh!
REEEEED!!
I DIDN'T...
...GET A SINGLE CHOCOLATE!!
I WAS SO LOOKING FORWARD TO SPENDING VALENTINE'S DAY WITH A NICE CHOCOLATE-INDUCED SLEEP!
WHY IS EVERYONE BEING SO DIFFICULT ...?
...
VALENTINE'S DAY IS A DAY YOU GIVE CHOCOLATE TO **SOMEONE** YOU LIKE.
...
...

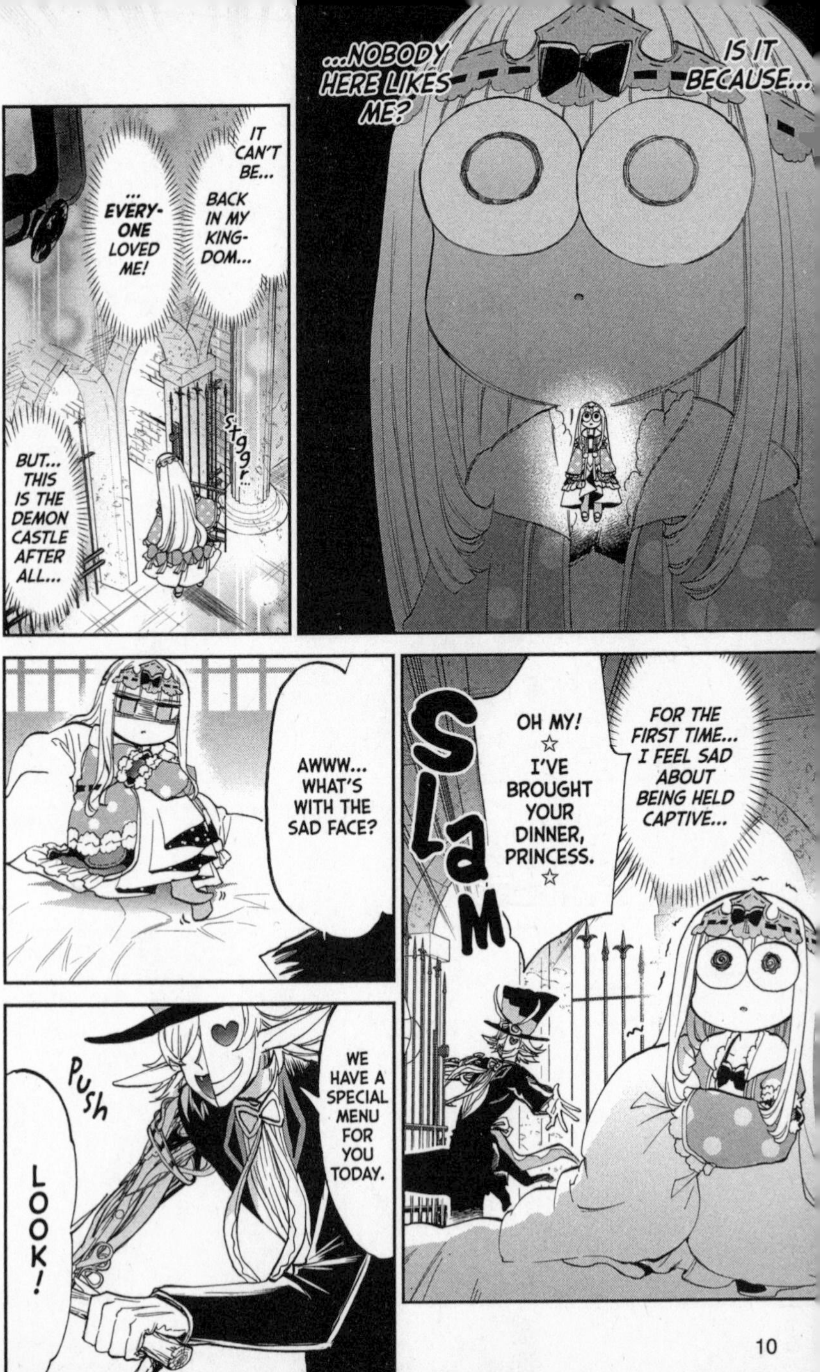
IS IT BECAUSE...
...NOBODY HERE LIKES ME?
IT CAN'T BE... BACK IN MY KINGDOM...
...EVERYONE LOVED ME!
sxggr...
BUT... THIS IS THE DEMON CASTLE AFTER ALL...
FOR THE FIRST TIME... I FEEL SAD ABOUT BEING HELD CAPTIVE...
SLAM
OH MY! ☆ I'VE BROUGHT YOUR DINNER, PRINCESS. ☆
AWWW... WHAT'S WITH THE SAD FACE?
WE HAVE A SPECIAL MENU FOR YOU TODAY.
Push
LOOK!

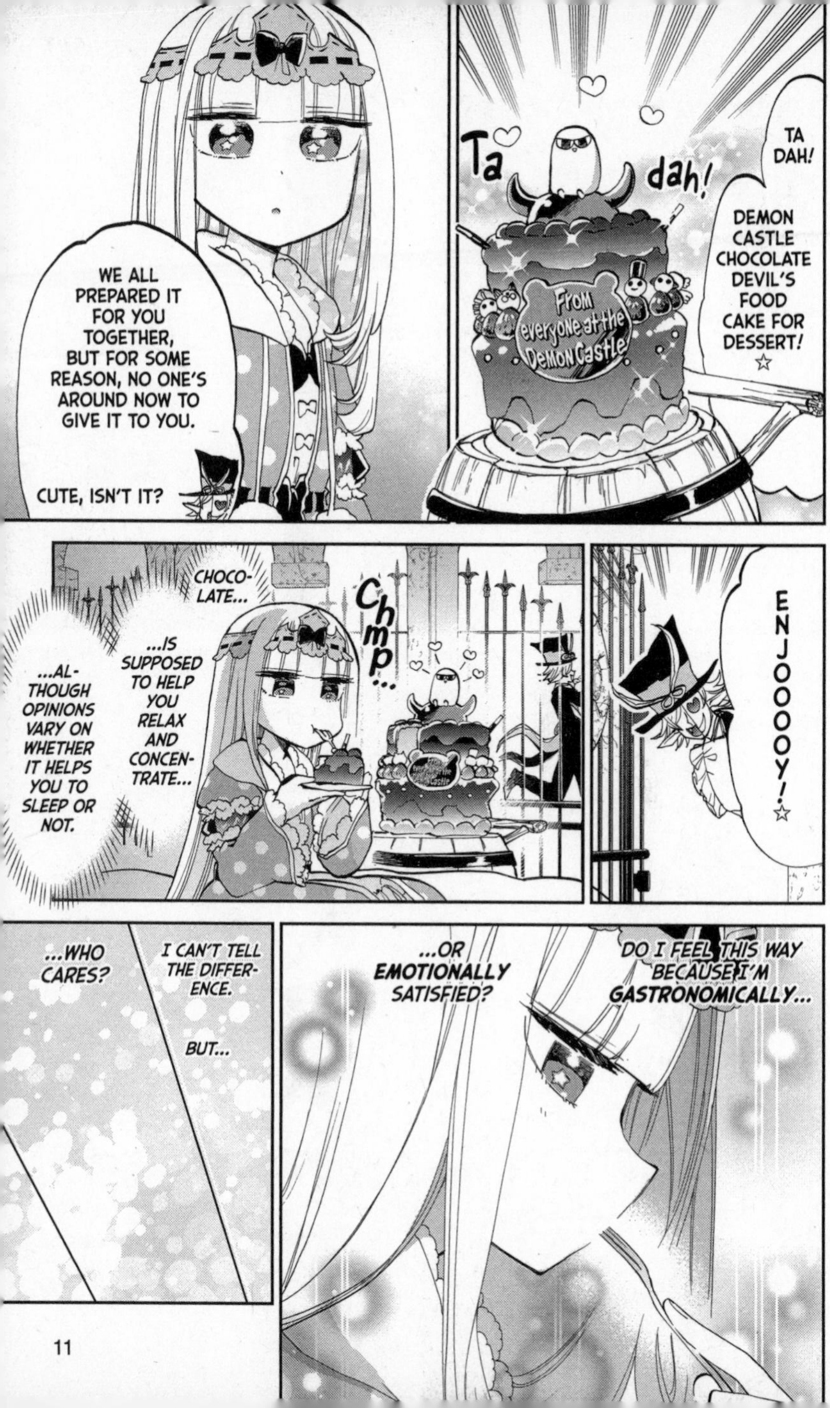
TA DAH!
Ta dah!
DEMON CASTLE CHOCOLATE DEVIL'S FOOD CAKE FOR DESSERT! ☆
From everyone at the Demon Castle
WE ALL PREPARED IT FOR YOU TOGETHER, BUT FOR SOME REASON, NO ONE'S AROUND NOW TO GIVE IT TO YOU.
CUTE, ISN'T IT?
ENJOOOOOY! ☆
Chmp...
CHOCOLATE...
...IS SUPPOSED TO HELP YOU RELAX AND CONCENTRATE...
...ALTHOUGH OPINIONS VARY ON WHETHER IT HELPS YOU TO SLEEP OR NOT.
DO I FEEL THIS WAY BECAUSE I'M GASTRONOMICALLY...
...OR EMOTIONALLY SATISFIED?
I CAN'T TELL THE DIFFERENCE.
BUT...
...WHO CARES?

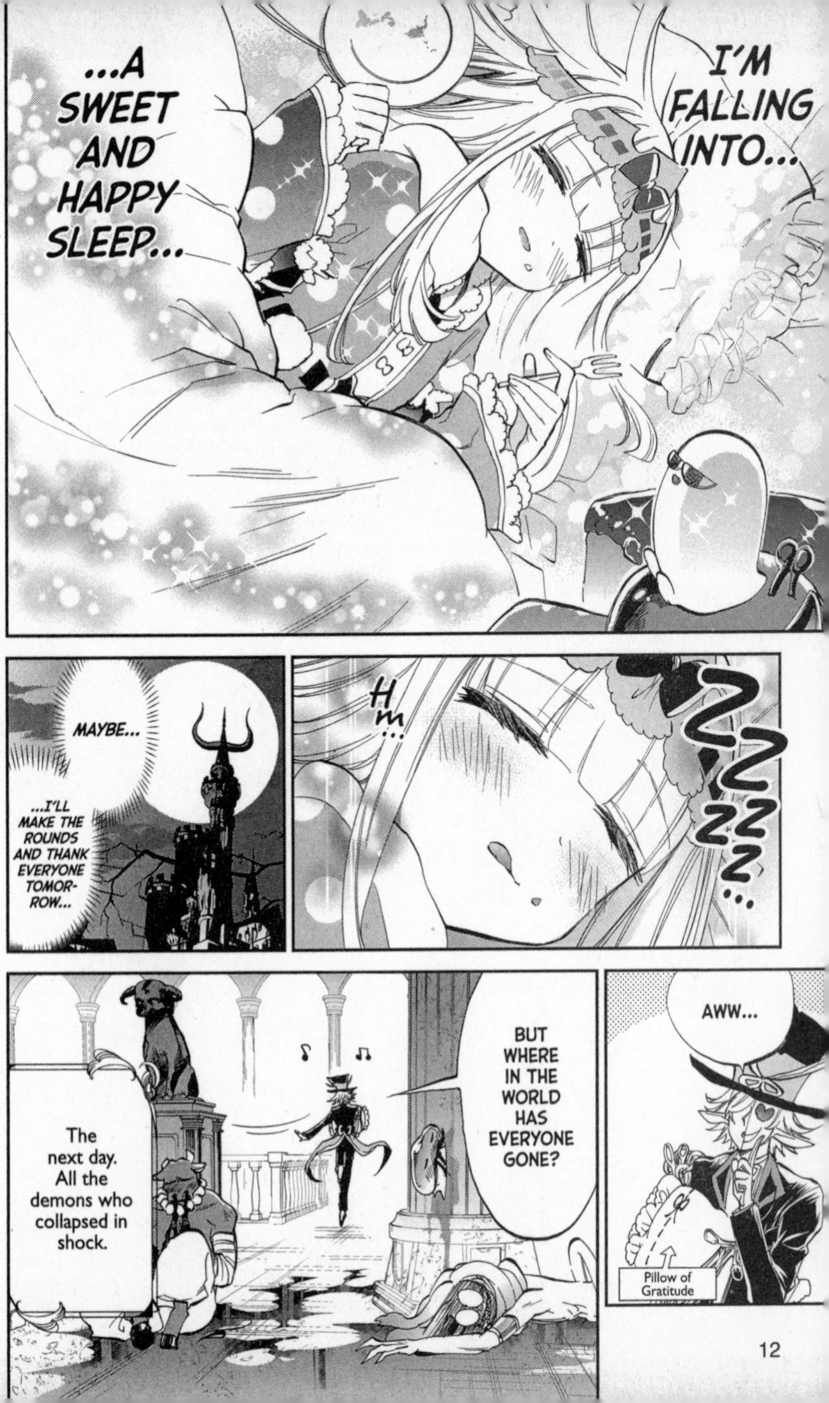
I'M FALLING INTO...
...A SWEET AND HAPPY SLEEP...
Hm...
ZZZZ...
MAYBE...
...I'LL MAKE THE ROUNDS AND THANK EVERYONE TOMOR-ROW...
AWW...
Pillow of Gratitude
BUT WHERE IN THE WORLD HAS EVERYONE GONE?
The next day. All the demons who collapsed in shock.

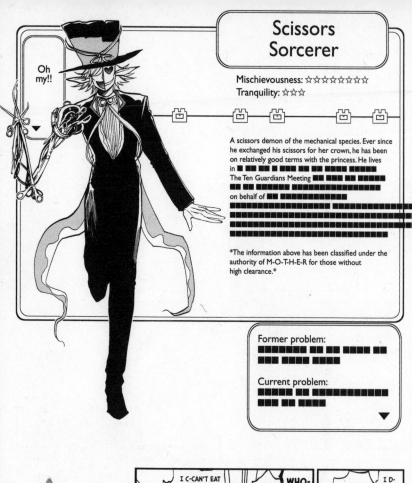

Oh my!!

Scissors Sorcerer

Mischievousness: ☆☆☆☆☆☆☆☆

Tranquility: ☆☆☆

A scissors demon of the mechanical species. Ever since he exchanged his scissors for her crown, he has been on relatively good terms with the princess. He lives in [redacted]
The Ten Guardians Meeting [redacted]
on behalf of [redacted]

The information above has been classified under the authority of M-O-T-H-E-R for those without high clearance.

Former problem:
[redacted]

Current problem:
[redacted]

I D-DON'T KNOW WHERE THEY CAME FROM...
...BUT SOMEONE HAS SENT US CHOCOLATES AND CARDS!
And mini sau-sages!
?!
WHO-OAA!
WHAT...? FOR ME...? WOW! (JOY)
I C-CAN'T EAT CHOCOLATE... BUT THE SAUSAGE SNACKS—
Since I'm a dog...
WHOAA!
I'M HEARING STRANGE JOYFUL CRIES!
THANK YOU SO MUCH!!

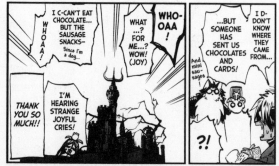

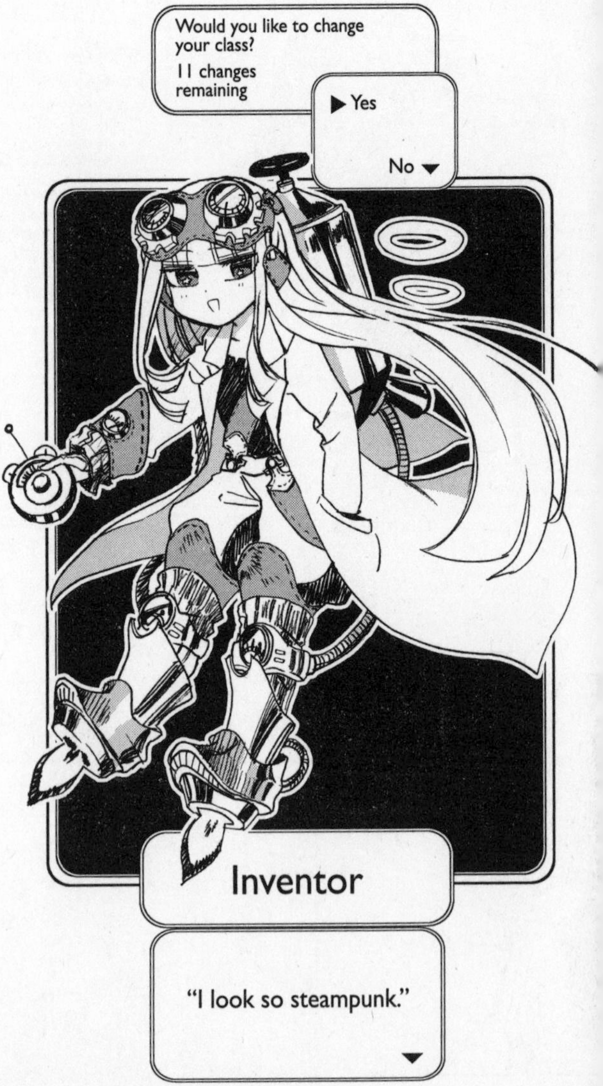
Would you like to change your class?
11 changes remaining
▶ Yes
No
Inventor
"I look so steampunk."

41st Night: Quilly Doesn't Hibernate

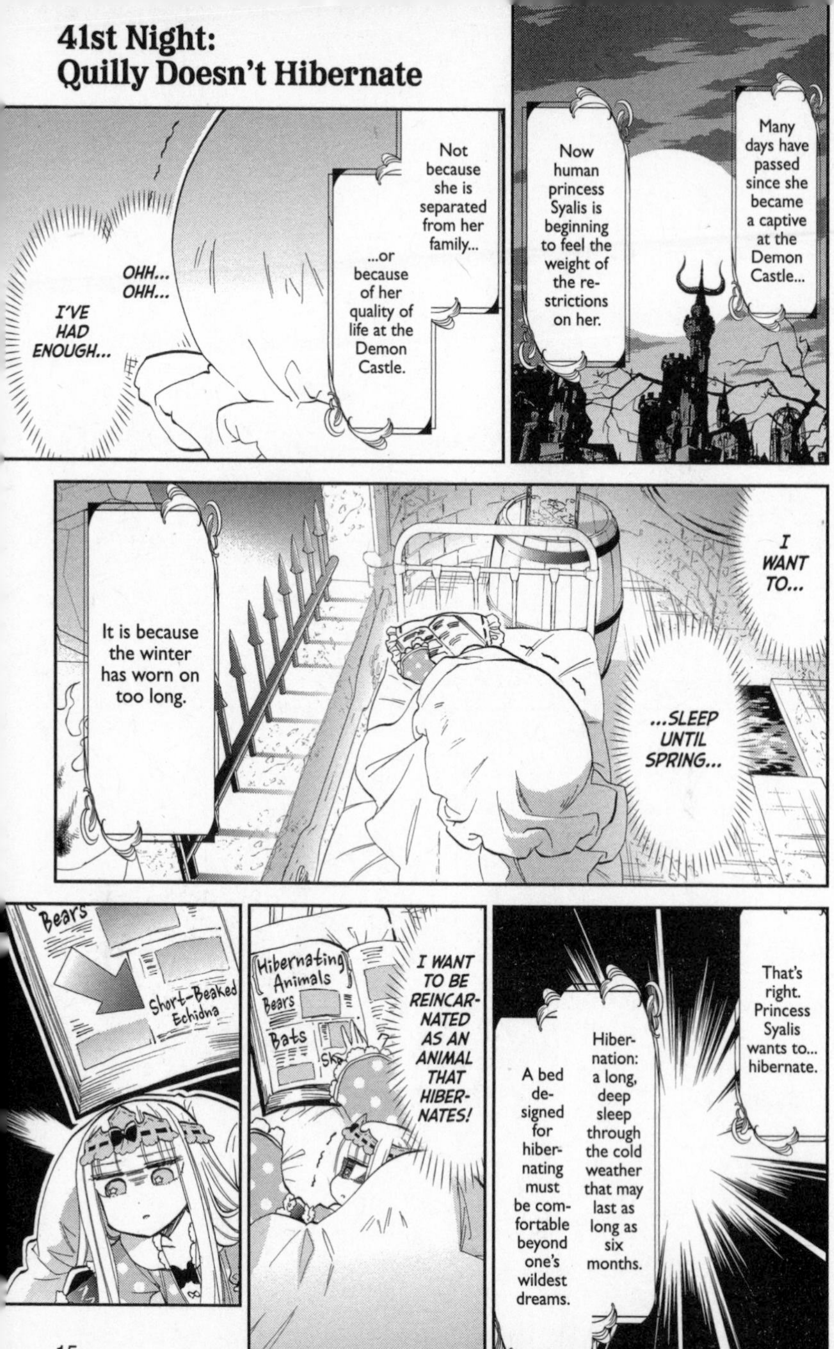

Many days have passed since she became a captive at the Demon Castle...
Now human princess Syalis is beginning to feel the weight of the restrictions on her.
Not because she is separated from her family...
...or because of her quality of life at the Demon Castle.
OHH... OHH...
I'VE HAD ENOUGH...
I WANT TO...
...SLEEP UNTIL SPRING...
It is because the winter has worn on too long.
That's right. Princess Syalis wants to... hibernate.
Hibernation: a long, deep sleep through the cold weather that may last as long as six months.
A bed designed for hibernating must be comfortable beyond one's wildest dreams.
I WANT TO BE REINCARNATED AS AN ANIMAL THAT HIBERNATES!
Hibernating Animals
Bears
Bats
Bears
Short-Beaked Echidna

41st Night: Quilly Doesn't Hibernate

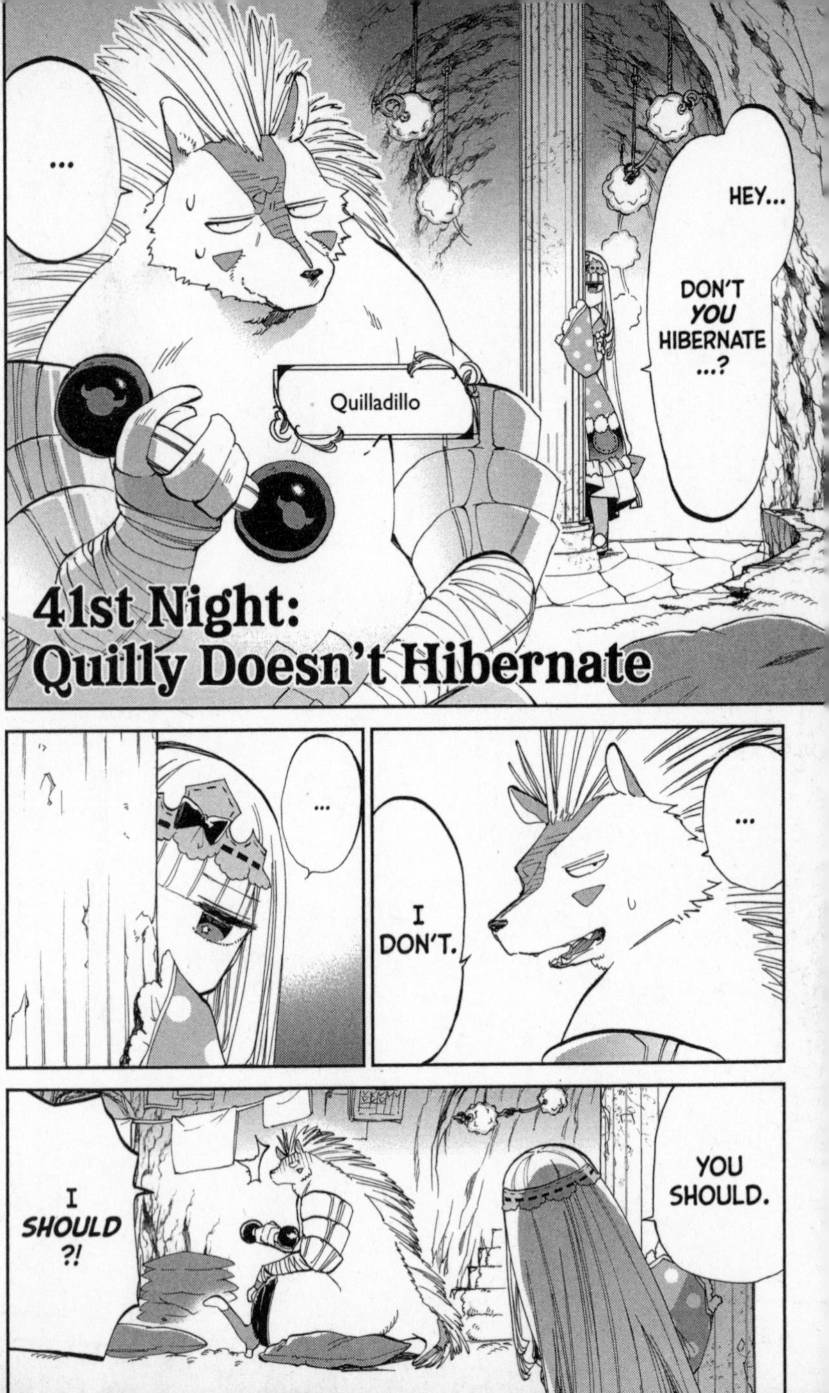
HEY... DON'T *YOU* HIBERNATE ...?
...
Quilladillo
...
I DON'T.
...
YOU SHOULD.
I *SHOULD* ?!

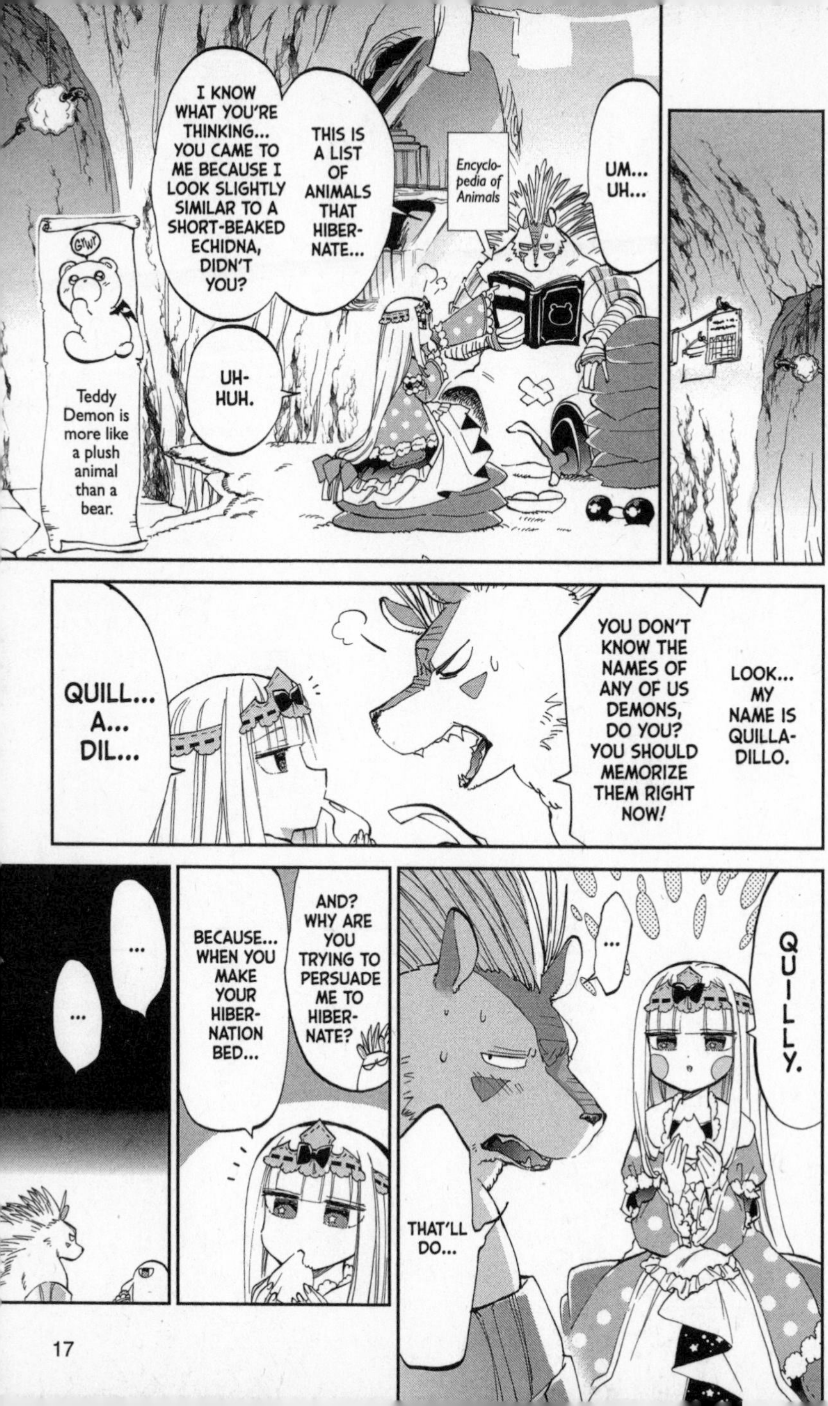
UM... UH...
Encyclopedia of Animals
THIS IS A LIST OF ANIMALS THAT HIBERNATE...
I KNOW WHAT YOU'RE THINKING... YOU CAME TO ME BECAUSE I LOOK SLIGHTLY SIMILAR TO A SHORT-BEAKED ECHIDNA, DIDN'T YOU?
UH-HUH.
Teddy Demon is more like a plush animal than a bear.
LOOK... MY NAME IS QUILLADILLO.
YOU DON'T KNOW THE NAMES OF ANY OF US DEMONS, DO YOU? YOU SHOULD MEMORIZE THEM RIGHT NOW!
QUILL... A... DIL...
QUILLY.
...
THAT'LL DO...
AND? WHY ARE YOU TRYING TO PERSUADE ME TO HIBERNATE?
BECAUSE... WHEN YOU MAKE YOUR HIBERNATION BED...
...
...

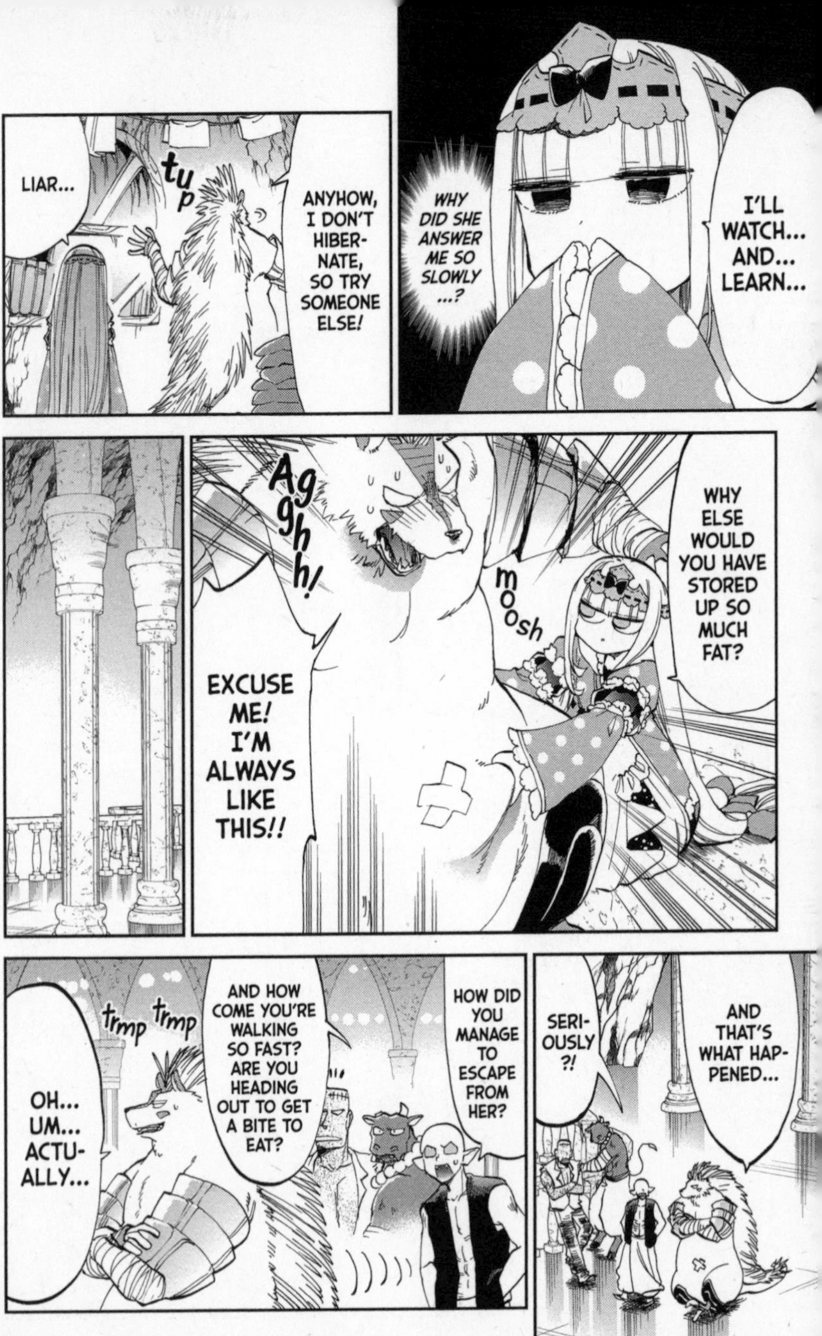
I'LL WATCH... AND... LEARN...
WHY DID SHE ANSWER ME SO SLOWLY ...?
ANYHOW, I DON'T HIBERNATE, SO TRY SOMEONE ELSE!
tup
LIAR...
WHY ELSE WOULD YOU HAVE STORED UP SO MUCH FAT?
moosh
Agghh!
EXCUSE ME! I'M ALWAYS LIKE THIS!!
AND THAT'S WHAT HAPPENED...
SERIOUSLY?!
HOW DID YOU MANAGE TO ESCAPE FROM HER?
AND HOW COME YOU'RE WALKING SO FAST? ARE YOU HEADING OUT TO GET A BITE TO EAT?
trmp trmp
OH... UM... ACTUALLY...

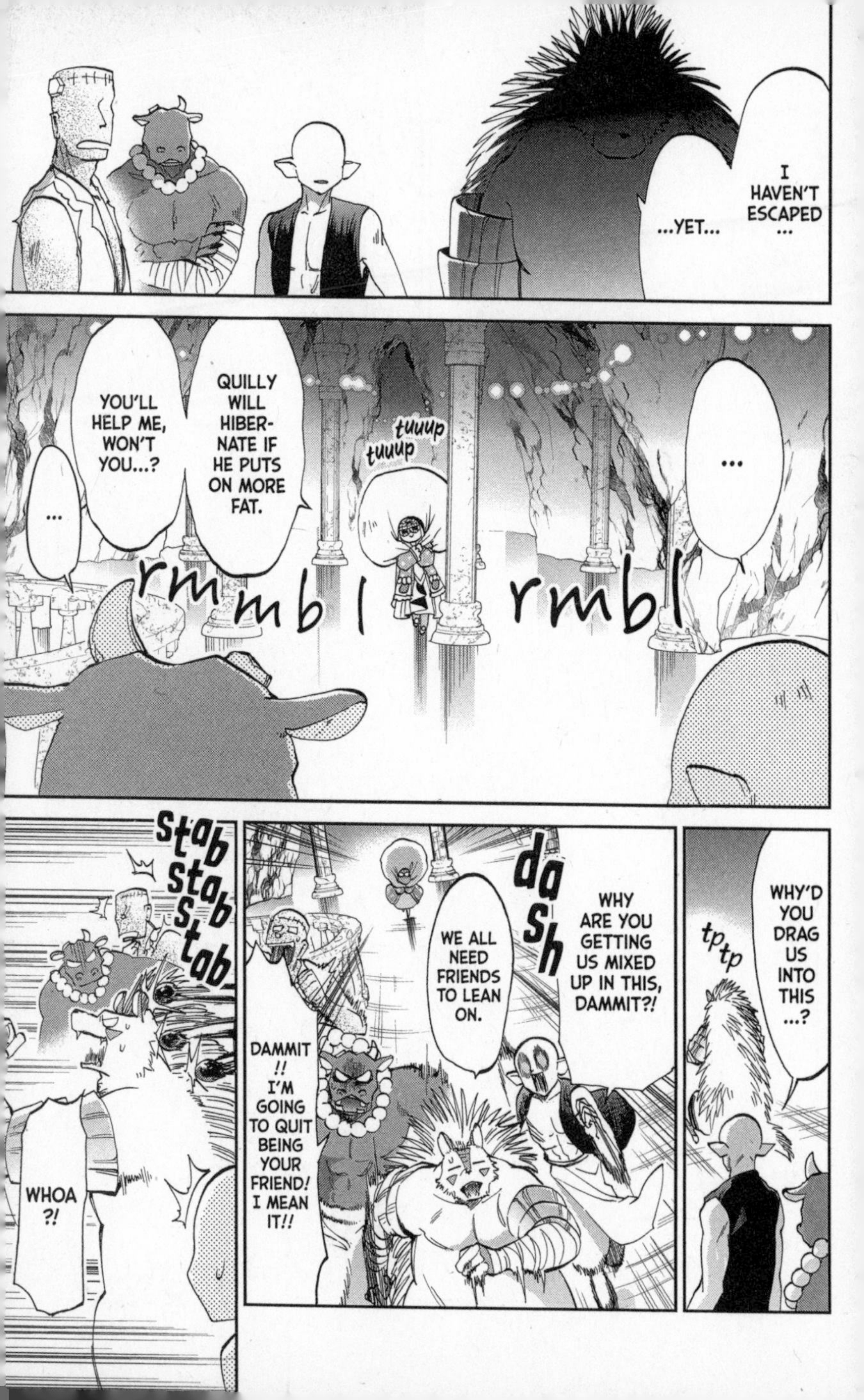
I HAVEN'T ESCAPED ...
...YET...
...
tuuup tuuup
QUILLY WILL HIBER-NATE IF HE PUTS ON MORE FAT.
YOU'LL HELP ME, WON'T YOU...?
...
rmbl rmbl
WHY'D YOU DRAG US INTO THIS ...?
tp tp
dash
WHY ARE YOU GETTING US MIXED UP IN THIS, DAMMIT?!
WE ALL NEED FRIENDS TO LEAN ON.
DAMMIT!! I'M GOING TO QUIT BEING YOUR FRIEND! I MEAN IT!!
stab stab stab stab
WHOA?!

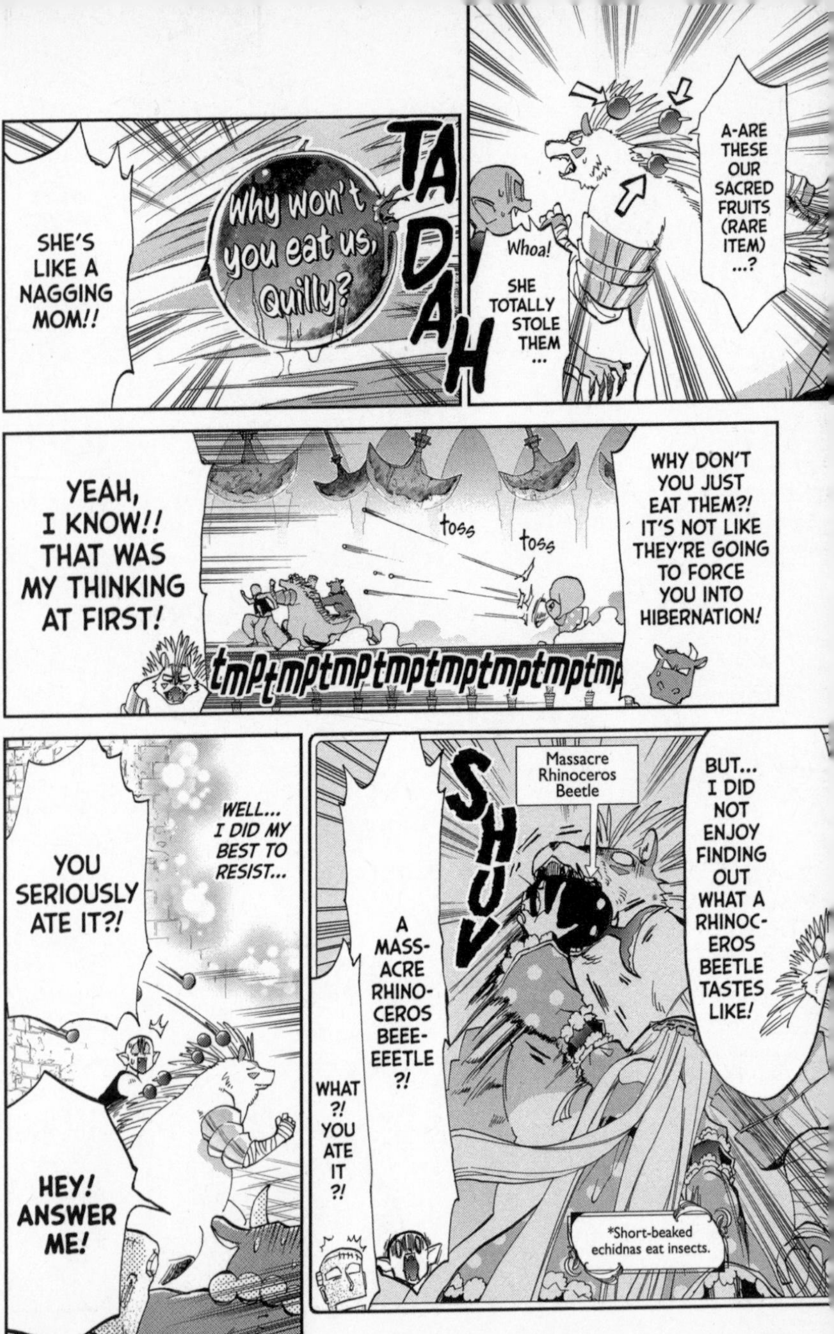
A-ARE THESE OUR SACRED FRUITS (RARE ITEM) ...?
Whoa!
SHE TOTALLY STOLE THEM ...
TADAH
Why won't you eat us, Quilly?
SHE'S LIKE A NAGGING MOM!!
WHY DON'T YOU JUST EAT THEM?! IT'S NOT LIKE THEY'RE GOING TO FORCE YOU INTO HIBERNATION!
toss
toss
YEAH, I KNOW!! THAT WAS MY THINKING AT FIRST!
tmptmptmptmptmptmptmptmp
BUT... I DID NOT ENJOY FINDING OUT WHAT A RHINOCEROS BEETLE TASTES LIKE!
Massacre Rhinoceros Beetle
SHUV
A MASSACRE RHINOCEROS BEEEEETLE?!
WHAT?! YOU ATE IT?!
*Short-beaked echidnas eat insects.
WELL... I DID MY BEST TO RESIST...
YOU SERIOUSLY ATE IT?!
HEY! ANSWER ME!

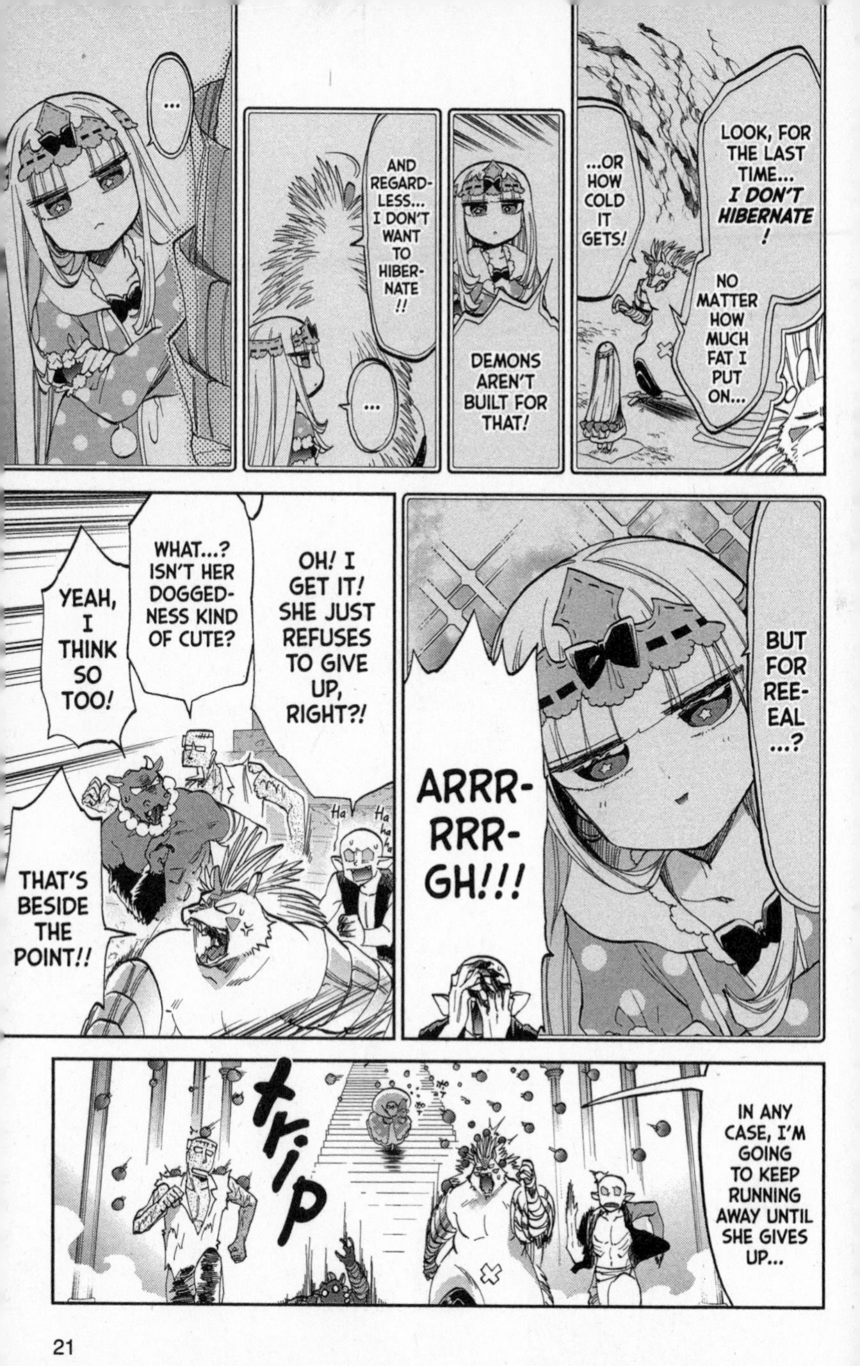
LOOK, FOR THE LAST TIME... *I DON'T HIBERNATE*!
NO MATTER HOW MUCH FAT I PUT ON...
...OR HOW COLD IT GETS!
DEMONS AREN'T BUILT FOR THAT!
AND REGARDLESS... I DON'T WANT TO HIBERNATE!!
...
...
BUT FOR REEEAL...?
ARRRRRRGH!!!
OH! I GET IT! SHE JUST REFUSES TO GIVE UP, RIGHT?!
WHAT...? ISN'T HER DOGGEDNESS KIND OF CUTE?
YEAH, I THINK SO TOO!
Ha Ha ha ha
THAT'S BESIDE THE POINT!!
IN ANY CASE, I'M GOING TO KEEP RUNNING AWAY UNTIL SHE GIVES UP...
TRIP

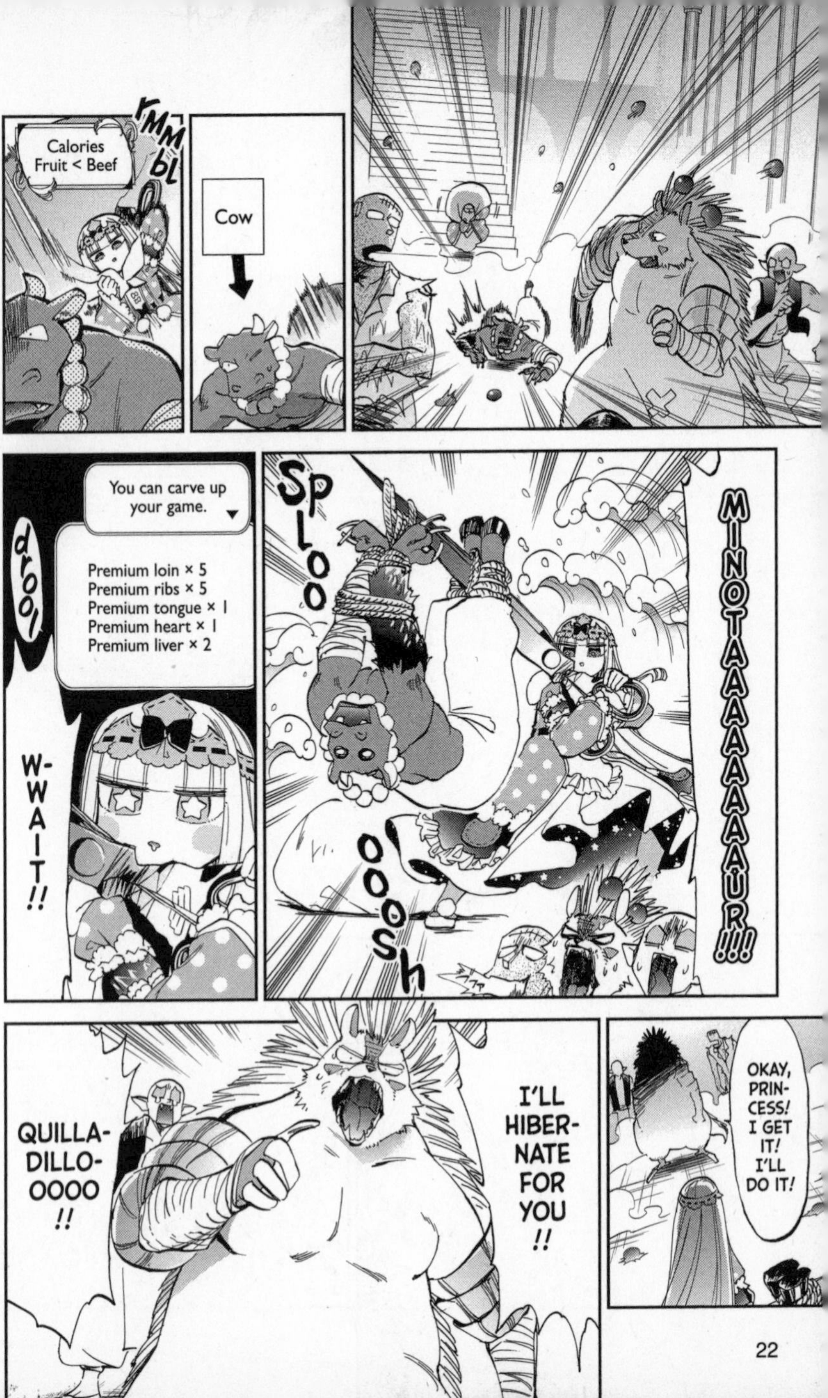
Cow
Calories
Fruit < Beef
RMMBL
MINOTAAAAAAAAUR!!!
SPLOO
OOOSH
You can carve up your game.
Premium loin × 5
Premium ribs × 5
Premium tongue × 1
Premium heart × 1
Premium liver × 2
drool
W-WAIT!!
OKAY, PRINCESS! I GET IT! I'LL DO IT!
I'LL HIBERNATE FOR YOU!!
QUILLADILLOOOOO!!

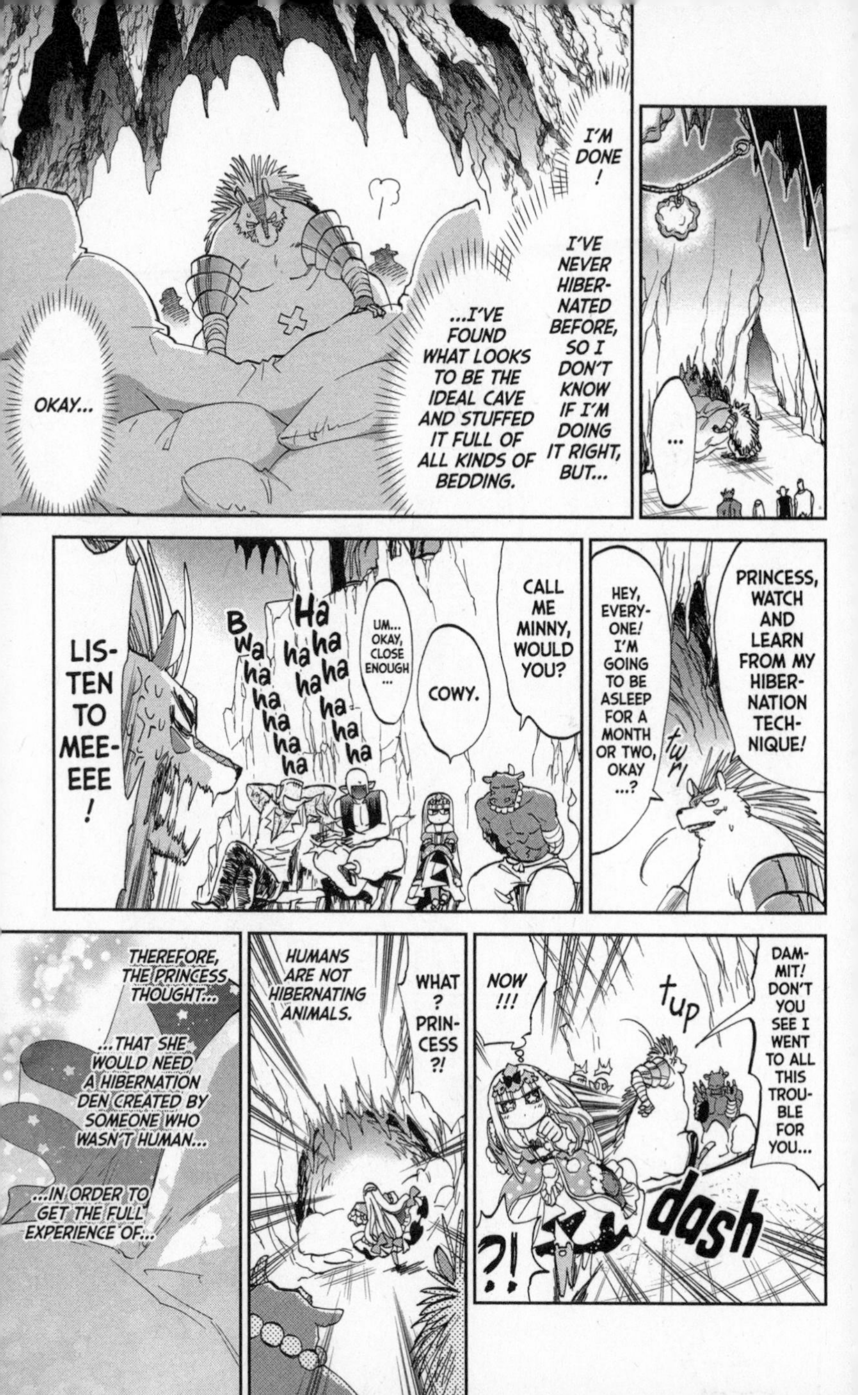
...
I'M DONE!
I'VE NEVER HIBERNATED BEFORE, SO I DON'T KNOW IF I'M DOING IT RIGHT, BUT...
...I'VE FOUND WHAT LOOKS TO BE THE IDEAL CAVE AND STUFFED IT FULL OF ALL KINDS OF BEDDING.
OKAY...
PRINCESS, WATCH AND LEARN FROM MY HIBERNATION TECHNIQUE!
twrl
HEY, EVERYONE! I'M GOING TO BE ASLEEP FOR A MONTH OR TWO, OKAY...?
CALL ME MINNY, WOULD YOU?
COWY.
UM... OKAY, CLOSE ENOUGH...
Ha ha ha ha ha ha ha ha ha
Bwa ha ha ha ha ha ha ha ha
LISTEN TO MEEEEE!
DAMMIT! DON'T YOU SEE I WENT TO ALL THIS TROUBLE FOR YOU...
tup
NOW!!!
dash
?!
WHAT? PRINCESS?!
HUMANS ARE NOT HIBERNATING ANIMALS.
THEREFORE, THE PRINCESS THOUGHT...
...THAT SHE WOULD NEED A HIBERNATION DEN CREATED BY SOMEONE WHO WASN'T HUMAN...
...IN ORDER TO GET THE FULL EXPERIENCE OF...

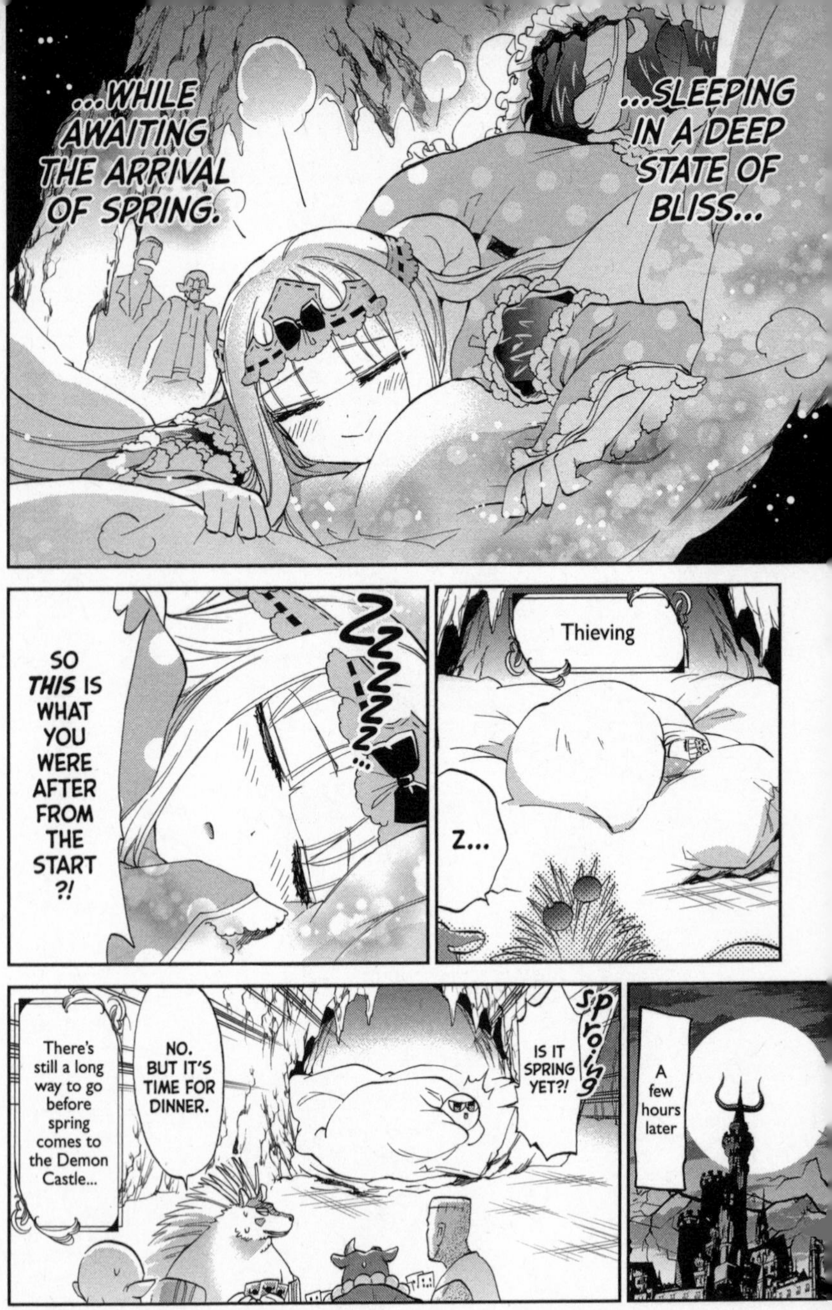
...SLEEPING IN A DEEP STATE OF BLISS...
...WHILE AWAITING THE ARRIVAL OF SPRING.
Thieving
Z...
ZZZZZ...
SO THIS IS WHAT YOU WERE AFTER FROM THE START?!
A few hours later
Sproing
IS IT SPRING YET?!
NO. BUT IT'S TIME FOR DINNER.
There's still a long way to go before spring comes to the Demon Castle...

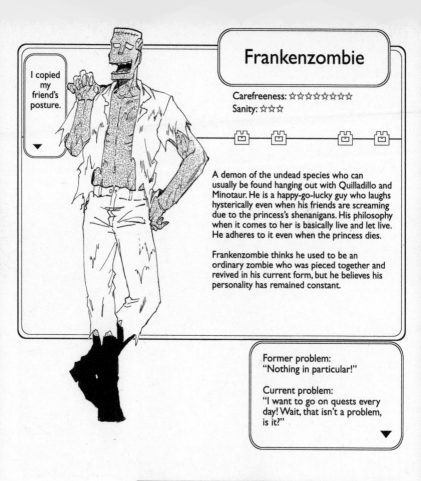

I copied my friend's posture.

Frankenzombie

Carefreeness: ☆☆☆☆☆☆☆☆☆
Sanity: ☆☆☆

A demon of the undead species who can usually be found hanging out with Quilladillo and Minotaur. He is a happy-go-lucky guy who laughs hysterically even when his friends are screaming due to the princess's shenanigans. His philosophy when it comes to her is basically live and let live. He adheres to it even when the princess dies.

Frankenzombie thinks he used to be an ordinary zombie who was pieced together and revived in his current form, but he believes his personality has remained constant.

Former problem:
"Nothing in particular!"

Current problem:
"I want to go on quests every day! Wait, that isn't a problem, is it?"

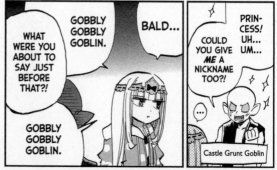

PRIN-CESS! UH... UM...
COULD YOU GIVE ***ME*** A NICKNAME TOO?!
...
Castle Grunt Goblin
BALD...
GOBBLY GOBBLY GOBLIN.
WHAT WERE YOU ABOUT TO SAY JUST BEFORE THAT?!
GOBBLY GOBBLY GOBLIN.

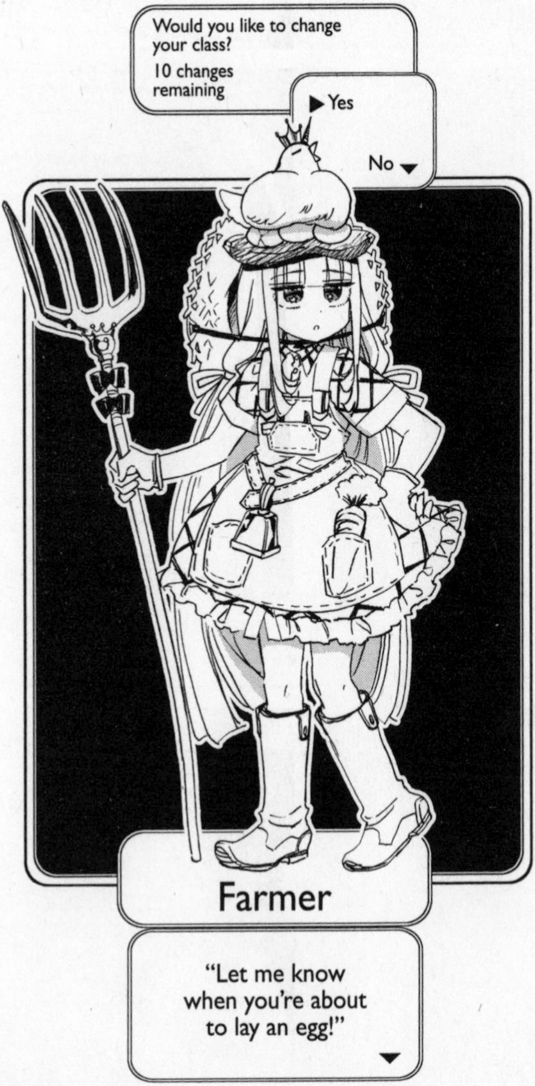
Would you like to change your class?
10 changes remaining
▶Yes
No
Farmer
"Let me know when you're about to lay an egg!"

42nd Night: Who's Been Sleeping Too Much?

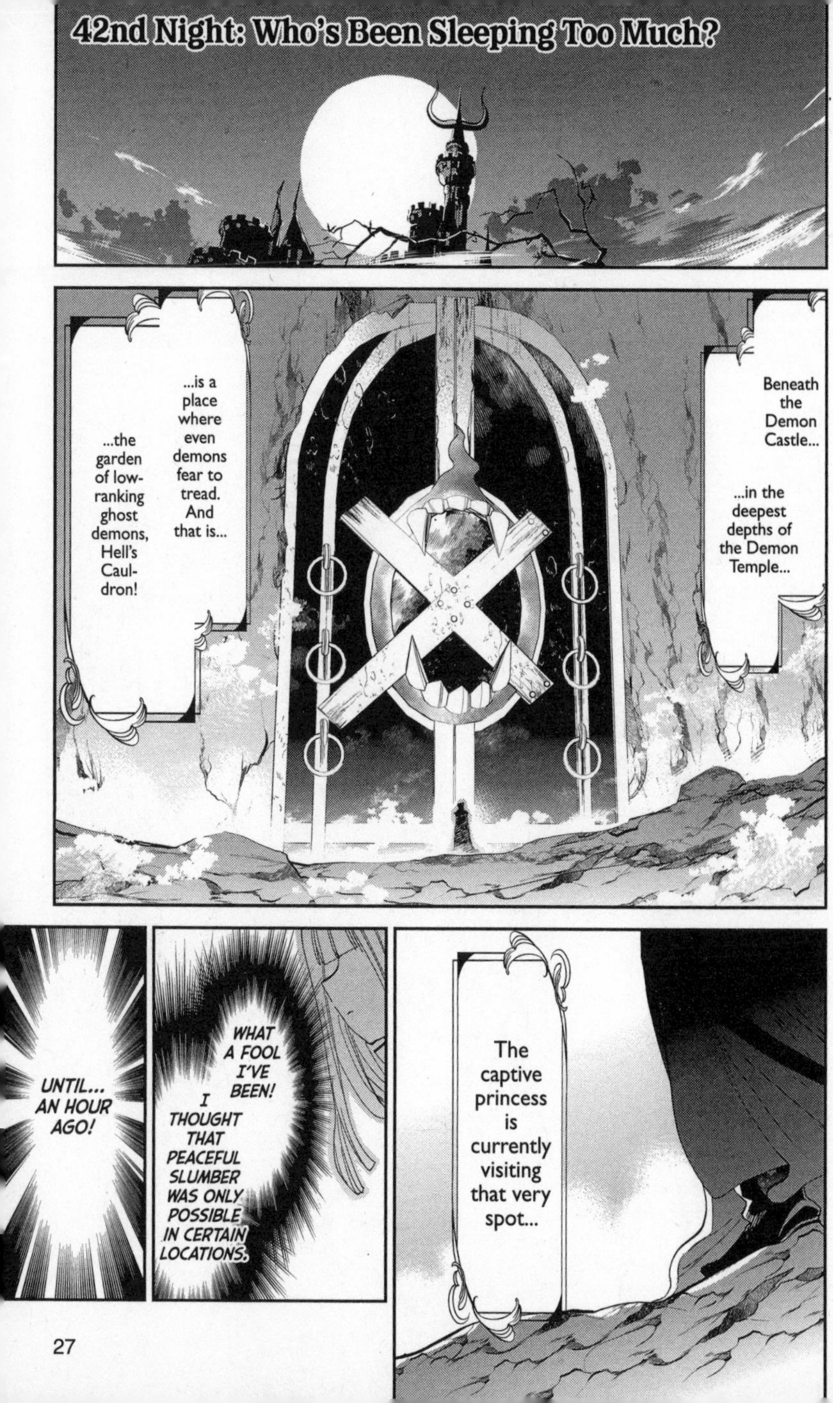

Beneath the Demon Castle...
...in the deepest depths of the Demon Temple...
...is a place where even demons fear to tread. And that is...
...the garden of low-ranking ghost demons, Hell's Cauldron!
The captive princess is currently visiting that very spot...
WHAT A FOOL I'VE BEEN!
I THOUGHT THAT PEACEFUL SLUMBER WAS ONLY POSSIBLE IN CERTAIN LOCATIONS.
UNTIL... AN HOUR AGO!

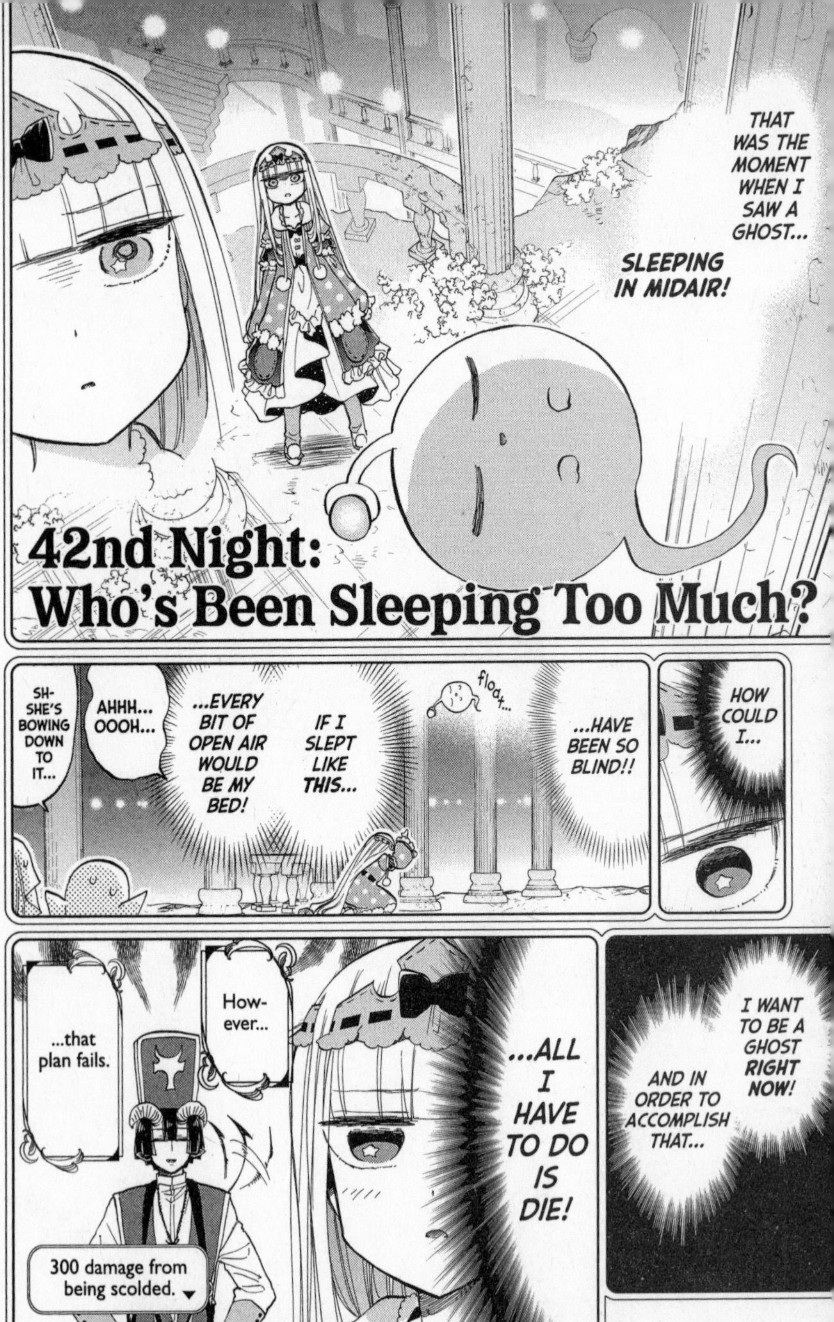
THAT WAS THE MOMENT WHEN I SAW A GHOST...
SLEEPING IN MIDAIR!
42nd Night: Who's Been Sleeping Too Much?
HOW COULD I...
...HAVE BEEN SO BLIND!!
float...
IF I SLEPT LIKE THIS...
...EVERY BIT OF OPEN AIR WOULD BE MY BED!
AHHH... OOOH...
SH-SHE'S BOWING DOWN TO IT...
I WANT TO BE A GHOST RIGHT NOW!
AND IN ORDER TO ACCOMPLISH THAT...
...ALL I HAVE TO DO IS DIE!
How-ever...
...that plan fails.
300 damage from being scolded.

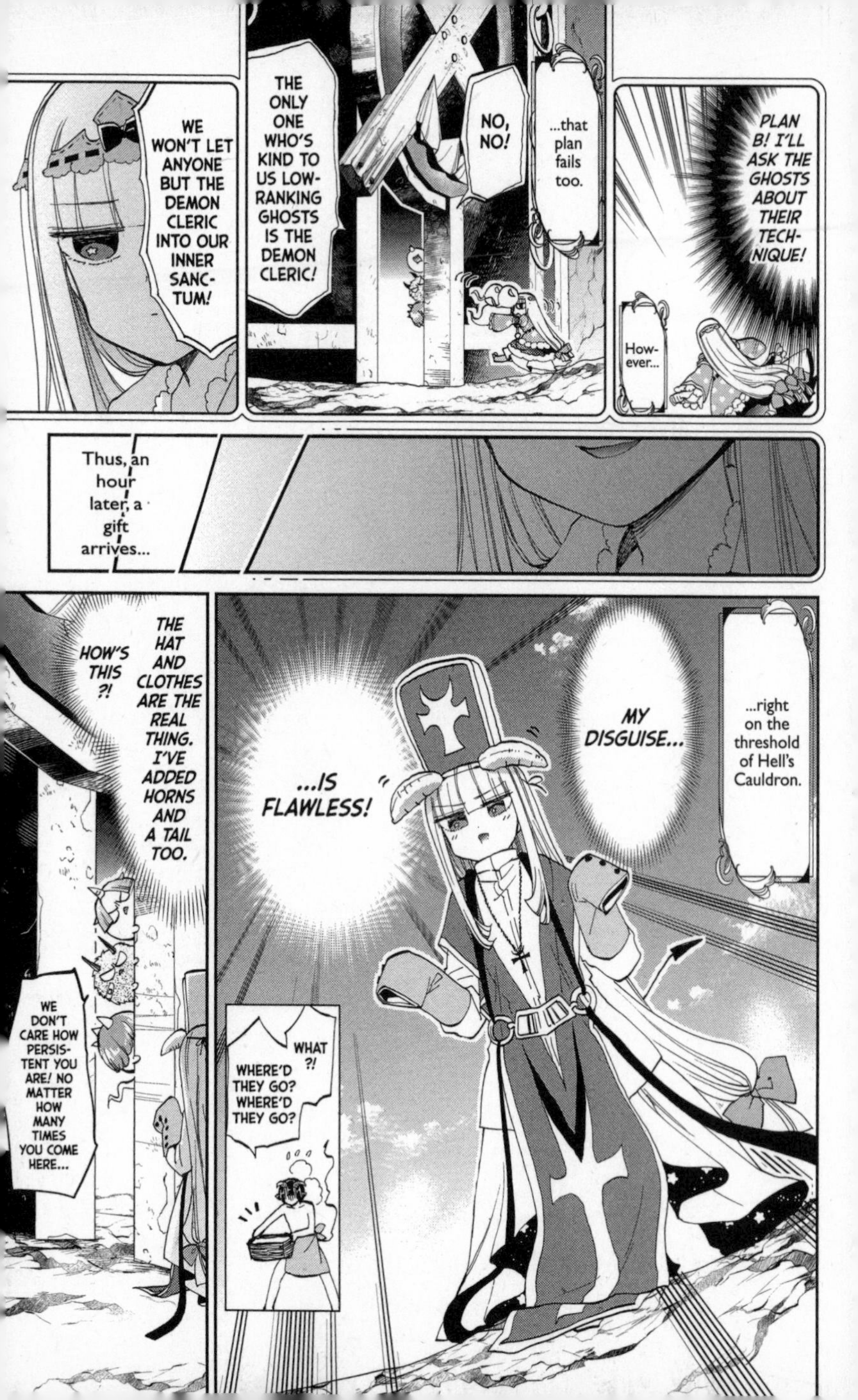
PLAN B! I'LL ASK THE GHOSTS ABOUT THEIR TECHNIQUE!
However...
...that plan fails too.
NO, NO!
THE ONLY ONE WHO'S KIND TO US LOW-RANKING GHOSTS IS THE DEMON CLERIC!
WE WON'T LET ANYONE BUT THE DEMON CLERIC INTO OUR INNER SANCTUM!
Thus, an hour later, a gift arrives...
...right on the threshold of Hell's Cauldron.
MY DISGUISE...
...IS FLAWLESS!
WHAT?!
WHERE'D THEY GO? WHERE'D THEY GO?
THE HAT AND CLOTHES ARE THE REAL THING. I'VE ADDED HORNS AND A TAIL TOO.
HOW'S THIS?!
WE DON'T CARE HOW PERSISTENT YOU ARE! NO MATTER HOW MANY TIMES YOU COME HERE...

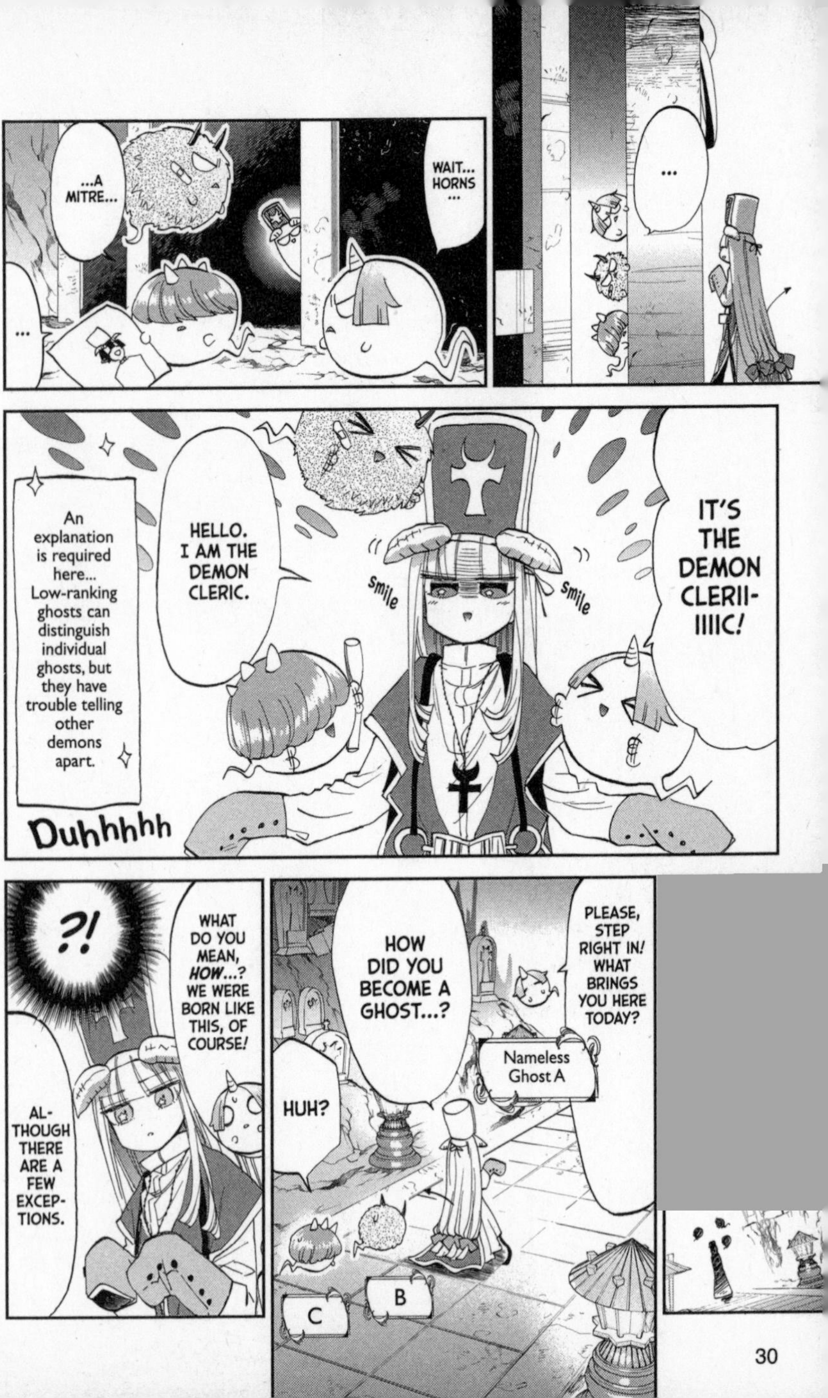
...
WAIT... HORNS ...
...A MITRE...
...
IT'S THE DEMON CLERIIIIIIC!
smile
smile
HELLO. I AM THE DEMON CLERIC.
An explanation is required here... Low-ranking ghosts can distinguish individual ghosts, but they have trouble telling other demons apart.
Duhhhhh
PLEASE, STEP RIGHT IN! WHAT BRINGS YOU HERE TODAY?
Nameless Ghost A
HOW DID YOU BECOME A GHOST...?
HUH?
B
C
WHAT DO YOU MEAN, *HOW*...? WE WERE BORN LIKE THIS, OF COURSE!
?!
ALTHOUGH THERE ARE A FEW EXCEPTIONS.

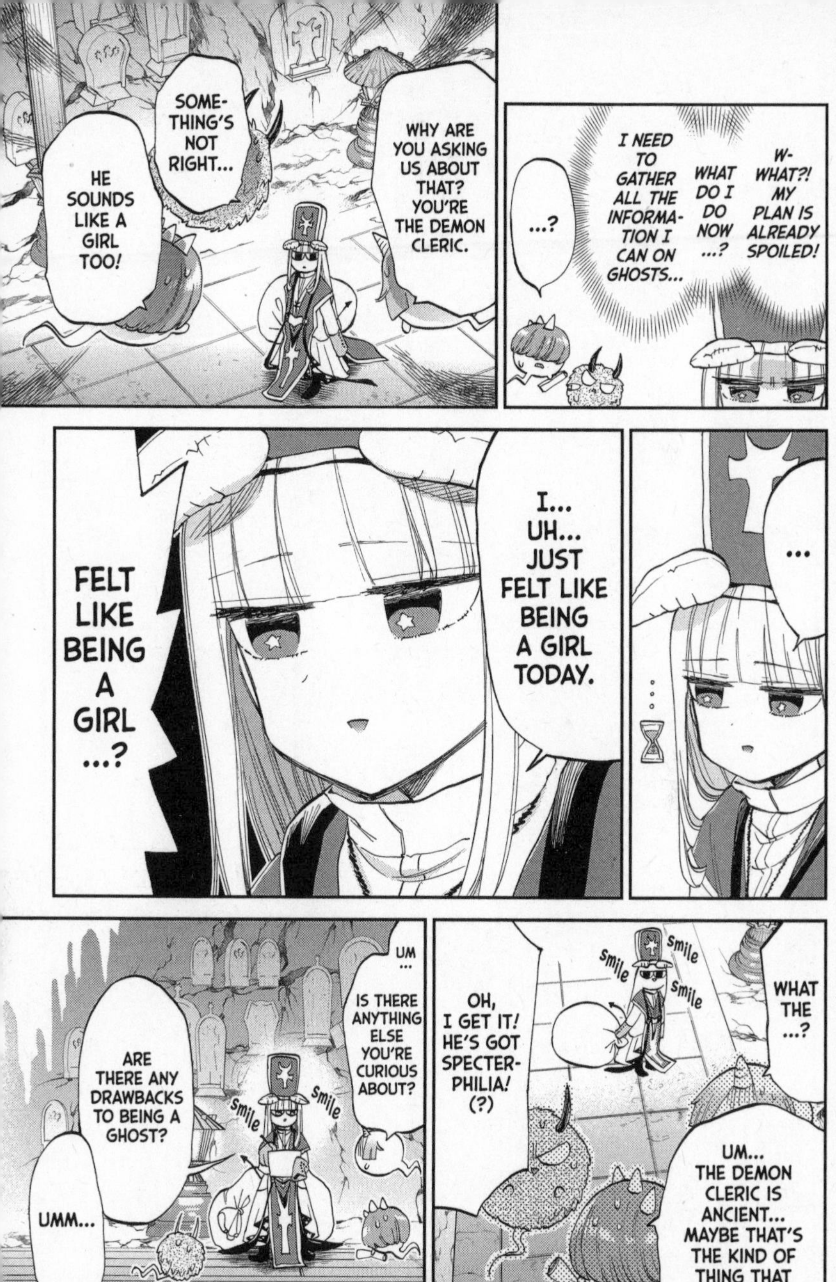
W-WHAT?! MY PLAN IS ALREADY SPOILED!
WHAT DO I DO NOW ...?
I NEED TO GATHER ALL THE INFORMATION I CAN ON GHOSTS...
...?
WHY ARE YOU ASKING US ABOUT THAT? YOU'RE THE DEMON CLERIC.
SOME-THING'S NOT RIGHT...
HE SOUNDS LIKE A GIRL TOO!
...
I... UH... JUST FELT LIKE BEING A GIRL TODAY.
FELT LIKE BEING A GIRL ...?
WHAT THE ...?
Smile
Smile
Smile
OH, I GET IT! HE'S GOT SPECTER-PHILIA! (?)
UM... THE DEMON CLERIC IS ANCIENT... MAYBE THAT'S THE KIND OF THING THAT HAPPENS AT HIS AGE..?
UM ...
IS THERE ANYTHING ELSE YOU'RE CURIOUS ABOUT?
Smile
Smile
ARE THERE ANY DRAWBACKS TO BEING A GHOST?
UMM...

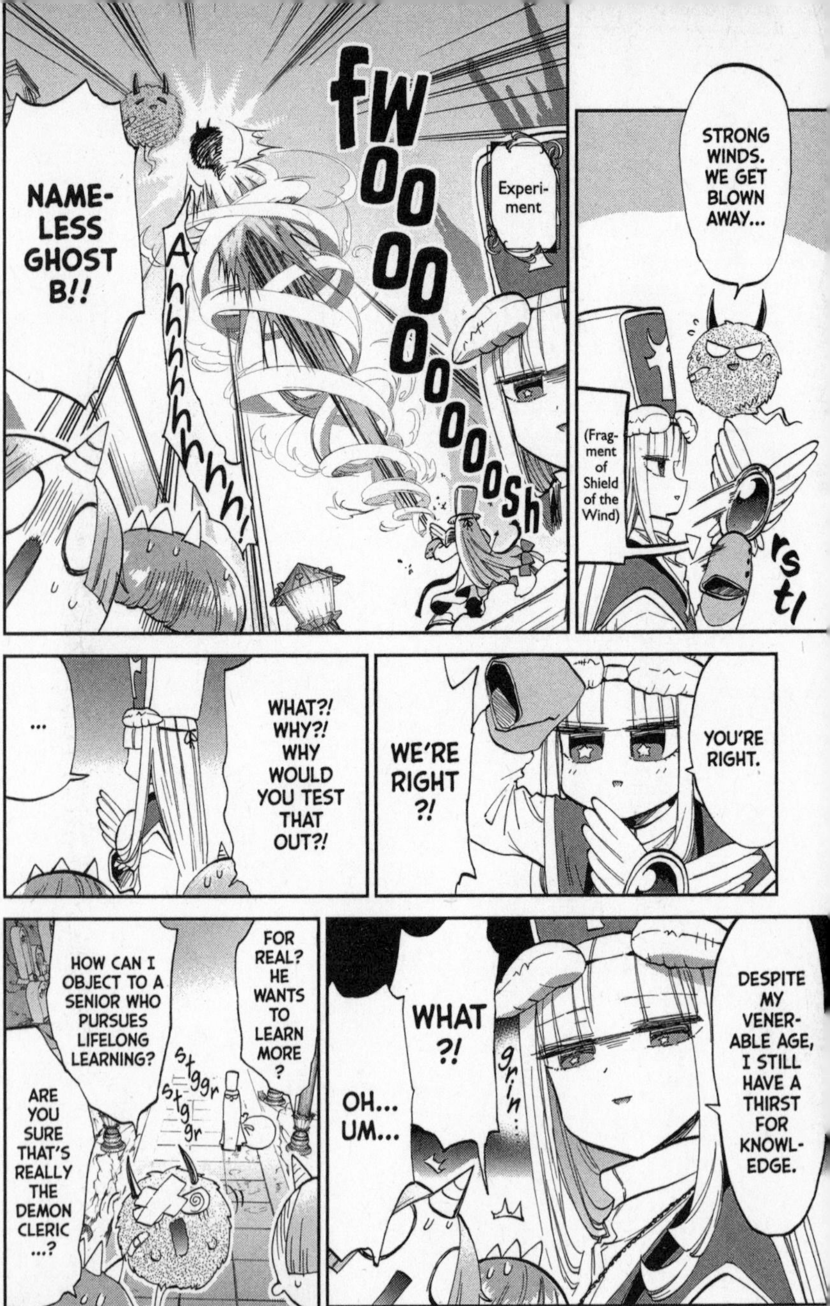
STRONG WINDS. WE GET BLOWN AWAY...
(Fragment of Shield of the Wind)
rstl
Experiment
FWOOOOOOOOOSH
Ahhhhhhhh!
NAMELESS GHOST B!!
YOU'RE RIGHT.
WE'RE RIGHT?!
WHAT?! WHY?! WHY WOULD YOU TEST THAT OUT?!
...
DESPITE MY VENERABLE AGE, I STILL HAVE A THIRST FOR KNOWLEDGE.
grin...
WHAT?!
OH... UM...
FOR REAL? HE WANTS TO LEARN MORE?
HOW CAN I OBJECT TO A SENIOR WHO PURSUES LIFELONG LEARNING?
stggr stggr
ARE YOU SURE THAT'S REALLY THE DEMON CLERIC...?

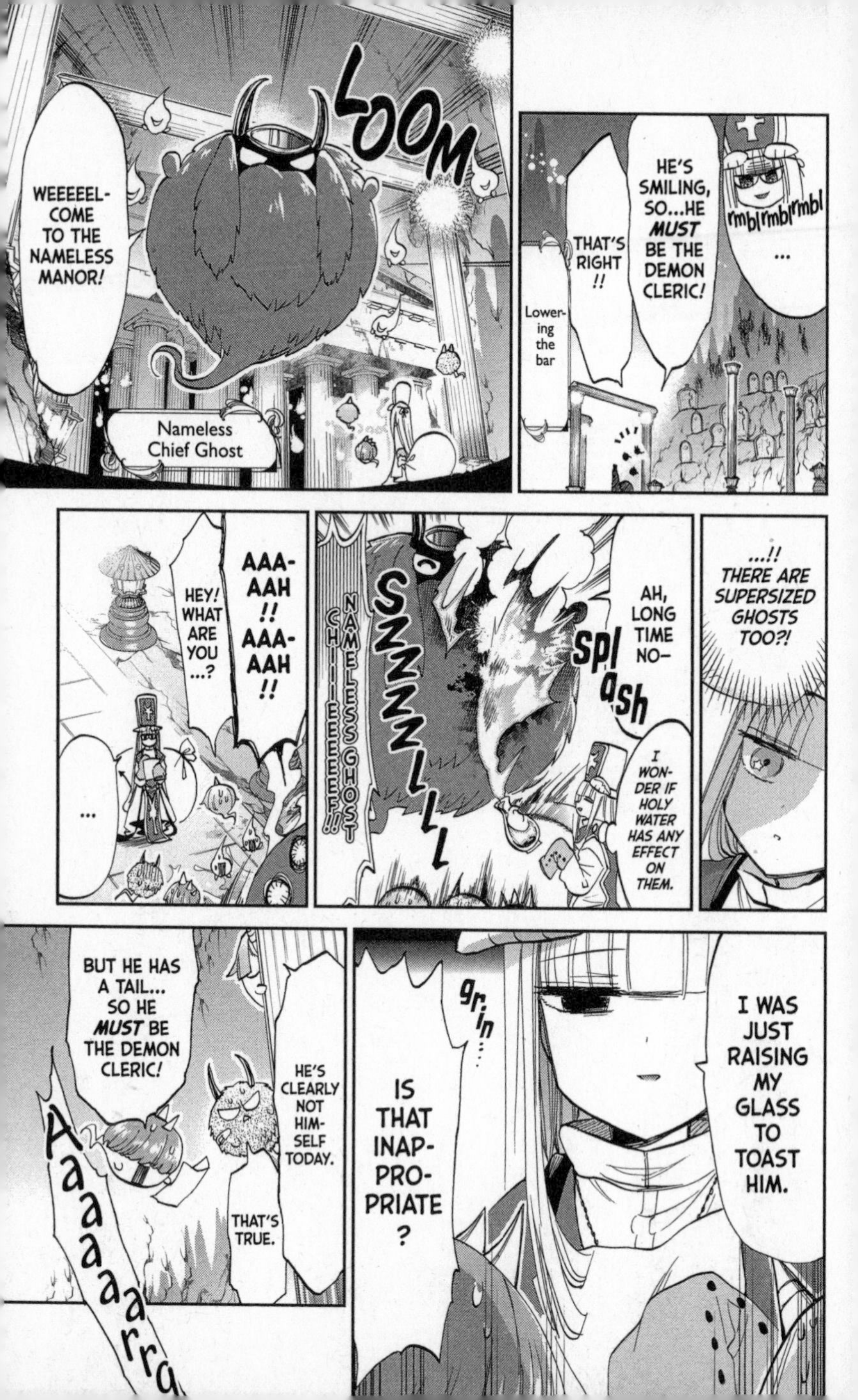
rmblrmblrmbl
...
HE'S SMILING, SO...HE *MUST* BE THE DEMON CLERIC!
THAT'S RIGHT!!
Lowering the bar
LOOM
WEEEEEL-COME TO THE NAMELESS MANOR!
Nameless Chief Ghost
...!! *THERE ARE SUPERSIZED GHOSTS TOO?!*
AH, LONG TIME NO—
splash
I WONDER IF HOLY WATER HAS ANY EFFECT ON THEM.
SZZZZLLLL
NAMELESS GHOST CHIIIEEEEEF!!
AAA-AAH!! AAA-AAH!!
HEY! WHAT ARE YOU...?
...
I WAS JUST RAISING MY GLASS TO TOAST HIM.
grin...
IS THAT INAPPROPRIATE?
HE'S CLEARLY NOT HIMSELF TODAY.
BUT HE HAS A TAIL... SO HE *MUST* BE THE DEMON CLERIC!
THAT'S TRUE.
Aaaaaarrg

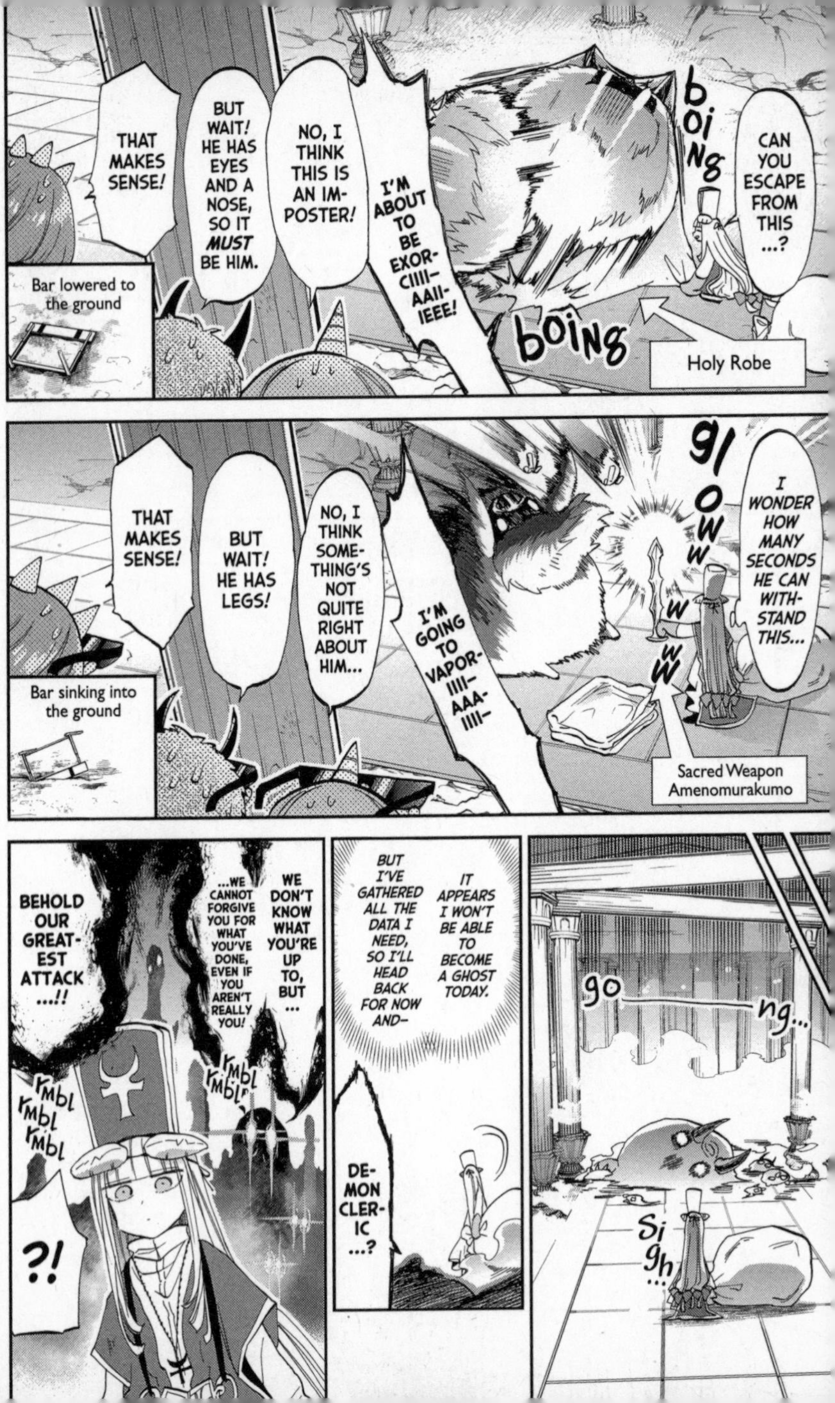
CAN YOU ESCAPE FROM THIS ...?
boing
I'M ABOUT TO BE EXOR-CIIII-AAII-IEEE!
NO, I THINK THIS IS AN IM-POSTER!
BUT WAIT! HE HAS EYES AND A NOSE, SO IT MUST BE HIM.
THAT MAKES SENSE!
boing
Holy Robe
Bar lowered to the ground
I WONDER HOW MANY SECONDS HE CAN WITH-STAND THIS...
glowwwww
I'M GOING TO VAPOR-IIII-AAA-IIII-
NO, I THINK SOME-THING'S NOT QUITE RIGHT ABOUT HIM...
BUT WAIT! HE HAS LEGS!
THAT MAKES SENSE!
Sacred Weapon Amenomurakumo
Bar sinking into the ground
go——ng...
Sigh...
IT APPEARS I WON'T BE ABLE TO BECOME A GHOST TODAY.
BUT I'VE GATHERED ALL THE DATA I NEED, SO I'LL HEAD BACK FOR NOW AND—
DE-MON CLER-IC ...?
WE DON'T KNOW WHAT YOU'RE UP TO, BUT ...
...WE CANNOT FORGIVE YOU FOR WHAT YOU'VE DONE, EVEN IF YOU AREN'T REALLY YOU!
rmbl rmbl
BEHOLD OUR GREAT-EST ATTACK ...!!
rmbl rmbl rmbl
?!

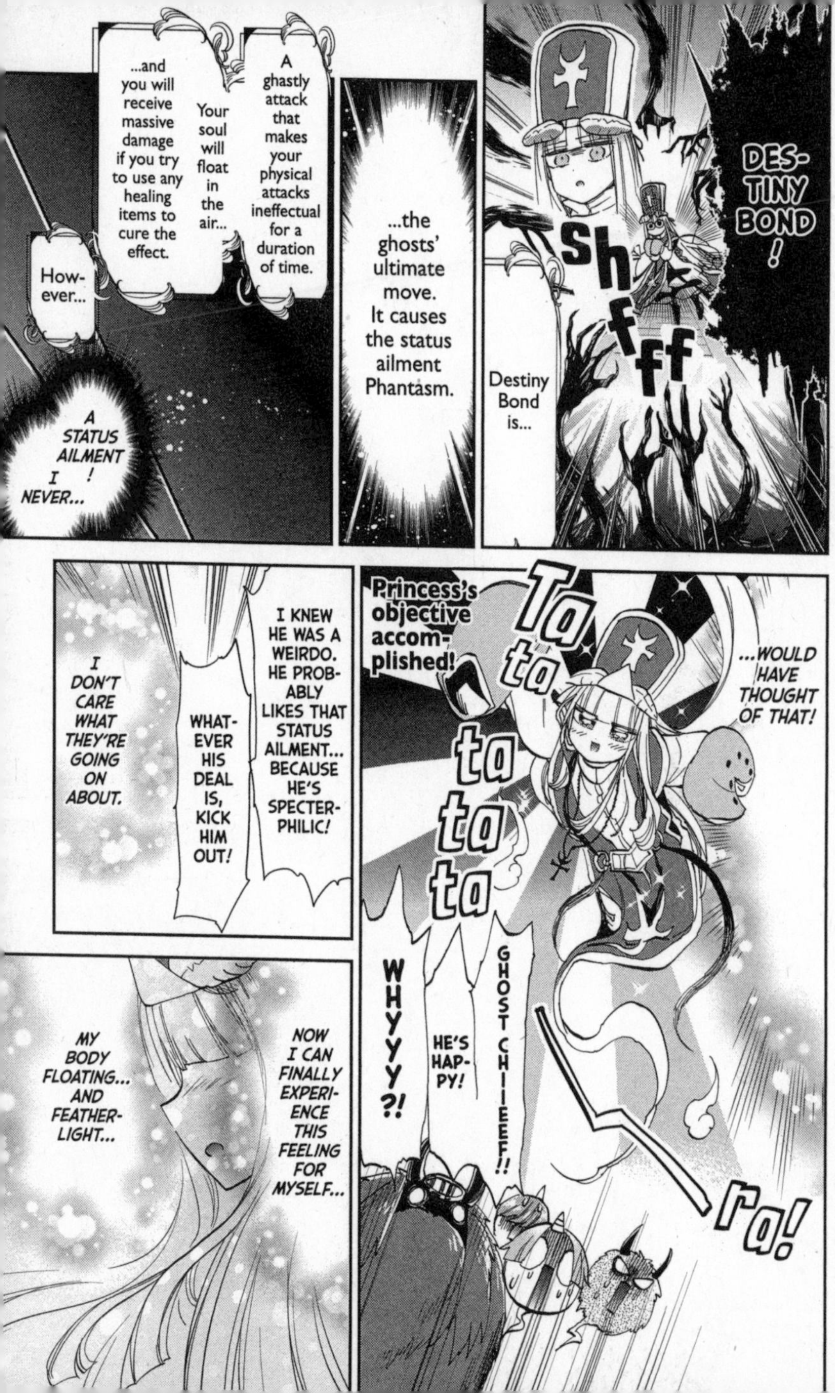
DES-TINY BOND!
Shfff
Destiny Bond is...
...the ghosts' ultimate move. It causes the status ailment Phantasm.
A ghastly attack that makes your physical attacks ineffectual for a duration of time.
Your soul will float in the air...
...and you will receive massive damage if you try to use any healing items to cure the effect.
How-ever...
A STATUS AILMENT! I NEVER...
Princess's objective accom-plished!
...WOULD HAVE THOUGHT OF THAT!
Tatatatata
ra!
GHOST CHIIEEF!!
HE'S HAP-PY!
WHYYY?!
I KNEW HE WAS A WEIRDO. HE PROB-ABLY LIKES THAT STATUS AILMENT... BECAUSE HE'S SPECTER-PHILIC!
WHAT-EVER HIS DEAL IS, KICK HIM OUT!
I DON'T CARE WHAT THEY'RE GOING ON ABOUT.
NOW I CAN FINALLY EXPERI-ENCE THIS FEELING FOR MYSELF...
MY BODY FLOATING... AND FEATHER-LIGHT...

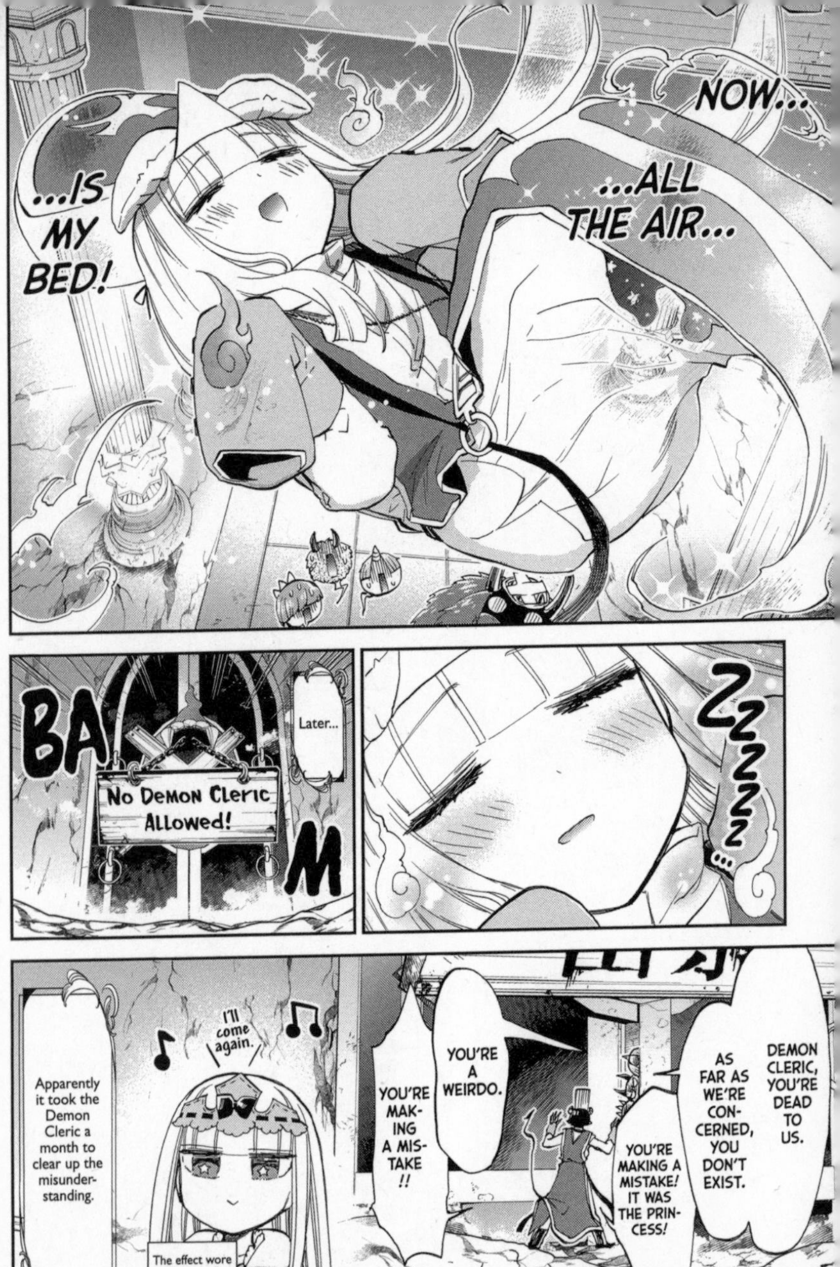
NOW...
...ALL THE AIR...
...IS MY BED!
Zzzzzz...
Later...
BAM
No Demon Cleric Allowed!
DEMON CLERIC, YOU'RE DEAD TO US.
AS FAR AS WE'RE CONCERNED, YOU DON'T EXIST.
YOU'RE MAKING A MISTAKE! IT WAS THE PRINCESS!
YOU'RE A WEIRDO.
YOU'RE MAKING A MISTAKE!!
Apparently it took the Demon Cleric a month to clear up the misunderstanding.
I'll come again.
The effect wore off eventually.

Nameless Ghost A, B, C

We would like to have names soon, thank you.

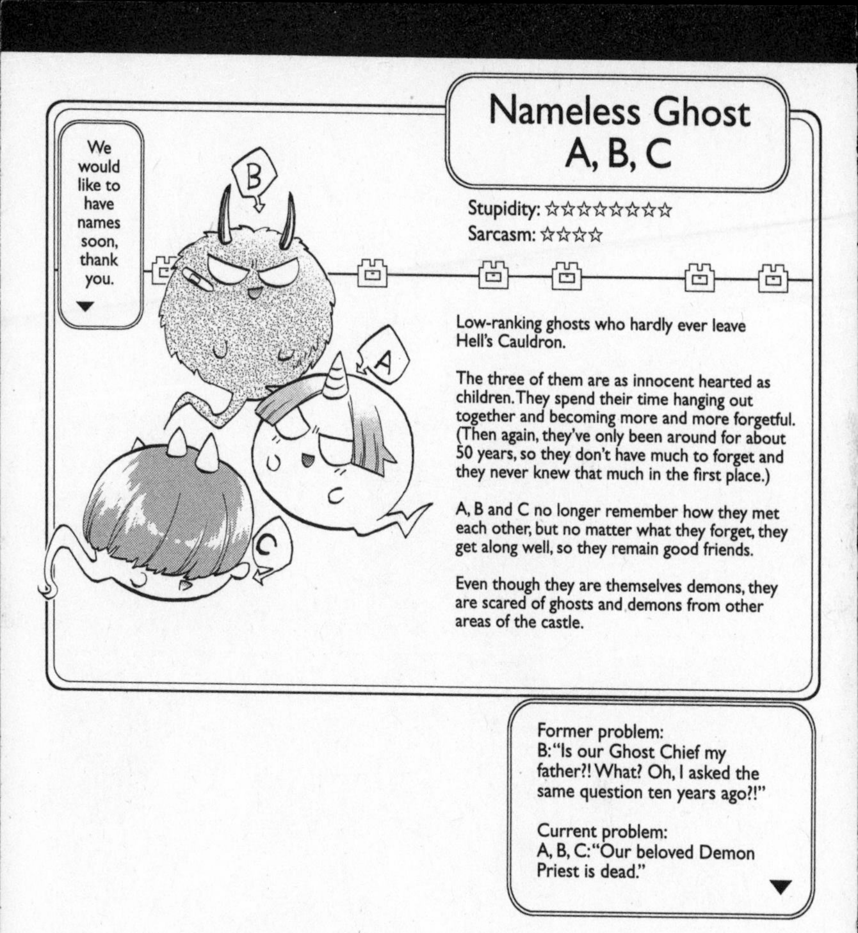
B
A
C

Stupidity: ☆☆☆☆☆☆☆☆☆

Sarcasm: ☆☆☆☆

Low-ranking ghosts who hardly ever leave Hell's Cauldron.

The three of them are as innocent hearted as children. They spend their time hanging out together and becoming more and more forgetful. (Then again, they've only been around for about 50 years, so they don't have much to forget and they never knew that much in the first place.)

A, B and C no longer remember how they met each other, but no matter what they forget, they get along well, so they remain good friends.

Even though they are themselves demons, they are scared of ghosts and demons from other areas of the castle.

Former problem:
B: "Is our Ghost Chief my father?! What? Oh, I asked the same question ten years ago?!"

Current problem:
A, B, C: "Our beloved Demon Priest is dead."

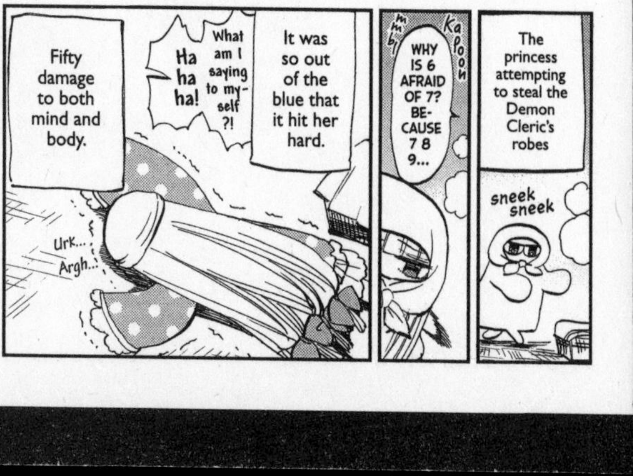
The princess attempting to steal the Demon Cleric's robes
sneek sneek
WHY IS 6 AFRAID OF 7? BE-CAUSE 7 8 9...
Kapoon
It was so out of the blue that it hit her hard.
What am I saying to my-self ?!
Ha ha ha!
Fifty damage to both mind and body.
Urk...
Argh...

Would you like to change your class?

9 changes remaining

▶Yes

No▼

Faux Cleric

"Focus on healing."

▼

43rd Night: Attack of the Teddy Demon Subspecies!

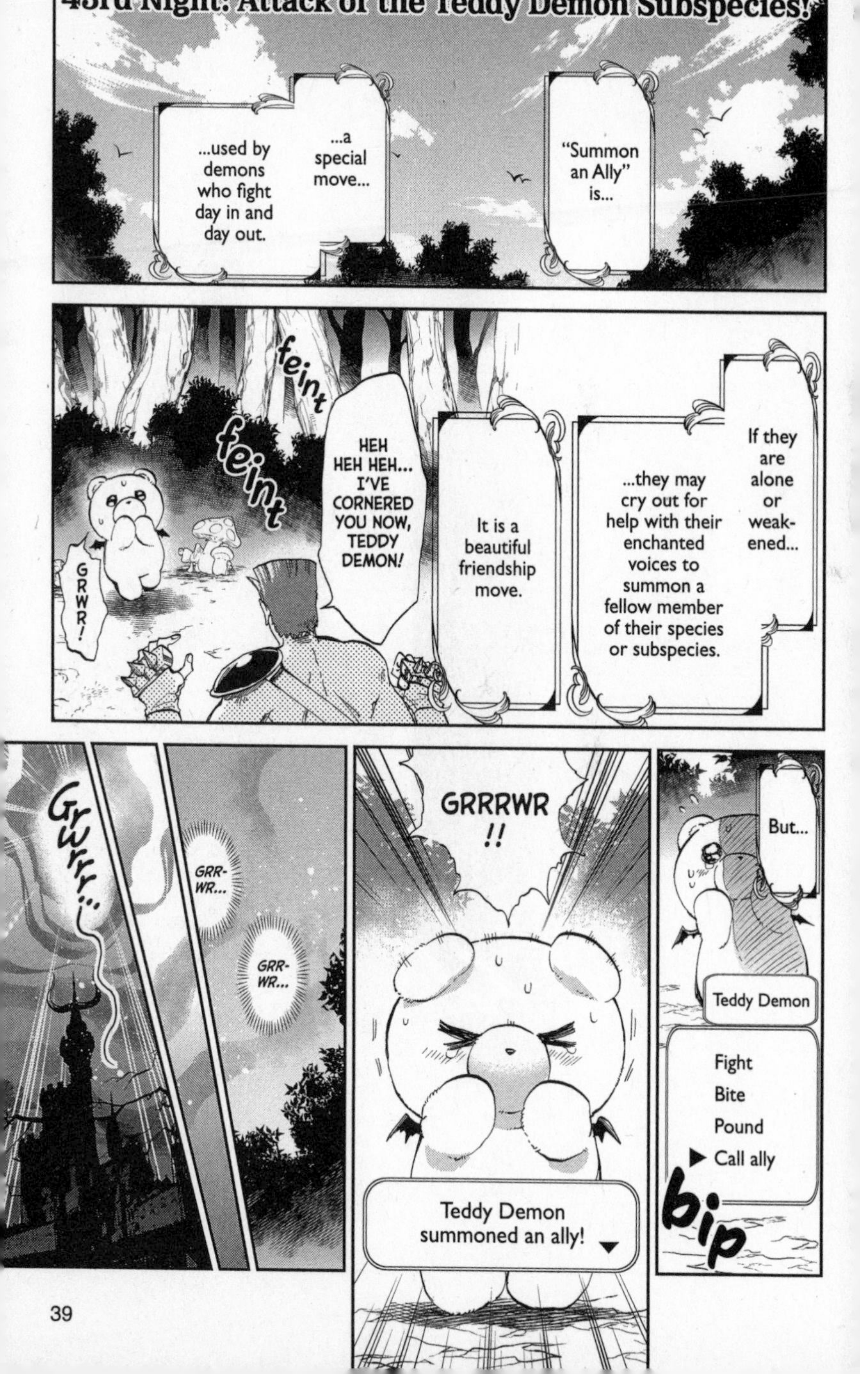
"Summon an Ally" is...
...a special move...
...used by demons who fight day in and day out.
If they are alone or weak-ened...
...they may cry out for help with their enchanted voices to summon a fellow member of their species or subspecies.
It is a beautiful friendship move.
HEH HEH HEH... I'VE CORNERED YOU NOW, TEDDY DEMON!
feint
feint
GRWR!
But...
Teddy Demon
Fight
Bite
Pound
▶ Call ally
bip
GRRRWR !!
Teddy Demon summoned an ally!
GRR-WR...
GRR-WR...
Grwrrr...

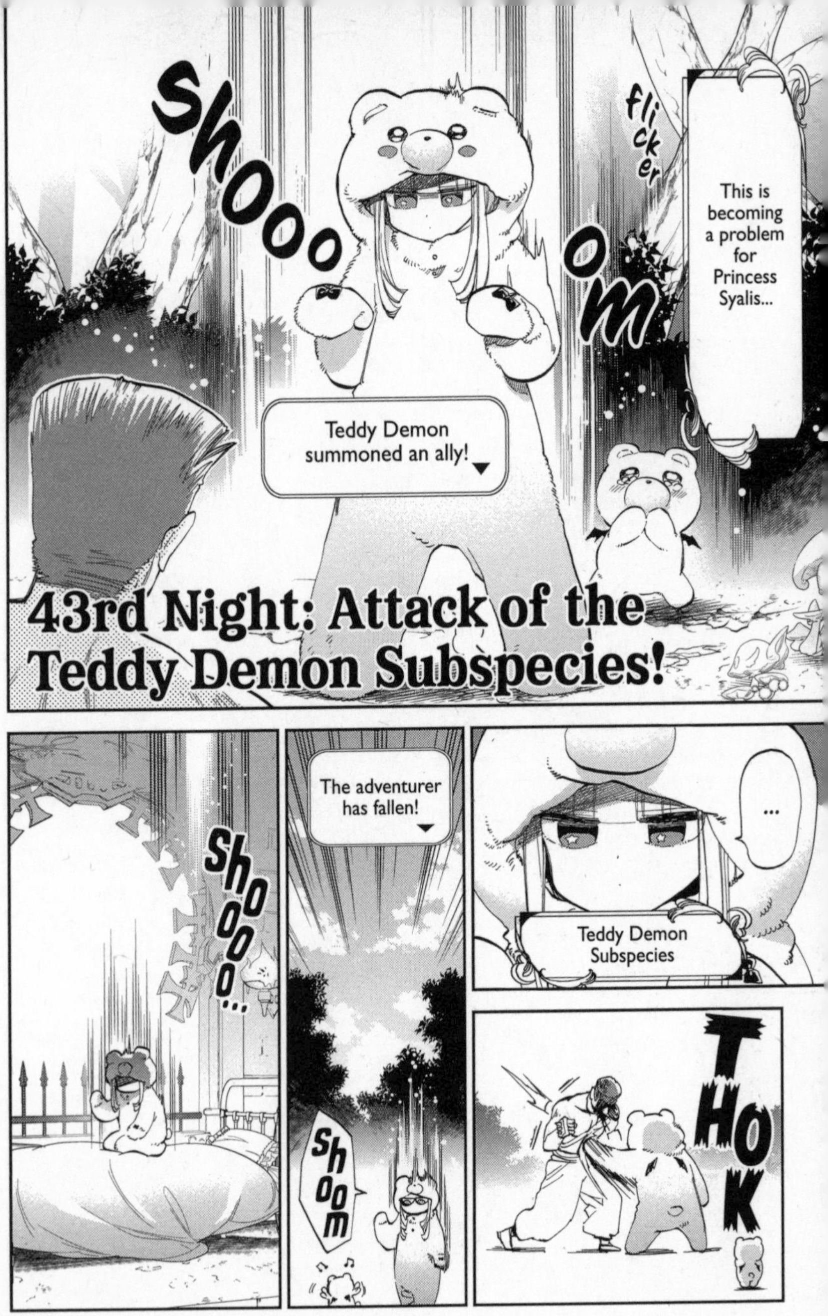
This is becoming a problem for Princess Syalis...
flicker
SHOOOOOM
Teddy Demon summoned an ally!
43rd Night: Attack of the Teddy Demon Subspecies!
...
Teddy Demon Subspecies
THOK
The adventurer has fallen!
Shoom
Shooooo...

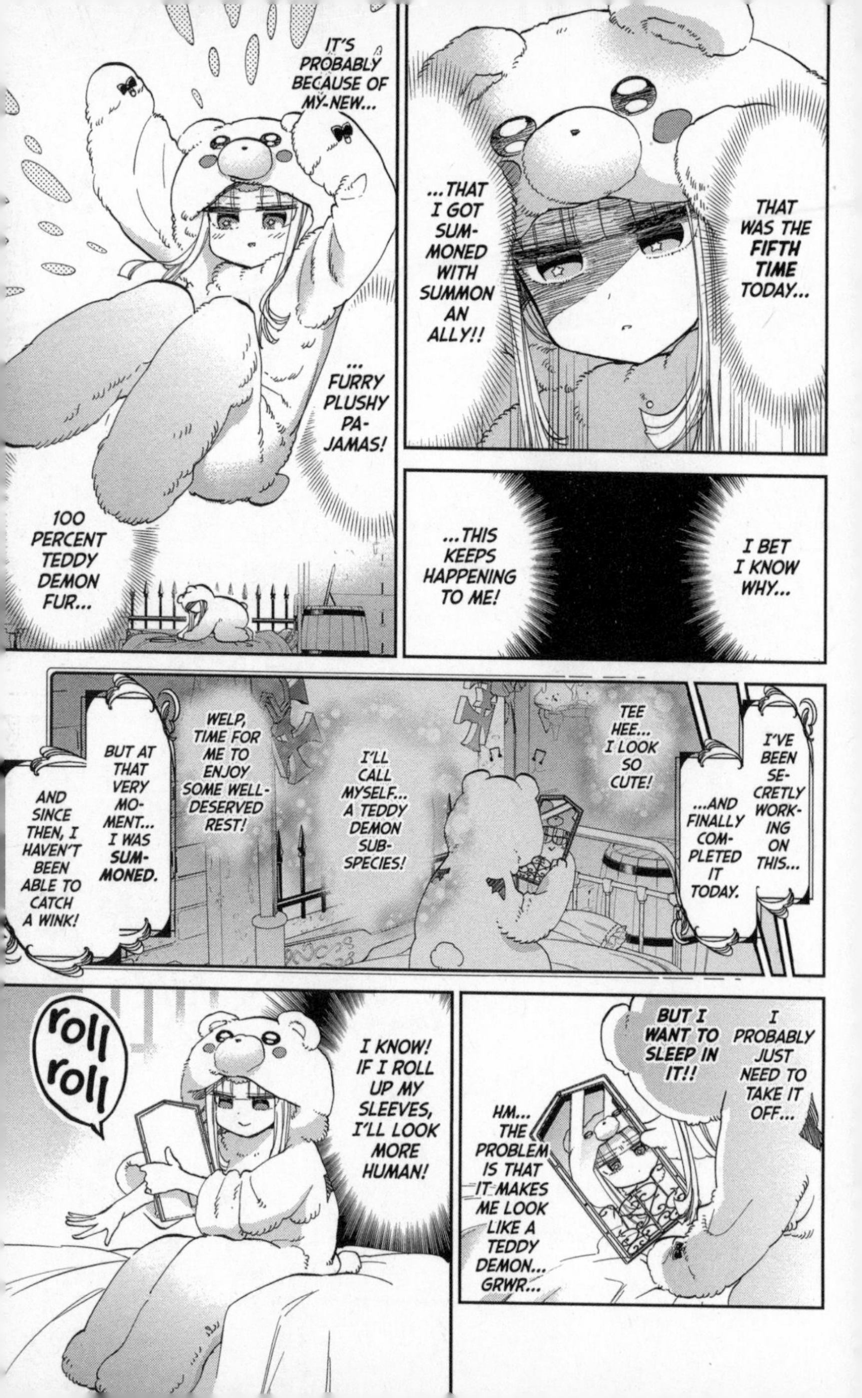
THAT WAS THE FIFTH TIME TODAY...
...THAT I GOT SUMMONED WITH SUMMON AN ALLY!!
...THIS KEEPS HAPPENING TO ME!
I BET I KNOW WHY...
IT'S PROBABLY BECAUSE OF MY-NEW...
...FURRY PLUSHY PAJAMAS!
100 PERCENT TEDDY DEMON FUR...
I'VE BEEN SECRETLY WORKING ON THIS...
...AND FINALLY COMPLETED IT TODAY.
TEE HEE... I LOOK SO CUTE!
I'LL CALL MYSELF... A TEDDY DEMON SUBSPECIES!
WELP, TIME FOR ME TO ENJOY SOME WELL-DESERVED REST!
BUT AT THAT VERY MOMENT... I WAS SUMMONED.
AND SINCE THEN, I HAVEN'T BEEN ABLE TO CATCH A WINK!
HM... THE PROBLEM IS THAT IT MAKES ME LOOK LIKE A TEDDY DEMON... GRWR...
I PROBABLY JUST NEED TO TAKE IT OFF...
BUT I WANT TO SLEEP IN IT!!
I KNOW! IF I ROLL UP MY SLEEVES, I'LL LOOK MORE HUMAN!
roll roll

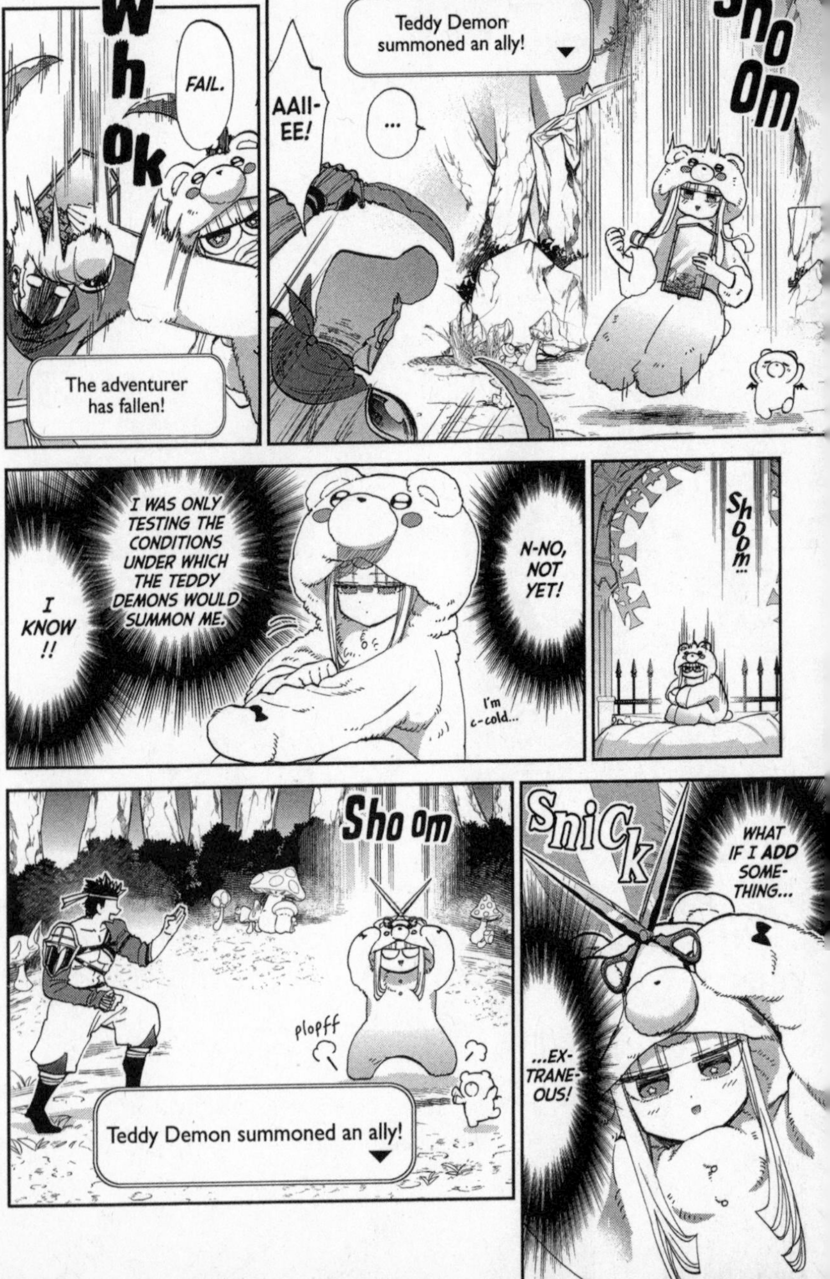
Shooom
Teddy Demon summoned an ally!
...
AAII-EE!
FAIL.
Whook
The adventurer has fallen!
Shoom...
N-NO, NOT YET!
I'm c-cold...
I WAS ONLY TESTING THE CONDITIONS UNDER WHICH THE TEDDY DEMONS WOULD SUMMON ME.
I KNOW!!
SniCk
WHAT IF I ADD SOME-THING...
...EX-TRANE-OUS!
Shoom
plopff
Teddy Demon summoned an ally!

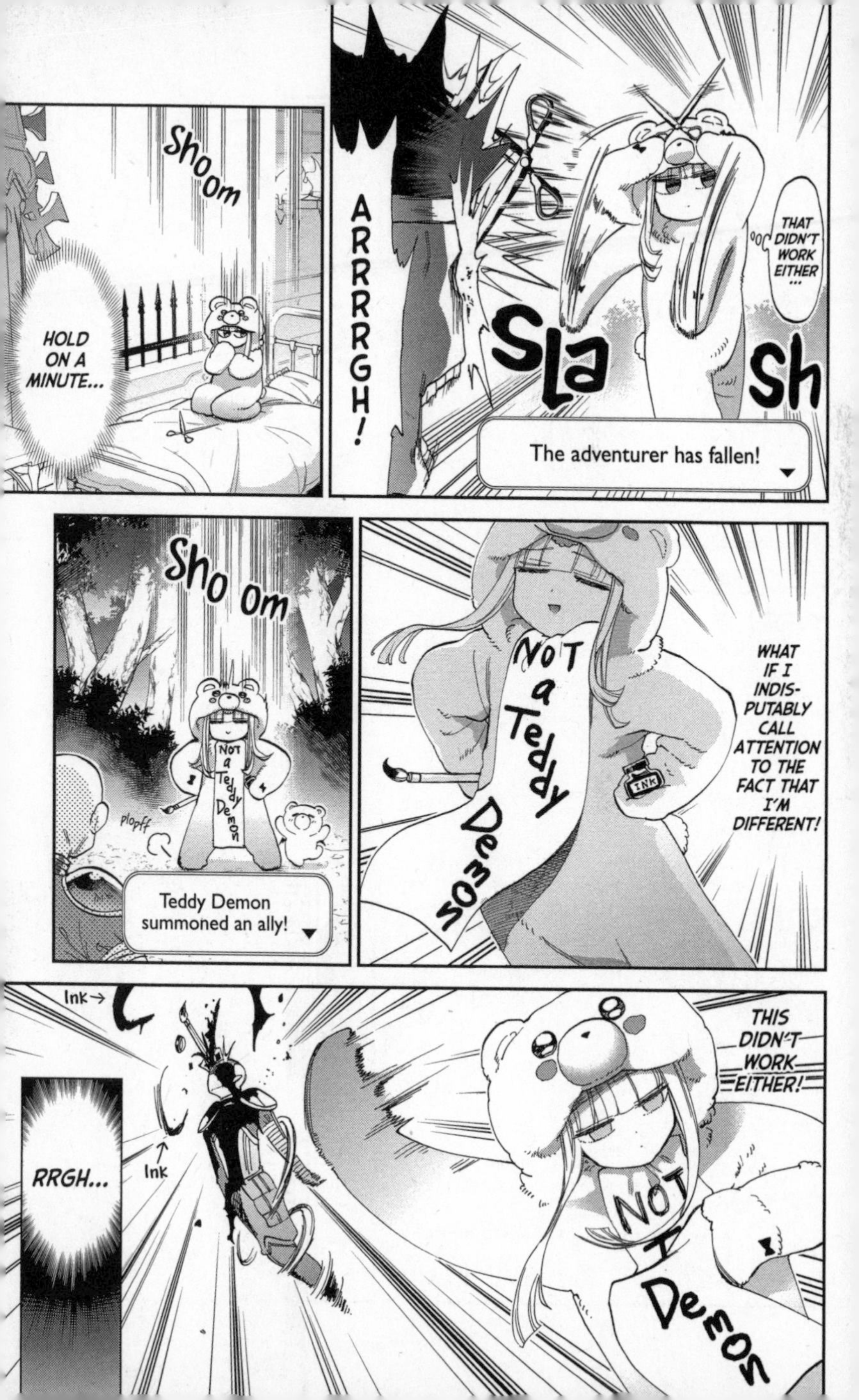
THAT DIDN'T WORK EITHER...
ARRRRRGH!
Slash
The adventurer has fallen!
Shoom
HOLD ON A MINUTE...
WHAT IF I INDISPUTABLY CALL ATTENTION TO THE FACT THAT I'M DIFFERENT!
NOT a Teddy Demon
INK
Shoom
NOT a Teddy Demon
plopff
Teddy Demon summoned an ally!
THIS DIDN'T WORK EITHER!
NOT
Demon
Ink→
Ink
RRGH...

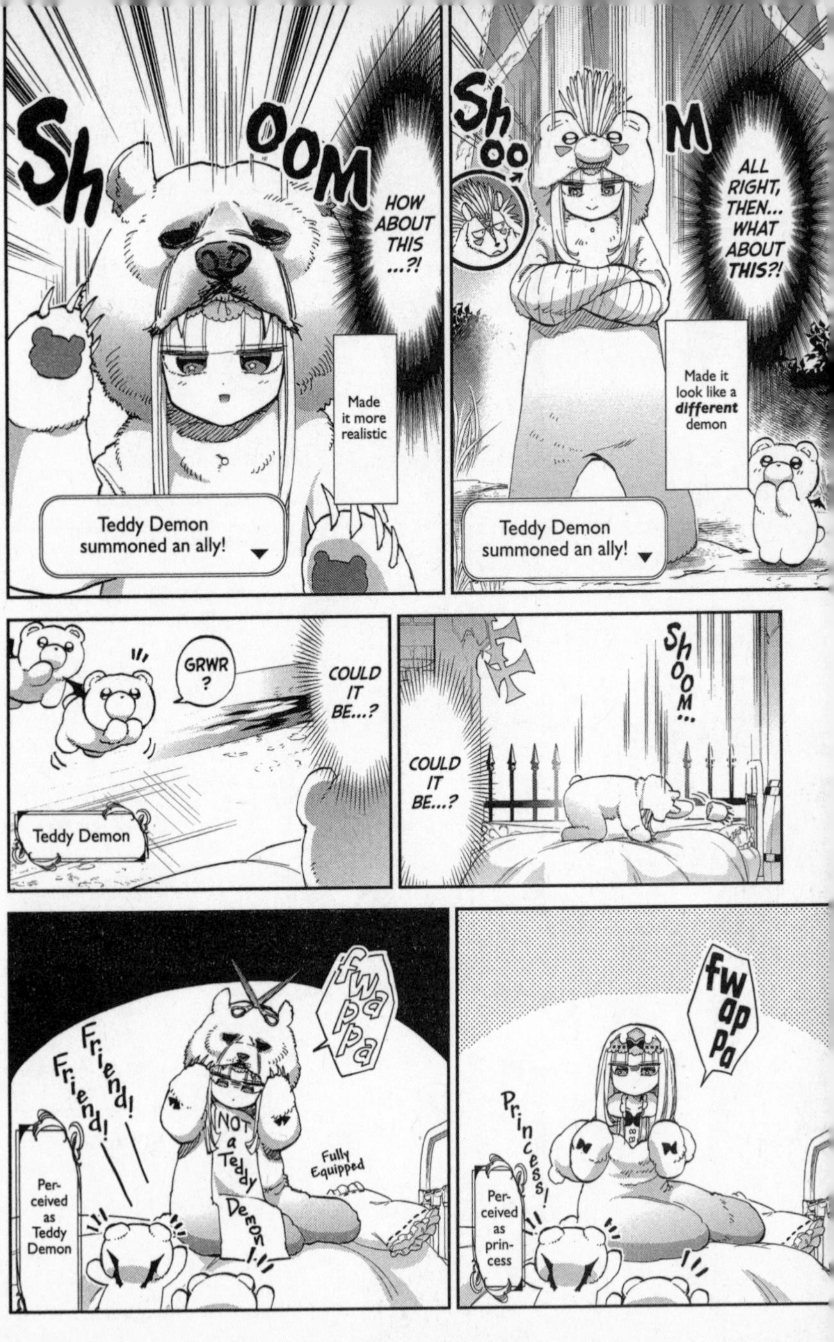
Sh oo M
ALL RIGHT, THEN... WHAT ABOUT THIS?!
Made it look like a **different** demon
Teddy Demon summoned an ally!
Sh OOM
HOW ABOUT THIS ...?!
Made it more realistic
Teddy Demon summoned an ally!
Shoom...
COULD IT BE...?
COULD IT BE...?
GRWR ?
Teddy Demon
fwappa
Princess!
Perceived as princess
fwappa
Friend! Friend!
NOT a Teddy Demon!
Fully Equipped
Perceived as Teddy Demon

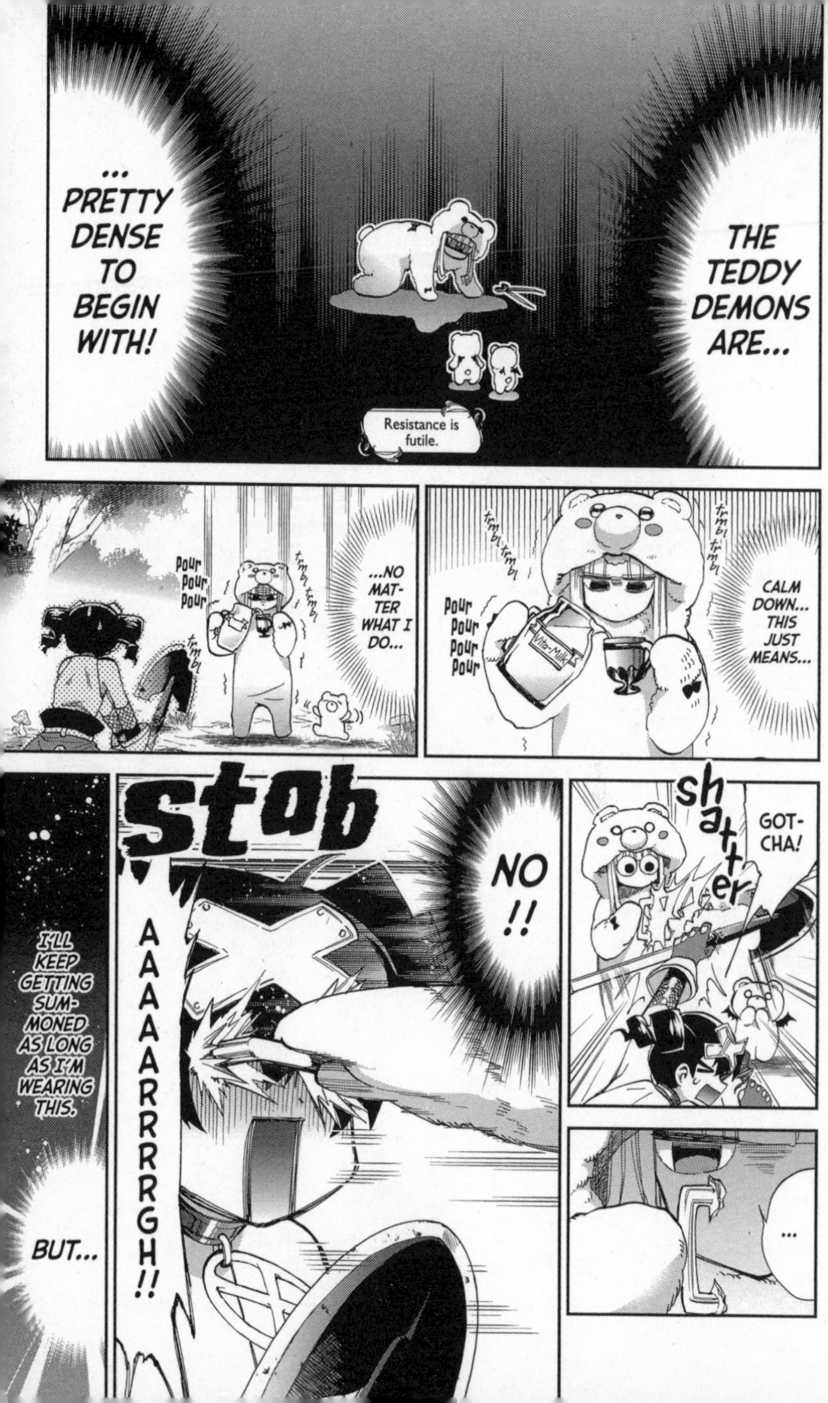
THE TEDDY DEMONS ARE...
... PRETTY DENSE TO BEGIN WITH!
Resistance is futile.
CALM DOWN... THIS JUST MEANS...
trmbl trmbl
trmbl trmbl
Pour Pour Pour Pour
Vita-Milk
...NO MATTER WHAT I DO...
trmbl trmbl
Pour Pour Pour
trmbl
shatter
GOT-CHA!
...
stab
NO !!
AAAAAARRRRRGH!!
I'LL KEEP GETTING SUMMONED AS LONG AS I'M WEARING THIS.
BUT...

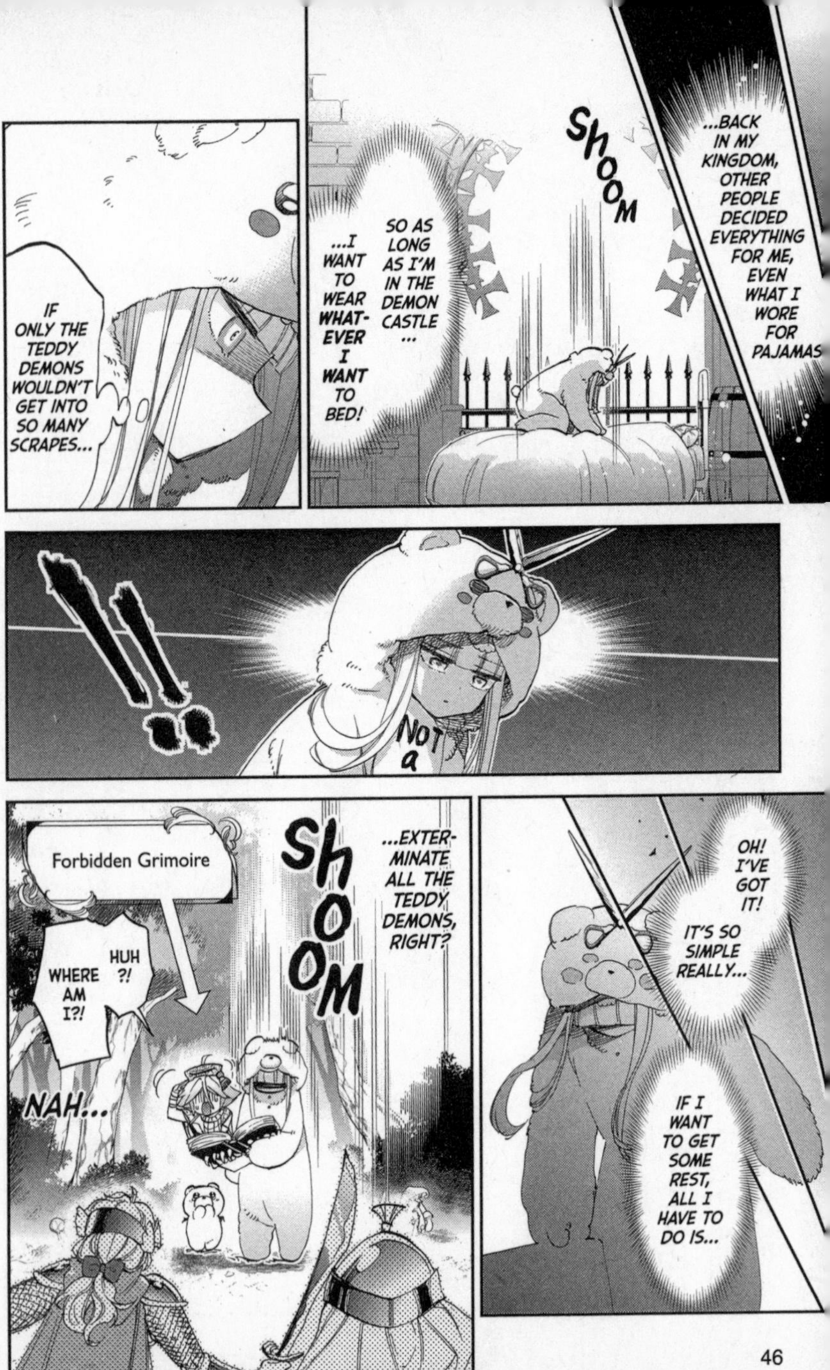
...BACK IN MY KINGDOM, OTHER PEOPLE DECIDED EVERYTHING FOR ME, EVEN WHAT I WORE FOR PAJAMAS
SHOOM
SO AS LONG AS I'M IN THE DEMON CASTLE...
...I WANT TO WEAR WHATEVER I WANT TO BED!
IF ONLY THE TEDDY DEMONS WOULDN'T GET INTO SO MANY SCRAPES...
!!
NOT a
OH! I'VE GOT IT!
IT'S SO SIMPLE REALLY...
IF I WANT TO GET SOME REST, ALL I HAVE TO DO IS...
...EXTERMINATE ALL THE TEDDY DEMONS, RIGHT?
SHOOM
Forbidden Grimoire
HUH ?!
WHERE AM I?!
NAH...

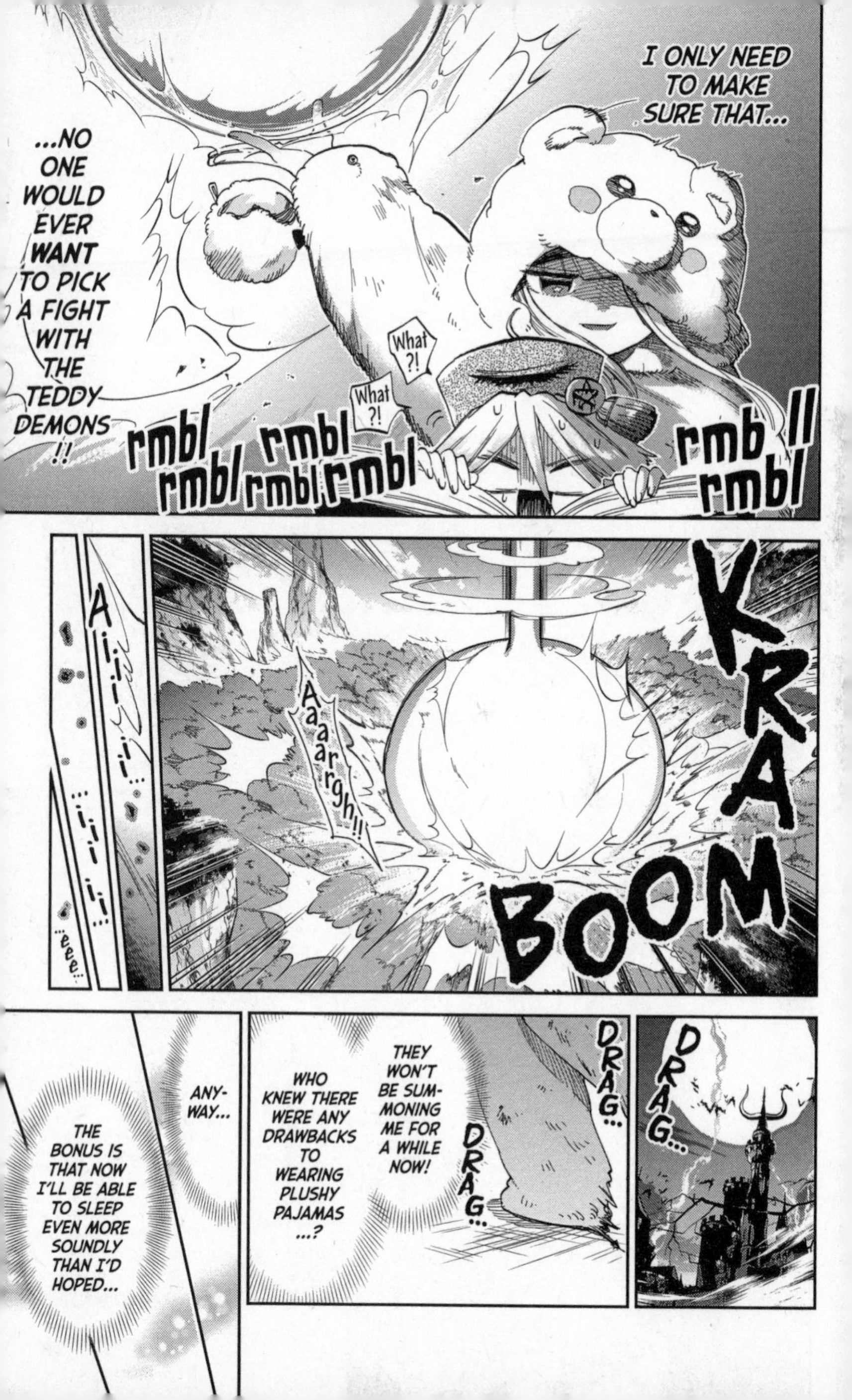
I ONLY NEED TO MAKE SURE THAT...
What?!
What?!
...NO ONE WOULD EVER WANT TO PICK A FIGHT WITH THE TEDDY DEMONS!!
rmbl rmbl
rmbl rmbl rmbl rmbl rmbl rmbl
KRA BOOM
Aaaargh!!
Aiiiii... ...iiiii... ...eee...
DRAG... DRAG...
DRAG... DRAG...
THEY WON'T BE SUMMONING ME FOR A WHILE NOW!
WHO KNEW THERE WERE ANY DRAWBACKS TO WEARING PLUSHY PAJAMAS...?
ANYWAY...
THE BONUS IS THAT NOW I'LL BE ABLE TO SLEEP EVEN MORE SOUNDLY THAN I'D HOPED...

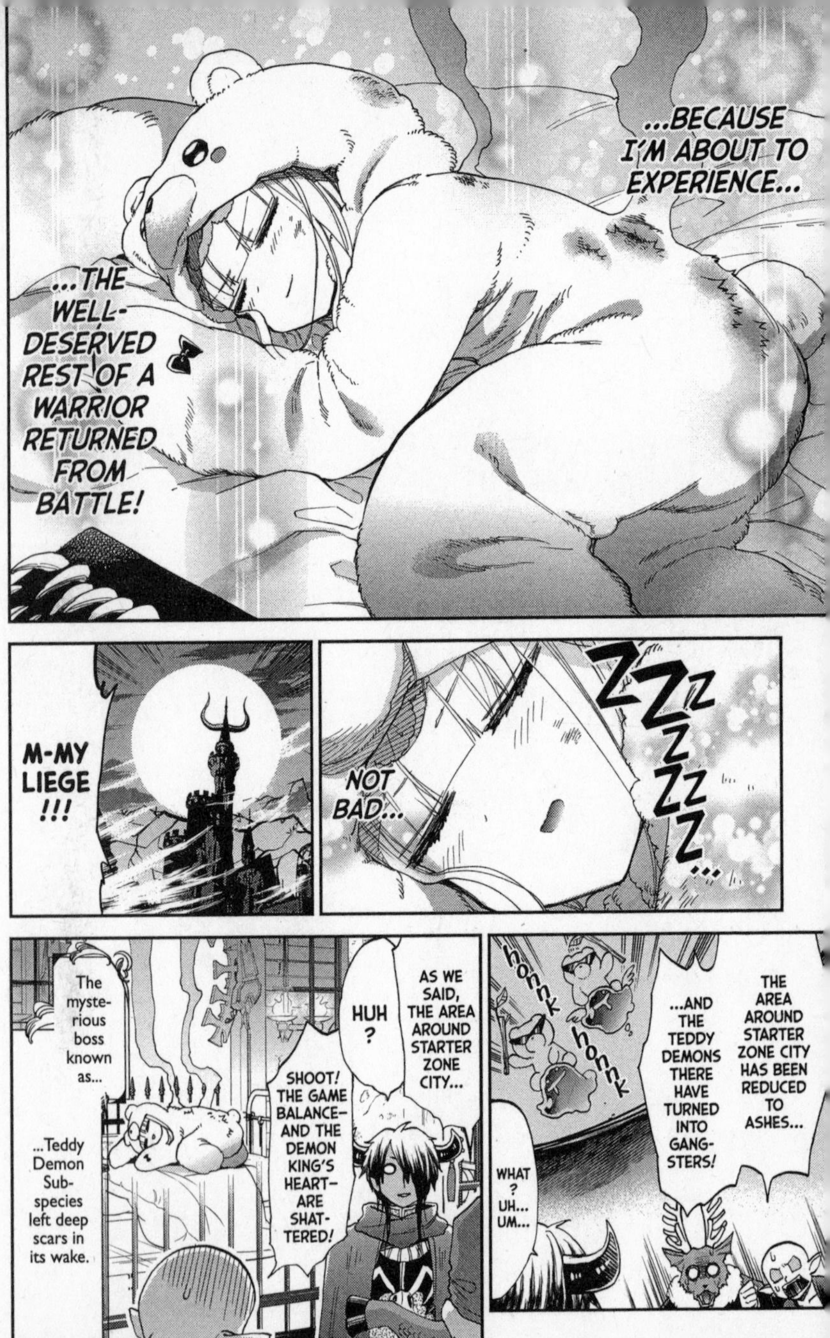
...BECAUSE I'M ABOUT TO EXPERIENCE...
...THE WELL-DESERVED REST OF A WARRIOR RETURNED FROM BATTLE!
NOT BAD...
ZZzzzz...
M-MY LIEGE!!!
THE AREA AROUND STARTER ZONE CITY HAS BEEN REDUCED TO ASHES...
...AND THE TEDDY DEMONS THERE HAVE TURNED INTO GANGSTERS!
honnk honnk
WHAT? UH... UM...
AS WE SAID, THE AREA AROUND STARTER ZONE CITY...
HUH?
SHOOT! THE GAME BALANCE—AND THE DEMON KING'S HEART—ARE SHATTERED!
The mysterious boss known as...
...Teddy Demon Subspecies left deep scars in its wake.

The Garden of Low-Ranking Ghosts

Hell's Cauldron

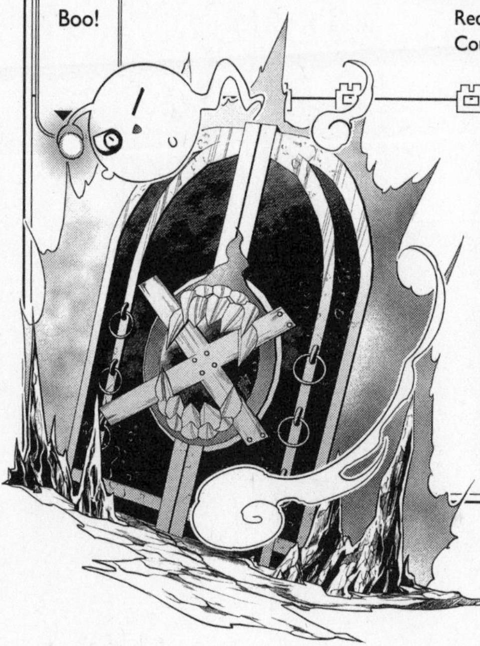
Boo!

Reclusiveness: ☆☆☆☆☆☆☆
Courage: ☆☆☆☆☆☆☆☆☆

Deep within the Demon Temple is nestled the Garden of Low-Ranking Ghosts. The area boss is known as the Nameless Ghost Chief. Since this region is inside the boundaries of the Demon Temple, the more elite ghosts and undead species of demons do not reside here.

Most of the garden's residents live out their days here without ever venturing farther afield. The Glow Wisps are some of the few who are more extroverted and have more friends and acquaintances than the Nameless Ghost Chief.

Excuse

"It's not what you think! You're making a mistake! I'm not specterphilic or anything like that... As a matter of fact, I don't really know where the line is between that and a normal interest in specters! But anyway, it's not like whatever you're thinking..."

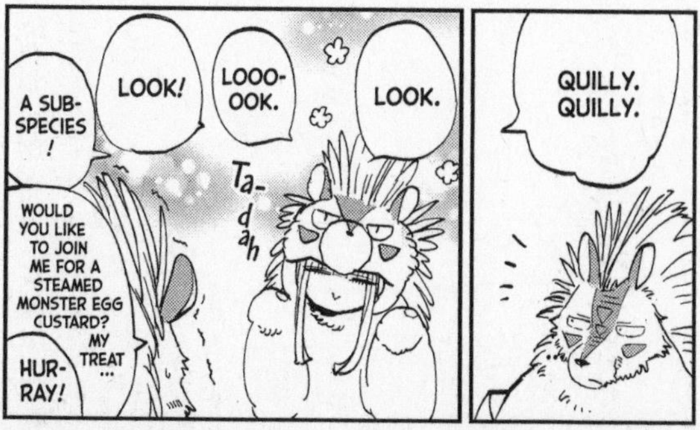
QUILLY. QUILLY.
LOOK.
LOOO-OOK.
LOOK!
A SUB-SPECIES!
Ta-da-dah
WOULD YOU LIKE TO JOIN ME FOR A STEAMED MONSTER EGG CUSTARD? MY TREAT...
HUR-RAY!

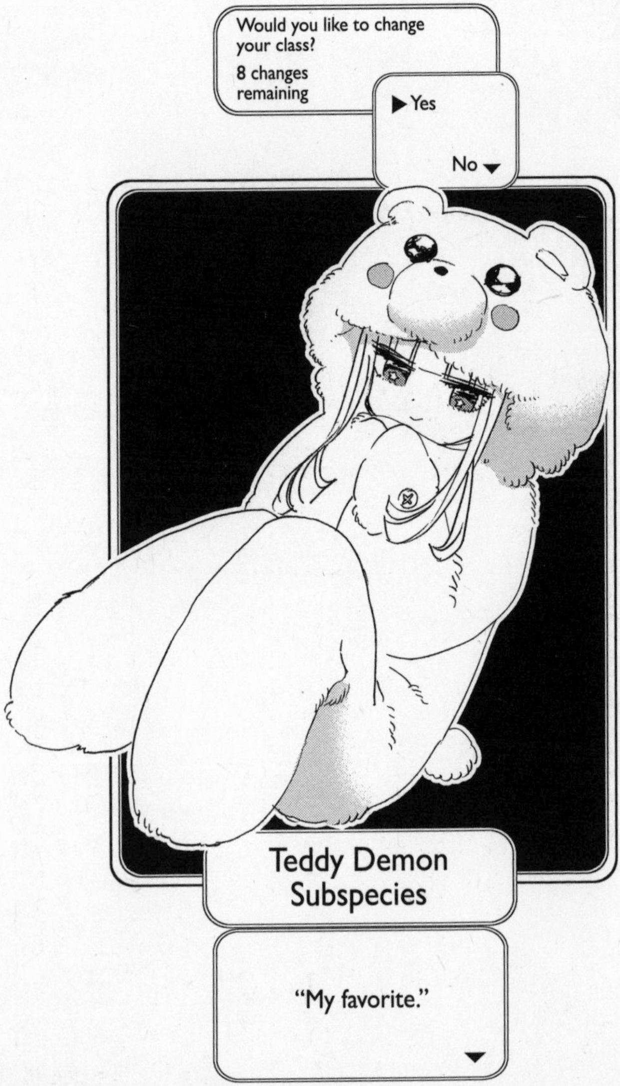
Would you like to change your class?
8 changes remaining
▶Yes
No
Teddy Demon Subspecies
"My favorite."

44th Night: Let's Have a Sing-Along

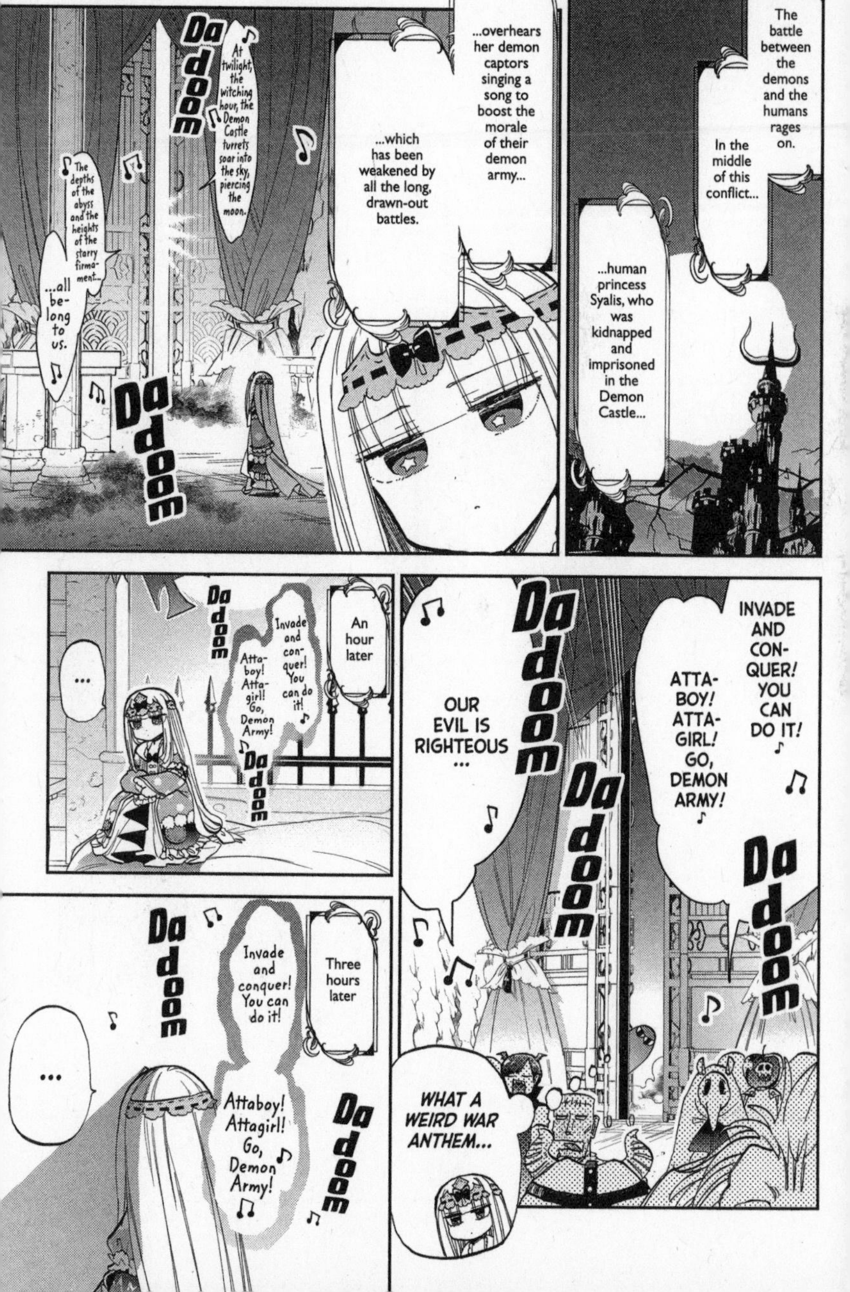
The battle between the demons and the humans rages on.
In the middle of this conflict...
...human princess Syalis, who was kidnapped and imprisoned in the Demon Castle...
...overhears her demon captors singing a song to boost the morale of their demon army...
...which has been weakened by all the long, drawn-out battles.
At twilight, the witching hour, the Demon Castle turrets soar into the sky, piercing the moon.
Da doom
The depths of the abyss and the heights of the starry firmament...
...all belong to us.
Da doom
INVADE AND CONQUER! YOU CAN DO IT!
ATTA-BOY! ATTA-GIRL! GO, DEMON ARMY!
Da doom
OUR EVIL IS RIGHTEOUS ...
Da doom
Da doom
WHAT A WEIRD WAR ANTHEM...
An hour later
Da doom
Invade and conquer! You can do it!
Attaboy! Attagirl! Go, Demon Army!
Da doom
...
Three hours later
Invade and conquer! You can do it!
Da doom
Attaboy! Attagirl! Go, Demon Army!
Da doom
...

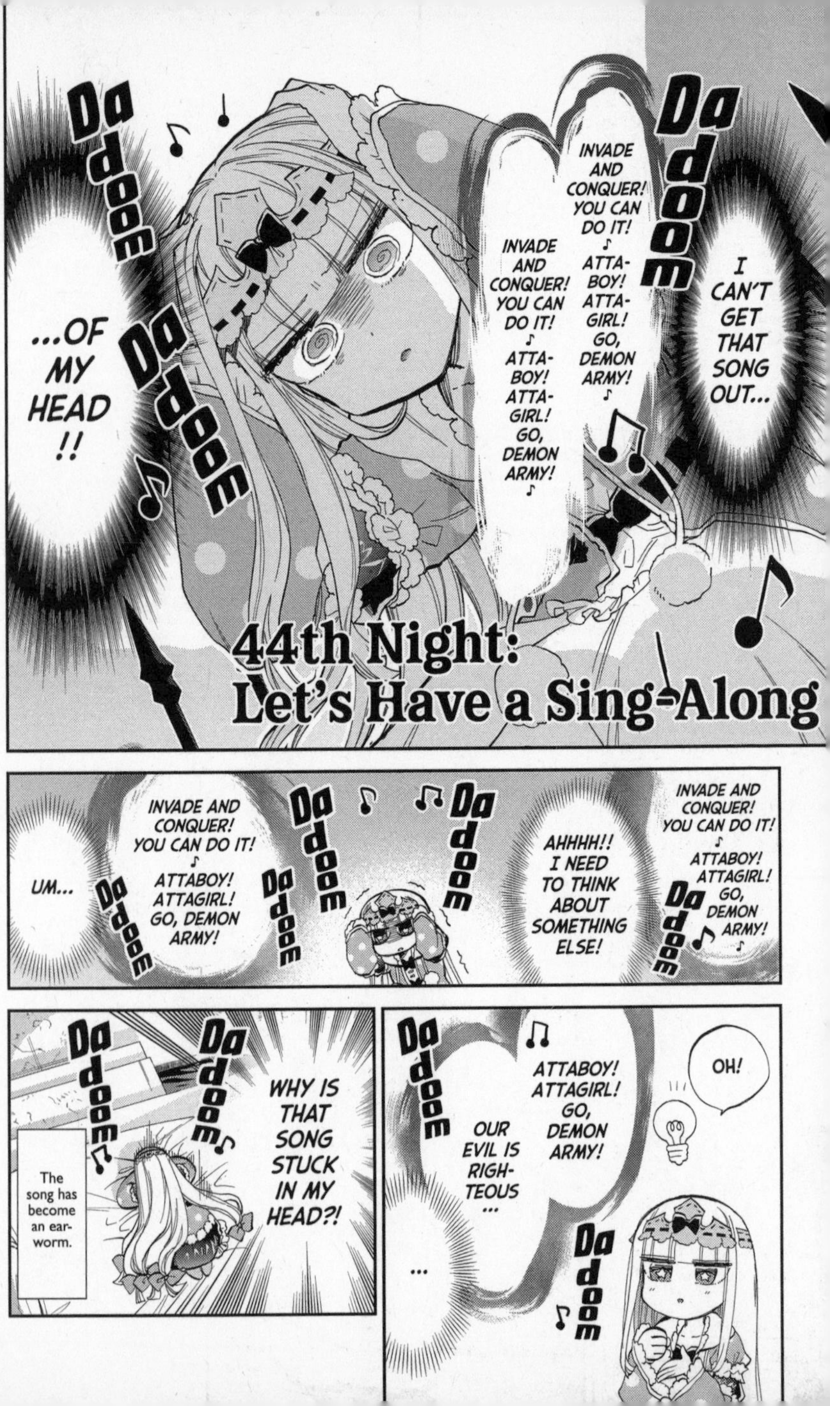
Da doom
I CAN'T GET THAT SONG OUT...
INVADE AND CONQUER! YOU CAN DO IT! ♪ ATTA-BOY! ATTA-GIRL! GO, DEMON ARMY! ♪
INVADE AND CONQUER! YOU CAN DO IT! ♪ ATTA-BOY! ATTA-GIRL! GO, DEMON ARMY! ♪
Da doom
Da doom
...OF MY HEAD!!
44th Night: Let's Have a Sing-Along
INVADE AND CONQUER! YOU CAN DO IT! ♪ ATTABOY! ATTAGIRL! GO, DEMON ARMY! ♪
Da doom
AHHHH!! I NEED TO THINK ABOUT SOMETHING ELSE!
Da doom
Da doom
INVADE AND CONQUER! YOU CAN DO IT! ♪ ATTABOY! ATTAGIRL! GO, DEMON ARMY!
Da doom
UM...
OH!
ATTABOY! ATTAGIRL! GO, DEMON ARMY!
Da doom
OUR EVIL IS RIGHTEOUS...
...
Da doom
Da doom
WHY IS THAT SONG STUCK IN MY HEAD?!
Da doom
The song has become an earworm.

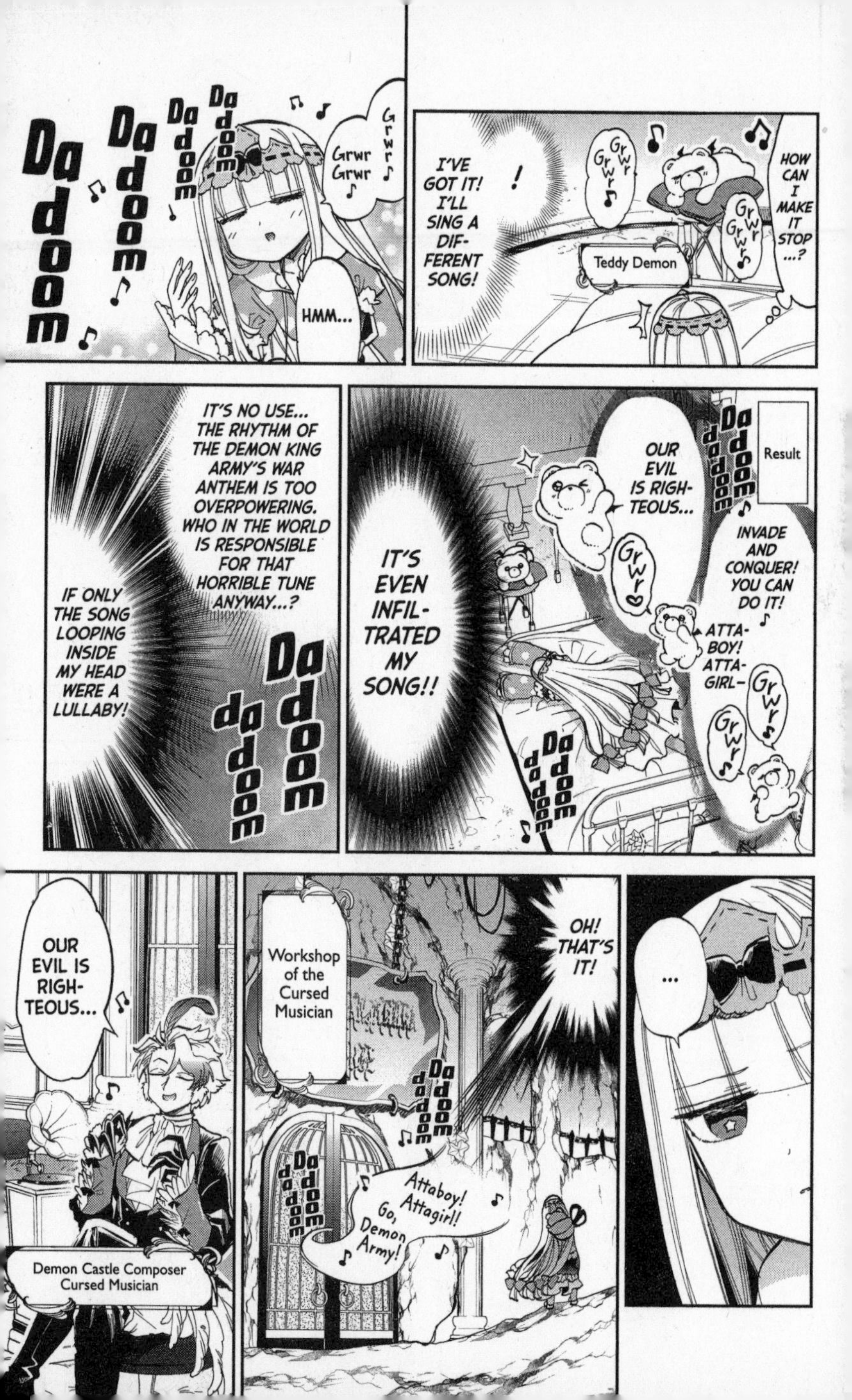
HOW CAN I MAKE IT STOP...?
Grwr Grwr♪
Teddy Demon
Grwr Grwr♪
!
I'VE GOT IT! I'LL SING A DIF-FERENT SONG!
Grwr Grwr♪
Grwr Grwr♪
HMM...
Da doom Da doom♪ Da doom♪ Da doom♪
Result
Da doom da doom♪
OUR EVIL IS RIGH-TEOUS...
Grwr
INVADE AND CONQUER! YOU CAN DO IT!♪
ATTA-BOY! ATTA-GIRL-
Grwr
Grwr
Da doom da doom
IT'S EVEN INFIL-TRATED MY SONG!!
IT'S NO USE... THE RHYTHM OF THE DEMON KING ARMY'S WAR ANTHEM IS TOO OVERPOWERING. WHO IN THE WORLD IS RESPONSIBLE FOR THAT HORRIBLE TUNE ANYWAY...?
IF ONLY THE SONG LOOPING INSIDE MY HEAD WERE A LULLABY!
Da doom da doom
...
OH! THAT'S IT!
Workshop of the Cursed Musician
Da doom da doom
Da doom da doom
Attaboy! Attagirl! Go, Demon Army!
OUR EVIL IS RIGH-TEOUS...♪
Demon Castle Composer Cursed Musician

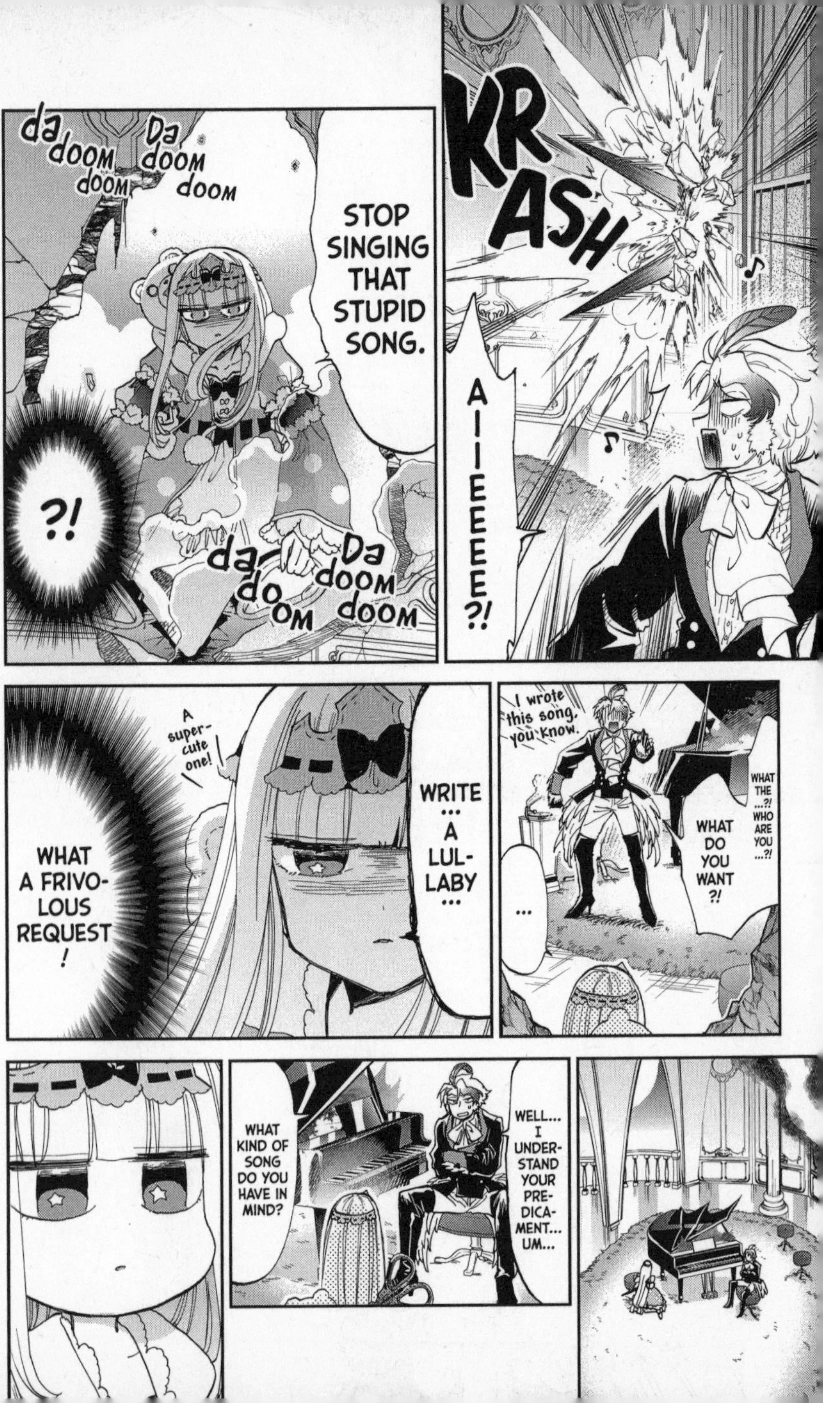
KRASH
AIIEEEEE?!
da doom doom
Da doom doom
STOP SINGING THAT STUPID SONG.
?!
da doom doom
Da doom doom
I wrote this song, you know.
WHAT THE ...?! WHO ARE YOU ...?!
WHAT DO YOU WANT ?!
...
WRITE ... A LUL-LABY ...
A super-cute one!
WHAT A FRIVO-LOUS REQUEST !
WELL... I UNDER-STAND YOUR PRE-DICA-MENT... UM...
WHAT KIND OF SONG DO YOU HAVE IN MIND?

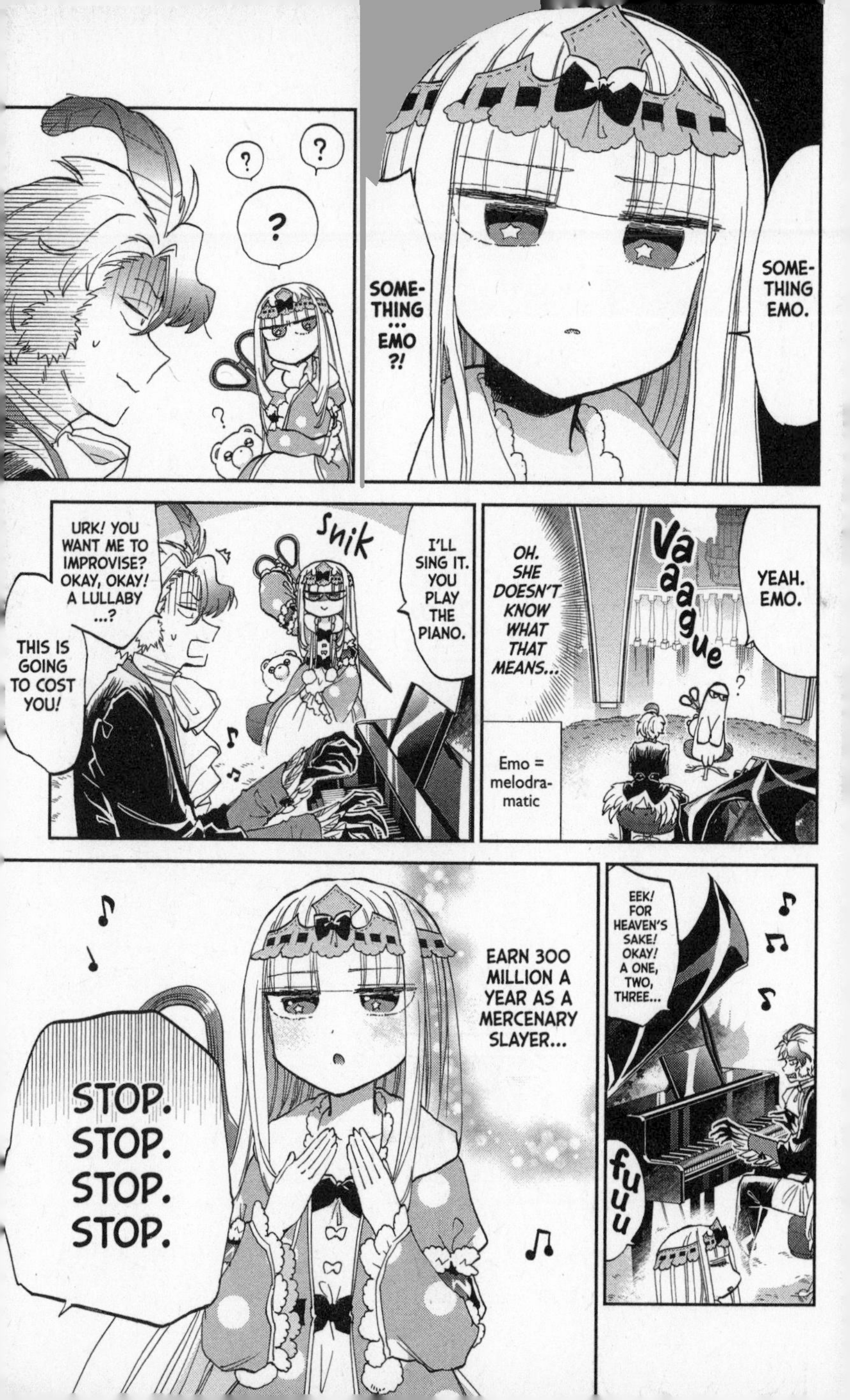
SOME-THING EMO.
SOME-THING ... EMO ?!
?
?
?
?
YEAH. EMO.
Vaague
OH. SHE DOESN'T KNOW WHAT THAT MEANS...
Emo = melodra-matic
?
I'LL SING IT. YOU PLAY THE PIANO.
Snik
URK! YOU WANT ME TO IMPROVISE? OKAY, OKAY! A LULLABY ...?
THIS IS GOING TO COST YOU!
EEK! FOR HEAVEN'S SAKE! OKAY! A ONE, TWO, THREE...
fuuu
EARN 300 MILLION A YEAR AS A MERCENARY SLAYER...
STOP. STOP. STOP. STOP.

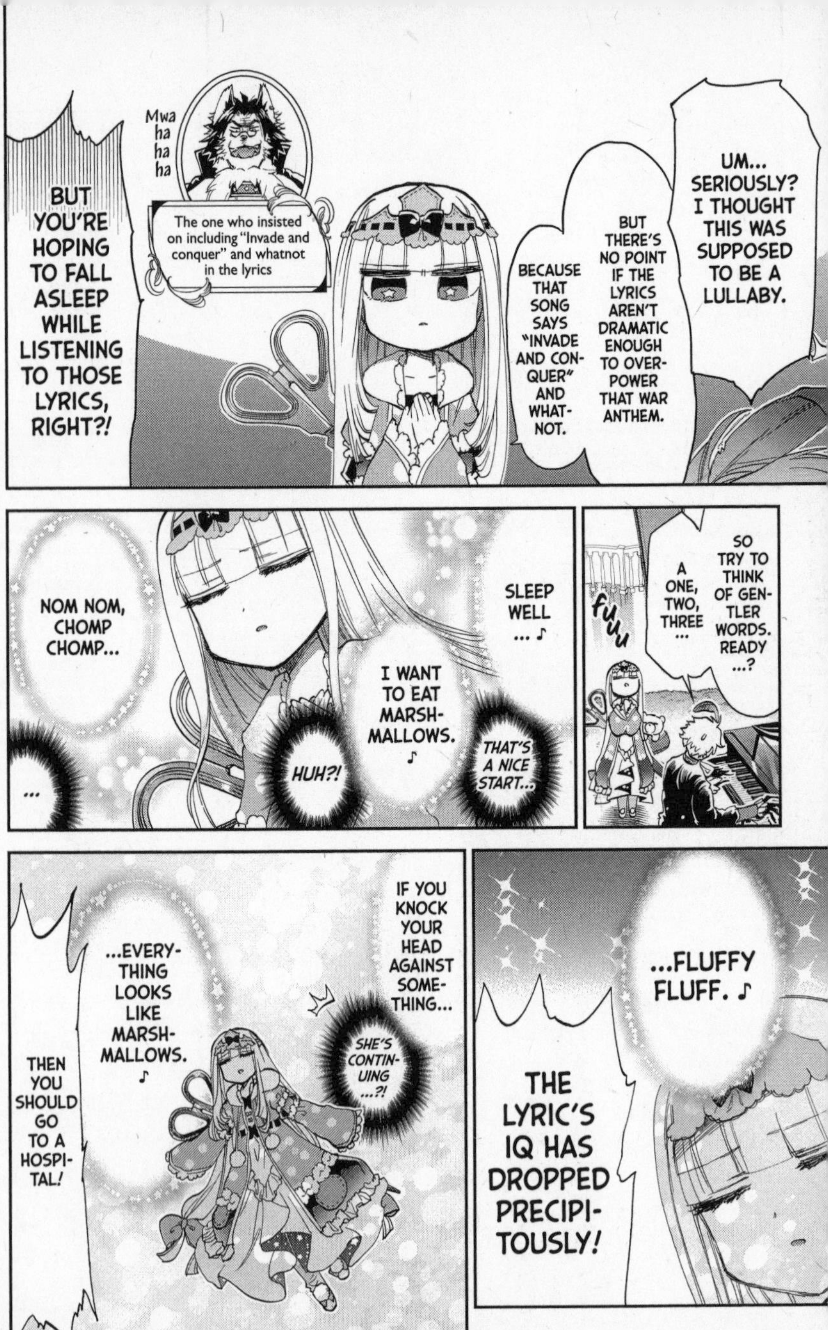
UM... SERIOUSLY? I THOUGHT THIS WAS SUPPOSED TO BE A LULLABY.
BUT THERE'S NO POINT IF THE LYRICS AREN'T DRAMATIC ENOUGH TO OVERPOWER THAT WAR ANTHEM.
BECAUSE THAT SONG SAYS "INVADE AND CONQUER" AND WHATNOT.
Mwa ha ha ha
The one who insisted on including "Invade and conquer" and whatnot in the lyrics
BUT YOU'RE HOPING TO FALL ASLEEP WHILE LISTENING TO THOSE LYRICS, RIGHT?!
SO TRY TO THINK OF GENTLER WORDS. READY ...?
A ONE, TWO, THREE ...
fuuu
SLEEP WELL ... ♪
THAT'S A NICE START...
I WANT TO EAT MARSHMALLOWS. ♪
HUH?!
NOM NOM, CHOMP CHOMP...
...
...FLUFFY FLUFF. ♪
THE LYRIC'S IQ HAS DROPPED PRECIPITOUSLY!
IF YOU KNOCK YOUR HEAD AGAINST SOMETHING...
SHE'S CONTINUING ...?!
...EVERYTHING LOOKS LIKE MARSHMALLOWS. ♪
THEN YOU SHOULD GO TO A HOSPITAL!

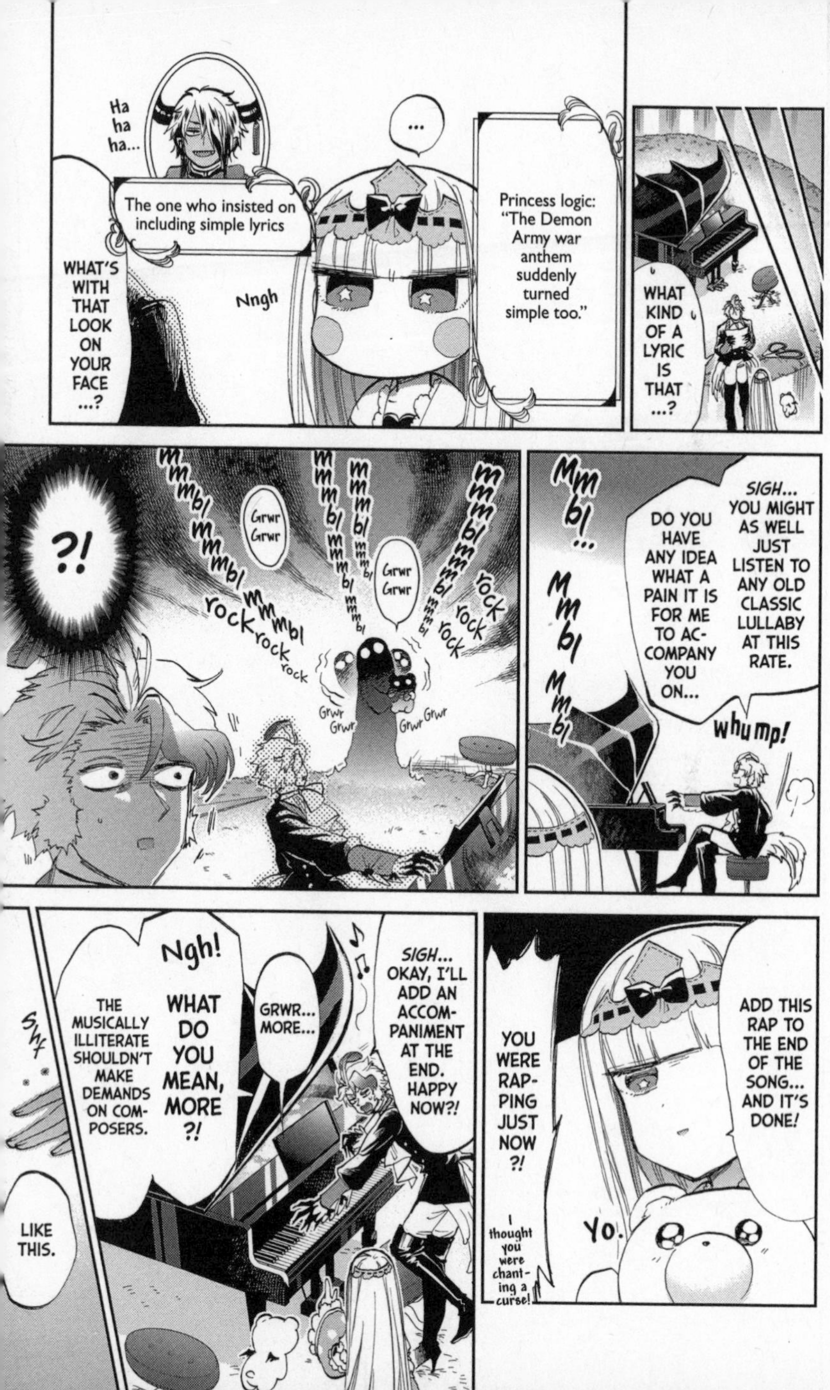
WHAT KIND OF A LYRIC IS THAT...?
Princess logic: "The Demon Army war anthem suddenly turned simple too."
...
Nngh
Ha ha ha...
The one who insisted on including simple lyrics
WHAT'S WITH THAT LOOK ON YOUR FACE...?
Mm bl...
Mm bl Mm bl
SIGH... YOU MIGHT AS WELL JUST LISTEN TO ANY OLD CLASSIC LULLABY AT THIS RATE.
DO YOU HAVE ANY IDEA WHAT A PAIN IT IS FOR ME TO ACCOMPANY YOU ON...
Whump!
Grwr Grwr
Grwr Grwr
Grwr Grwr Grwr Grwr
?!
ADD THIS RAP TO THE END OF THE SONG... AND IT'S DONE!
Yo.
YOU WERE RAPPING JUST NOW?!
I thought you were chanting a curse!
SIGH... OKAY, I'LL ADD AN ACCOMPANIMENT AT THE END. HAPPY NOW?!
GRWR... MORE...
Ngh! WHAT DO YOU MEAN, MORE?!
THE MUSICALLY ILLITERATE SHOULDN'T MAKE DEMANDS ON COMPOSERS.
LIKE THIS.

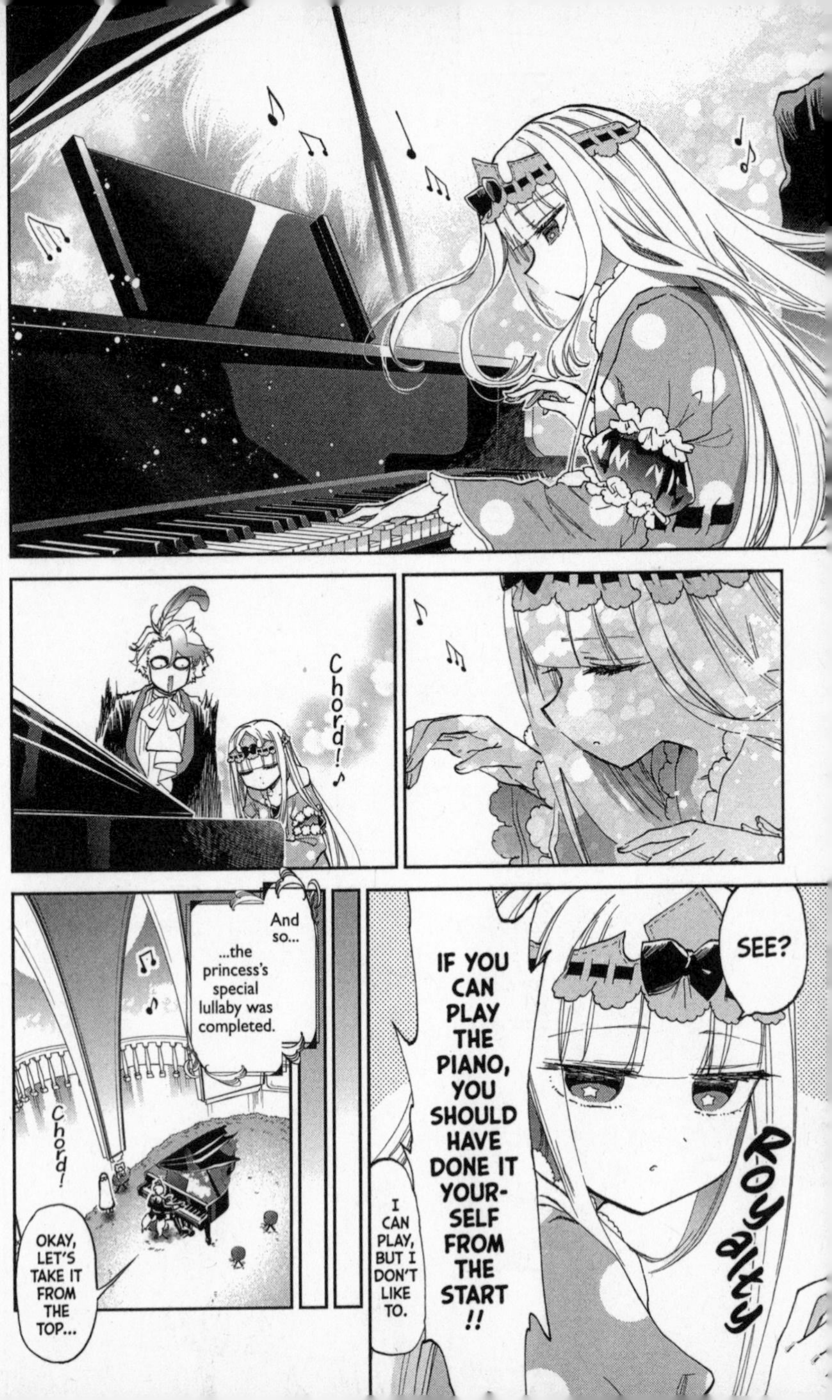
Chord!♪
SEE?
IF YOU CAN PLAY THE PIANO, YOU SHOULD HAVE DONE IT YOURSELF FROM THE START!!
Royalty
I CAN PLAY, BUT I DON'T LIKE TO.
And so... ...the princess's special lullaby was completed.
Chord!
OKAY, LET'S TAKE IT FROM THE TOP...

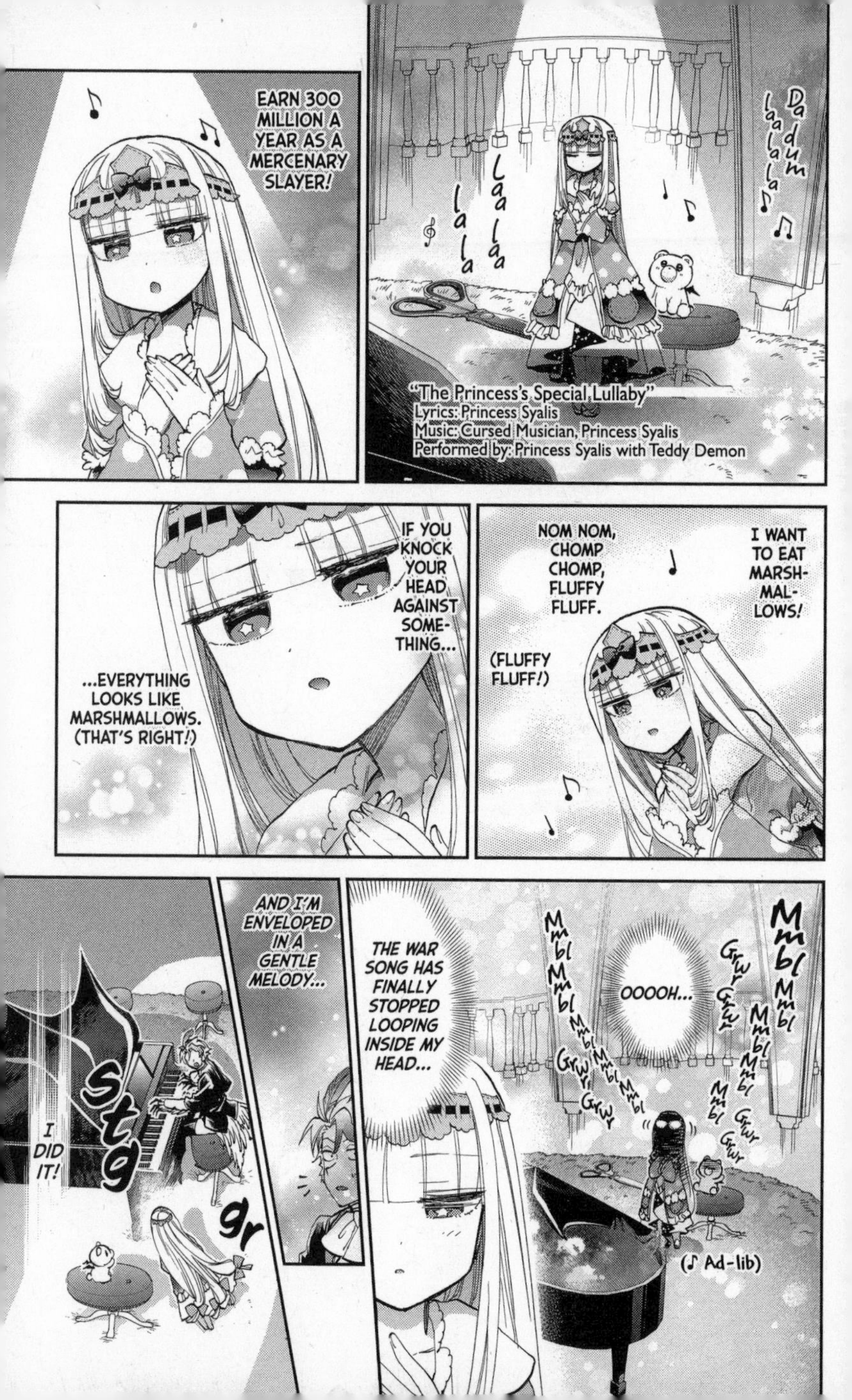
Da dum laa la la la
Laa laa la la la
"The Princess's Special Lullaby"
Lyrics: Princess Syalis
Music: Cursed Musician, Princess Syalis
Performed by: Princess Syalis with Teddy Demon
EARN 300 MILLION A YEAR AS A MERCENARY SLAYER!
I WANT TO EAT MARSH-MAL-LOWS!
NOM NOM, CHOMP CHOMP, FLUFFY FLUFF.
(FLUFFY FLUFF!)
IF YOU KNOCK YOUR HEAD AGAINST SOME-THING...
...EVERYTHING LOOKS LIKE MARSHMALLOWS. (THAT'S RIGHT!)
Mmbl Mmbl
Grwr Grwr
OOOOH...
THE WAR SONG HAS FINALLY STOPPED LOOPING INSIDE MY HEAD...
(♪ Ad-lib)
AND I'M ENVELOPED IN A GENTLE MELODY...
stg
gr
I DID IT!

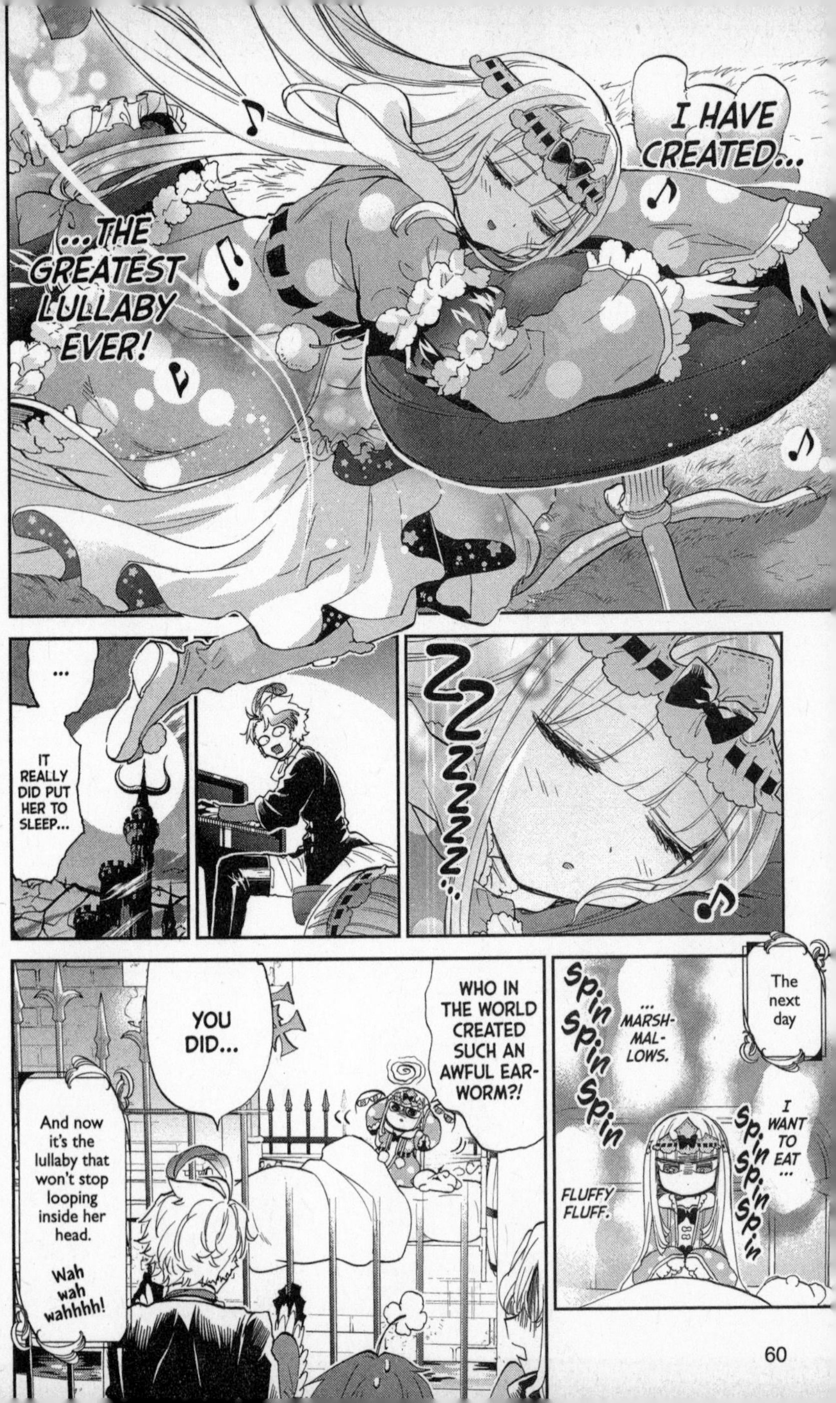
I HAVE CREATED...
...THE GREATEST LULLABY EVER!
ZZZZZZ...
...
IT REALLY DID PUT HER TO SLEEP...
The next day
Spin Spin Spin
... MARSH-MAL-LOWS.
I WANT TO EAT ...
Spin Spin Spin
FLUFFY FLUFF.
WHO IN THE WORLD CREATED SUCH AN AWFUL EAR-WORM?!
YOU DID...
And now it's the lullaby that won't stop looping inside her head.
Wah wah wahhhh!

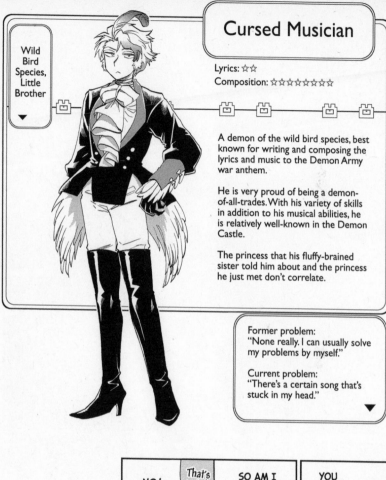

Wild Bird Species, Little Brother

Cursed Musician

Lyrics: ☆☆
Composition: ☆☆☆☆☆☆☆☆☆

A demon of the wild bird species, best known for writing and composing the lyrics and music to the Demon Army war anthem.

He is very proud of being a demon-of-all-trades. With his variety of skills in addition to his musical abilities, he is relatively well-known in the Demon Castle.

The princess that his fluffy-brained sister told him about and the princess he just met don't correlate.

Former problem:
"None really. I can usually solve my problems by myself."

Current problem:
"There's a certain song that's stuck in my head."

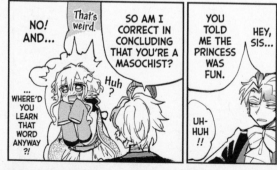

HEY, SIS...
YOU TOLD ME THE PRINCESS WAS FUN.
UH-HUH !!
SO AM I CORRECT IN CONCLUDING THAT YOU'RE A MASOCHIST?
Huh?
That's weird.
NO! AND...
...WHERE'D YOU LEARN THAT WORD ANYWAY?!

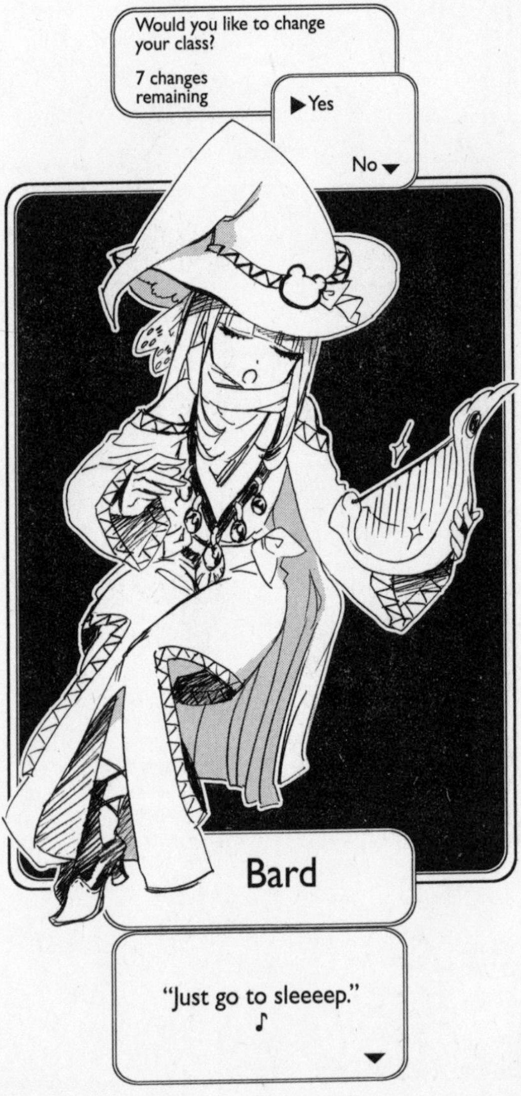
Would you like to change your class?
7 changes remaining
▶Yes
No
Bard
"Just go to sleeeep."
♪

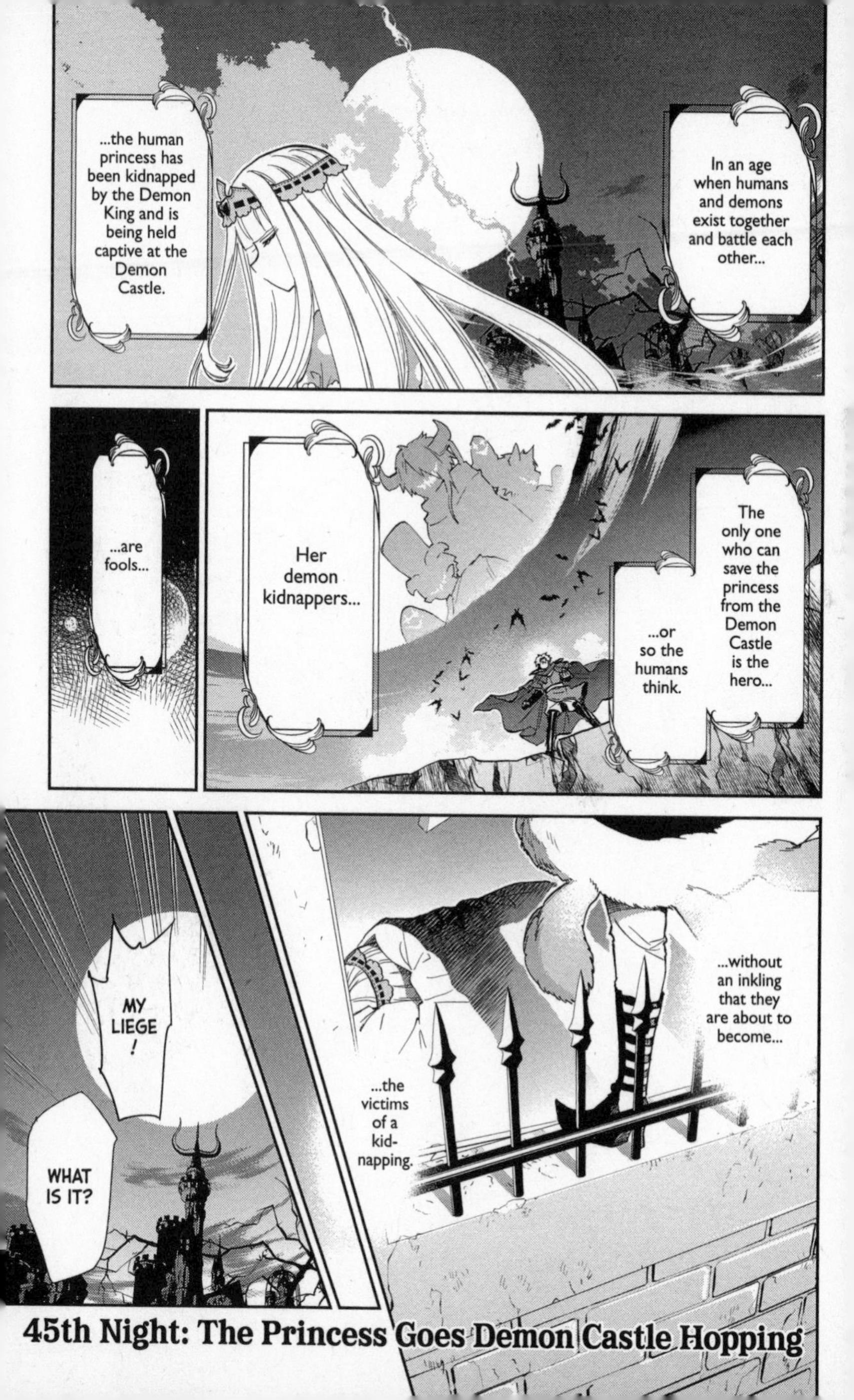
In an age when humans and demons exist together and battle each other...
...the human princess has been kidnapped by the Demon King and is being held captive at the Demon Castle.
The only one who can save the princess from the Demon Castle is the hero...
...or so the humans think.
Her demon kidnappers...
...are fools...
...without an inkling that they are about to become...
...the victims of a kid-napping.
MY LIEGE!
WHAT IS IT?

45th Night: The Princess Goes Demon Castle Hopping

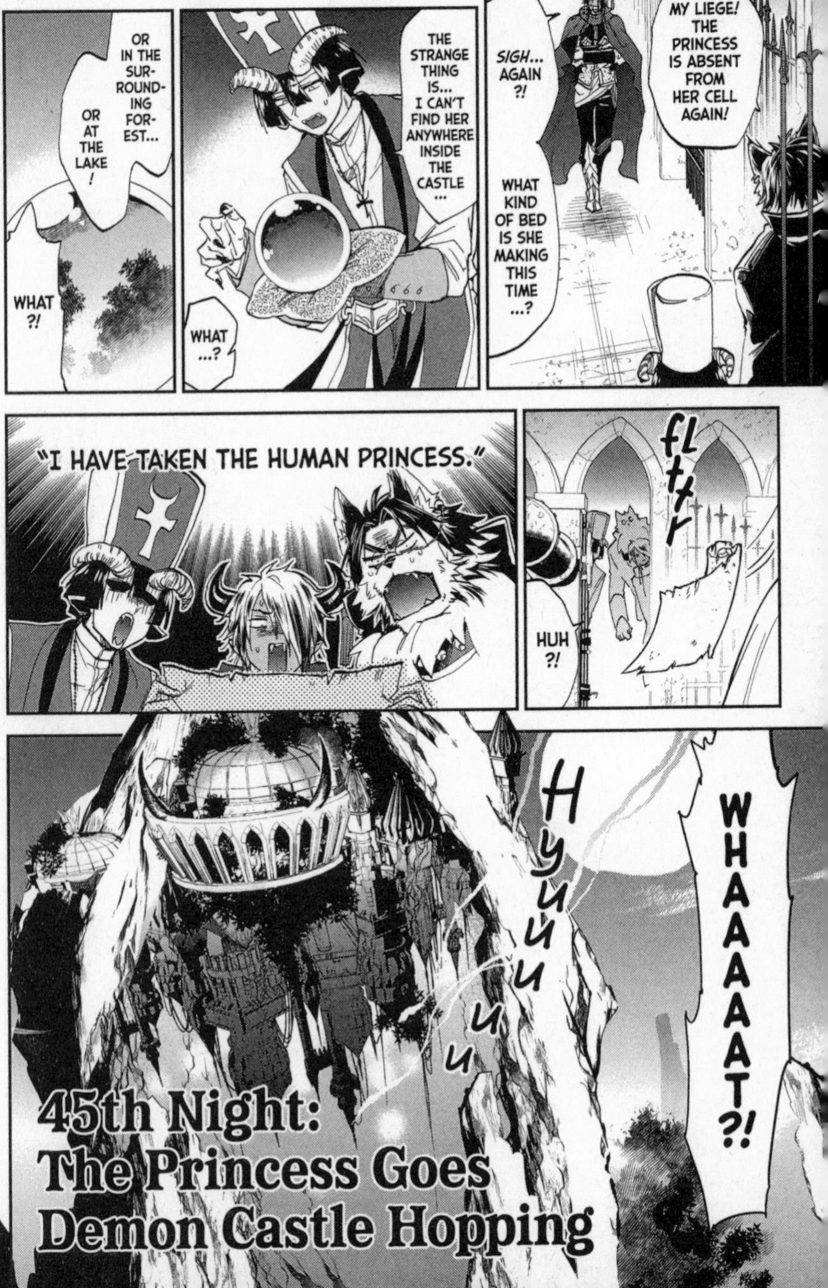
MY LIEGE! THE PRINCESS IS ABSENT FROM HER CELL AGAIN!
SIGH... AGAIN?!
WHAT KIND OF BED IS SHE MAKING THIS TIME...?
THE STRANGE THING IS... I CAN'T FIND HER ANYWHERE INSIDE THE CASTLE...
WHAT...?
OR IN THE SURROUNDING FOREST...
OR AT THE LAKE!
WHAT?!
flttr
HUH?!
"I HAVE TAKEN THE HUMAN PRINCESS."
WHAAAAAAT?!
Hyuuuuuu

45th Night: The Princess Goes Demon Castle Hopping

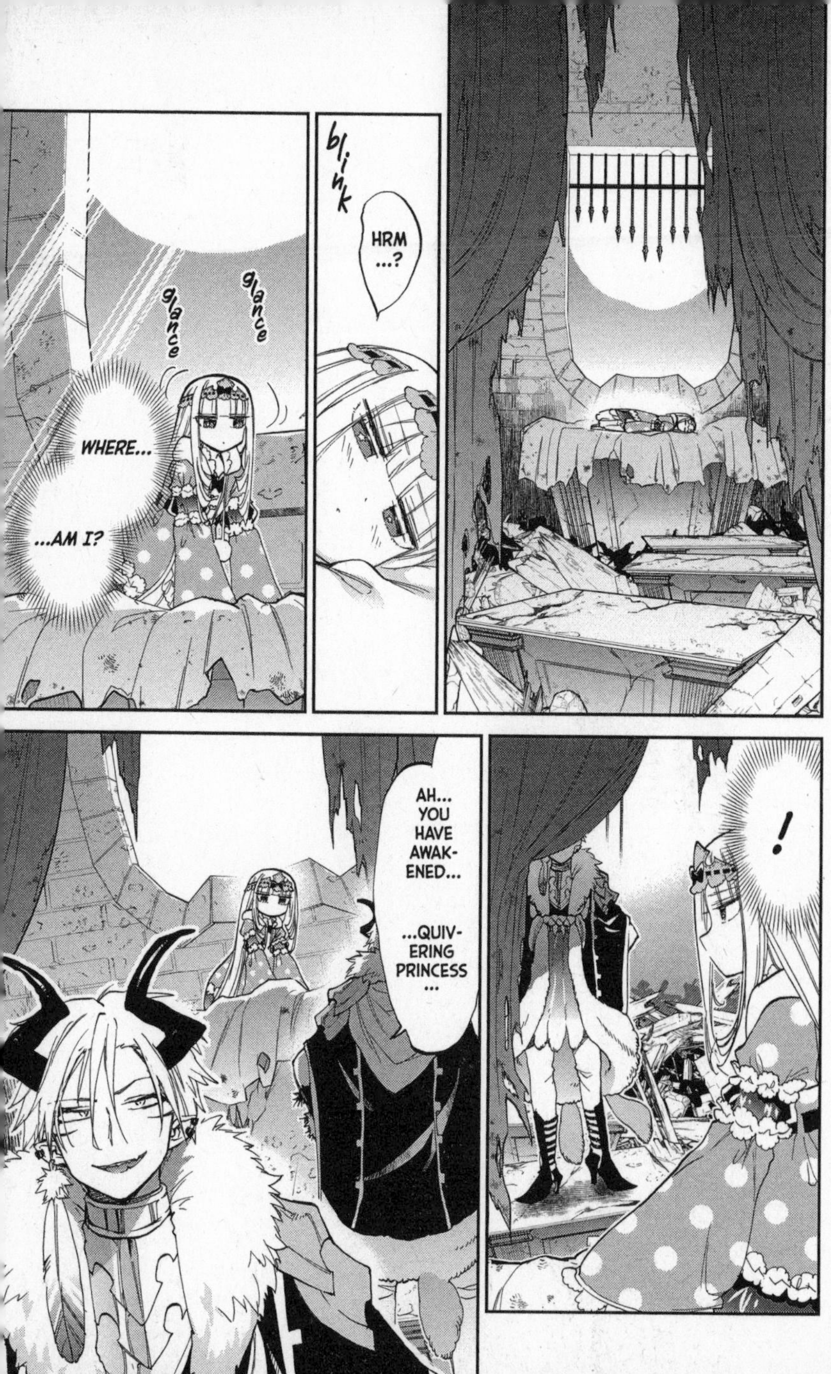
blink
HRM ...?
glance
glance
WHERE...
...AM I?
!
AH... YOU HAVE AWAKENED...
...QUIVERING PRINCESS ...

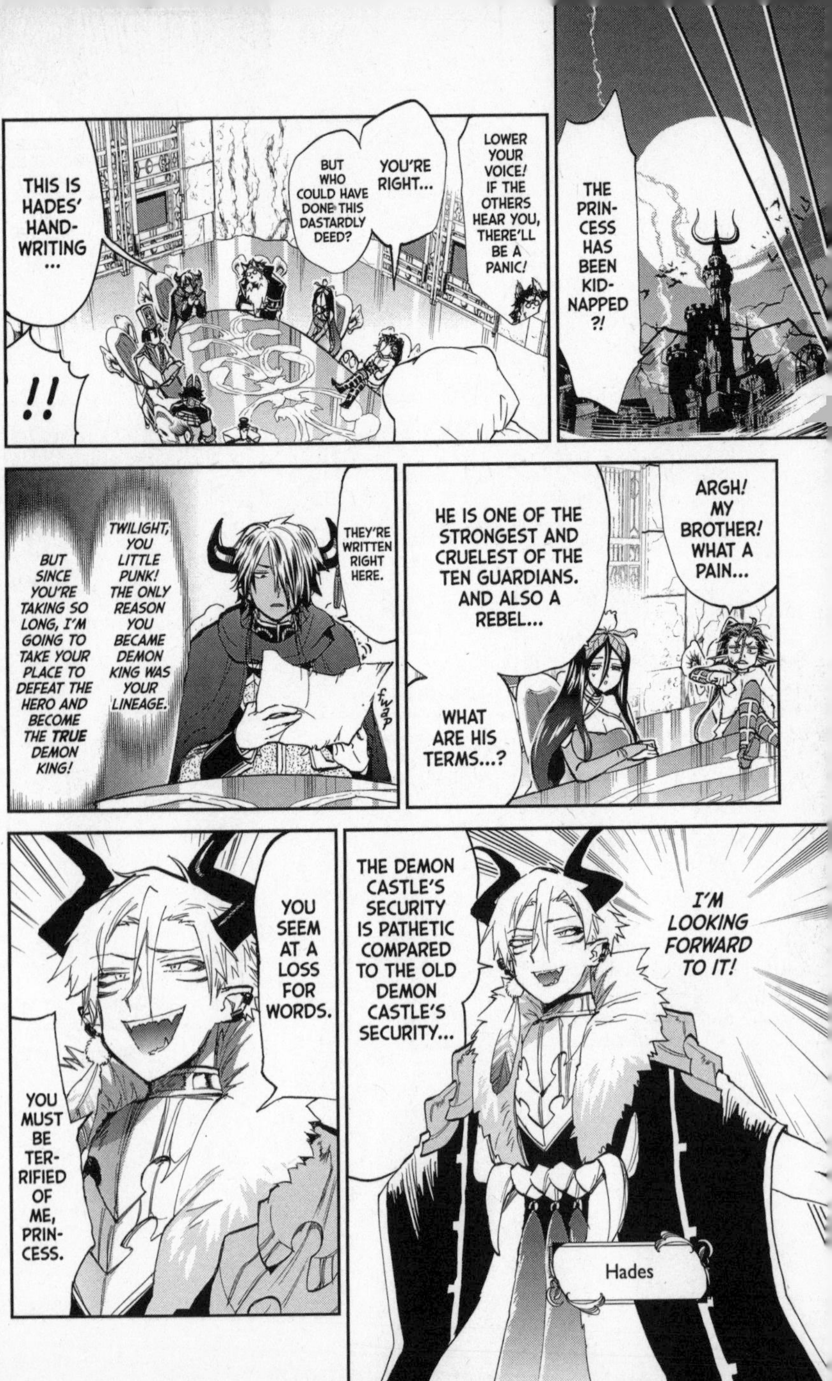
THE PRINCESS HAS BEEN KIDNAPPED?!
LOWER YOUR VOICE! IF THE OTHERS HEAR YOU, THERE'LL BE A PANIC!
YOU'RE RIGHT...
BUT WHO COULD HAVE DONE THIS DASTARDLY DEED?
THIS IS HADES' HAND-WRITING ...
!!
ARGH! MY BROTHER! WHAT A PAIN...
HE IS ONE OF THE STRONGEST AND CRUELEST OF THE TEN GUARDIANS. AND ALSO A REBEL...
WHAT ARE HIS TERMS...?
THEY'RE WRITTEN RIGHT HERE.
fwap
TWILIGHT, YOU LITTLE PUNK! THE ONLY REASON YOU BECAME DEMON KING WAS YOUR LINEAGE.
BUT SINCE YOU'RE TAKING SO LONG, I'M GOING TO TAKE YOUR PLACE TO DEFEAT THE HERO AND BECOME THE TRUE DEMON KING!
THE DEMON CASTLE'S SECURITY IS PATHETIC COMPARED TO THE OLD DEMON CASTLE'S SECURITY...
I'M LOOKING FORWARD TO IT!
Hades
YOU SEEM AT A LOSS FOR WORDS.
YOU MUST BE TERRIFIED OF ME, PRINCESS.

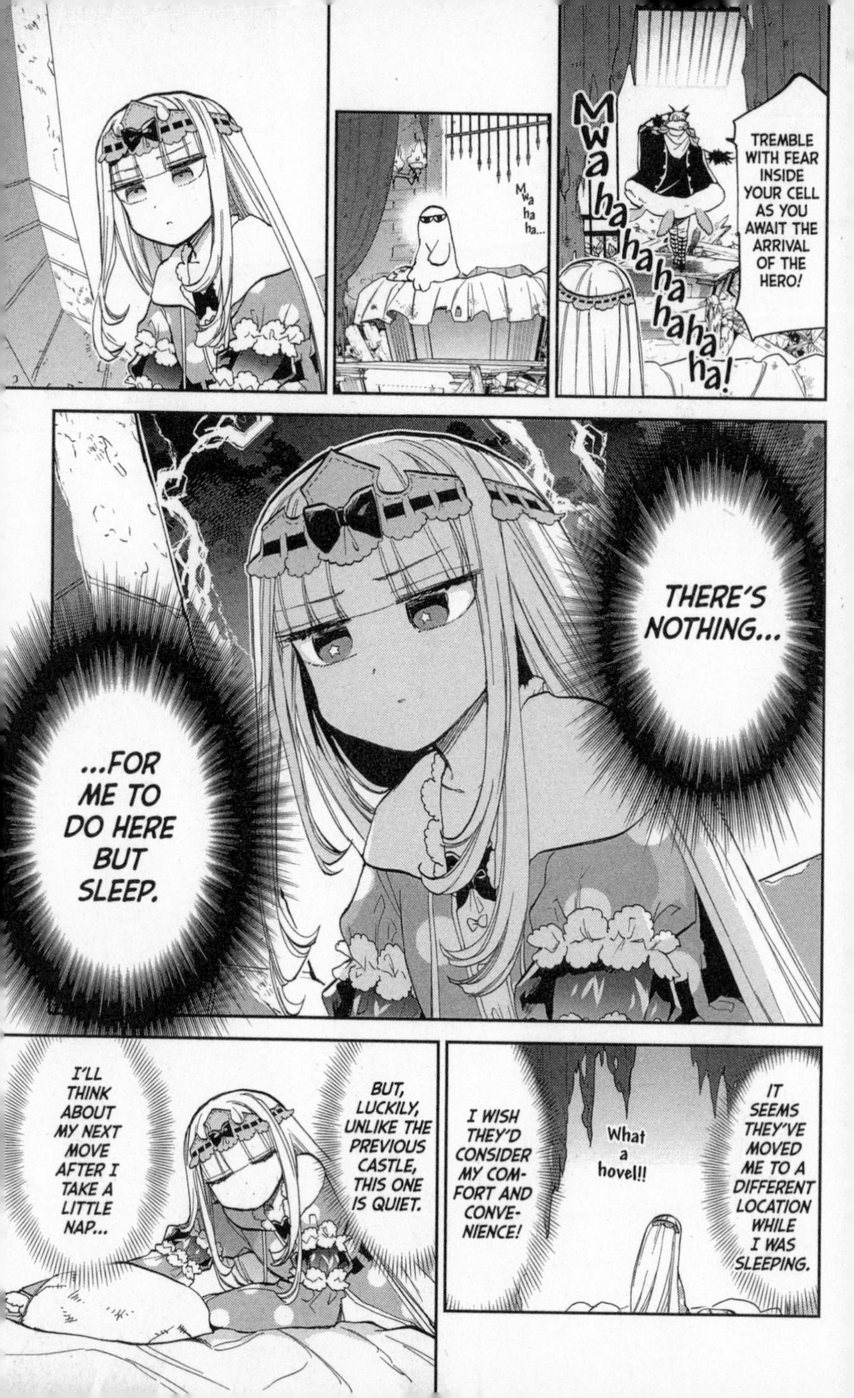
Mwahahahahahahahaha!
TREMBLE WITH FEAR INSIDE YOUR CELL AS YOU AWAIT THE ARRIVAL OF THE HERO!
Mwa ha ha ha...
THERE'S NOTHING...
...FOR ME TO DO HERE BUT SLEEP.
IT SEEMS THEY'VE MOVED ME TO A DIFFERENT LOCATION WHILE I WAS SLEEPING.
What a hovel!!
I WISH THEY'D CONSIDER MY COM-FORT AND CONVE-NIENCE!
BUT, LUCKILY, UNLIKE THE PREVIOUS CASTLE, THIS ONE IS QUIET.
I'LL THINK ABOUT MY NEXT MOVE AFTER I TAKE A LITTLE NAP...

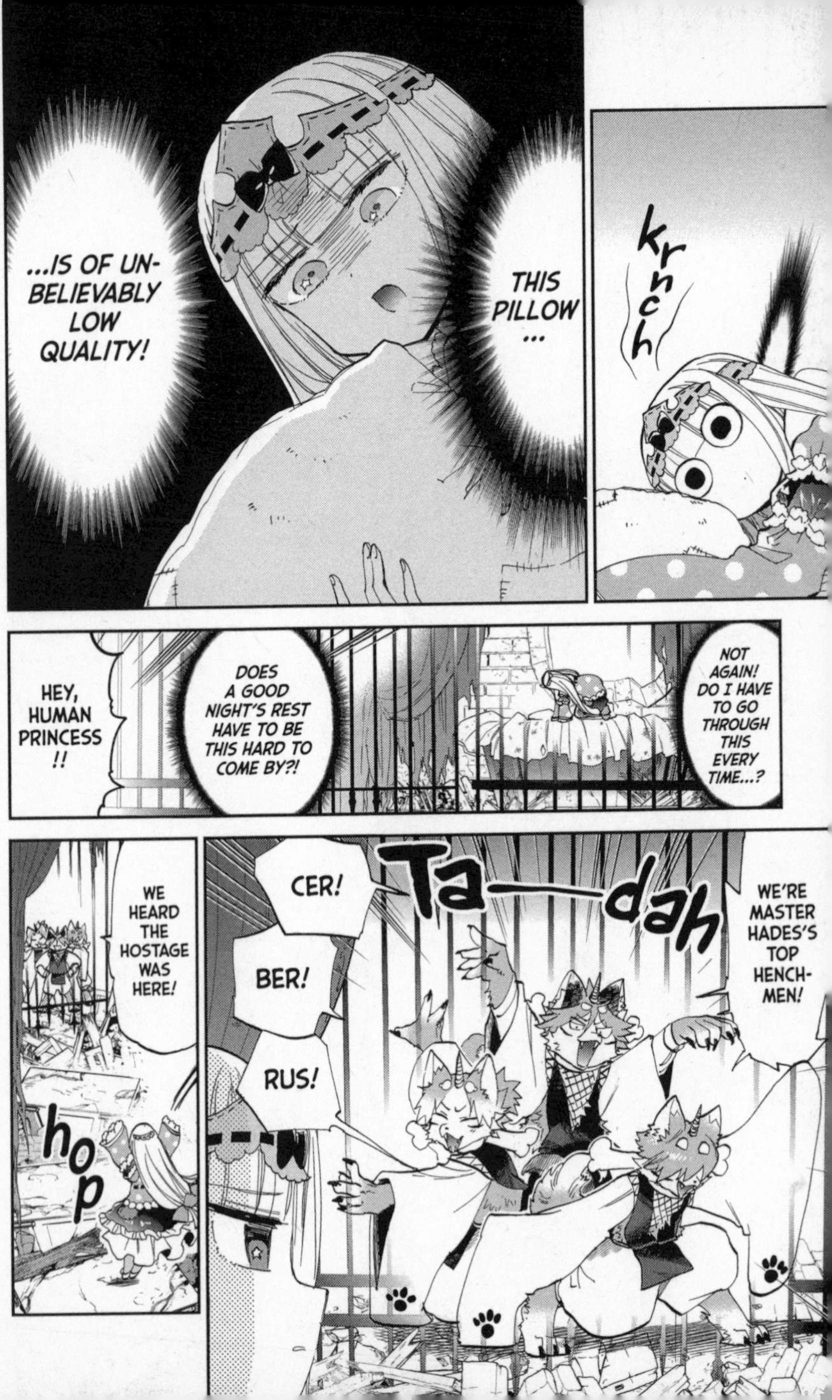
krnch
THIS PILLOW ...
...IS OF UN-BELIEVABLY LOW QUALITY!
NOT AGAIN! DO I HAVE TO GO THROUGH THIS EVERY TIME...?
DOES A GOOD NIGHT'S REST HAVE TO BE THIS HARD TO COME BY?!
HEY, HUMAN PRINCESS !!
WE'RE MASTER HADES'S TOP HENCH-MEN!
Ta—dah
CER!
BER!
RUS!
WE HEARD THE HOSTAGE WAS HERE!
hop

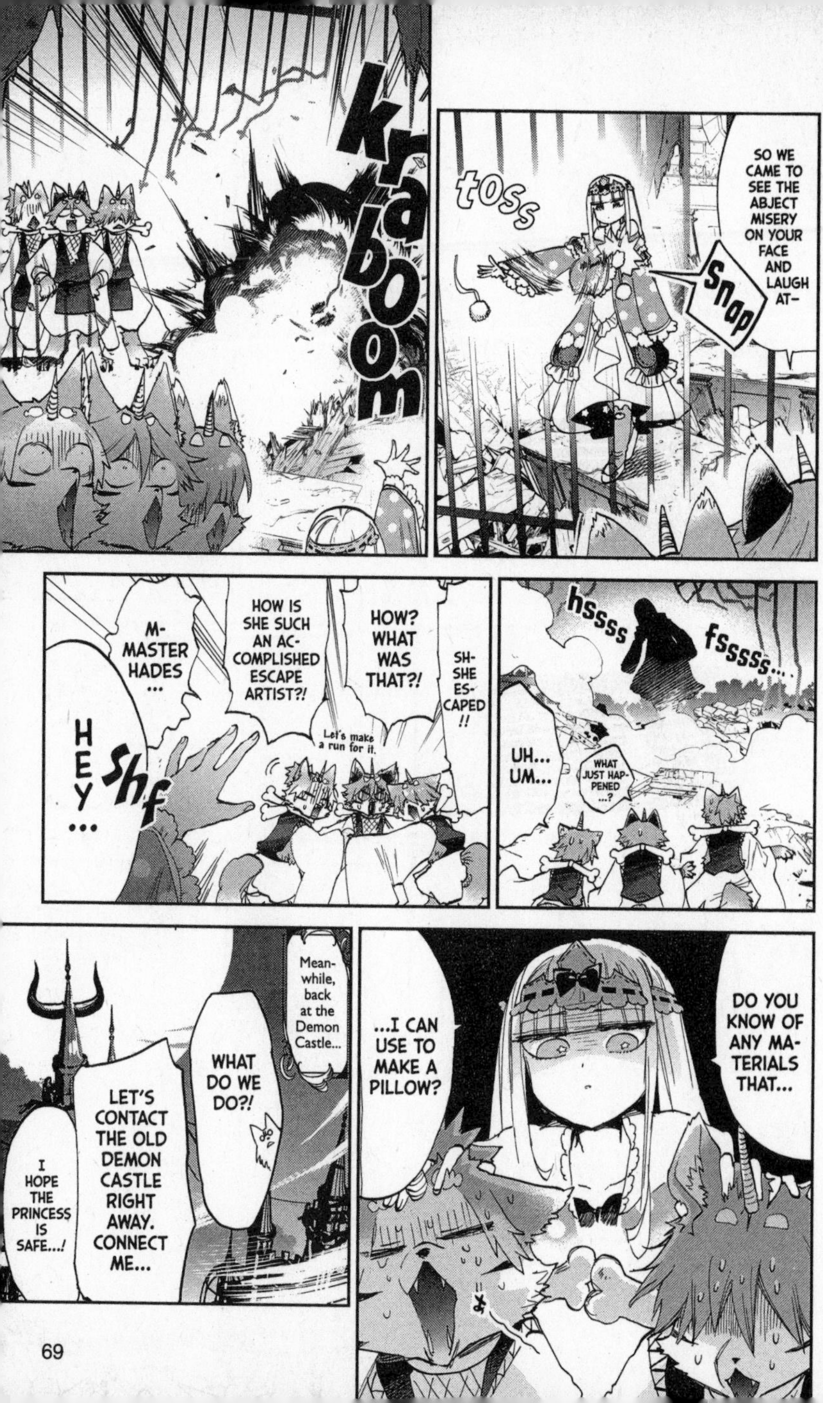
toss
SO WE CAME TO SEE THE ABJECT MISERY ON YOUR FACE AND LAUGH AT—
Snap
kraboom
hsssss
fsssss...
UH... UM...
WHAT JUST HAPPENED...?
SH-SHE ESCAPED!!
HOW? WHAT WAS THAT?!
HOW IS SHE SUCH AN ACCOMPLISHED ESCAPE ARTIST?!
Let's make a run for it.
M-MASTER HADES...
HEY...
Shf
DO YOU KNOW OF ANY MATERIALS THAT...
...I CAN USE TO MAKE A PILLOW?
Meanwhile, back at the Demon Castle...
WHAT DO WE DO?!
LET'S CONTACT THE OLD DEMON CASTLE RIGHT AWAY. CONNECT ME...
I HOPE THE PRINCESS IS SAFE...!

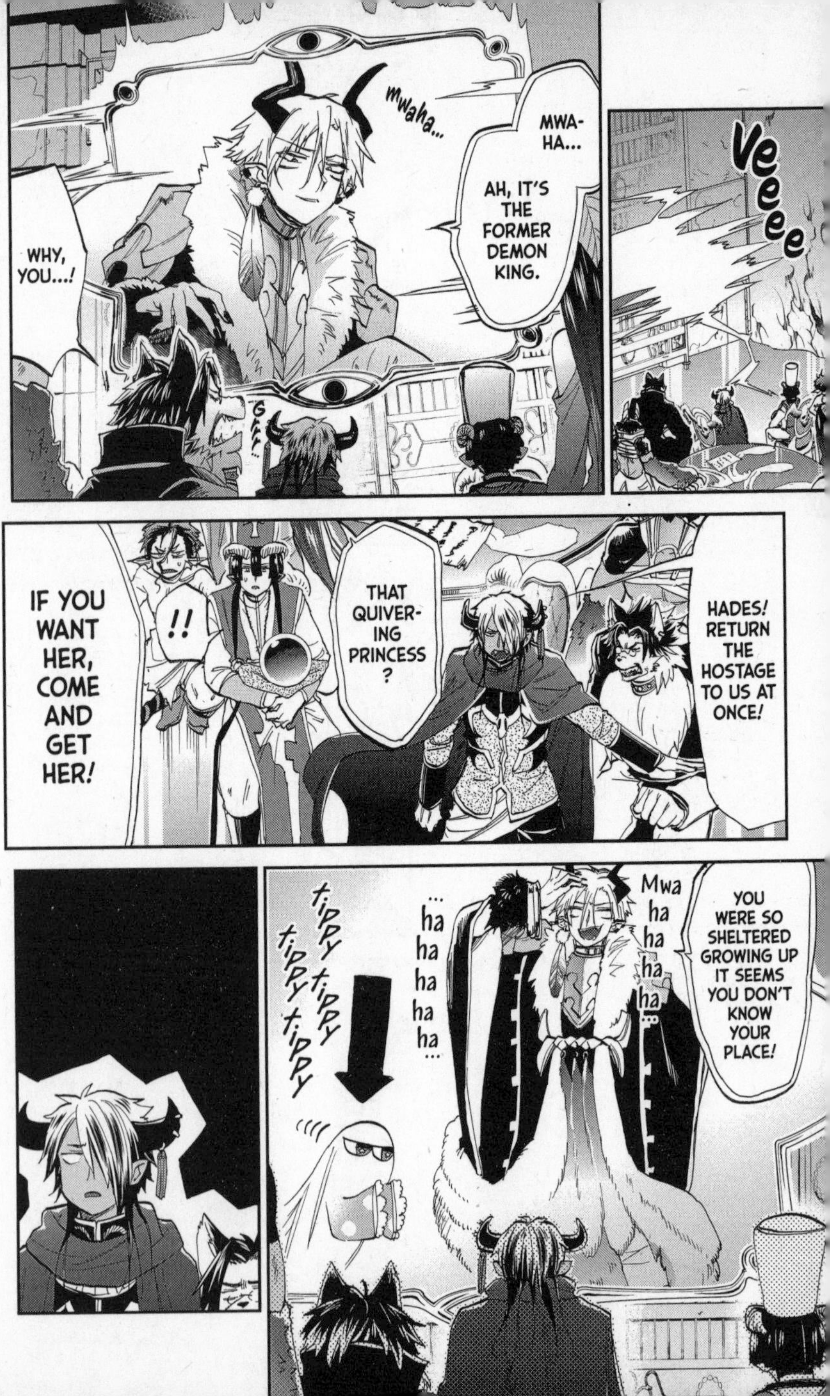
Veeee
MWA-HA...
AH, IT'S THE FORMER DEMON KING.
mwaha...
WHY, YOU...!
Grrr...
HADES! RETURN THE HOSTAGE TO US AT ONCE!
THAT QUIVERING PRINCESS?
!!
IF YOU WANT HER, COME AND GET HER!
YOU WERE SO SHELTERED GROWING UP IT SEEMS YOU DON'T KNOW YOUR PLACE!
Mwa ha ha ha ha...
...ha ha ha ha ha ha...
tippy tippy tippy tippy

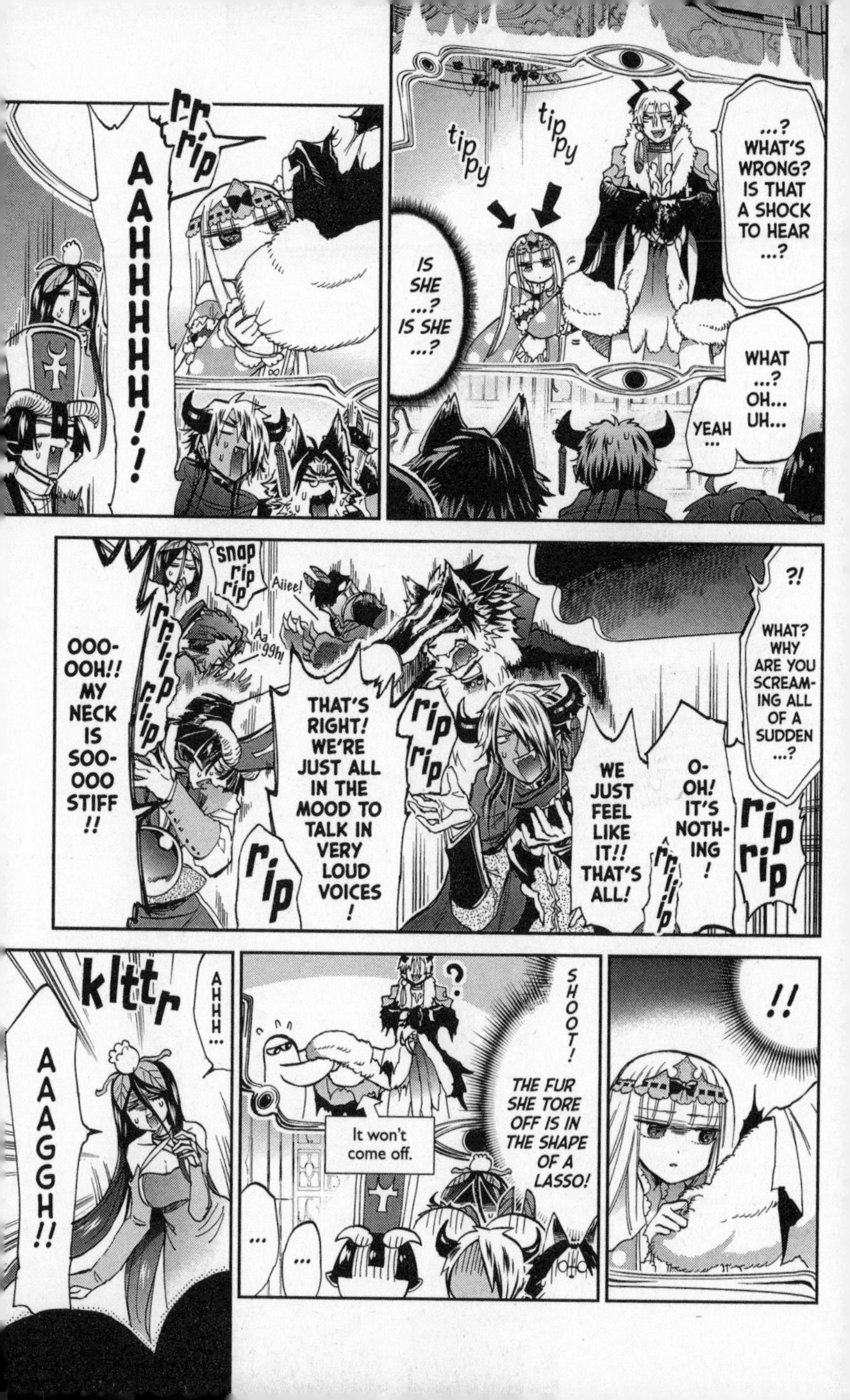
...? WHAT'S WRONG? IS THAT A SHOCK TO HEAR ...?
tippy
tippy
IS SHE ...? IS SHE ...?
WHAT ...? OH... UH...
YEAH ...
rr rip
AAHHHHHH!!
?!
WHAT? WHY ARE YOU SCREAMING ALL OF A SUDDEN ...?
rip rip
O-OH! IT'S NOTHING!
rrrip
WE JUST FEEL LIKE IT!! THAT'S ALL!
rip rip
Aiiee!
THAT'S RIGHT! WE'RE JUST ALL IN THE MOOD TO TALK IN VERY LOUD VOICES!
rip
Aaggh!
snap rip rip
rrrip rrrip
OOO-OOH!! MY NECK IS SOO-OOO STIFF!!
!!
SHOOT!
THE FUR SHE TORE OFF IS IN THE SHAPE OF A LASSO!
?
It won't come off.
...
...
AHHH...
klttr
AAAAGGH!!

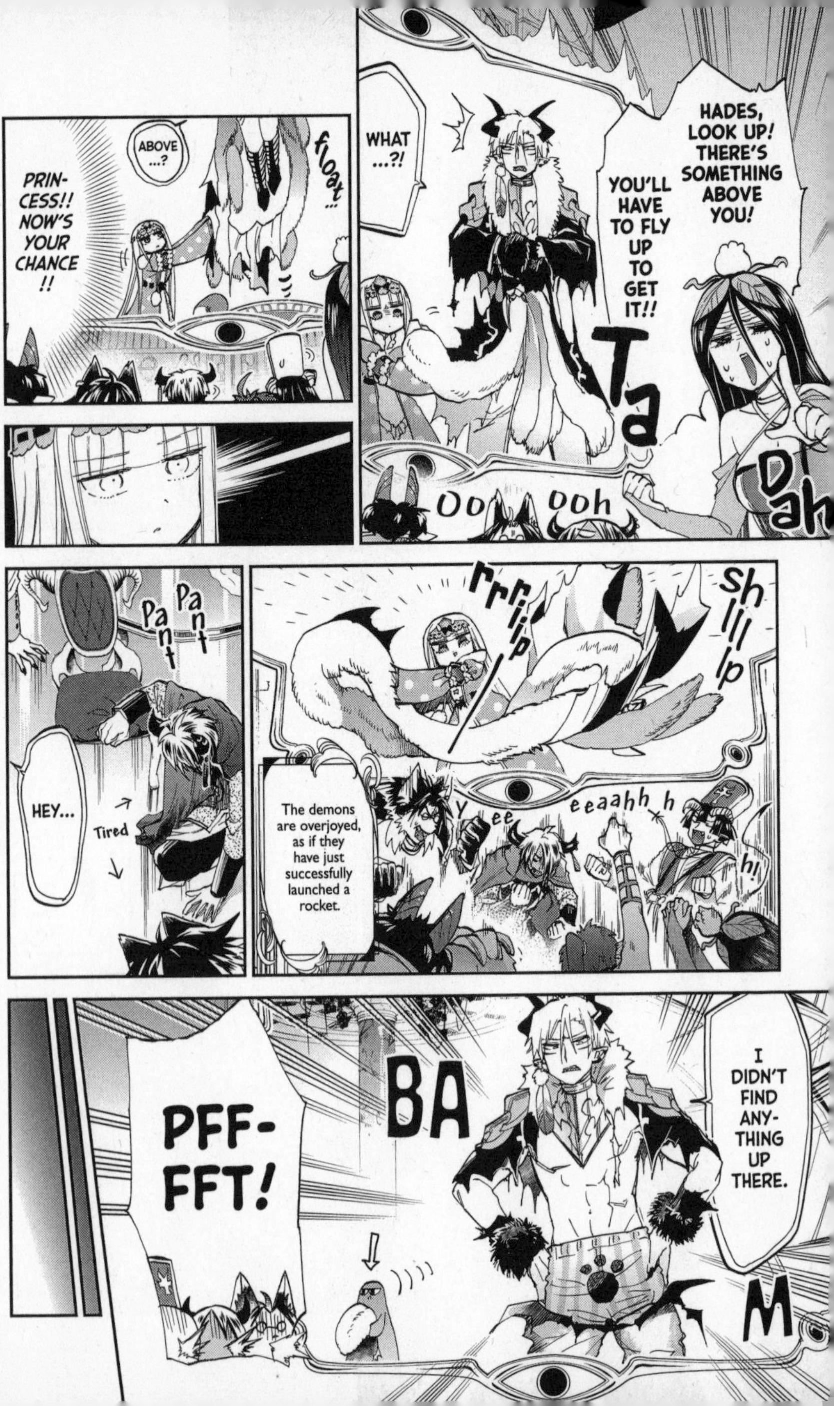
HADES, LOOK UP! THERE'S SOMETHING ABOVE YOU!
YOU'LL HAVE TO FLY UP TO GET IT!!
Ta
Dah
WHAT ...?!
Oo ooh
ABOVE ...?
PRIN-CESS!! NOW'S YOUR CHANCE !!
float...
shlllp
rrriip
Yeeeaahh h
hi!
The demons are overjoyed, as if they have just successfully launched a rocket.
Pant Pant
HEY...
Tired
I DIDN'T FIND ANY-THING UP THERE.
BA
M
PFF-FFT!

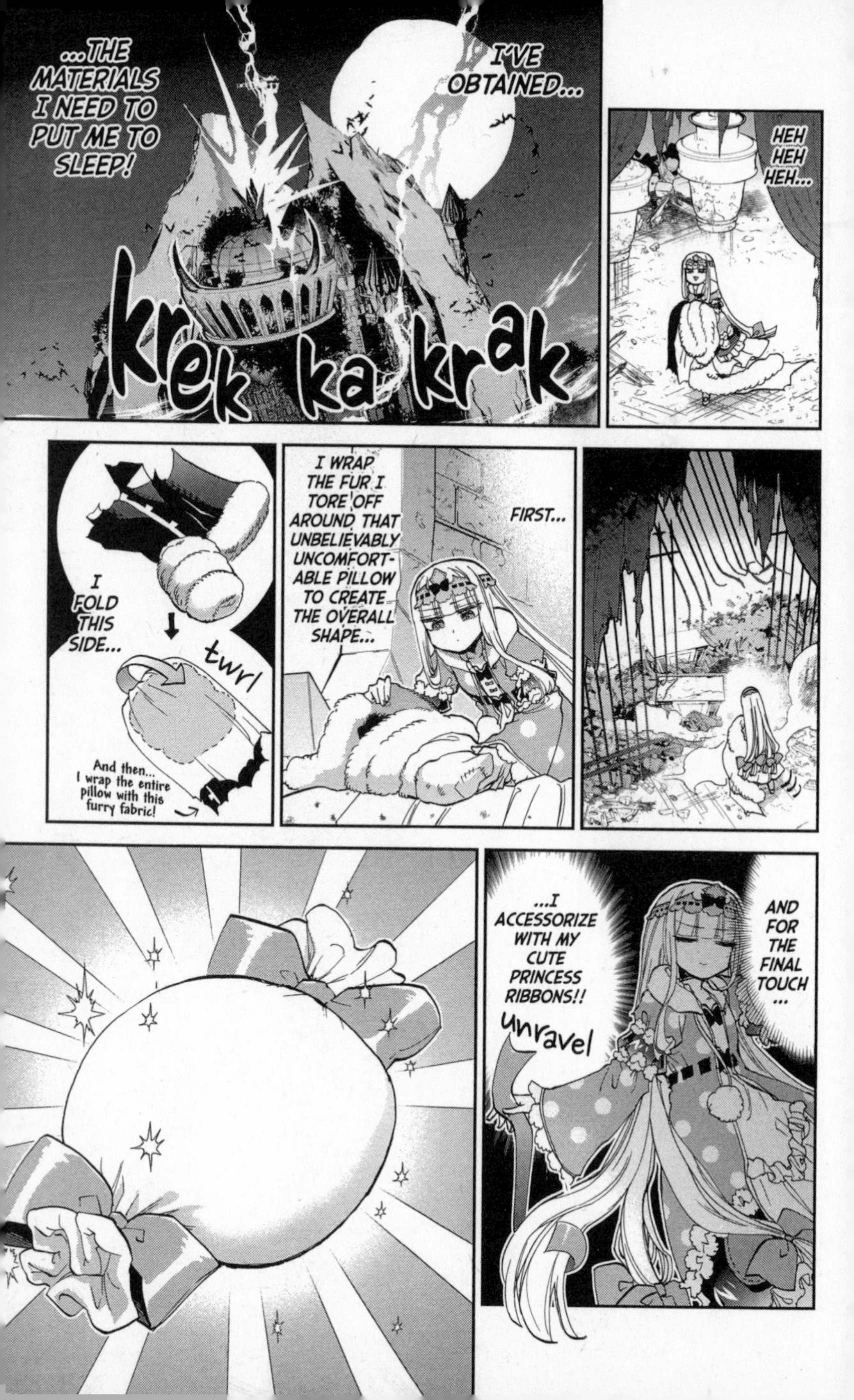
HEH HEH HEH...
I'VE OBTAINED...
...THE MATERIALS I NEED TO PUT ME TO SLEEP!
krek ka-krak
FIRST...
I WRAP THE FUR I TORE OFF AROUND THAT UNBELIEVABLY UNCOMFORTABLE PILLOW TO CREATE THE OVERALL SHAPE...
I FOLD THIS SIDE...
twrl
And then... I wrap the entire pillow with this furry fabric!
AND FOR THE FINAL TOUCH...
...I ACCESSORIZE WITH MY CUTE PRINCESS RIBBONS!!
unravel

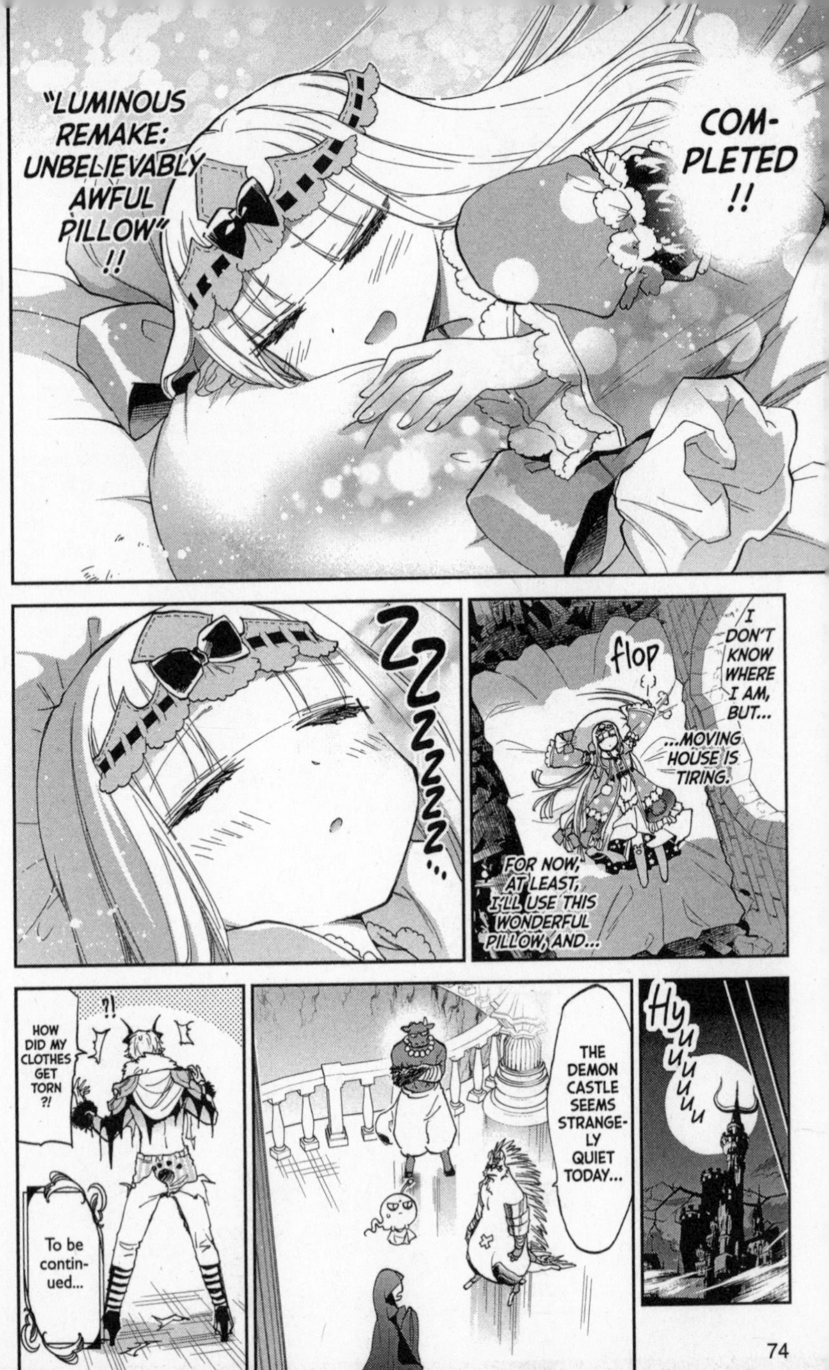
"LUMINOUS REMAKE: UNBELIEVABLY AWFUL PILLOW"!!
COM-PLETED!!
I DON'T KNOW WHERE I AM, BUT...
flop
...MOVING HOUSE IS TIRING.
FOR NOW, AT LEAST, I'LL USE THIS WONDERFUL PILLOW, AND...
ZZZZZ...
Hyuuuuuuu
THE DEMON CASTLE SEEMS STRANGE-LY QUIET TODAY...
?!
HOW DID MY CLOTHES GET TORN?!
To be contin-ued...

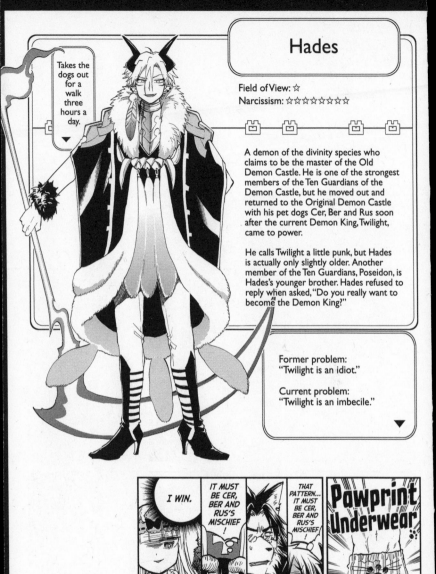

Hades

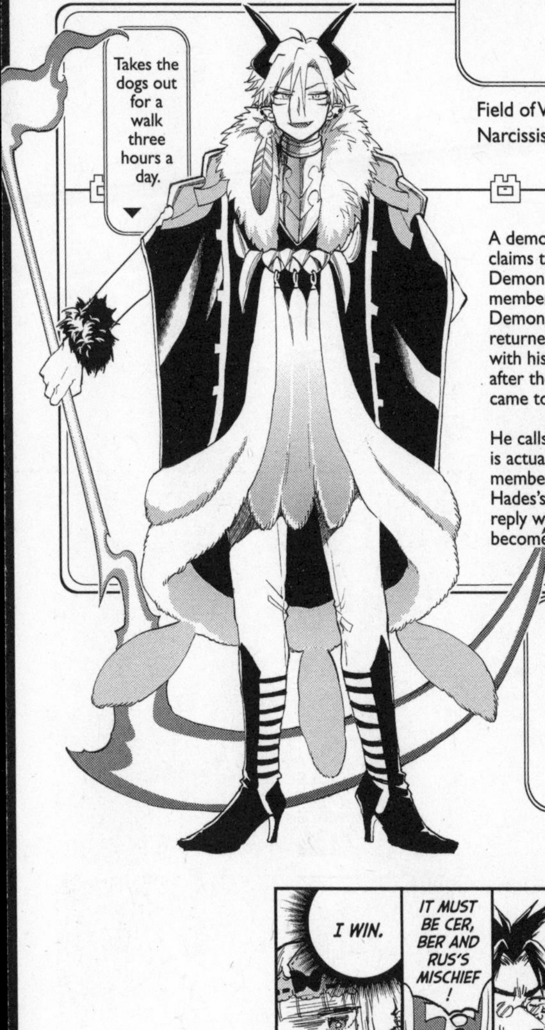

Takes the dogs out for a walk three hours a day.

Field of View: ☆
Narcissism: ☆☆☆☆☆☆☆☆☆

A demon of the divinity species who claims to be the master of the Old Demon Castle. He is one of the strongest members of the Ten Guardians of the Demon Castle, but he moved out and returned to the Original Demon Castle with his pet dogs Cer, Ber and Rus soon after the current Demon King, Twilight, came to power.

He calls Twilight a little punk, but Hades is actually only slightly older. Another member of the Ten Guardians, Poseidon, is Hades's younger brother. Hades refused to reply when asked, "Do you really want to become the Demon King?"

Former problem:
"Twilight is an idiot."

Current problem:
"Twilight is an imbecile."

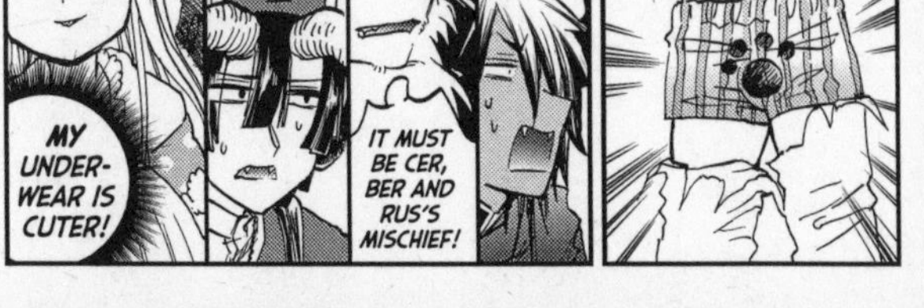
Pawprint Underwear
THAT PATTERN... IT MUST BE CER, BER AND RUS'S MISCHIEF!
IT MUST BE CER, BER AND RUS'S MISCHIEF!
IT MUST BE CER, BER AND RUS'S MISCHIEF!
I WIN.
MY UNDER-WEAR IS CUTER!

Would you like to change your class?

6 changes remaining

▶ Yes

No ▼

Gardener

"My special move is pruning."

▼

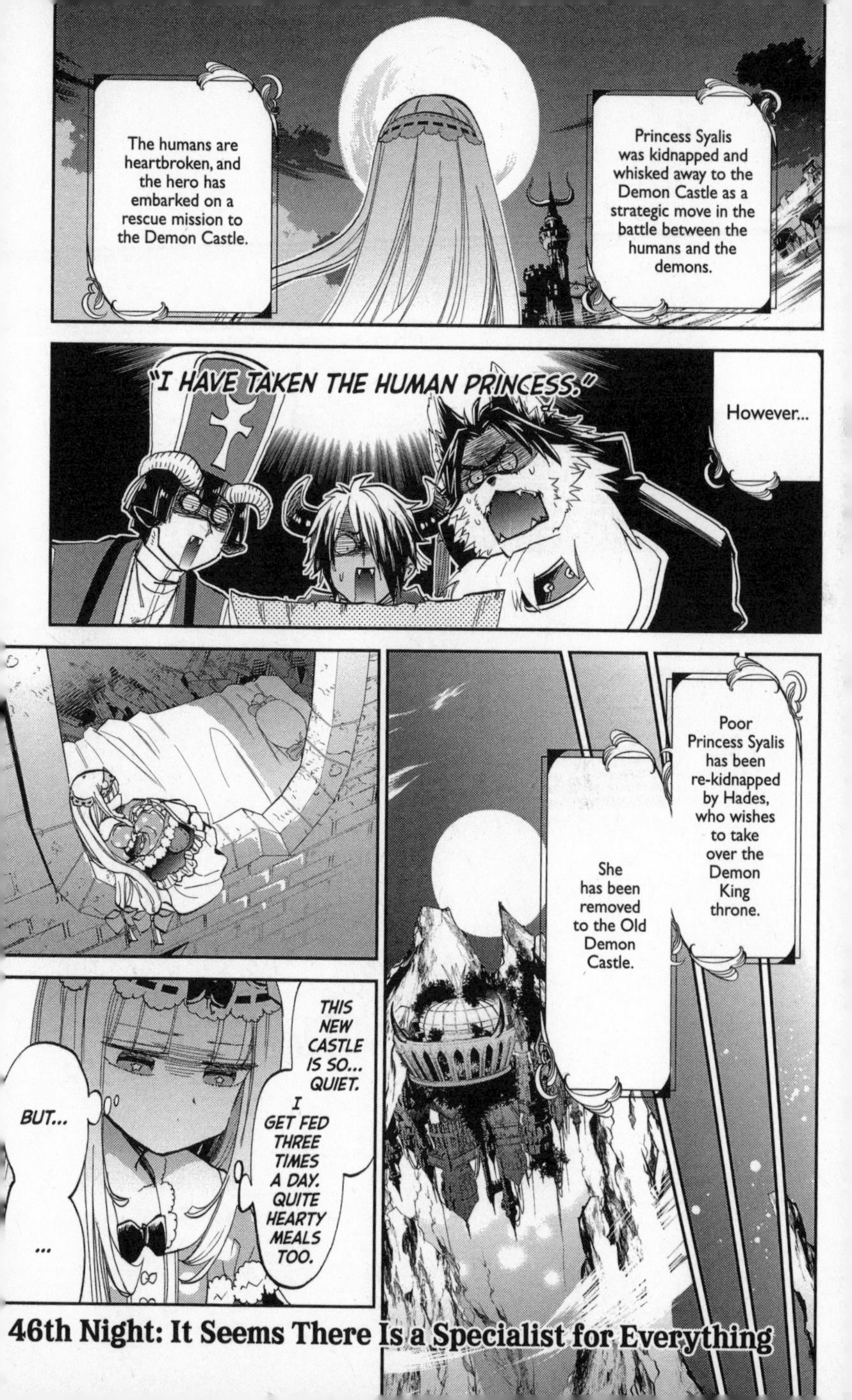
Princess Syalis was kidnapped and whisked away to the Demon Castle as a strategic move in the battle between the humans and the demons.
The humans are heartbroken, and the hero has embarked on a rescue mission to the Demon Castle.
However...
"I HAVE TAKEN THE HUMAN PRINCESS."
Poor Princess Syalis has been re-kidnapped by Hades, who wishes to take over the Demon King throne.
She has been removed to the Old Demon Castle.
THIS NEW CASTLE IS SO... QUIET.
I GET FED THREE TIMES A DAY. QUITE HEARTY MEALS TOO.
BUT...
...

46th Night: It Seems There Is a Specialist for Everything

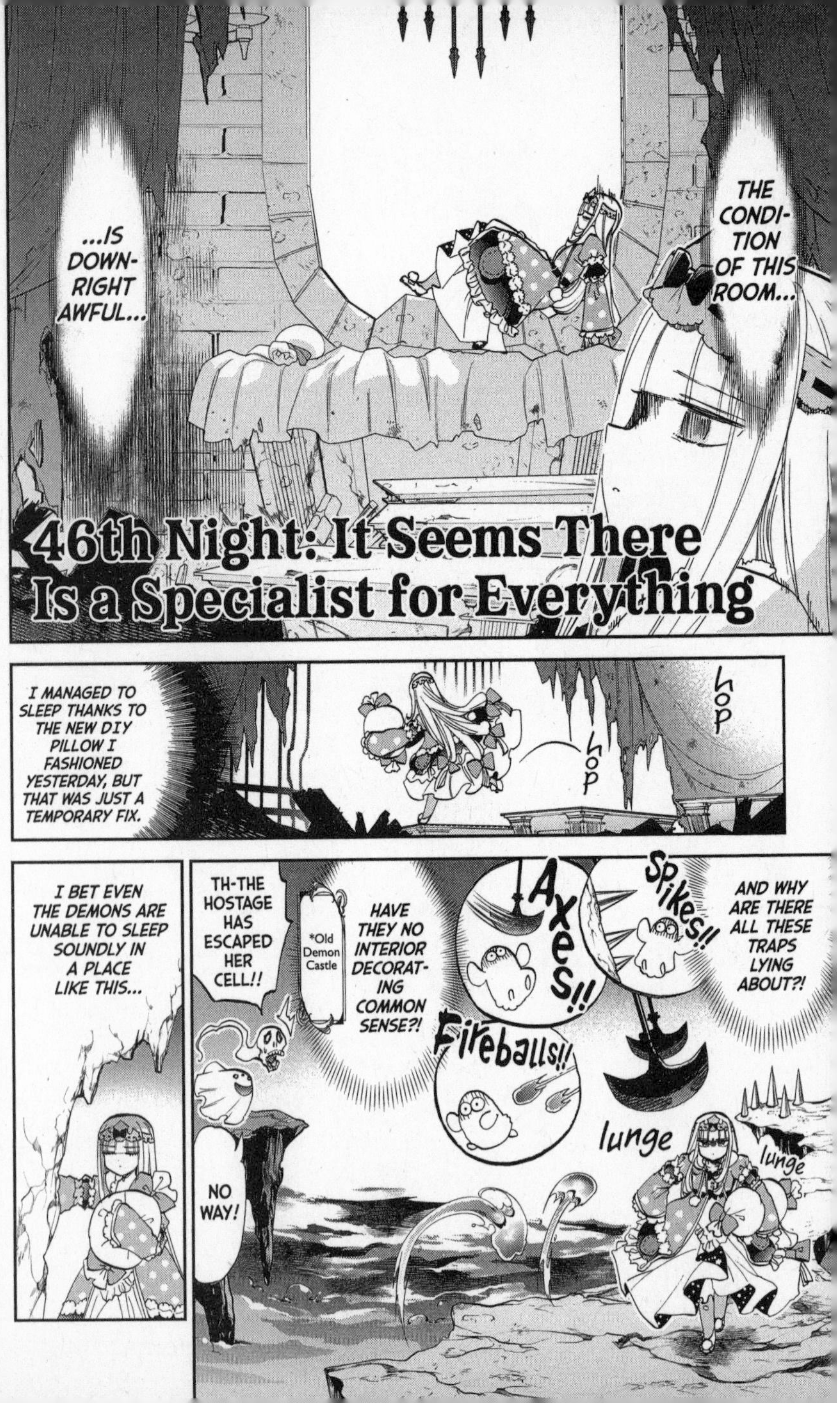
THE CONDITION OF THIS ROOM...
...IS DOWNRIGHT AWFUL...
46th Night: It Seems There Is a Specialist for Everything
hop
hop
I MANAGED TO SLEEP THANKS TO THE NEW DIY PILLOW I FASHIONED YESTERDAY, BUT THAT WAS JUST A TEMPORARY FIX.
AND WHY ARE THERE ALL THESE TRAPS LYING ABOUT?!
Spikes!!
Axes!!
Fireballs!!
HAVE THEY NO INTERIOR DECORATING COMMON SENSE?!
*Old Demon Castle
TH-THE HOSTAGE HAS ESCAPED HER CELL!!
NO WAY!
lunge
lunge
I BET EVEN THE DEMONS ARE UNABLE TO SLEEP SOUNDLY IN A PLACE LIKE THIS...

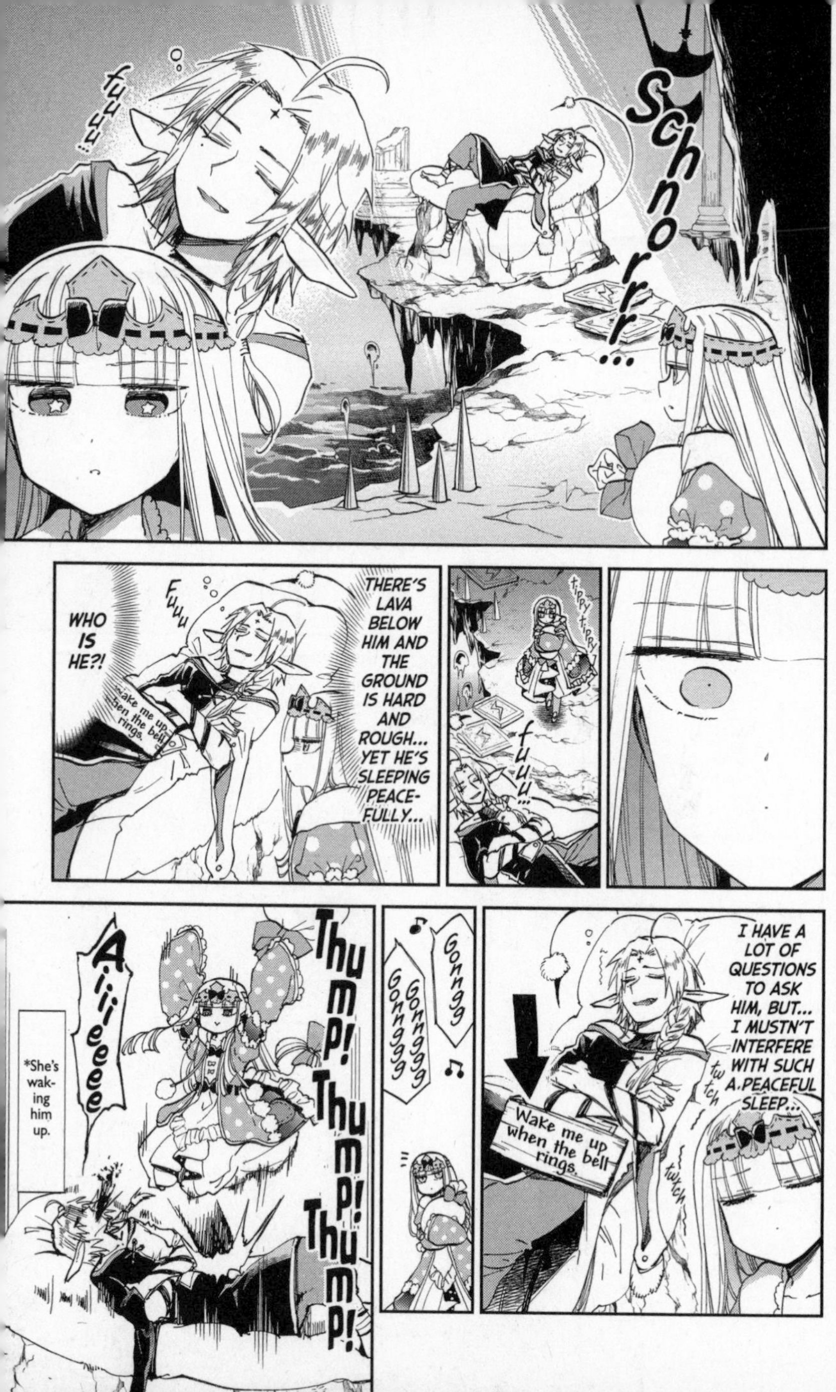
Schnorrr...!
fuuuu...
tippy tippy
fuuu...
THERE'S LAVA BELOW HIM AND THE GROUND IS HARD AND ROUGH... YET HE'S SLEEPING PEACEFULLY...
WHO IS HE?!
Fuuu
I HAVE A LOT OF QUESTIONS TO ASK HIM, BUT... I MUSTN'T INTERFERE WITH SUCH A PEACEFUL SLEEP...
twitch
twitch
Wake me up when the bell rings.
Gonngg
Gonnggg Gonnggg
Thump! Thump! Thump!
Aiiieeee
*She's waking him up.

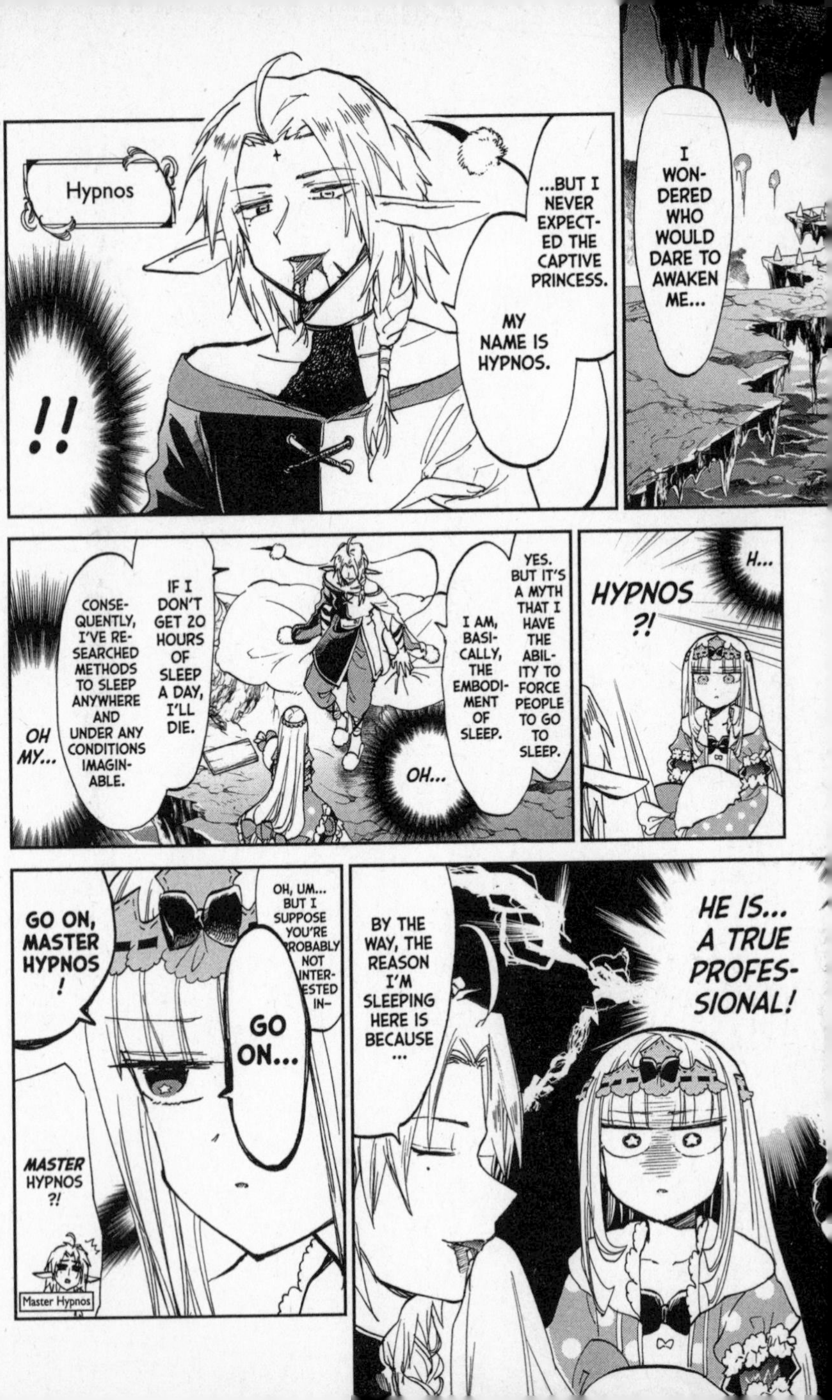
I WONDERED WHO WOULD DARE TO AWAKEN ME...
...BUT I NEVER EXPECTED THE CAPTIVE PRINCESS.
MY NAME IS HYPNOS.
Hypnos
!!
H...
HYPNOS ?!
YES. BUT IT'S A MYTH THAT I HAVE THE ABILITY TO FORCE PEOPLE TO GO TO SLEEP.
I AM, BASICALLY, THE EMBODIMENT OF SLEEP.
OH...
IF I DON'T GET 20 HOURS OF SLEEP A DAY, I'LL DIE.
CONSEQUENTLY, I'VE RESEARCHED METHODS TO SLEEP ANYWHERE AND UNDER ANY CONDITIONS IMAGINABLE.
OH MY...
HE IS... A TRUE PROFESSIONAL!
BY THE WAY, THE REASON I'M SLEEPING HERE IS BECAUSE ...
OH, UM... BUT I SUPPOSE YOU'RE PROBABLY NOT INTERESTED IN-
GO ON...
GO ON, MASTER HYPNOS!
MASTER HYPNOS ?!
Master Hypnos

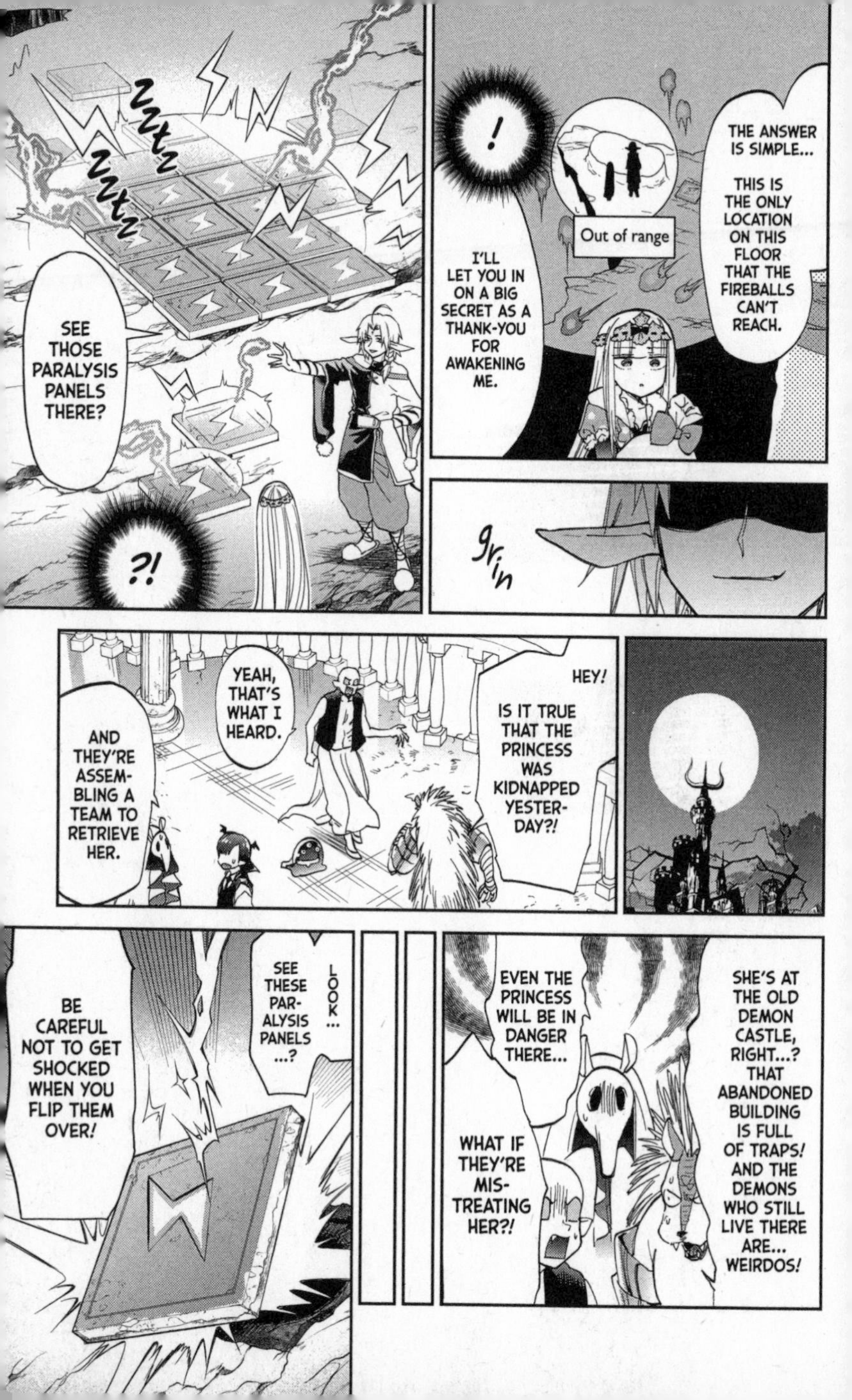
I'LL LET YOU IN ON A BIG SECRET AS A THANK-YOU FOR AWAKENING ME.
THE ANSWER IS SIMPLE...
THIS IS THE ONLY LOCATION ON THIS FLOOR THAT THE FIREBALLS CAN'T REACH.
Out of range
!
grin
ZZZtz
ZZZtz
SEE THOSE PARALYSIS PANELS THERE?
?!
HEY!
IS IT TRUE THAT THE PRINCESS WAS KIDNAPPED YESTERDAY?!
YEAH, THAT'S WHAT I HEARD.
AND THEY'RE ASSEMBLING A TEAM TO RETRIEVE HER.
SHE'S AT THE OLD DEMON CASTLE, RIGHT...? THAT ABANDONED BUILDING IS FULL OF TRAPS! AND THE DEMONS WHO STILL LIVE THERE ARE... WEIRDOS!
EVEN THE PRINCESS WILL BE IN DANGER THERE...
WHAT IF THEY'RE MISTREATING HER?!
LOOK...
SEE THESE PARALYSIS PANELS...?
BE CAREFUL NOT TO GET SHOCKED WHEN YOU FLIP THEM OVER!

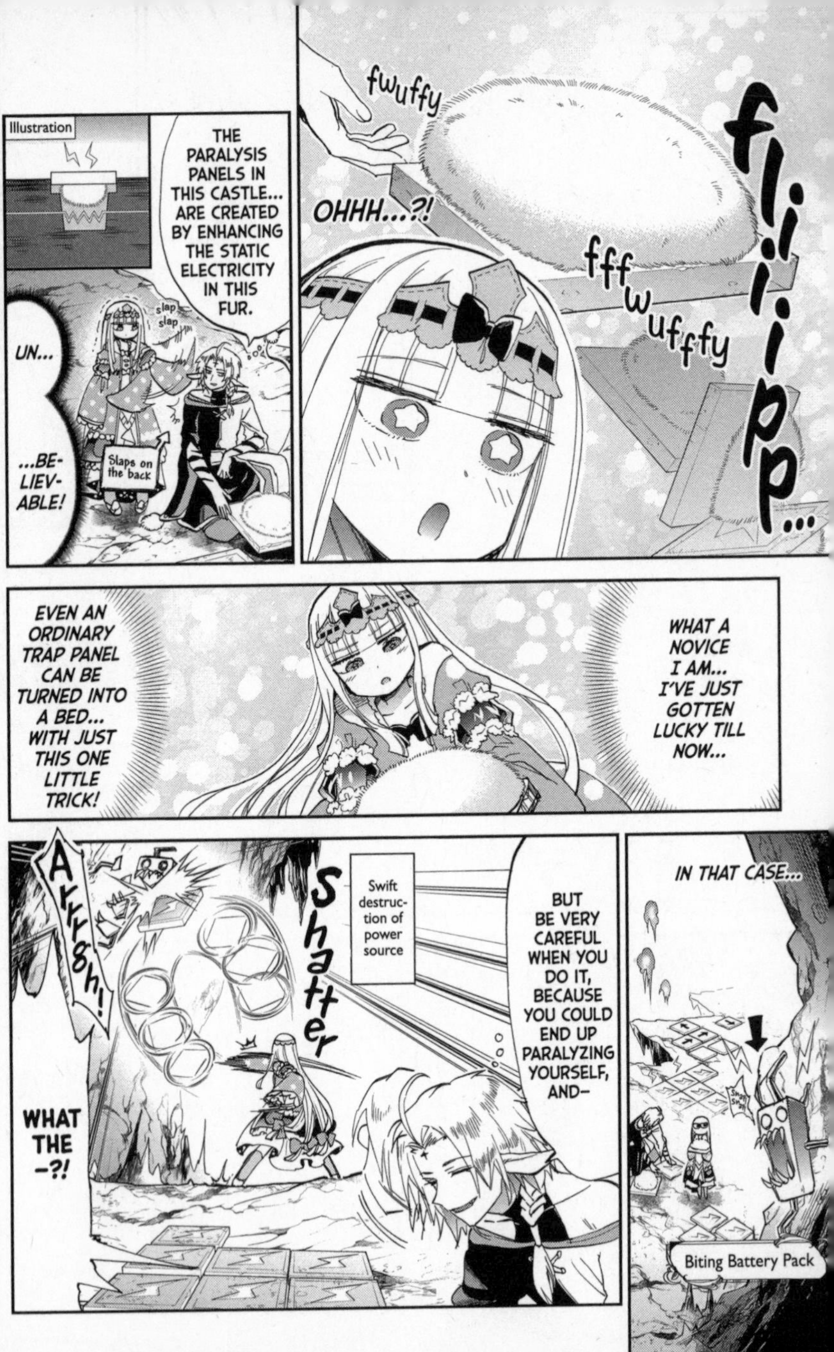
fwuffy
OHHH...?!
fffwuffy
fliiiipp...
Illustration
THE PARALYSIS PANELS IN THIS CASTLE... ARE CREATED BY ENHANCING THE STATIC ELECTRICITY IN THIS FUR.
slap slap
UN...
...BE-LIEV-ABLE!
Slaps on the back
WHAT A NOVICE I AM... I'VE JUST GOTTEN LUCKY TILL NOW...
EVEN AN ORDINARY TRAP PANEL CAN BE TURNED INTO A BED... WITH JUST THIS ONE LITTLE TRICK!
IN THAT CASE...
Biting Battery Pack
BUT BE VERY CAREFUL WHEN YOU DO IT, BECAUSE YOU COULD END UP PARALYZING YOURSELF, AND—
Swift destruction of power source
Shatter
Arrrgh!
WHAT THE —?!

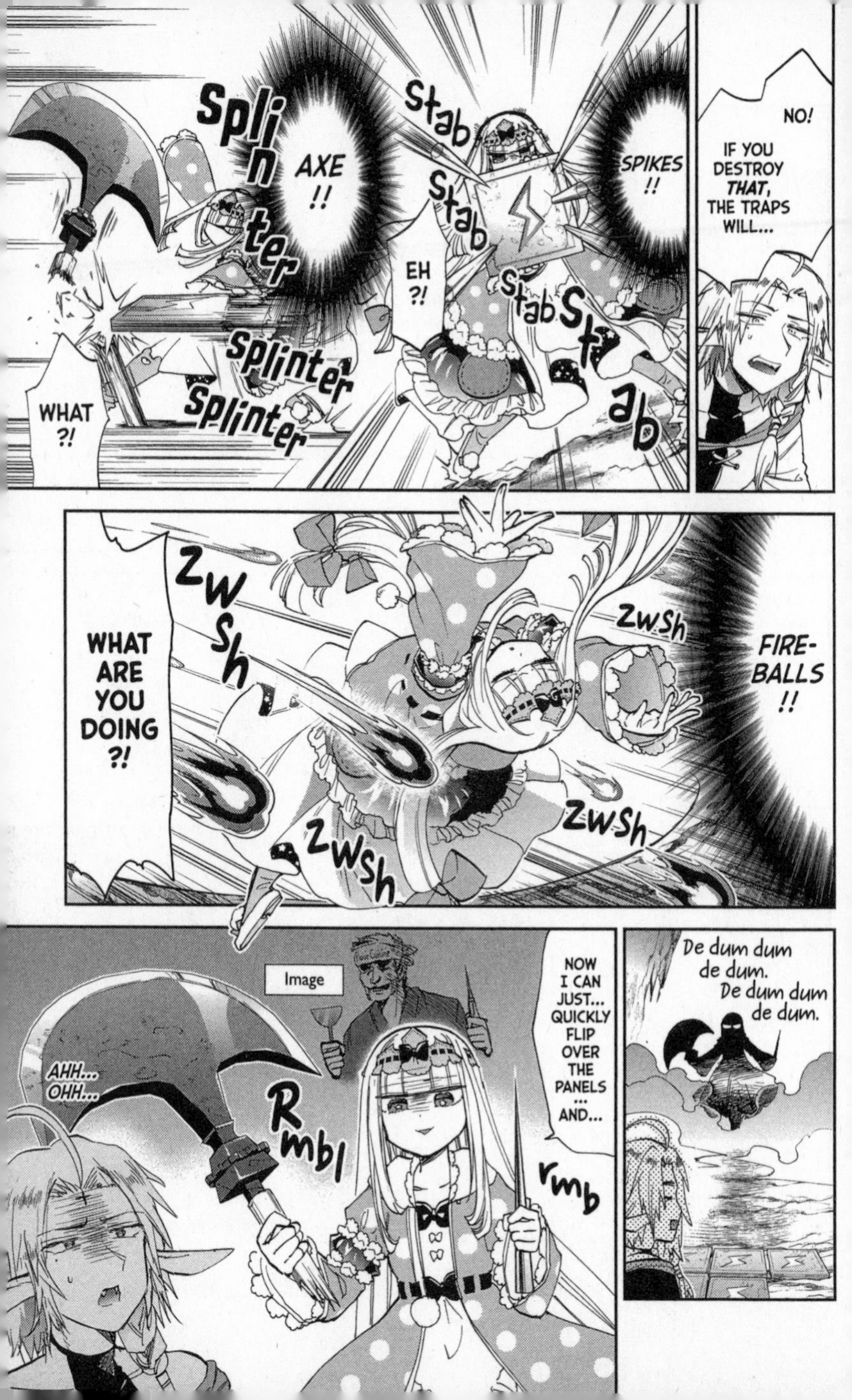
NO!
IF YOU DESTROY *THAT*, THE TRAPS WILL...
Stab
Stab
SPIKES !!
AXE !!
Splinter
EH ?!
Stab Stab
WHAT ?!
splinter
splinter
FIRE-BALLS !!
zwsh
zwsh
WHAT ARE YOU DOING ?!
zwsh
zwsh
De dum dum de dum.
De dum dum de dum.
NOW I CAN JUST... QUICKLY FLIP OVER THE PANELS ... AND...
Image
Rmbl
rmb
AHH... OHH...

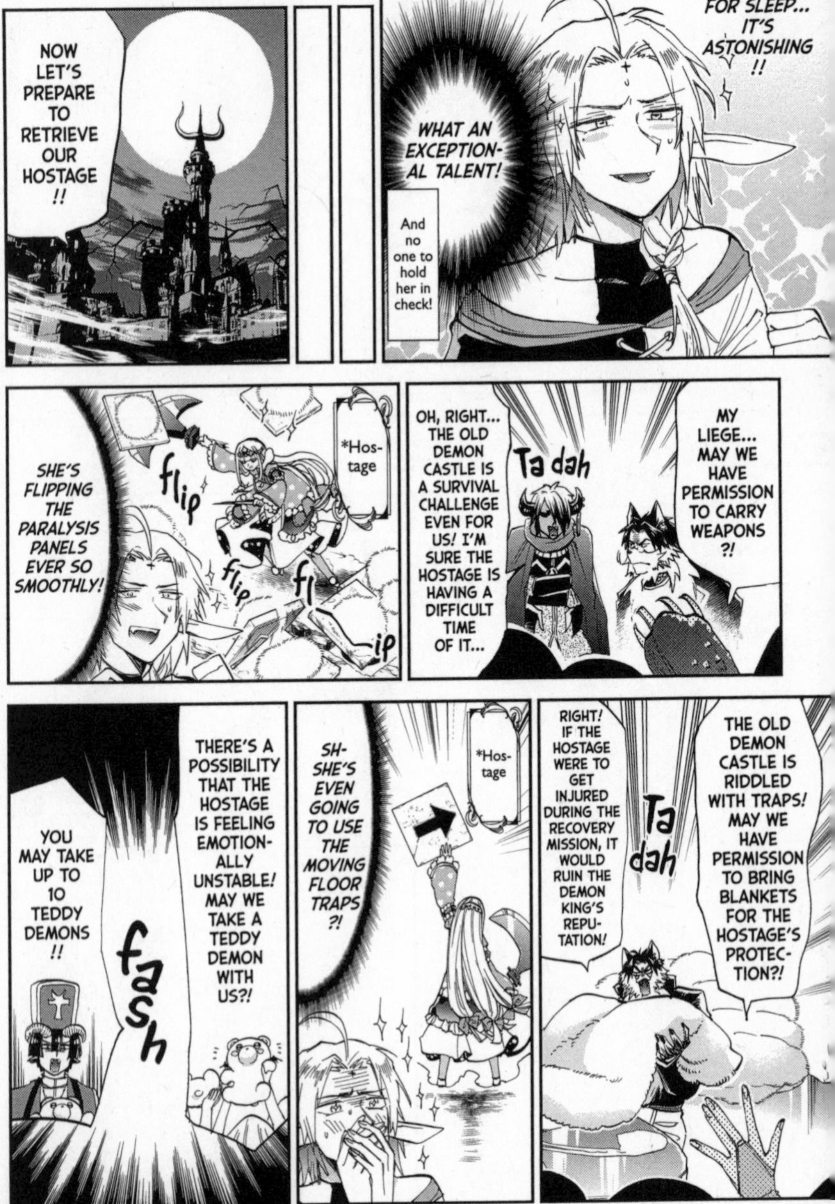
HER PASSION FOR SLEEP... IT'S ASTONISHING!!
WHAT AN EXCEPTIONAL TALENT!
And no one to hold her in check!
NOW LET'S PREPARE TO RETRIEVE OUR HOSTAGE!!
MY LIEGE... MAY WE HAVE PERMISSION TO CARRY WEAPONS?!
Ta dah
OH, RIGHT... THE OLD DEMON CASTLE IS A SURVIVAL CHALLENGE EVEN FOR US! I'M SURE THE HOSTAGE IS HAVING A DIFFICULT TIME OF IT...
*Hostage
SHE'S FLIPPING THE PARALYSIS PANELS EVER SO SMOOTHLY!
flip
flip
fl
ip
THE OLD DEMON CASTLE IS RIDDLED WITH TRAPS! MAY WE HAVE PERMISSION TO BRING BLANKETS FOR THE HOSTAGE'S PROTECTION?!
Ta dah
RIGHT! IF THE HOSTAGE WERE TO GET INJURED DURING THE RECOVERY MISSION, IT WOULD RUIN THE DEMON KING'S REPUTATION!
*Hostage
SH-SHE'S EVEN GOING TO USE THE MOVING FLOOR TRAPS?!
THERE'S A POSSIBILITY THAT THE HOSTAGE IS FEELING EMOTIONALLY UNSTABLE! MAY WE TAKE A TEDDY DEMON WITH US?!
fash
YOU MAY TAKE UP TO 10 TEDDY DEMONS!!

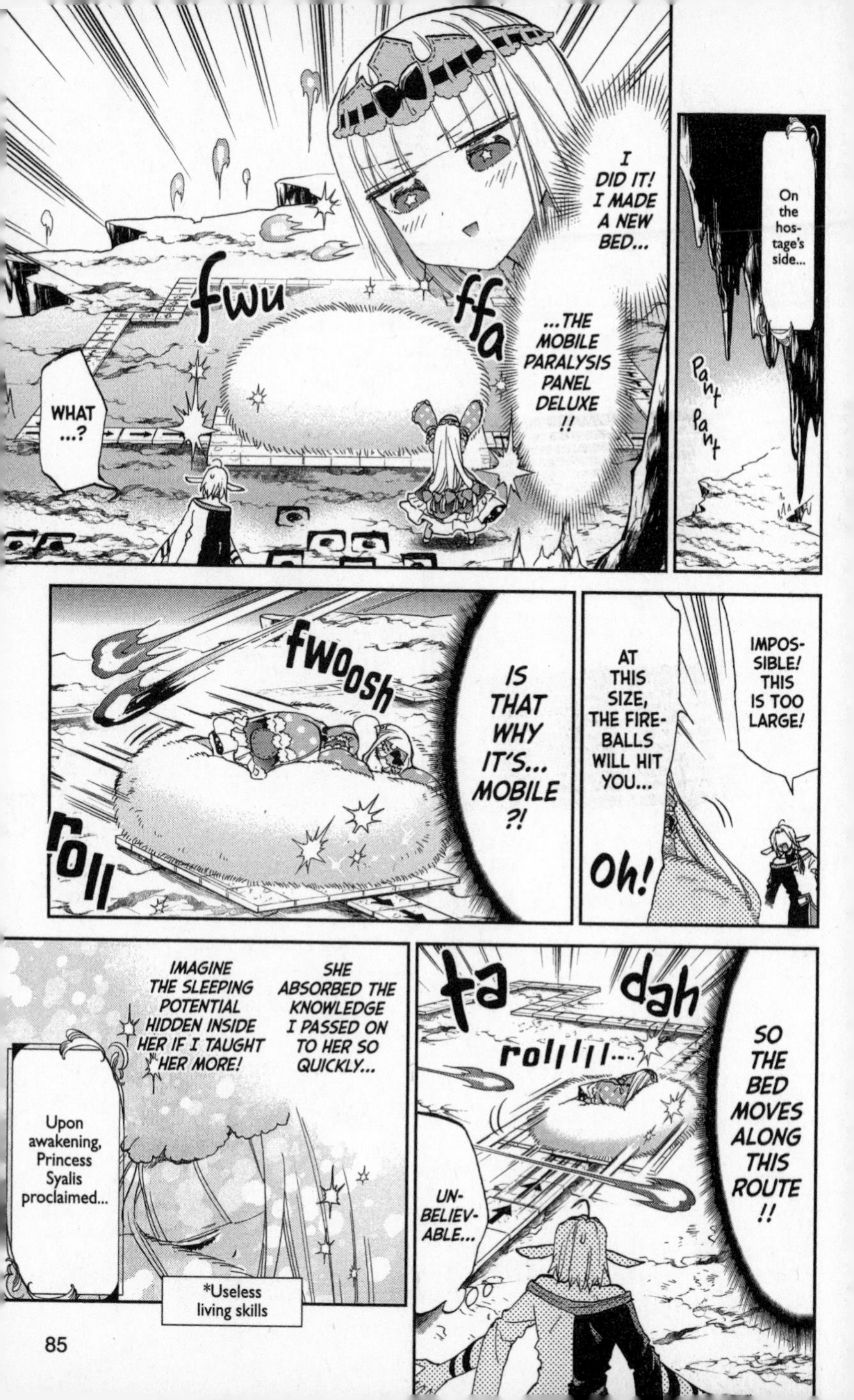
On the hostage's side...
Pant Pant
I DID IT! I MADE A NEW BED...
...THE MOBILE PARALYSIS PANEL DELUXE!!
fwu ffa
WHAT...?
IMPOSSIBLE! THIS IS TOO LARGE!
AT THIS SIZE, THE FIREBALLS WILL HIT YOU...
Oh!
IS THAT WHY IT'S... MOBILE?!
fwoosh
roll
ta dah
SO THE BED MOVES ALONG THIS ROUTE!!
rolllll...
UNBELIEVABLE...
SHE ABSORBED THE KNOWLEDGE I PASSED ON TO HER SO QUICKLY...
IMAGINE THE SLEEPING POTENTIAL HIDDEN INSIDE HER IF I TAUGHT HER MORE!
Upon awakening, Princess Syalis proclaimed...
*Useless living skills

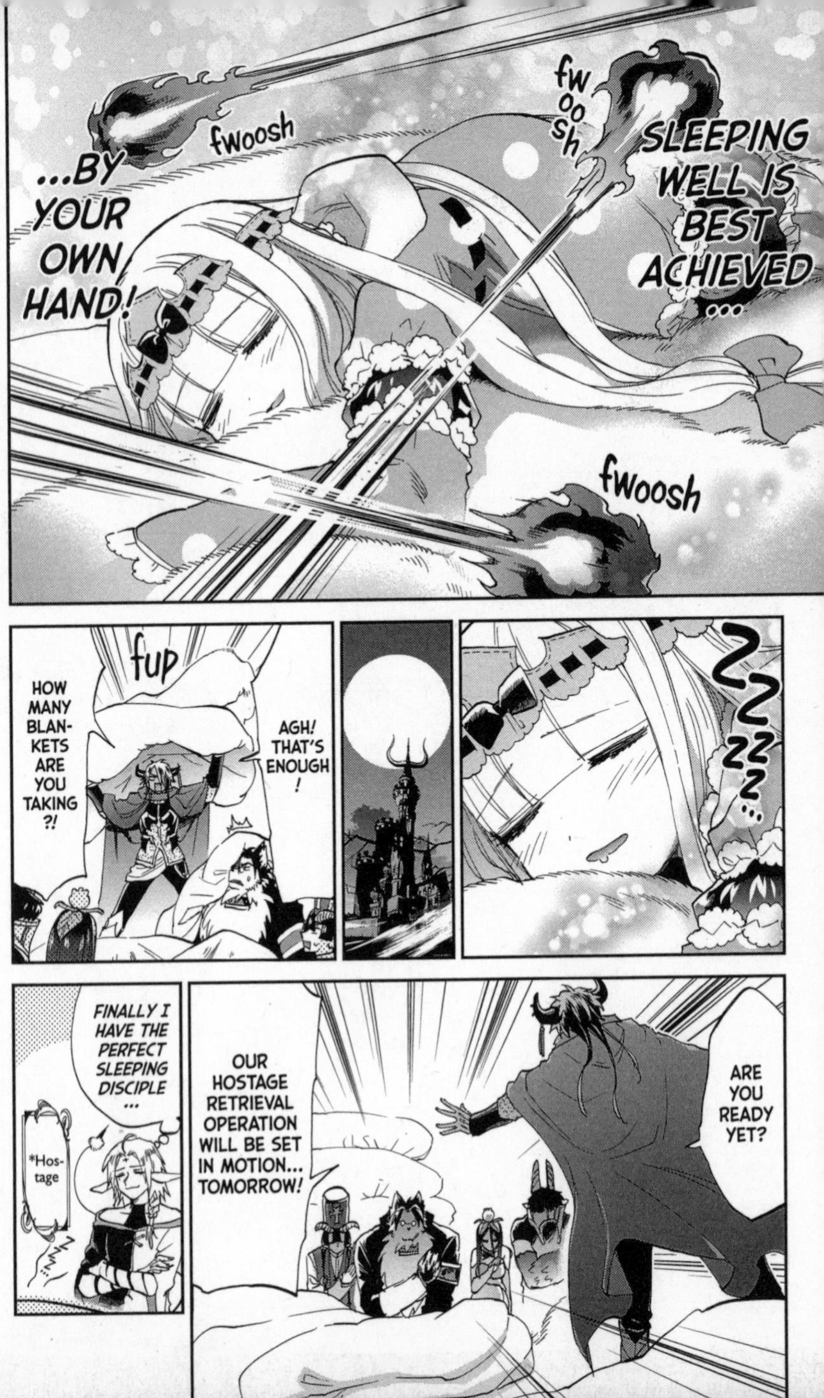
fwoosh
SLEEPING WELL IS BEST ACHIEVED...
fwoosh
...BY YOUR OWN HAND!
fwoosh
ZZZZZ...
fup
AGH! THAT'S ENOUGH!
HOW MANY BLANKETS ARE YOU TAKING?!
ARE YOU READY YET?
OUR HOSTAGE RETRIEVAL OPERATION WILL BE SET IN MOTION... TOMORROW!
FINALLY I HAVE THE PERFECT SLEEPING DISCIPLE...
*Hostage

Hypnos

I'm really ill-suited to be a mentor.

Sleepiness: ☆☆☆☆☆☆☆☆☆☆☆
Discipline: ☆☆

A demon of the spirit species who must sleep 20 hours a day. He will die if he does not sleep enough, so he is devoted to sleep research. He has been living in the Old Demon Castle since the days of the previous Demon King, but not because he has anything against the current regime, only because it's quieter than the New Demon Castle.

He is very happy now because his new disciple is putting the wisdom he has passed down to her to good use.

Problem he had until a few hundred years ago:
"The seasons fly by."

Current problem:
"Small dogs don't like me."

fwoosh
nod
fwip
WATCHING MY DISCIPLE SLEEP IN HER BED MAKES ME SLEEPY ...
fwoosh
nod
fwoosh
nod
fwoosh
nod
ZZZZZZ
fwoosh
fwoosh
THAT GUY SCARES ME.
I CAN SEE WHY.

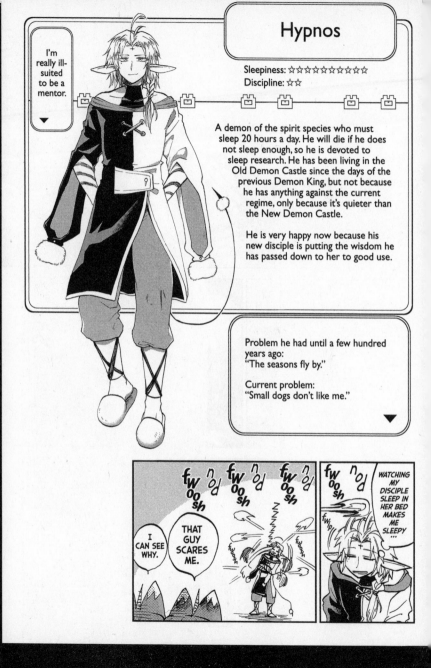

Would you like to change
your class?

5 changes
remaining

▶Yes

No ▼

Postman

"Attack with
threatening letters."

▼

47th Night: Retrieve the Princess (A Demon Castle Monster)

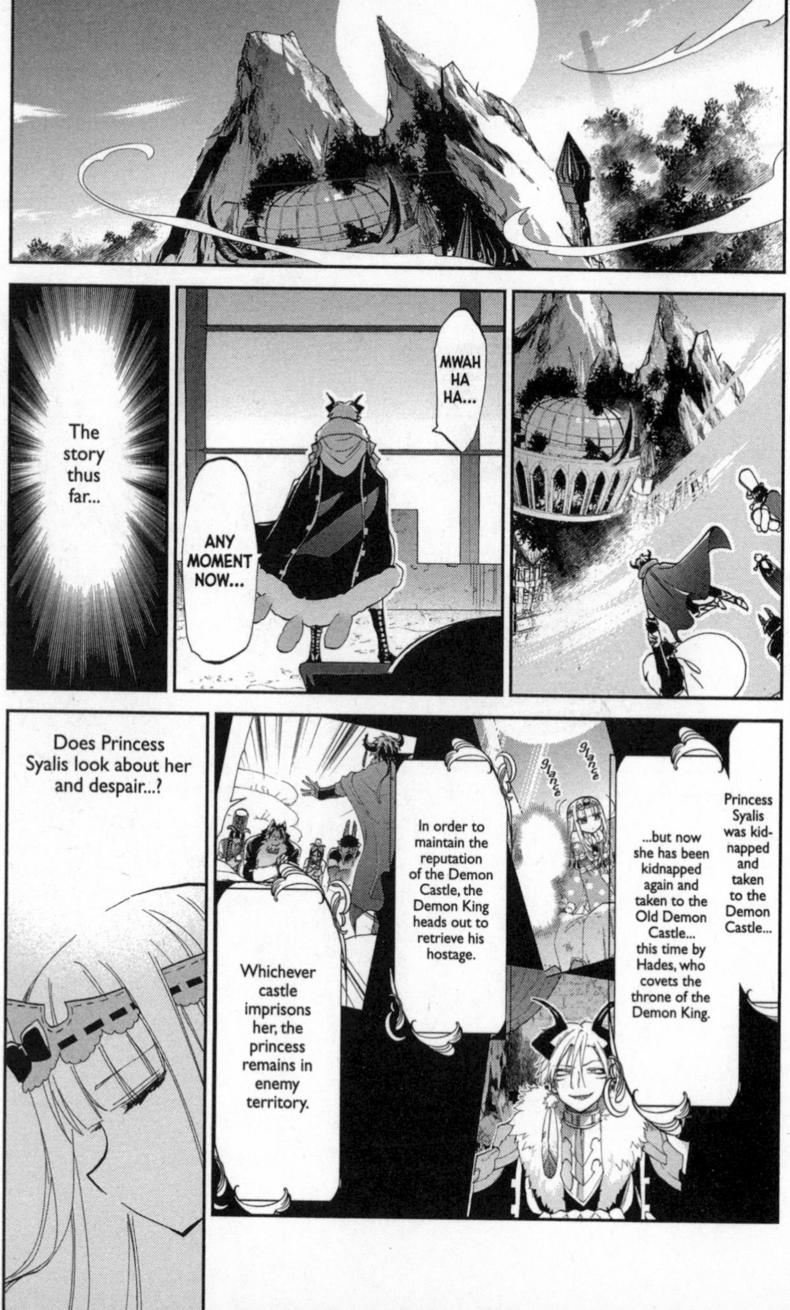
MWAH HA HA...
ANY MOMENT NOW...
The story thus far...
Princess Syalis was kid-napped and taken to the Demon Castle...
glance glance
...but now she has been kidnapped again and taken to the Old Demon Castle... this time by Hades, who covets the throne of the Demon King.
In order to maintain the reputation of the Demon Castle, the Demon King heads out to retrieve his hostage.
Whichever castle imprisons her, the princess remains in enemy territory.
Does Princess Syalis look about her and despair...?

47th Night: Retrieve the Princess (A Demon Castle Monster)

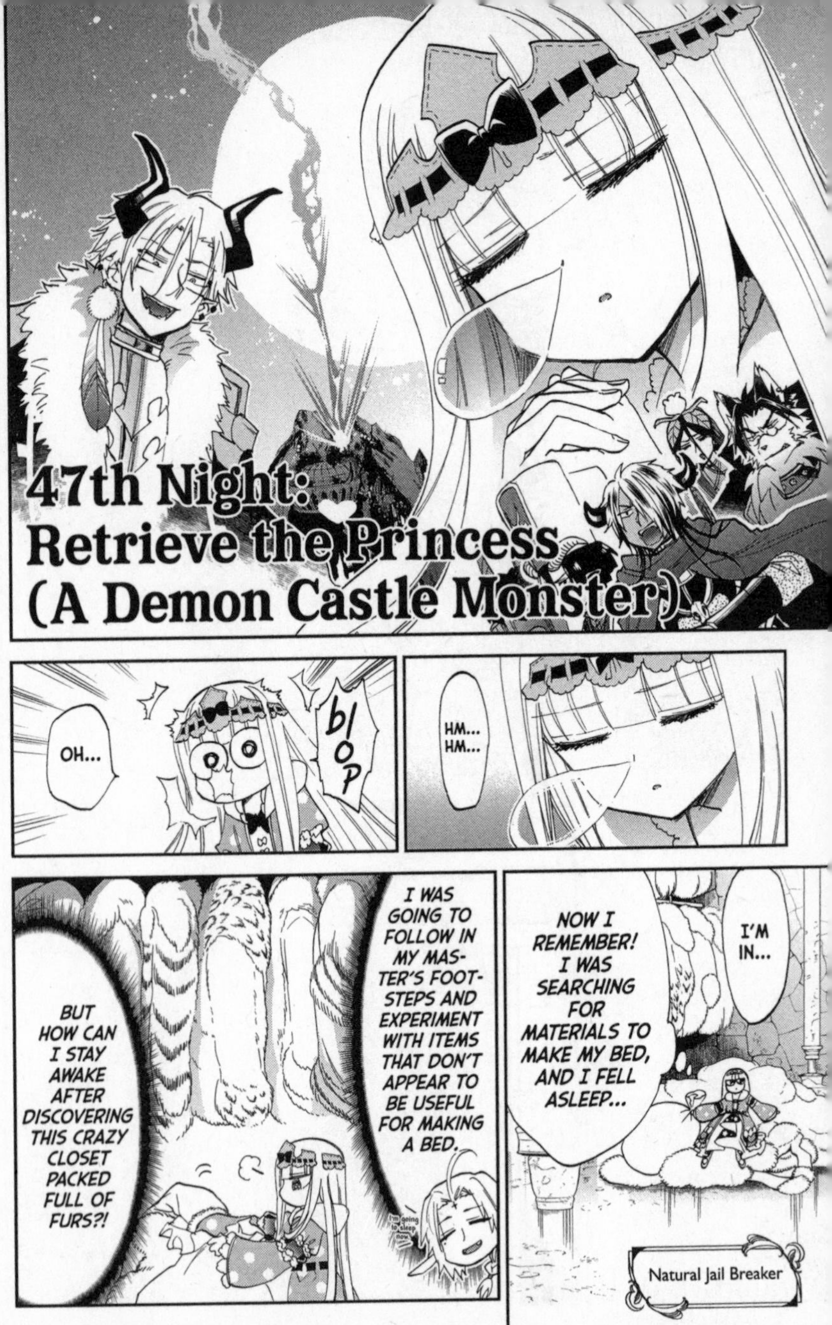
HM... HM...
OH...
blop
I'M IN...
NOW I REMEMBER! I WAS SEARCHING FOR MATERIALS TO MAKE MY BED, AND I FELL ASLEEP...
Natural Jail Breaker
I WAS GOING TO FOLLOW IN MY MASTER'S FOOTSTEPS AND EXPERIMENT WITH ITEMS THAT DON'T APPEAR TO BE USEFUL FOR MAKING A BED.
BUT HOW CAN I STAY AWAKE AFTER DISCOVERING THIS CRAZY CLOSET PACKED FULL OF FURS?!
I'm going to sleep now.

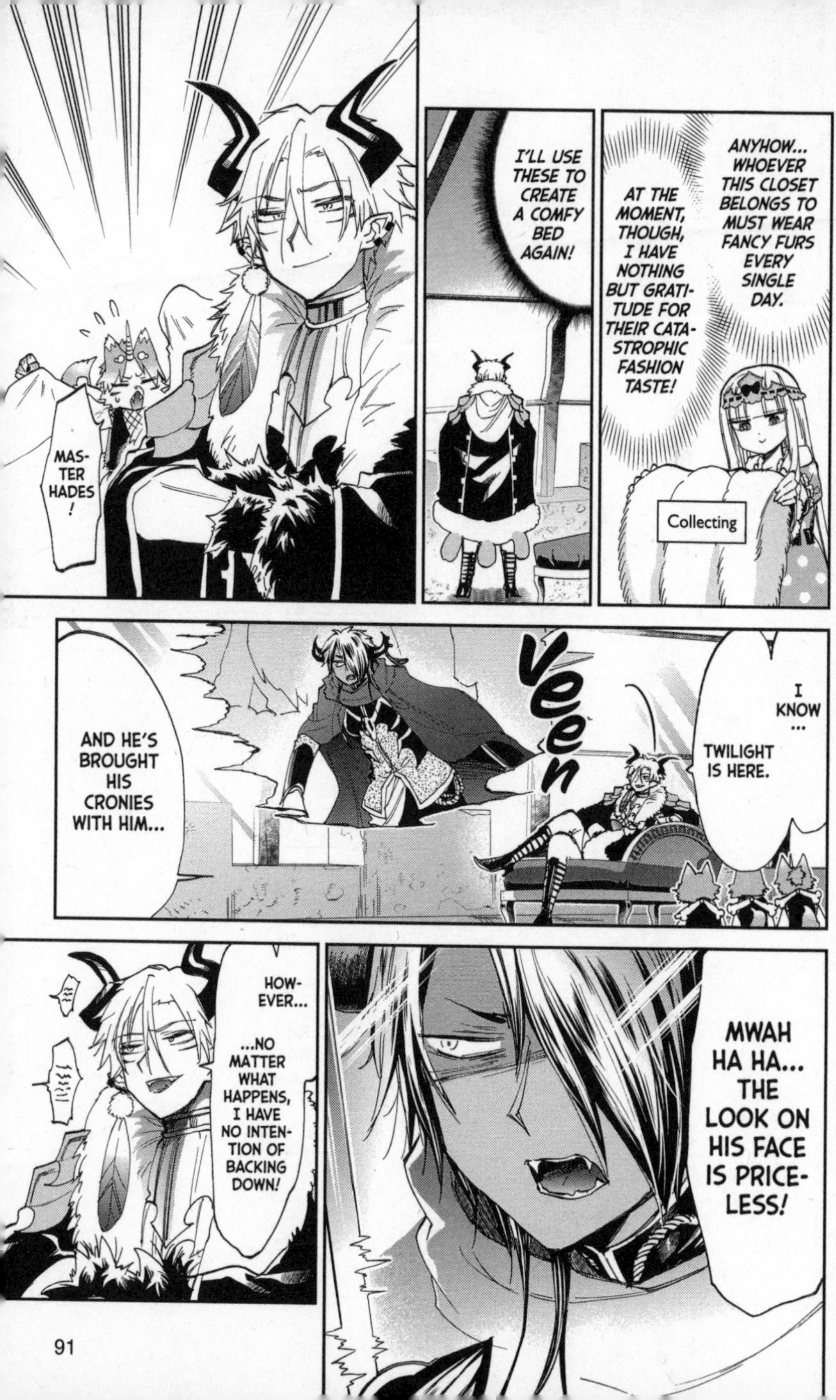
ANYHOW... WHOEVER THIS CLOSET BELONGS TO MUST WEAR FANCY FURS EVERY SINGLE DAY.
AT THE MOMENT, THOUGH, I HAVE NOTHING BUT GRATITUDE FOR THEIR CATASTROPHIC FASHION TASTE!
Collecting
I'LL USE THESE TO CREATE A COMFY BED AGAIN!
MASTER HADES!
I KNOW...
TWILIGHT IS HERE.
Veen
AND HE'S BROUGHT HIS CRONIES WITH HIM...
MWAH HA HA... THE LOOK ON HIS FACE IS PRICELESS!
HOWEVER...
...NO MATTER WHAT HAPPENS, I HAVE NO INTENTION OF BACKING DOWN!

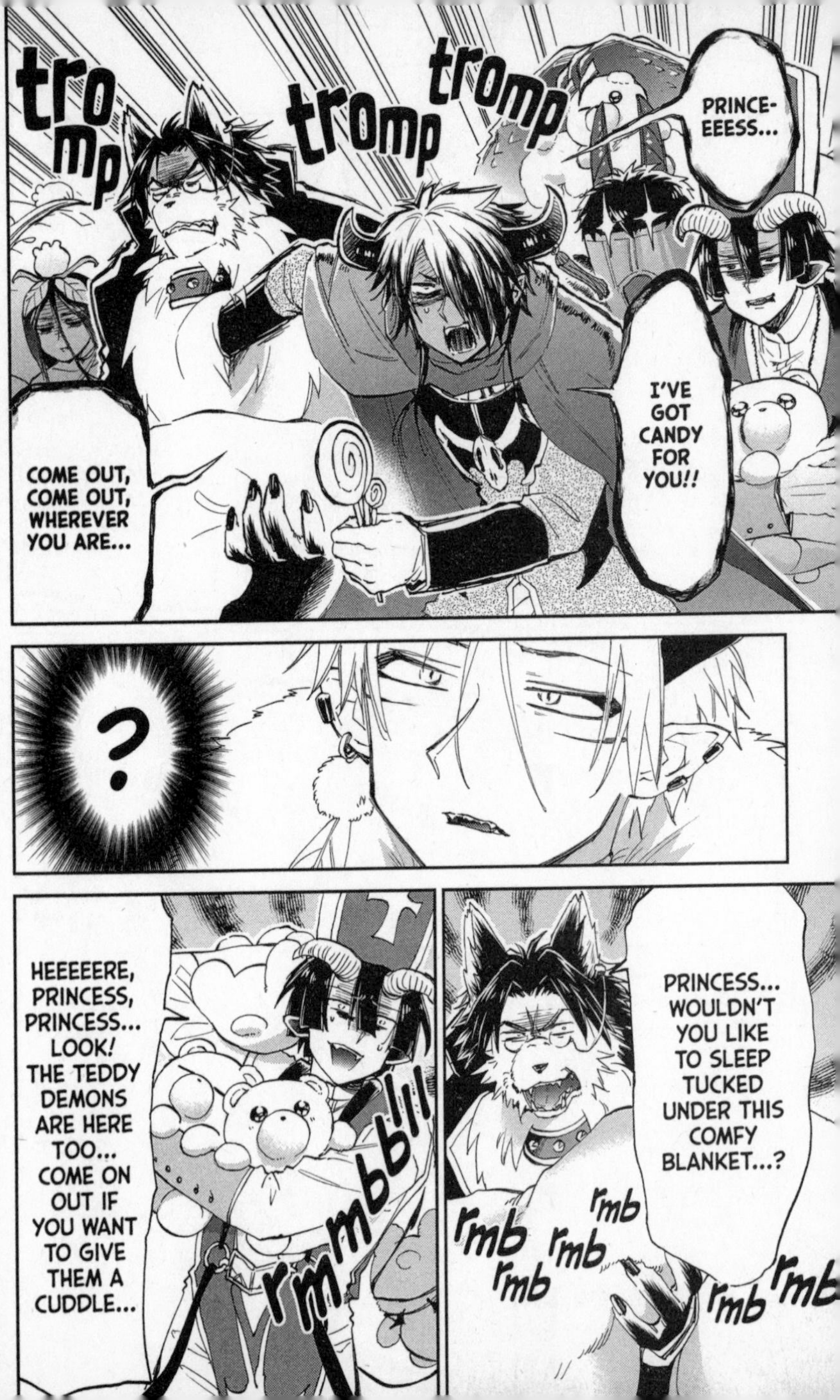
PRINCE-EEESS...
tromp tromp
I'VE GOT CANDY FOR YOU!!
tromp
tromp
COME OUT, COME OUT, WHEREVER YOU ARE...
?
PRINCESS... WOULDN'T YOU LIKE TO SLEEP TUCKED UNDER THIS COMFY BLANKET...?
rmb rmb rmb rmb rmb rmb rmb
HEEEEERE, PRINCESS, PRINCESS... LOOK! THE TEDDY DEMONS ARE HERE TOO... COME ON OUT IF YOU WANT TO GIVE THEM A CUDDLE...
rmmbbl

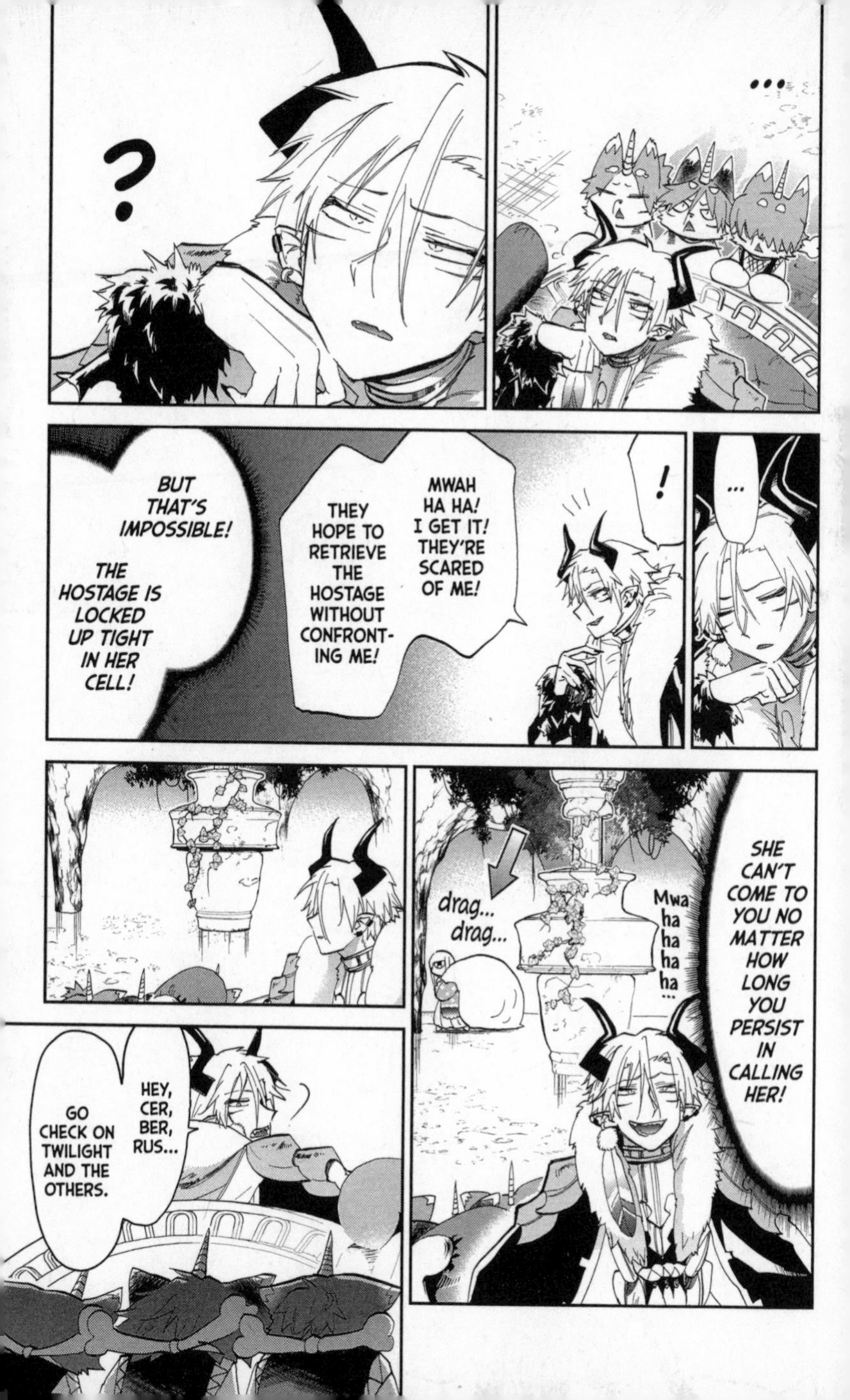
...
?
...
!
MWAH HA HA! I GET IT! THEY'RE SCARED OF ME!
THEY HOPE TO RETRIEVE THE HOSTAGE WITHOUT CONFRONTING ME!
BUT THAT'S IMPOSSIBLE! THE HOSTAGE IS LOCKED UP TIGHT IN HER CELL!
SHE CAN'T COME TO YOU NO MATTER HOW LONG YOU PERSIST IN CALLING HER!
Mwa ha ha ha ha ha...
drag... drag...
HEY, CER, BER, RUS...
GO CHECK ON TWILIGHT AND THE OTHERS.

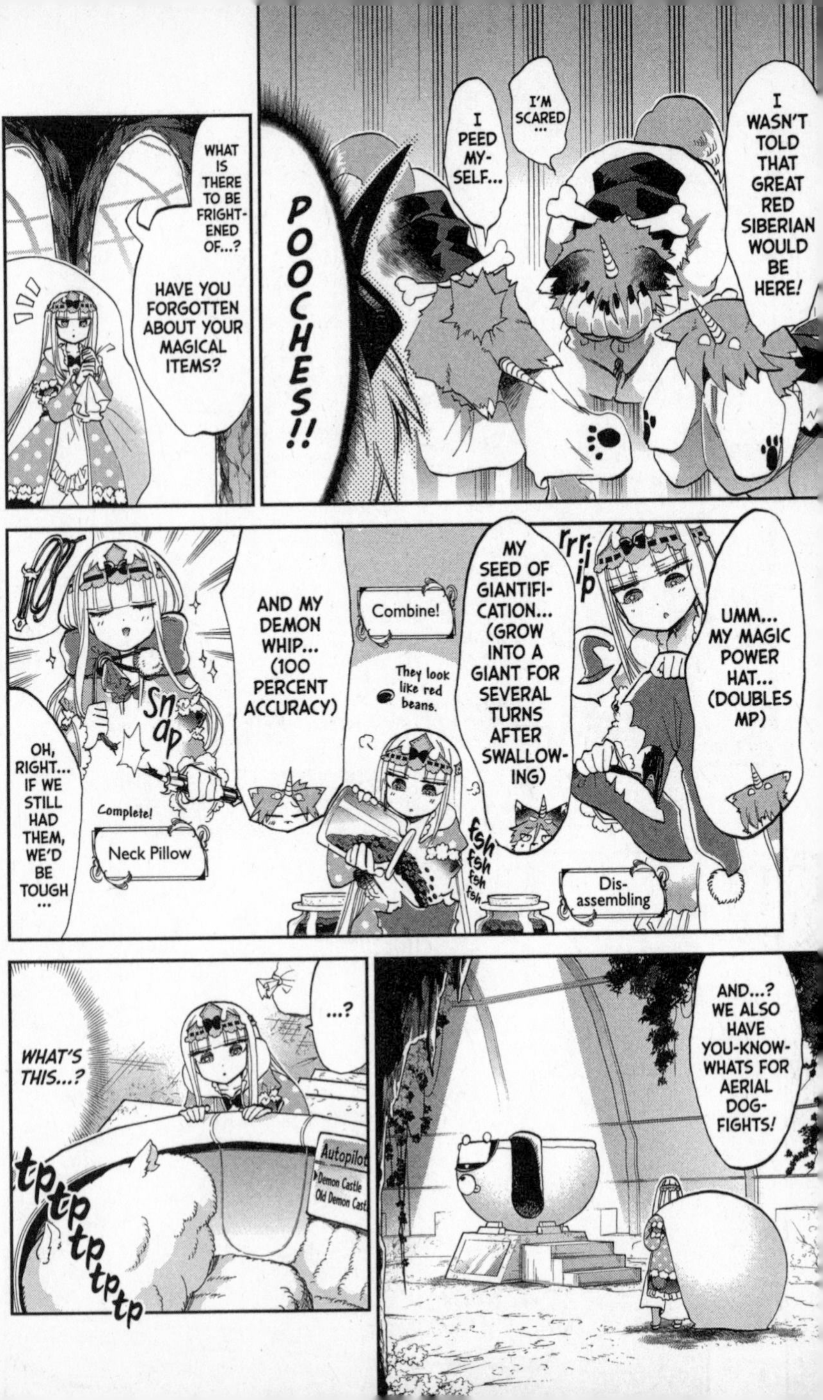
I WASN'T TOLD THAT GREAT RED SIBERIAN WOULD BE HERE!
I'M SCARED...
I PEED MY-SELF...
POOCHES!!
WHAT IS THERE TO BE FRIGHT-ENED OF...?
HAVE YOU FORGOTTEN ABOUT YOUR MAGICAL ITEMS?
UMM... MY MAGIC POWER HAT... (DOUBLES MP)
Dis-assembling
rrrip
MY SEED OF GIANTIFI-CATION... (GROW INTO A GIANT FOR SEVERAL TURNS AFTER SWALLOW-ING)
fsh fsh fsh fsh
They look like red beans.
Combine!
AND MY DEMON WHIP... (100 PERCENT ACCURACY)
snap
Complete!
Neck Pillow
OH, RIGHT... IF WE STILL HAD THEM, WE'D BE TOUGH...
AND...? WE ALSO HAVE YOU-KNOW-WHATS FOR AERIAL DOG-FIGHTS!
...?
WHAT'S THIS...?
Autopilot
Demon Castle
tptptptptp

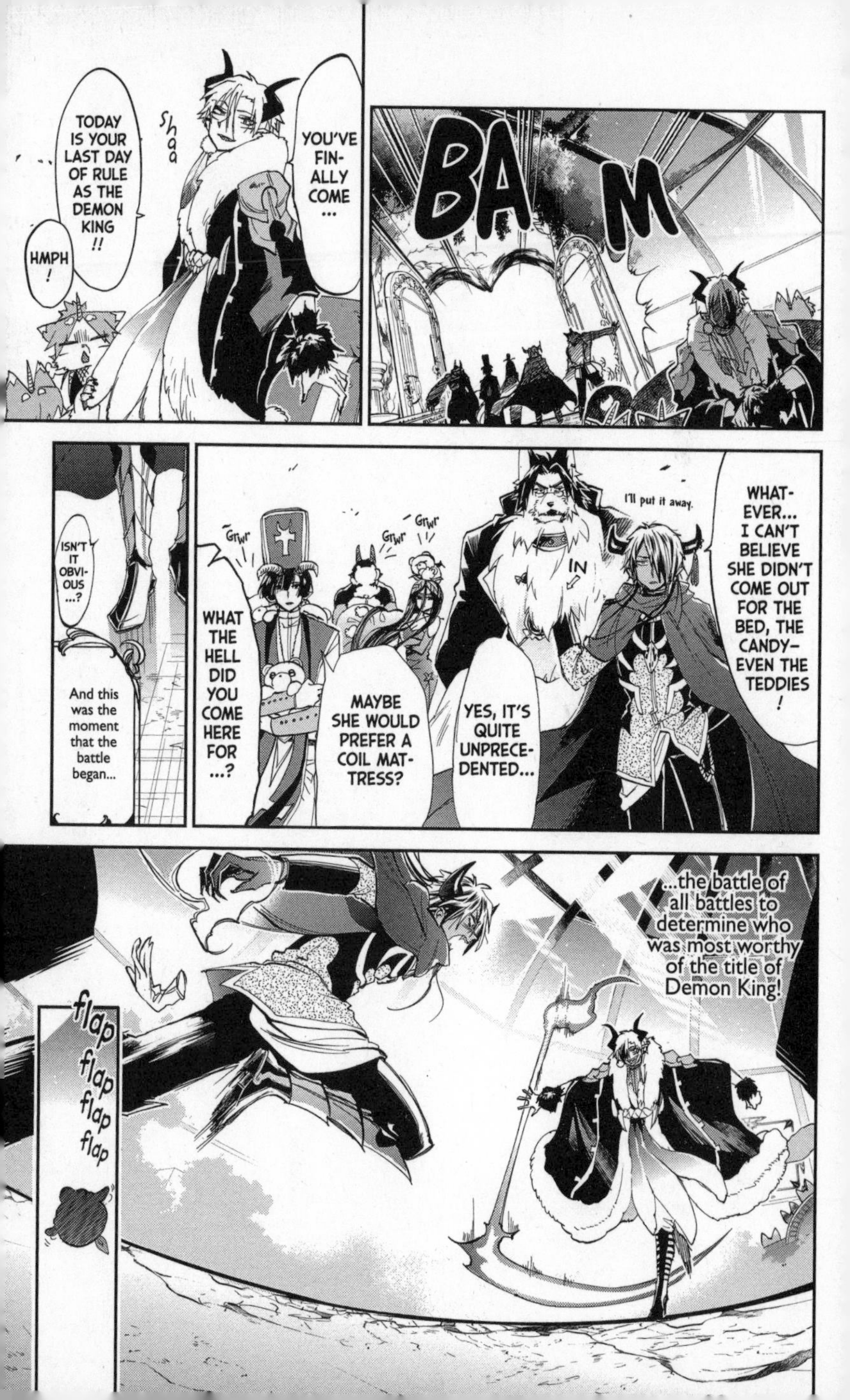
BAM
YOU'VE FIN-ALLY COME...
Shaa
TODAY IS YOUR LAST DAY OF RULE AS THE DEMON KING!!
HMPH!
WHAT-EVER... I CAN'T BELIEVE SHE DIDN'T COME OUT FOR THE BED, THE CANDY— EVEN THE TEDDIES!
I'll put it away.
IN
YES, IT'S QUITE UNPRECE-DENTED...
MAYBE SHE WOULD PREFER A COIL MAT-TRESS?
Grwr
Grwr
Grwr
WHAT THE HELL DID YOU COME HERE FOR...?
ISN'T IT OBVI-OUS...?
And this was the moment that the battle began...
...the battle of all battles to determine who was most worthy of the title of Demon King!
flap flap flap flap

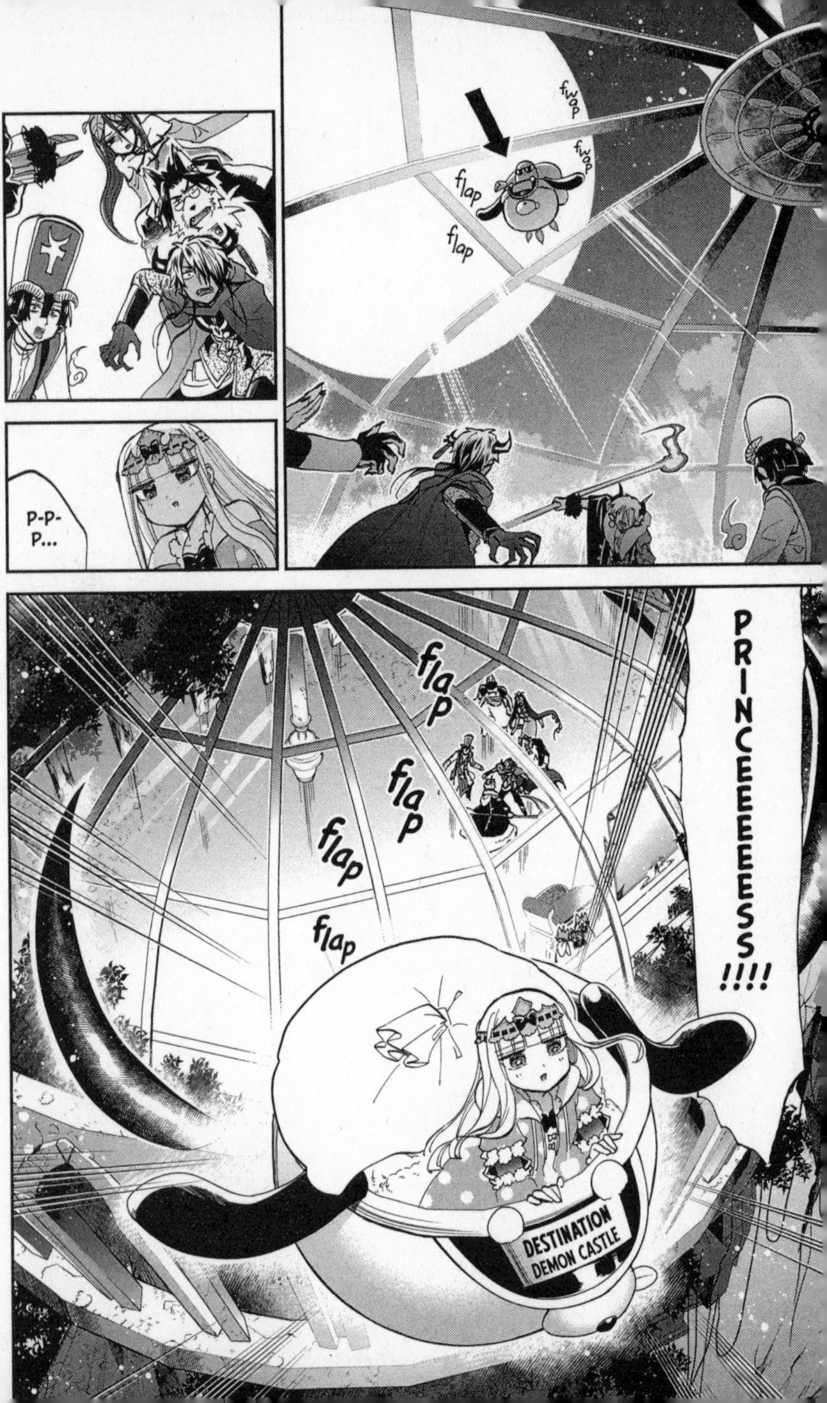
fwap
fwap
flap
flap
P-P-P...
PRINCEEEEESS!!!!
flap
flap
flap
flap
DESTINATION
DEMON CASTLE

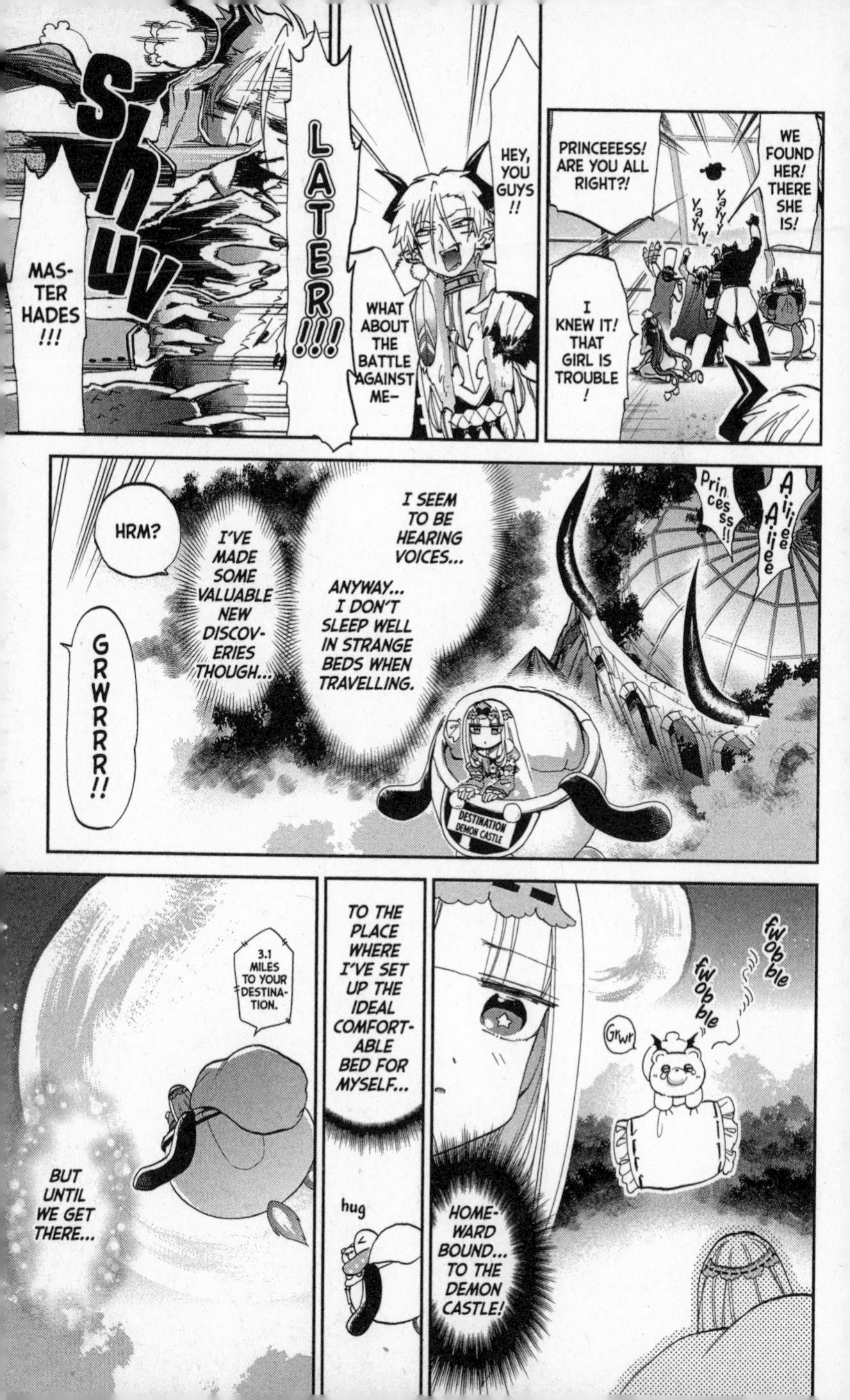
WE FOUND HER! THERE SHE IS!
PRINCEEESS! ARE YOU ALL RIGHT?!
Yayyy Yayyy
I KNEW IT! THAT GIRL IS TROUBLE!
HEY, YOU GUYS!!
WHAT ABOUT THE BATTLE AGAINST ME–
LATER!!!
SHUUV
MASTER HADES!!!
Aiiee Aiiee
Princess!!
I SEEM TO BE HEARING VOICES...
ANYWAY... I DON'T SLEEP WELL IN STRANGE BEDS WHEN TRAVELLING.
I'VE MADE SOME VALUABLE NEW DISCOVERIES THOUGH...
HRM?
GRWRRRR!!
DESTINATION DEMON CASTLE
fwobble fwobble
Grwr
HOMEWARD BOUND... TO THE DEMON CASTLE!
TO THE PLACE WHERE I'VE SET UP THE IDEAL COMFORTABLE BED FOR MYSELF...
hug
3.1 MILES TO YOUR DESTINATION.
BUT UNTIL WE GET THERE...

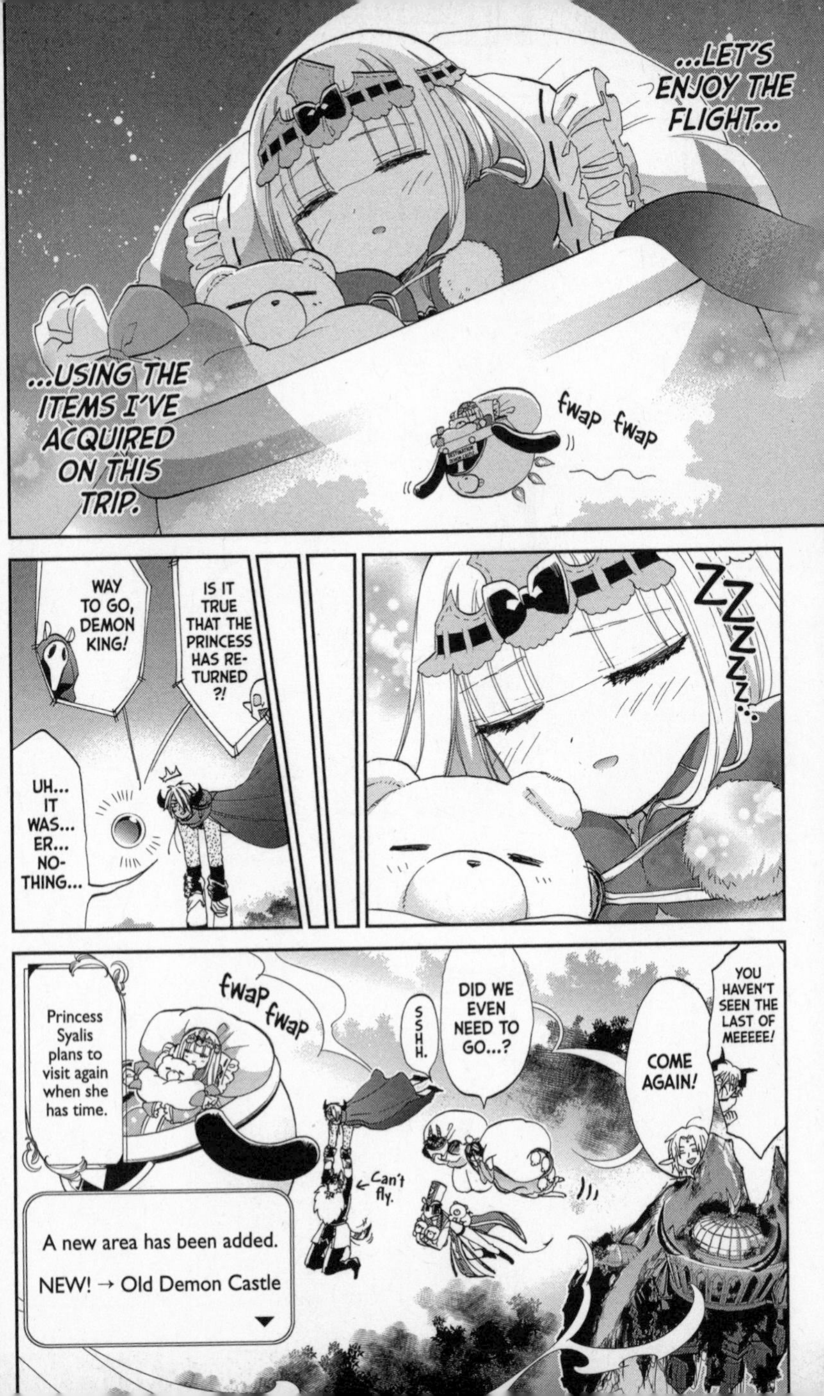
...LET'S ENJOY THE FLIGHT...
...USING THE ITEMS I'VE ACQUIRED ON THIS TRIP.
fwap fwap
ZZZZZ...
IS IT TRUE THAT THE PRINCESS HAS RE-TURNED?!
WAY TO GO, DEMON KING!
UH... IT WAS... ER... NO-THING...
YOU HAVEN'T SEEN THE LAST OF MEEEEE!
COME AGAIN!
DID WE EVEN NEED TO GO...?
SSHH.
fwap fwap
Princess Syalis plans to visit again when she has time.
Can't fly.
A new area has been added.
NEW! → Old Demon Castle

Cer, Ber, Rus

Three spoiled siblings.

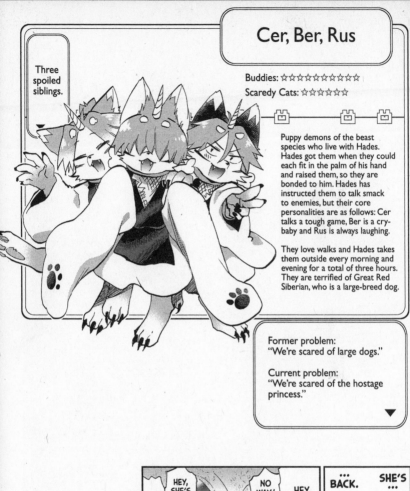

Buddies: ☆☆☆☆☆☆☆☆☆☆

Scaredy Cats: ☆☆☆☆☆☆

Puppy demons of the beast species who live with Hades. Hades got them when they could each fit in the palm of his hand and raised them, so they are bonded to him. Hades has instructed them to talk smack to enemies, but their core personalities are as follows: Cer talks a tough game, Ber is a cry-baby and Rus is always laughing.

They love walks and Hades takes them outside every morning and evening for a total of three hours. They are terrified of Great Red Siberian, who is a large-breed dog.

Former problem:
"We're scared of large dogs."

Current problem:
"We're scared of the hostage princess."

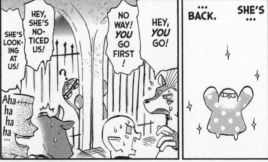

SHE'S ...
... BACK.

HEY, YOU GO!
NO WAY! YOU GO FIRST!
HEY, SHE'S NOTICED US!
SHE'S LOOKING AT US!
Aha ha ha ha ...

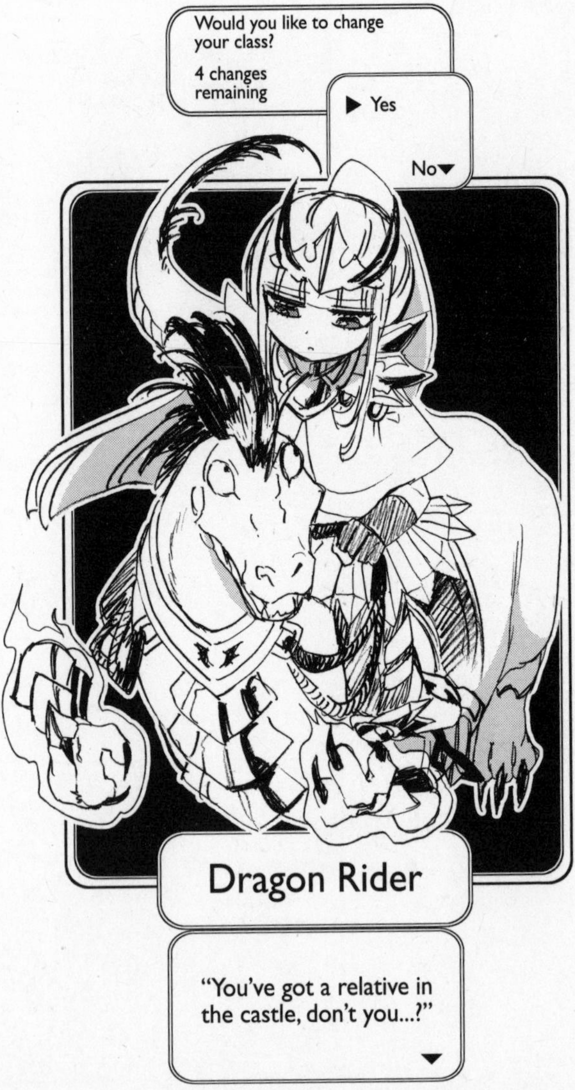
Would you like to change your class?
4 changes remaining
▶ Yes
No
Dragon Rider
"You've got a relative in the castle, don't you...?"

48th Night: Extreme Training Magic Tournament of Monsters

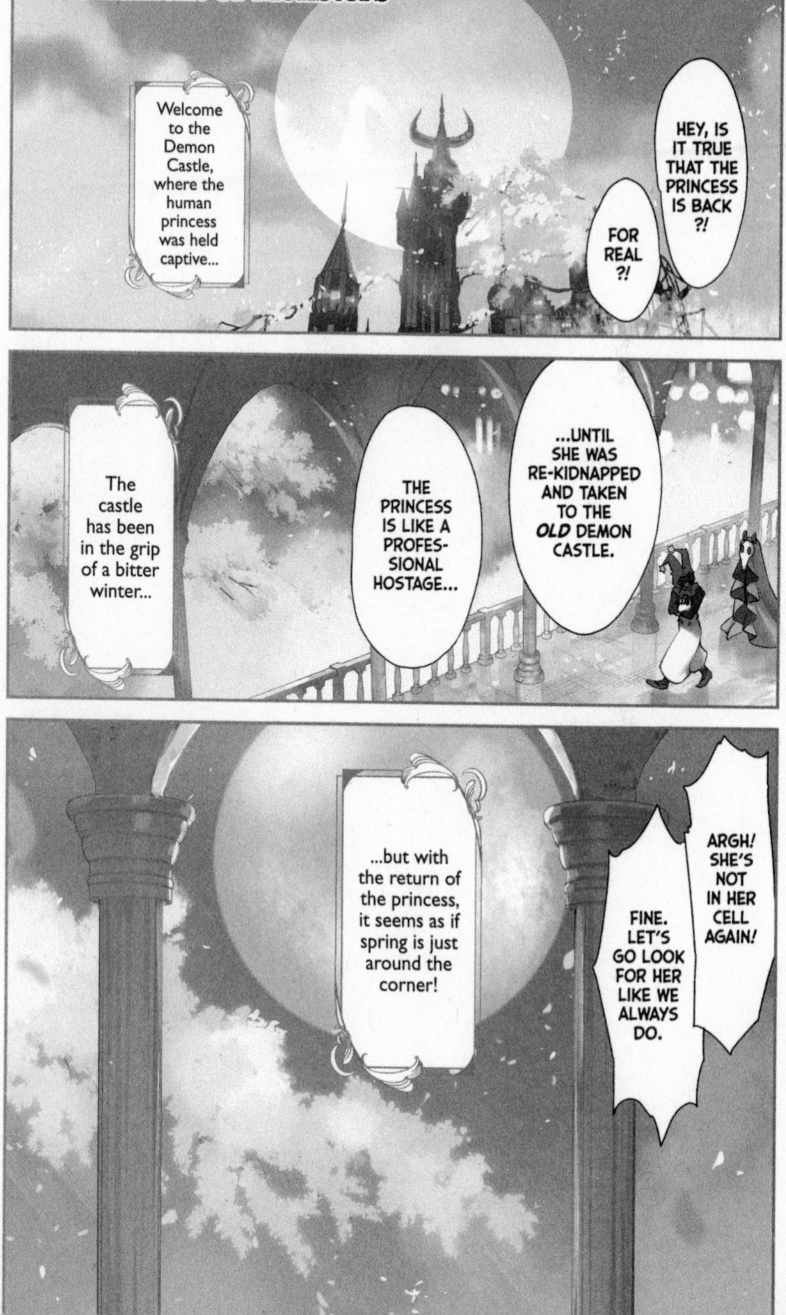
HEY, IS IT TRUE THAT THE PRINCESS IS BACK?!
FOR REAL?!
Welcome to the Demon Castle, where the human princess was held captive...
...UNTIL SHE WAS RE-KIDNAPPED AND TAKEN TO THE *OLD* DEMON CASTLE.
THE PRINCESS IS LIKE A PROFES-SIONAL HOSTAGE...
The castle has been in the grip of a bitter winter...
ARGH! SHE'S NOT IN HER CELL AGAIN!
FINE. LET'S GO LOOK FOR HER LIKE WE ALWAYS DO.
...but with the return of the princess, it seems as if spring is just around the corner!

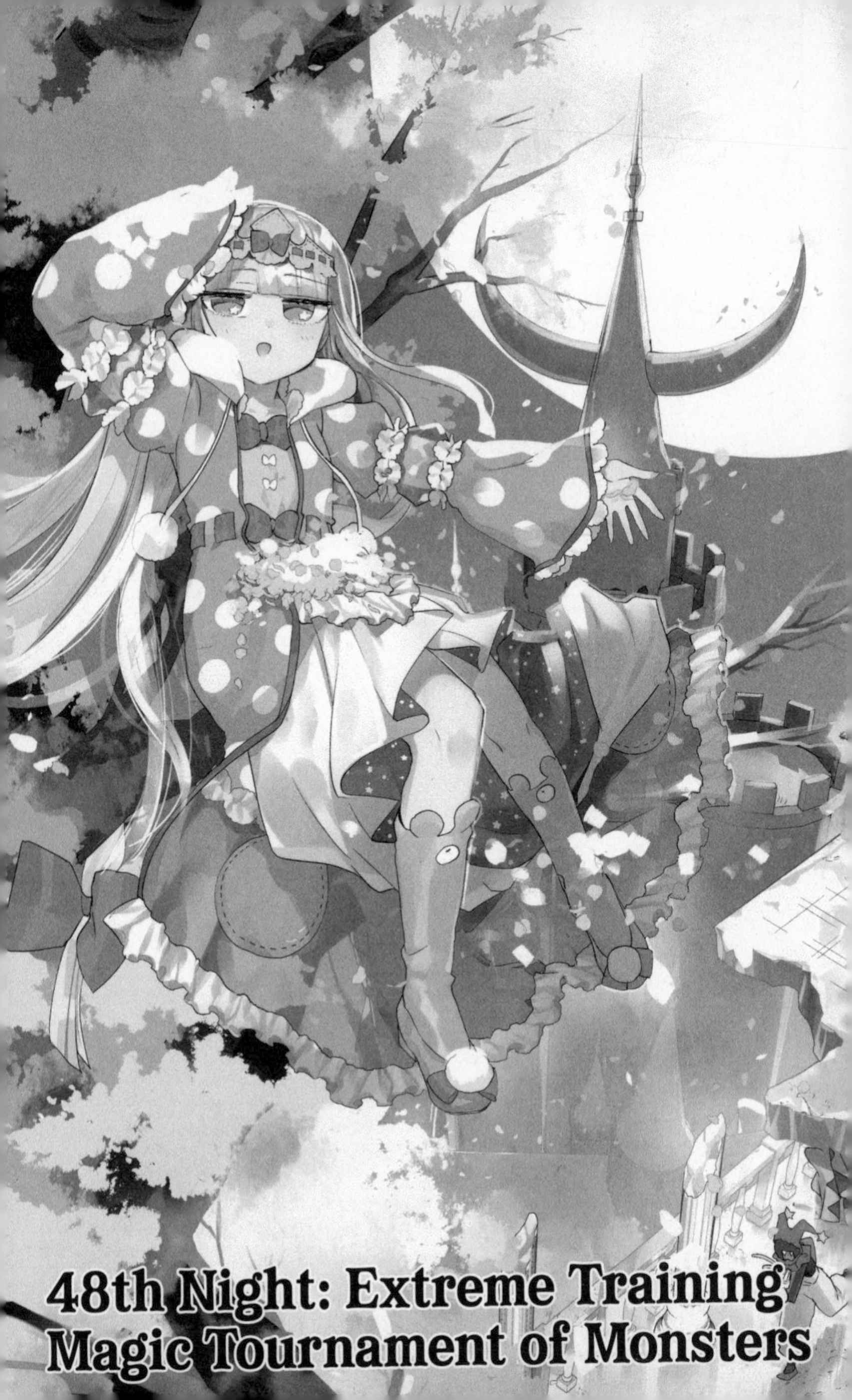

48th Night: Extreme Training Magic Tournament of Monsters

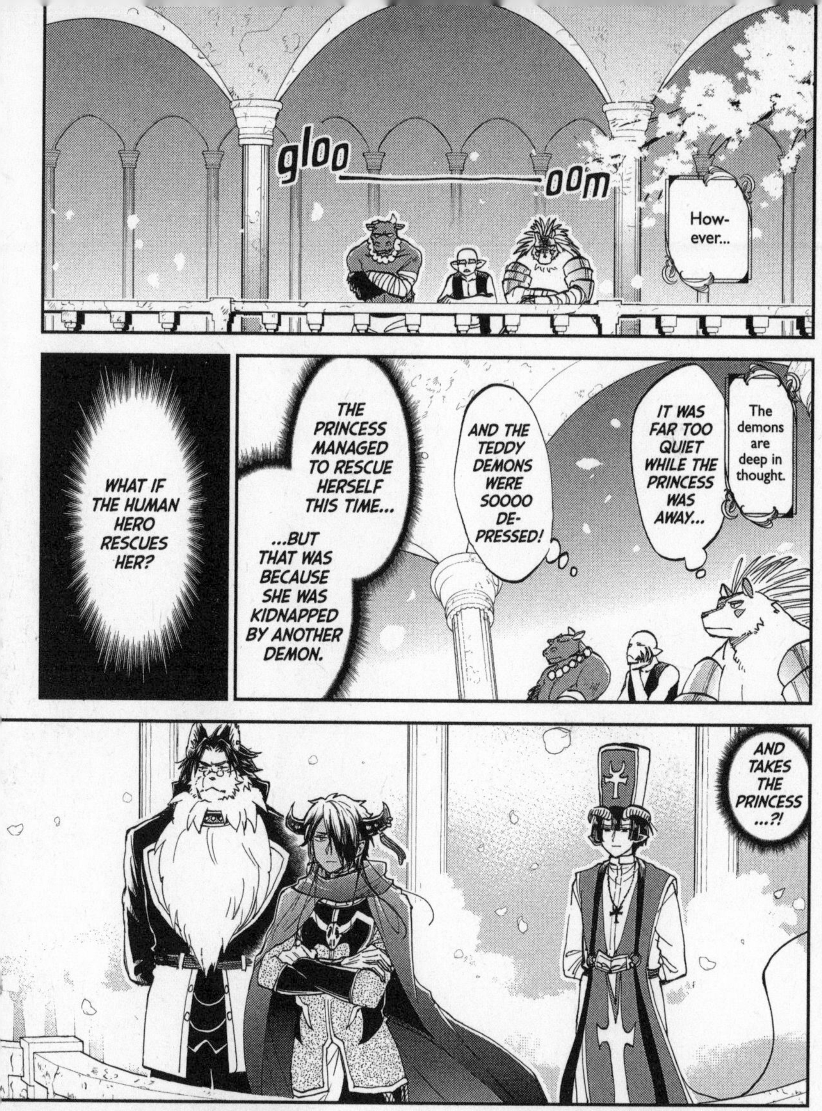
How-ever...
gloo——oom
The demons are deep in thought.
IT WAS FAR TOO QUIET WHILE THE PRINCESS WAS AWAY...
AND THE TEDDY DEMONS WERE SOOOO DE-PRESSED!
THE PRINCESS MANAGED TO RESCUE HERSELF THIS TIME...
...BUT THAT WAS BECAUSE SHE WAS KIDNAPPED BY ANOTHER DEMON.
WHAT IF THE HUMAN HERO RESCUES HER?
AND TAKES THE PRINCESS ...?!

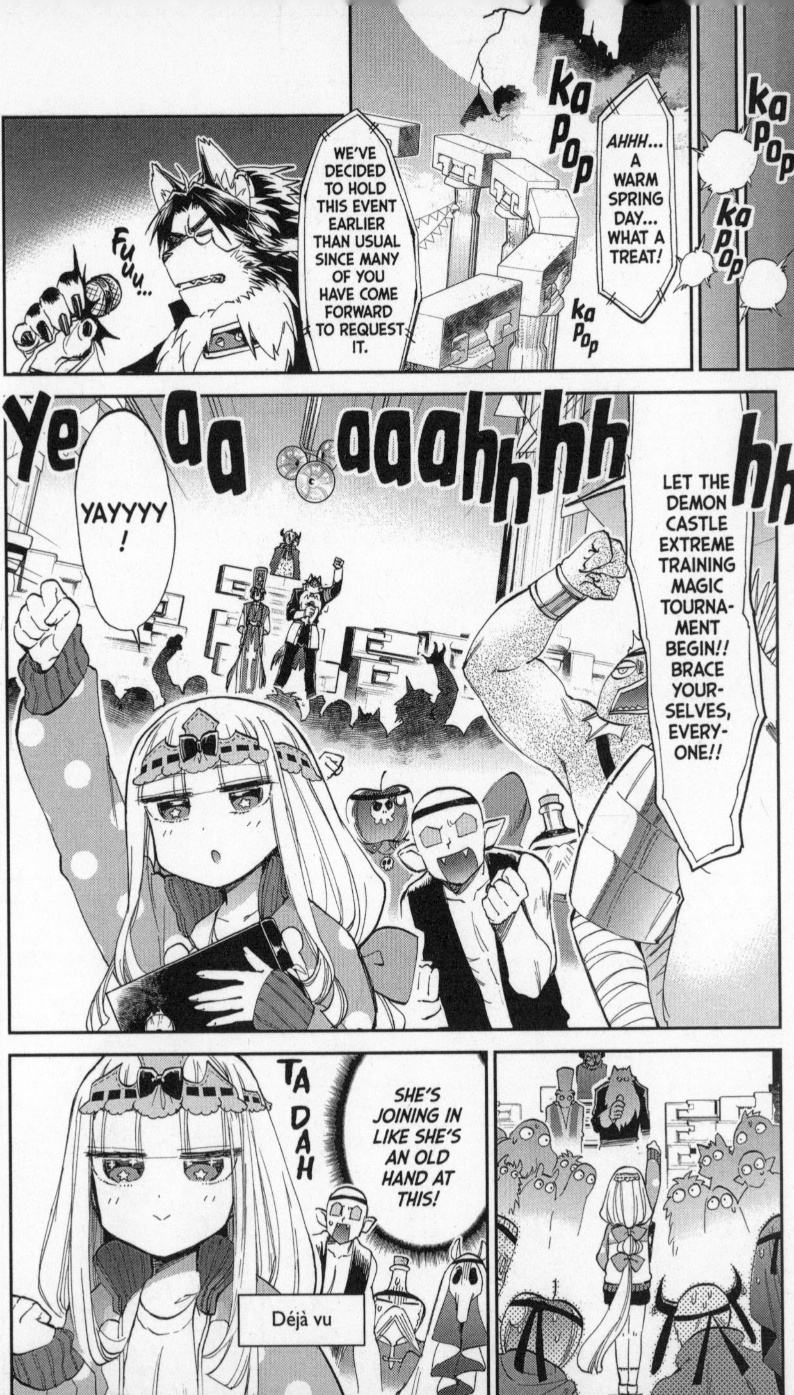
kapop
kapop
kapop
AHHH... A WARM SPRING DAY... WHAT A TREAT!
kapop
kapop
WE'VE DECIDED TO HOLD THIS EVENT EARLIER THAN USUAL SINCE MANY OF YOU HAVE COME FORWARD TO REQUEST IT.
Fuuu...
Yeaaaaahhhhhh
LET THE DEMON CASTLE EXTREME TRAINING MAGIC TOURNAMENT BEGIN!! BRACE YOURSELVES, EVERYONE!!
YAYYYY!
SHE'S JOINING IN LIKE SHE'S AN OLD HAND AT THIS!
TA DAH
Déjà vu

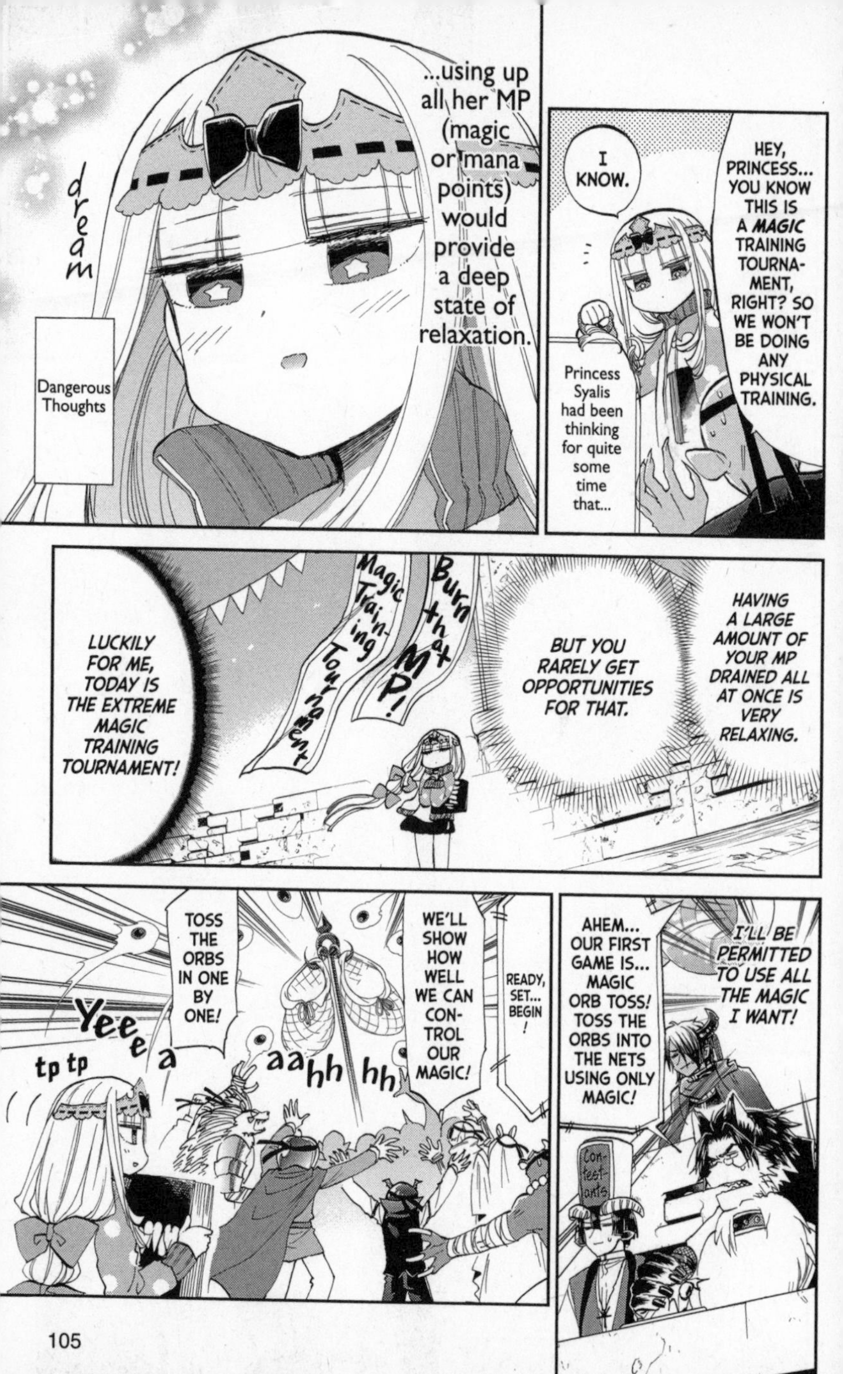
HEY, PRINCESS... YOU KNOW THIS IS A *MAGIC* TRAINING TOURNAMENT, RIGHT? SO WE WON'T BE DOING ANY PHYSICAL TRAINING.
I KNOW.
Princess Syalis had been thinking for quite some time that...
...using up all her MP (magic or mana points) would provide a deep state of relaxation.
dream
Dangerous Thoughts
HAVING A LARGE AMOUNT OF YOUR MP DRAINED ALL AT ONCE IS VERY RELAXING.
BUT YOU RARELY GET OPPORTUNITIES FOR THAT.
Burn that MP!
Magic Training Tournament
LUCKILY FOR ME, TODAY IS THE EXTREME MAGIC TRAINING TOURNAMENT!
I'LL BE PERMITTED TO USE ALL THE MAGIC I WANT!
AHEM... OUR FIRST GAME IS... MAGIC ORB TOSS! TOSS THE ORBS INTO THE NETS USING ONLY MAGIC!
Contestants
READY, SET... BEGIN!
WE'LL SHOW HOW WELL WE CAN CONTROL OUR MAGIC!
TOSS THE ORBS IN ONE BY ONE!
aahhhh
Yeeeea
tp tp

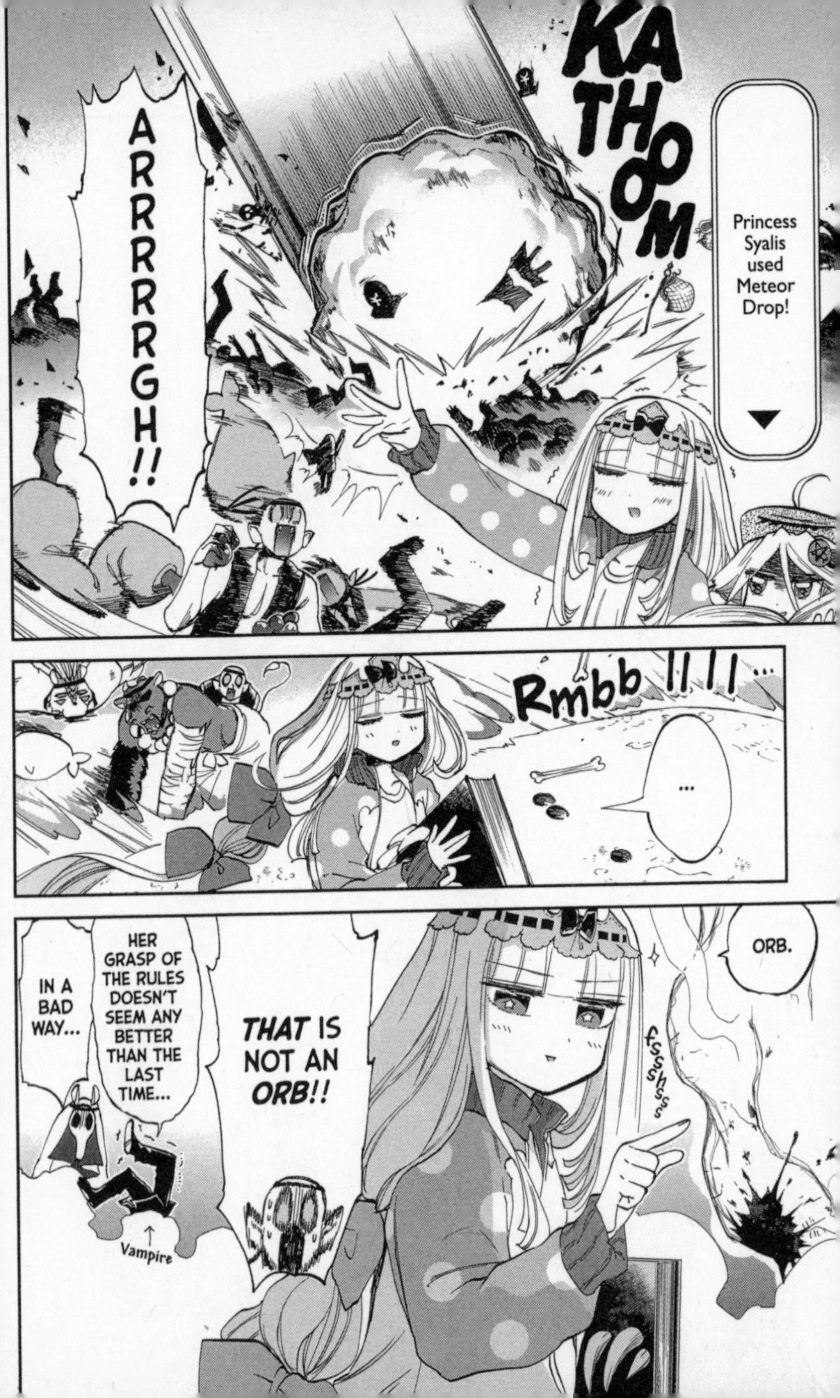
Princess Syalis used Meteor Drop!
KATHOOM
ARRRRRRGH!!
Rmbb !!!!...
...
ORB.
fsssssss
THAT IS NOT AN ORB!!
HER GRASP OF THE RULES DOESN'T SEEM ANY BETTER THAN THE LAST TIME...
IN A BAD WAY...
Vampire

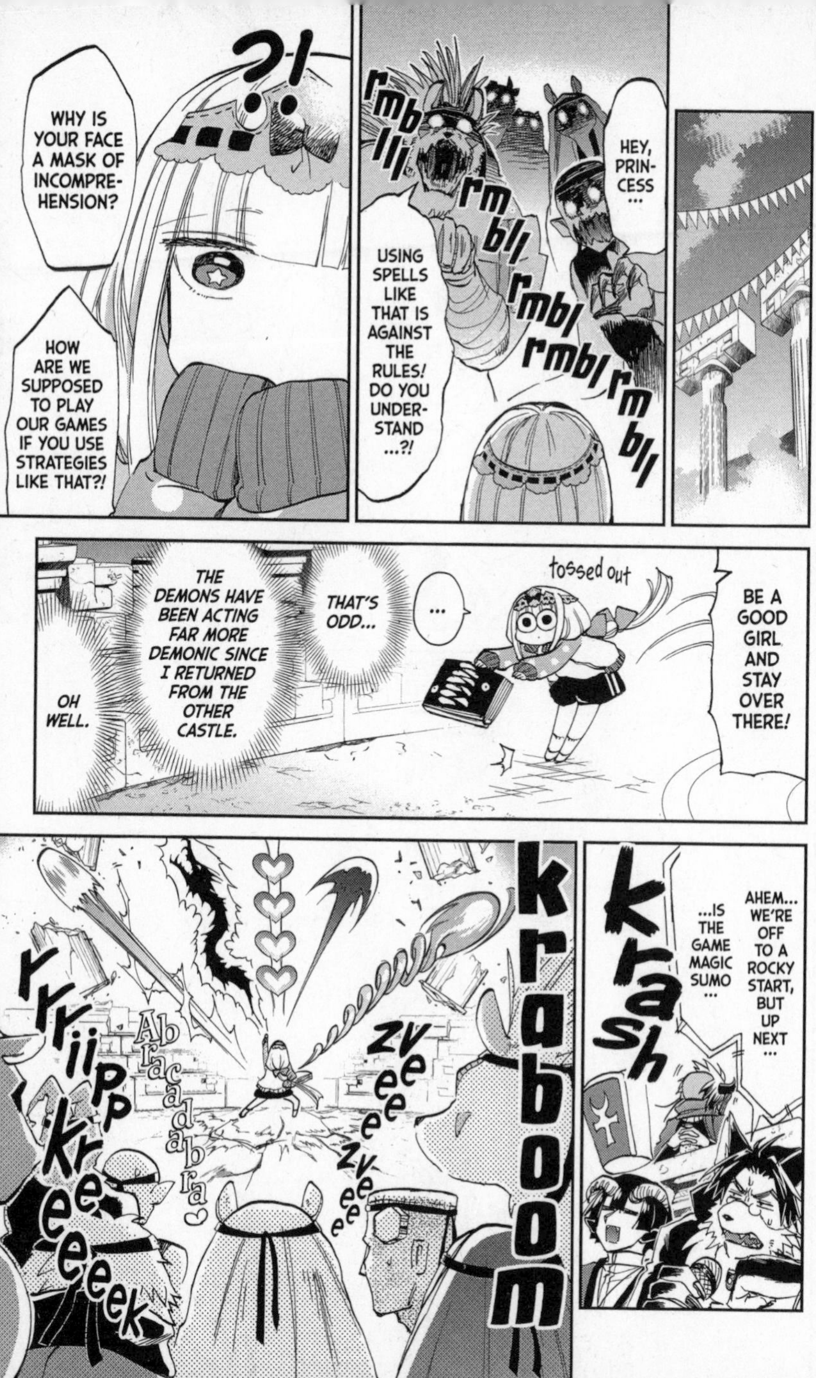
HEY, PRINCESS...
USING SPELLS LIKE THAT IS AGAINST THE RULES! DO YOU UNDERSTAND...?!
rmblll rmbll rmbl rmbl rmbll
?!
WHY IS YOUR FACE A MASK OF INCOMPREHENSION?
HOW ARE WE SUPPOSED TO PLAY OUR GAMES IF YOU USE STRATEGIES LIKE THAT?!
BE A GOOD GIRL AND STAY OVER THERE!
tossed out
...
THAT'S ODD...
THE DEMONS HAVE BEEN ACTING FAR MORE DEMONIC SINCE I RETURNED FROM THE OTHER CASTLE.
OH WELL.
AHEM... WE'RE OFF TO A ROCKY START, BUT UP NEXT...
...IS THE GAME MAGIC SUMO...
krash
kraboom
zveeee
zveeee
Abracadabra
rrriipp
kreeeeeek

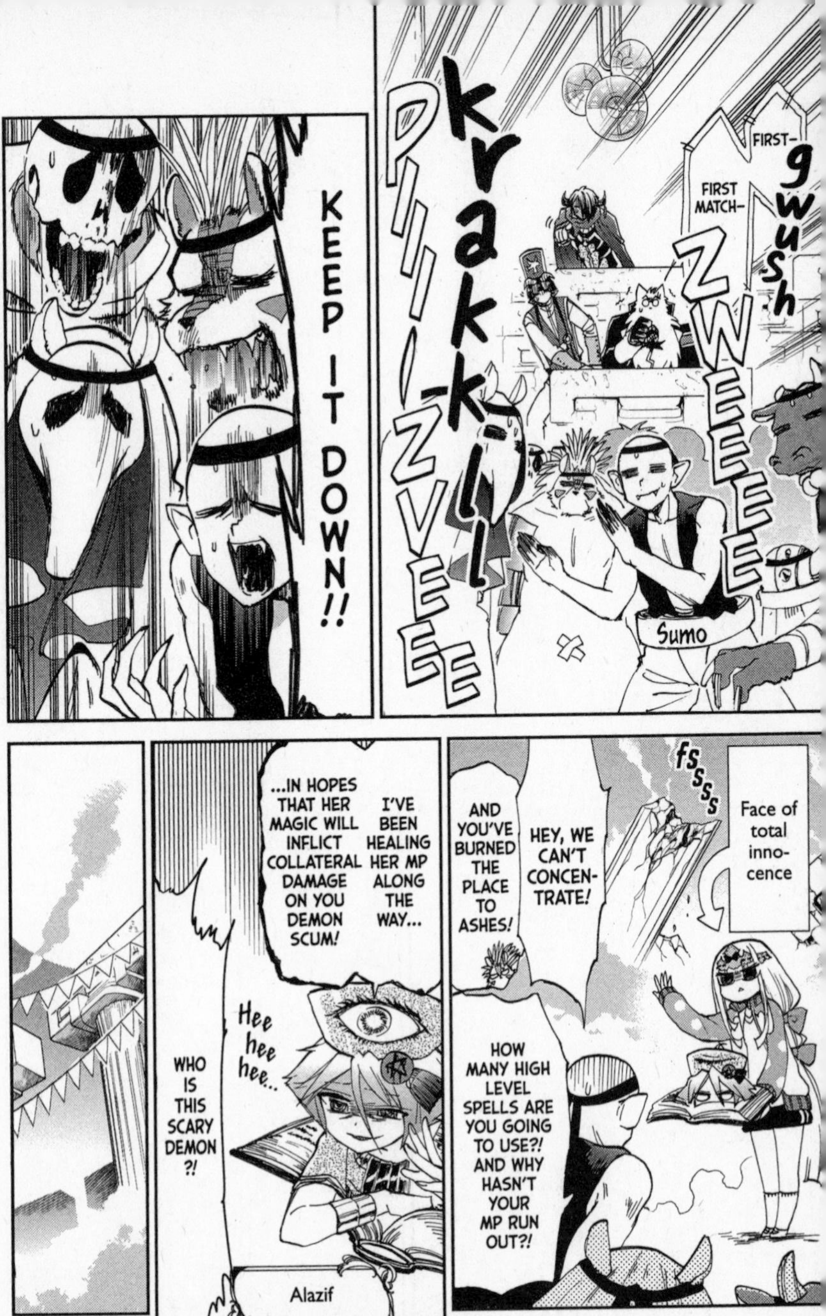
FIRST—
FIRST MATCH—
gwush
ZWEEEEEE
krakk-iil
PIIII-ZZVEEE
Sumo
KEEP IT DOWN!!
fssss
Face of total innocence
HEY, WE CAN'T CONCENTRATE!
AND YOU'VE BURNED THE PLACE TO ASHES!
HOW MANY HIGH LEVEL SPELLS ARE YOU GOING TO USE?! AND WHY HASN'T YOUR MP RUN OUT?!
I'VE BEEN HEALING HER MP ALONG THE WAY...
...IN HOPES THAT HER MAGIC WILL INFLICT COLLATERAL DAMAGE ON YOU DEMON SCUM!
Hee hee hee...
WHO IS THIS SCARY DEMON?!
Alazif

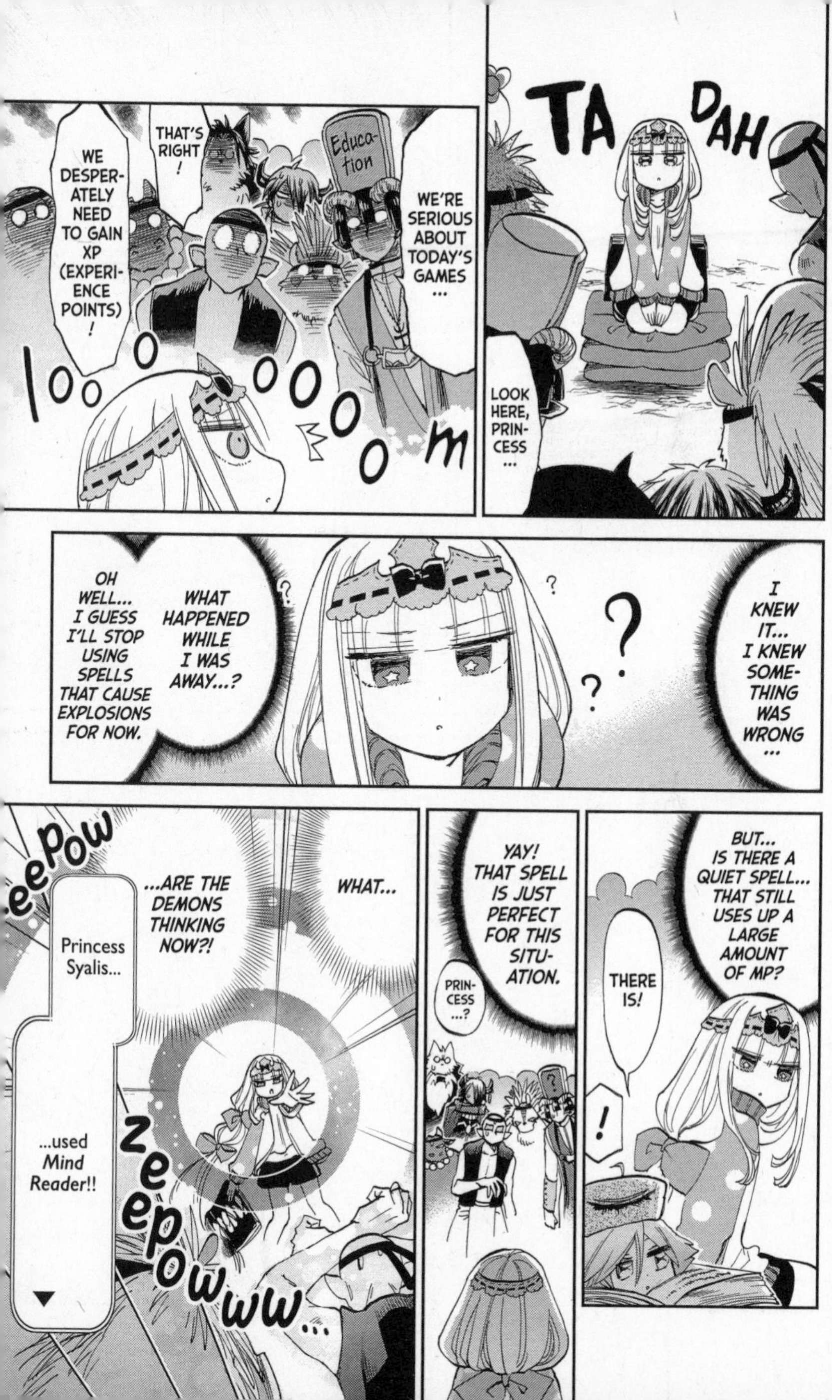
TA DAH
LOOK HERE, PRINCESS...
WE'RE SERIOUS ABOUT TODAY'S GAMES...
THAT'S RIGHT!
WE DESPERATELY NEED TO GAIN XP (EXPERIENCE POINTS)!
Education
LOOOOOOOOM
I KNEW IT... I KNEW SOMETHING WAS WRONG...
WHAT HAPPENED WHILE I WAS AWAY...?
OH WELL... I GUESS I'LL STOP USING SPELLS THAT CAUSE EXPLOSIONS FOR NOW.
BUT... IS THERE A QUIET SPELL... THAT STILL USES UP A LARGE AMOUNT OF MP?
THERE IS!
!
YAY! THAT SPELL IS JUST PERFECT FOR THIS SITUATION.
PRINCESS...?
WHAT...
...ARE THE DEMONS THINKING NOW?!
Princess Syalis...
...used Mind Reader!!
eePOW
zeepowww...

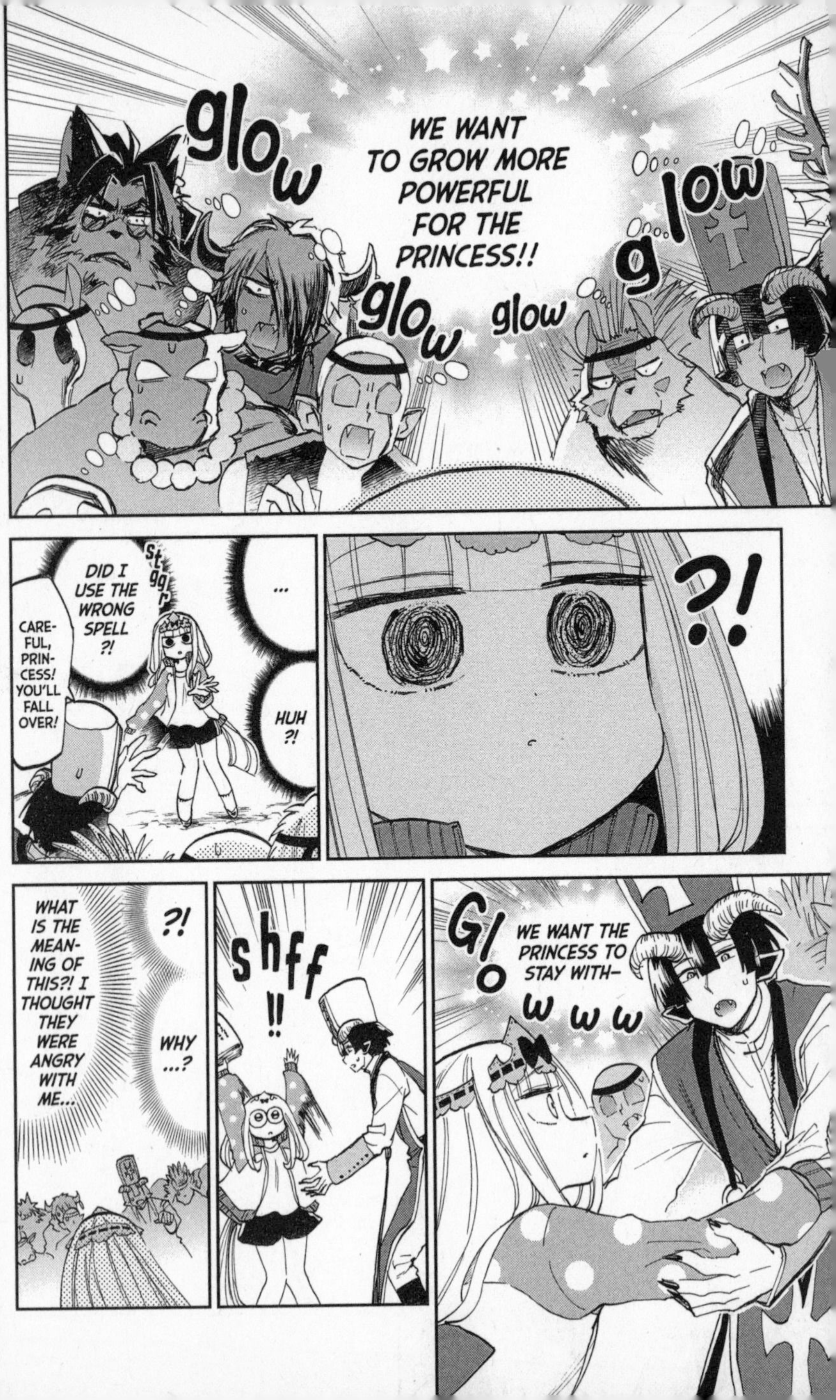
glow
glow
WE WANT TO GROW MORE POWERFUL FOR THE PRINCESS!!
glow
glow
?!
...
HUH ?!
DID I USE THE WRONG SPELL ?!
stggr
CARE-FUL, PRIN-CESS! YOU'LL FALL OVER!
Glowww
WE WANT THE PRINCESS TO STAY WITH–
shff
!!
?!
WHY ...?
WHAT IS THE MEANING OF THIS?! I THOUGHT THEY WERE ANGRY WITH ME...

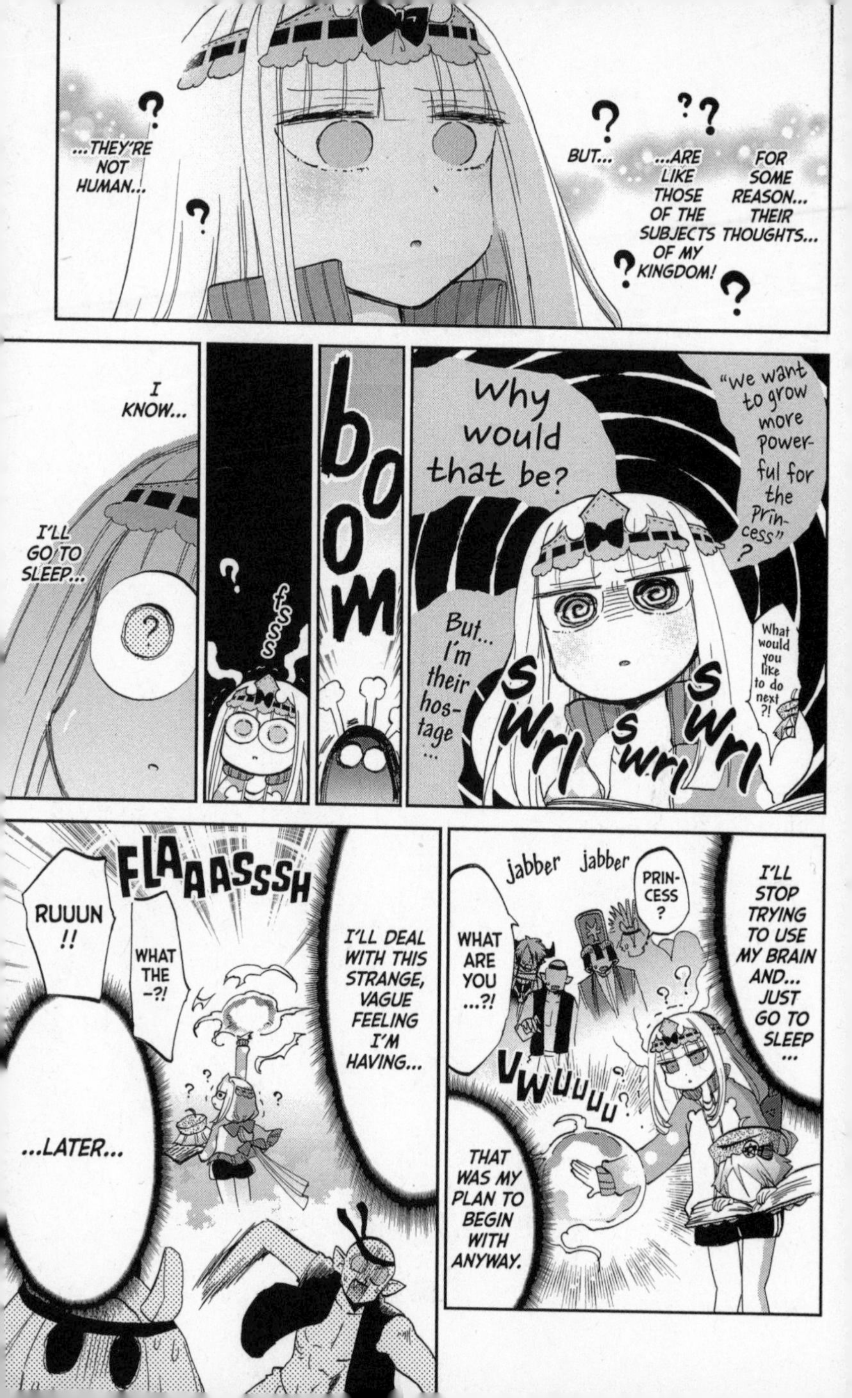
FOR SOME REASON... THEIR THOUGHTS...
...ARE LIKE THOSE OF THE SUBJECTS OF MY KINGDOM!
BUT...
...THEY'RE NOT HUMAN...
"we want to grow more power-ful for the Prin-cess"?
Why would that be?
What would you like to do next?!
But... I'm their hos-tage...
swrl swrl swrl
boom
fsss
I KNOW...
I'LL GO TO SLEEP...
I'LL STOP TRYING TO USE MY BRAIN AND... JUST GO TO SLEEP...
PRIN-CESS?
jabber jabber
WHAT ARE YOU...?!
VWUUUUU
THAT WAS MY PLAN TO BEGIN WITH ANYWAY.
I'LL DEAL WITH THIS STRANGE, VAGUE FEELING I'M HAVING...
FLAAASSSH
WHAT THE-?!
RUUUN!!
...LATER...

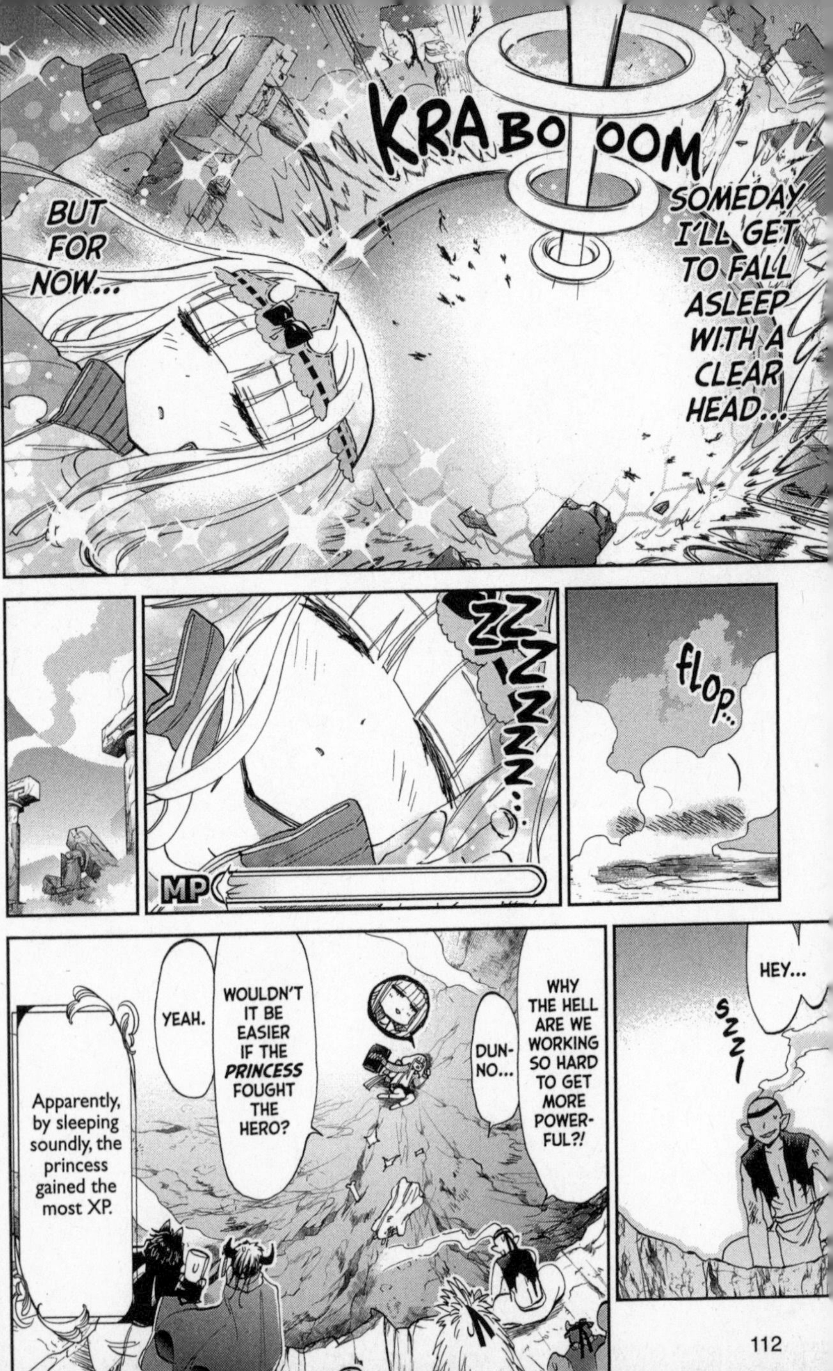

KRABOOOM
SOMEDAY I'LL GET TO FALL ASLEEP WITH A CLEAR HEAD...
BUT FOR NOW...
flop...
ZZZZZZZ...
MP
HEY...
SZZ
WHY THE HELL ARE WE WORKING SO HARD TO GET MORE POWER-FUL?!
DUN-NO...
WOULDN'T IT BE EASIER IF THE *PRINCESS* FOUGHT THE HERO?
YEAH.
Apparently, by sleeping soundly, the princess gained the most XP.

Demon Castle Extreme Training Magic Tournament of Monsters

Event will be held rain or shine.

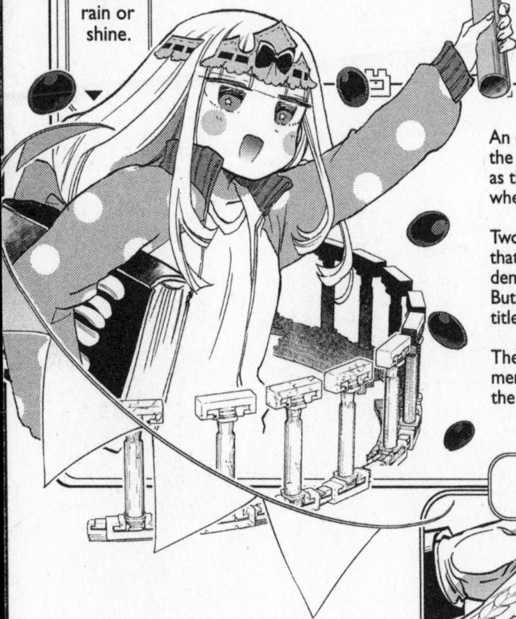

Bloom of Youthfulness: ☆☆☆☆☆☆☆

Guts: ☆☆☆☆

An event for the demons who work in the Demon Castle to gain as much XP as they can during the spring and autumn when the weather is nice.

Two types of tournaments are held so that both the physical and the intellectual demons can make full use of their abilities. But recently the hostage has stolen the title of XP Champion.

The planning committee of the tournament consists of the Demon King and the Ten Guardians.

Tournament Leaflet

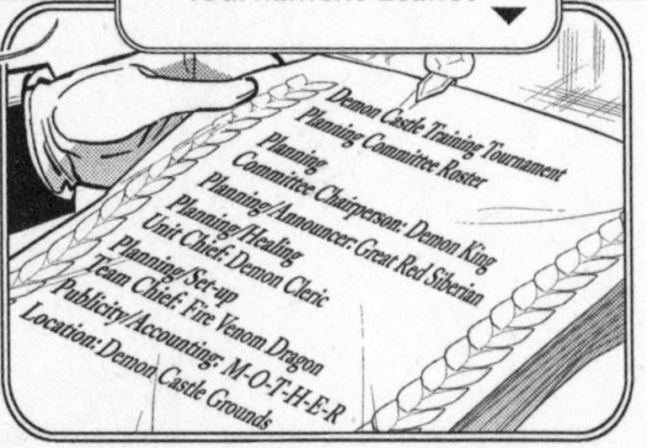
Demon Castle Training Tournament
Planning Committee Roster
Planning
Committee Chairperson: Demon King
Planning/Announcer: Great Red Siberian
Planning/Healing
Unit Chief: Demon Cleric
Planning/Set-up
Team Chief: Fire Venom Dragon
Publicity/Accounting: M-O-T-H-E-R
Location: Demon Castle Grounds

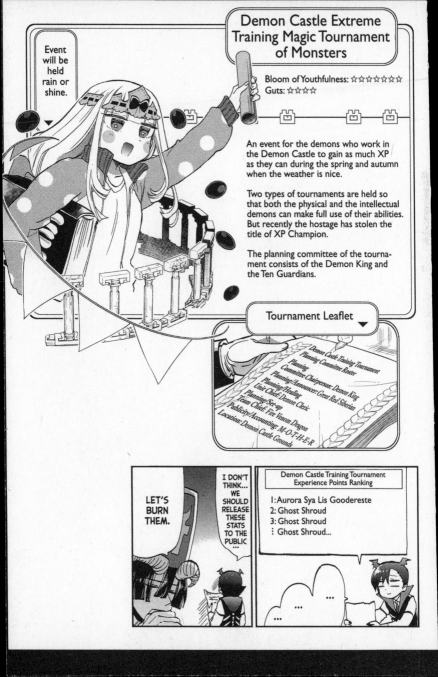

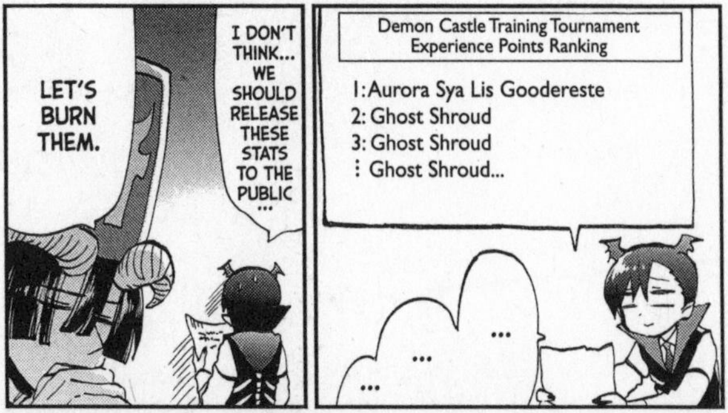
Demon Castle Training Tournament
Experience Points Ranking
1: Aurora Sya Lis Goodereste
2: Ghost Shroud
3: Ghost Shroud
⋮ Ghost Shroud...
...
...
...
I DON'T THINK... WE SHOULD RELEASE THESE STATS TO THE PUBLIC...
LET'S BURN THEM.

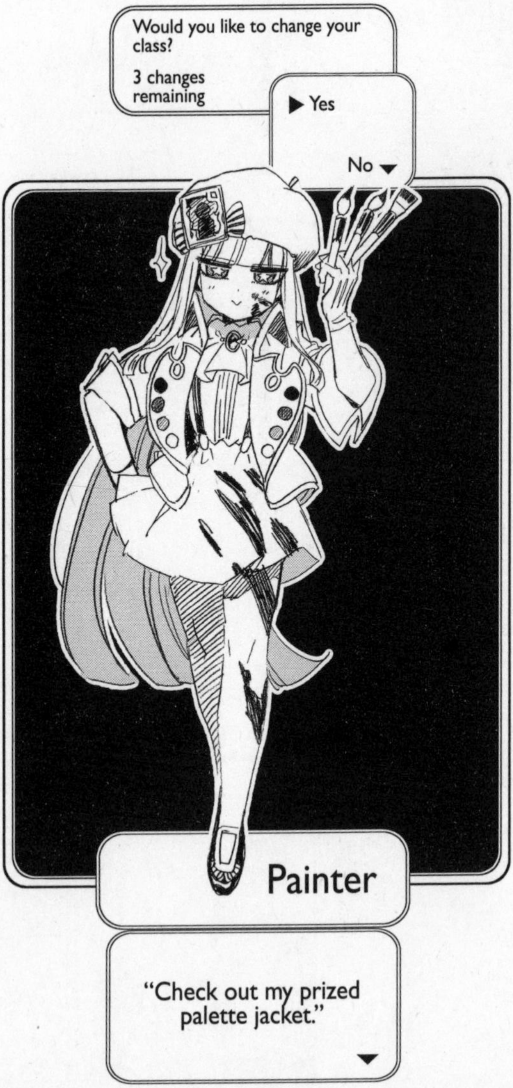
Would you like to change your class?
3 changes remaining
▶ Yes
No
Painter
"Check out my prized palette jacket."

49th Night: Better Living Through Gadgets

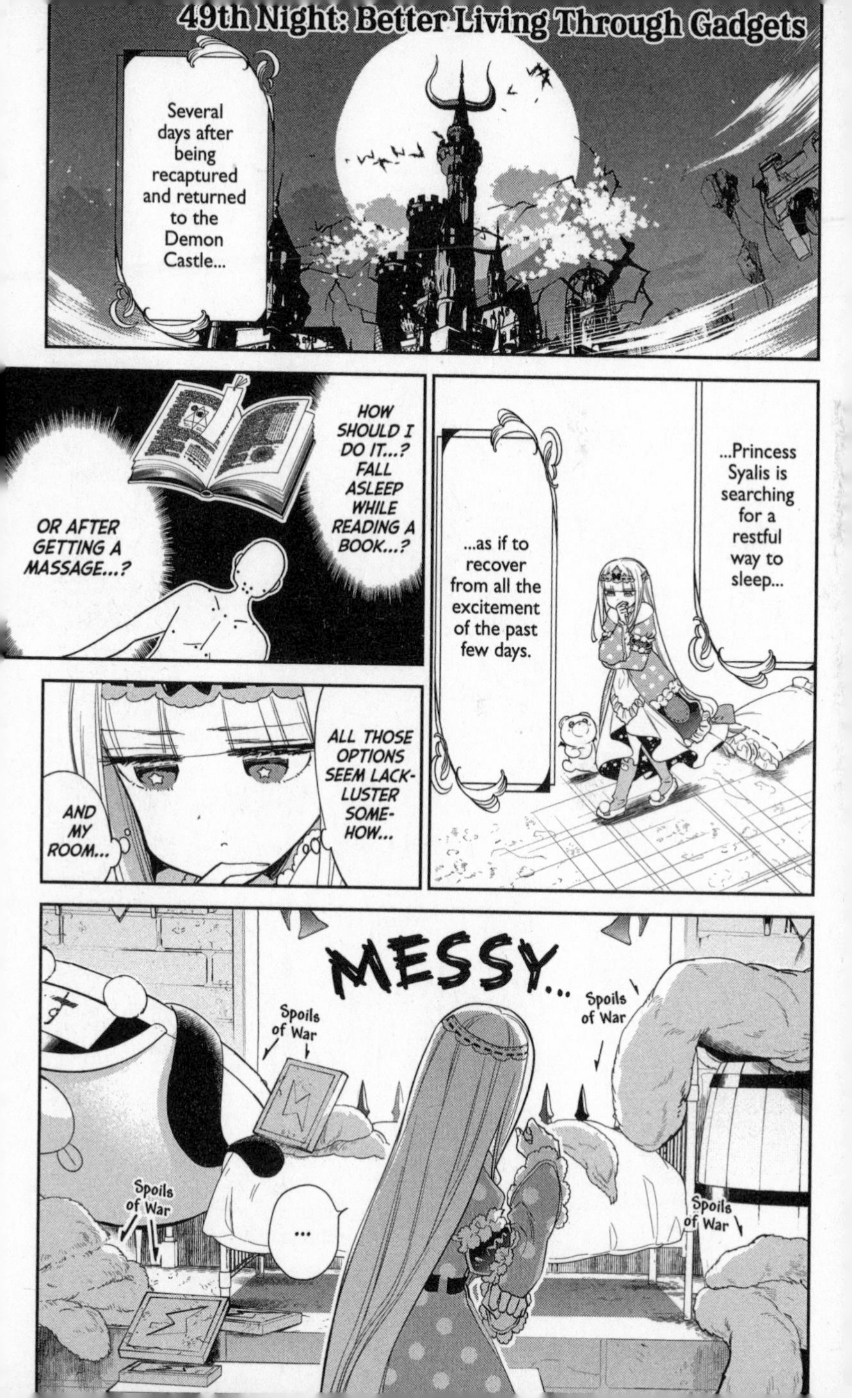
Several days after being recaptured and returned to the Demon Castle...
...Princess Syalis is searching for a restful way to sleep...
...as if to recover from all the excitement of the past few days.
HOW SHOULD I DO IT...? FALL ASLEEP WHILE READING A BOOK...?
OR AFTER GETTING A MASSAGE...?
ALL THOSE OPTIONS SEEM LACK-LUSTER SOME-HOW...
AND MY ROOM...
MESSY...
Spoils of War
Spoils of War
Spoils of War
Spoils of War
...

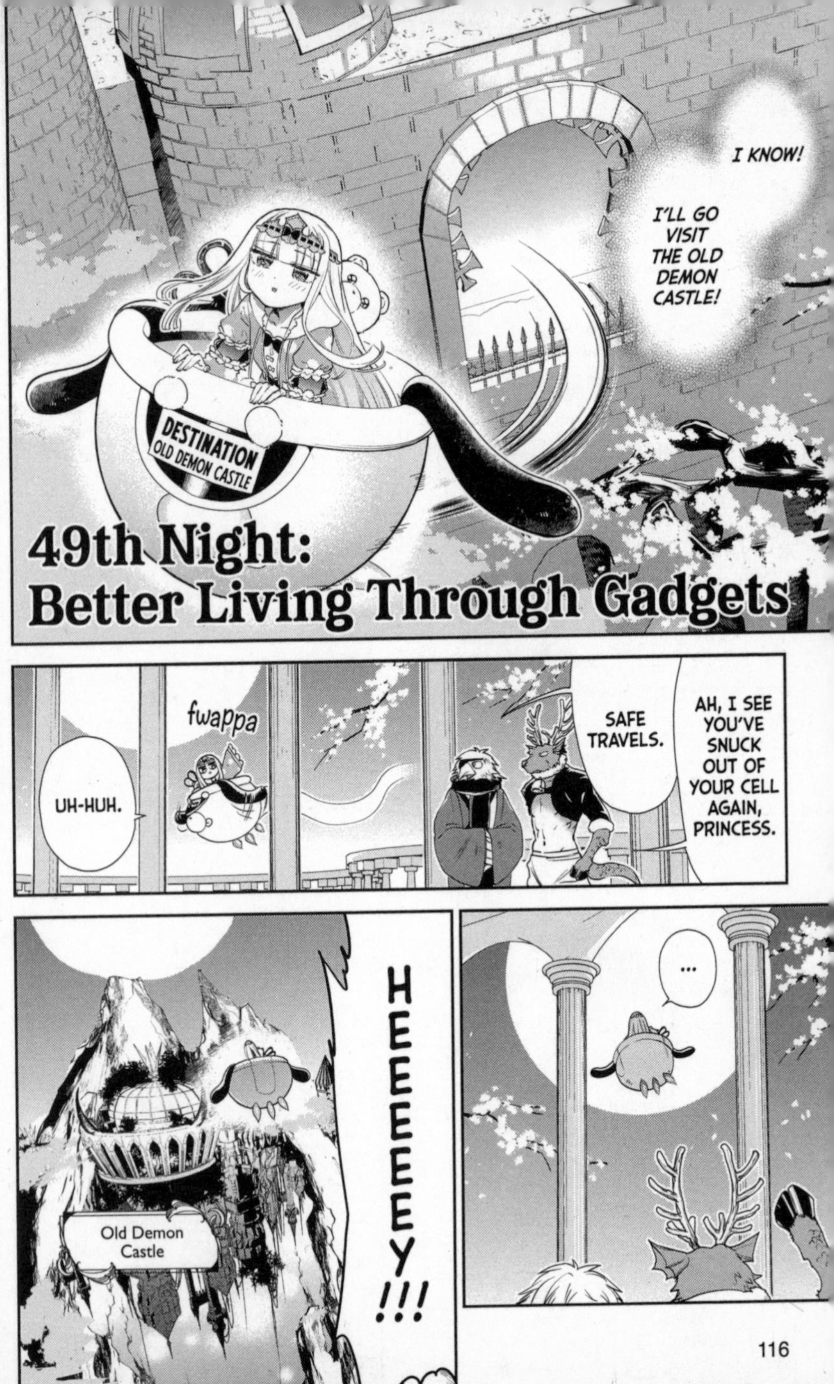

I KNOW!
I'LL GO VISIT THE OLD DEMON CASTLE!
DESTINATION OLD DEMON CASTLE
49th Night: Better Living Through Gadgets
AH, I SEE YOU'VE SNUCK OUT OF YOUR CELL AGAIN, PRINCESS.
SAFE TRAVELS.
fwappa
UH-HUH.
...
HEEEEEEY!!!
Old Demon Castle

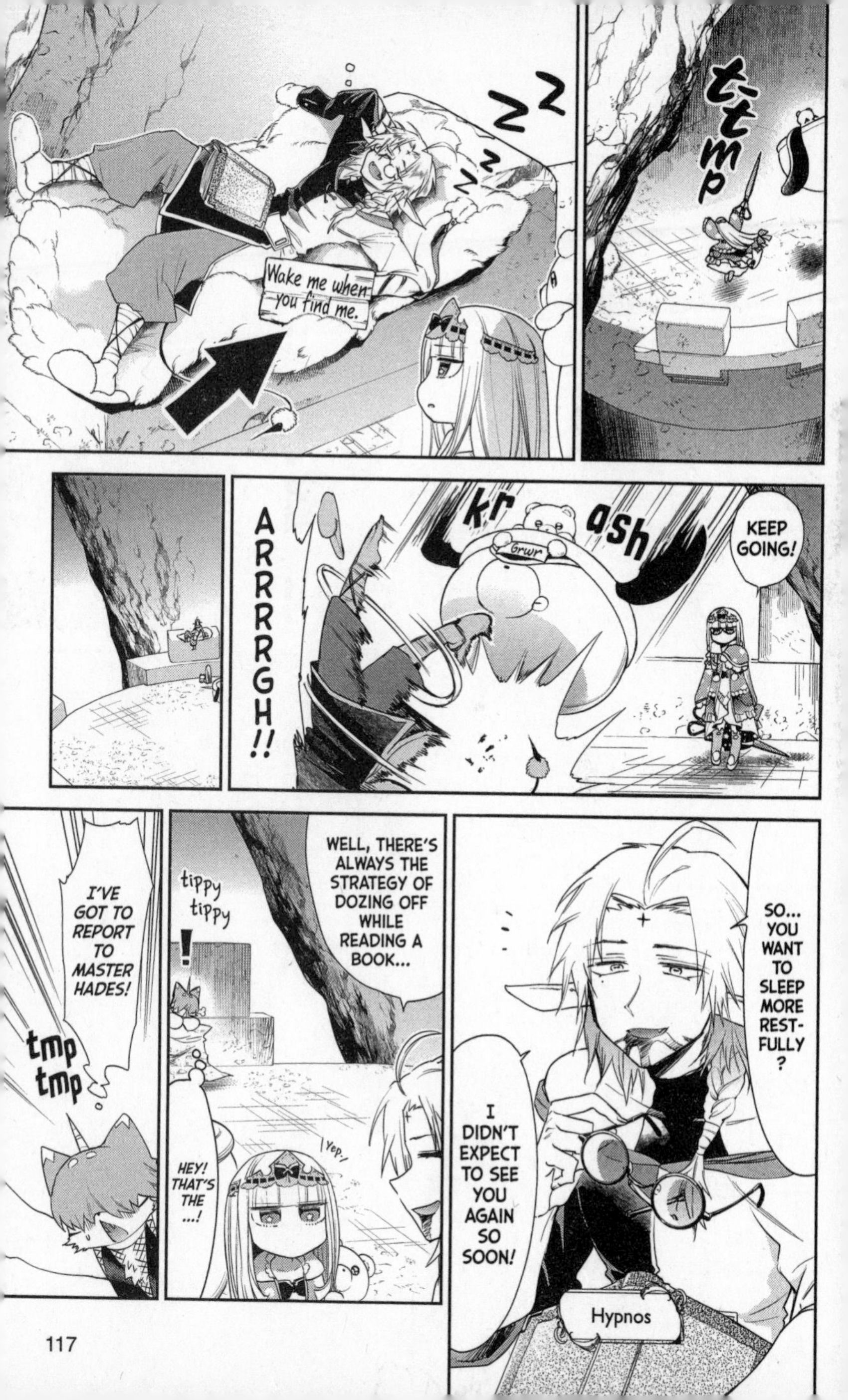
t-tmp
Zzz
Wake me when you find me.
KEEP GOING!
krash
Grwr
ARRRRGH!!
SO... YOU WANT TO SLEEP MORE REST-FULLY?
I DIDN'T EXPECT TO SEE YOU AGAIN SO SOON!
Hypnos
WELL, THERE'S ALWAYS THE STRATEGY OF DOZING OFF WHILE READING A BOOK...
tippy tippy
!
HEY! THAT'S THE ...!
Yep.
I'VE GOT TO REPORT TO MASTER HADES!
tmp tmp

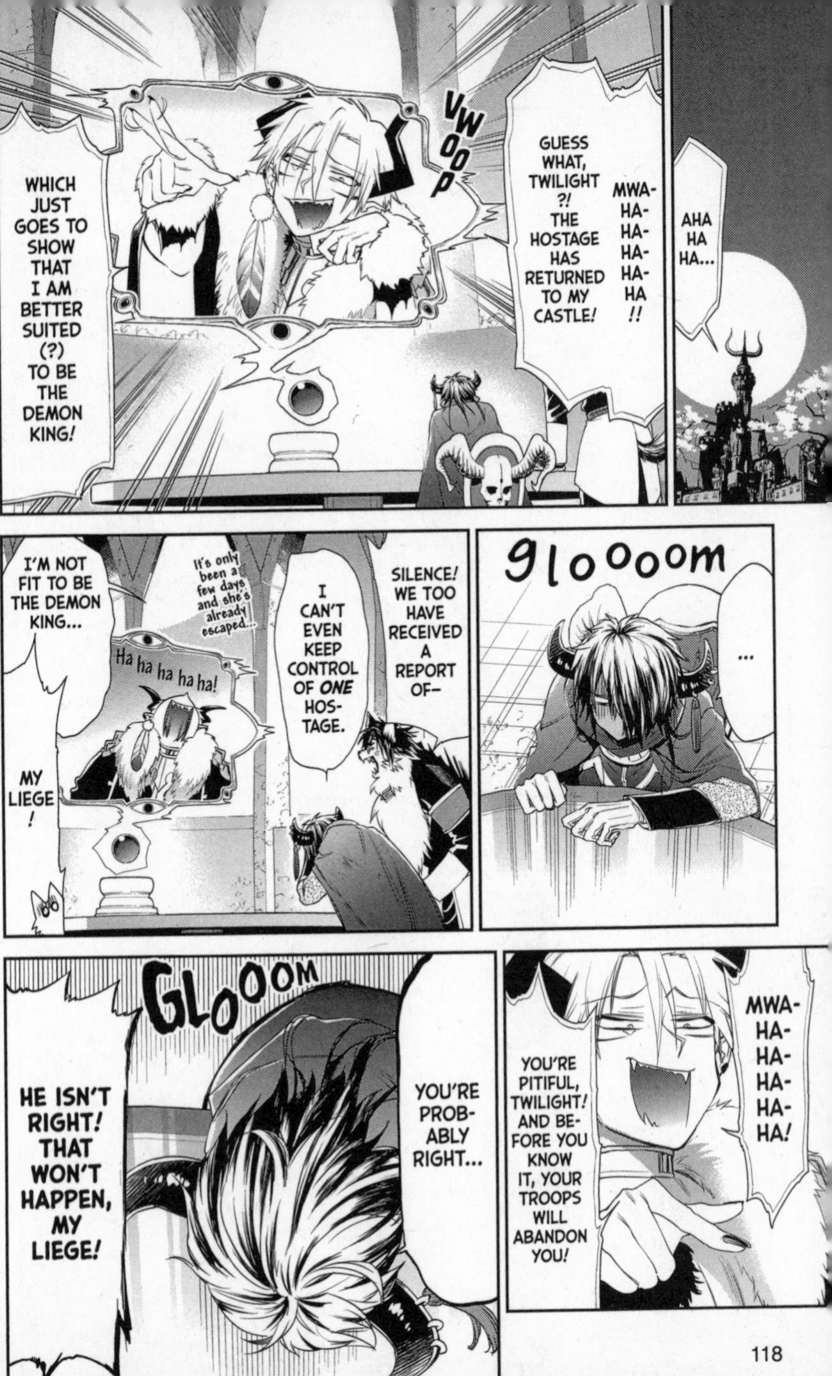
AHA HA HA...
MWA-HA-HA-HA-HA-HA!!
GUESS WHAT, TWILIGHT?! THE HOSTAGE HAS RETURNED TO MY CASTLE!
VWOOP
WHICH JUST GOES TO SHOW THAT I AM BETTER SUITED (?) TO BE THE DEMON KING!
gloooom
...
SILENCE! WE TOO HAVE RECEIVED A REPORT OF–
I CAN'T EVEN KEEP CONTROL OF *ONE* HOSTAGE.
It's only been a few days and she's already escaped...
Ha ha ha ha ha!
I'M NOT FIT TO BE THE DEMON KING...
MY LIEGE!
MWA-HA-HA-HA-HA-HA!
YOU'RE PITIFUL, TWILIGHT! AND BEFORE YOU KNOW IT, YOUR TROOPS WILL ABANDON YOU!
GLOOOM
YOU'RE PROBABLY RIGHT...
HE ISN'T RIGHT! THAT WON'T HAPPEN, MY LIEGE!

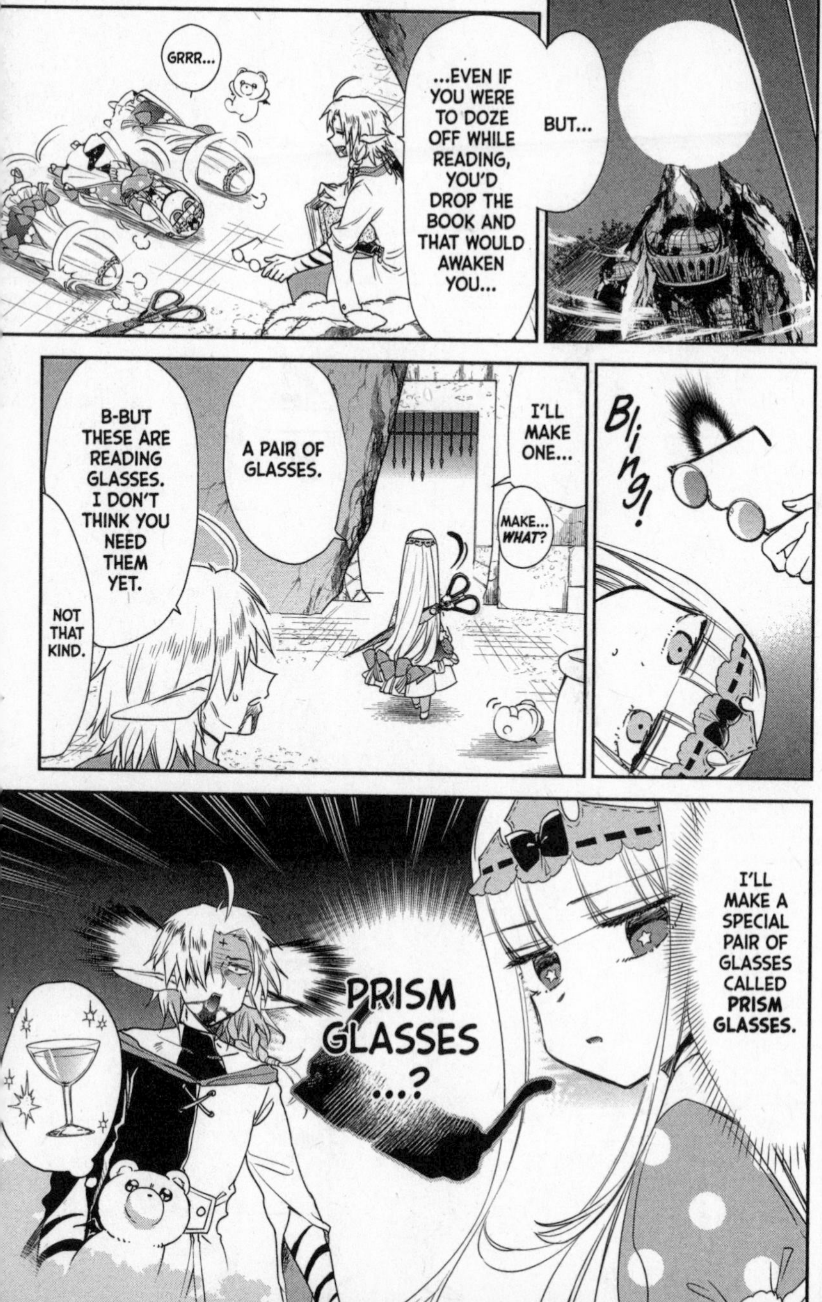
BUT...
...EVEN IF YOU WERE TO DOZE OFF WHILE READING, YOU'D DROP THE BOOK AND THAT WOULD AWAKEN YOU...
GRRR...
Bling!
I'LL MAKE ONE...
MAKE... *WHAT?*
A PAIR OF GLASSES.
B-BUT THESE ARE READING GLASSES. I DON'T THINK YOU NEED THEM YET.
NOT THAT KIND.
I'LL MAKE A SPECIAL PAIR OF GLASSES CALLED **PRISM** GLASSES.
PRISM GLASSES ...?

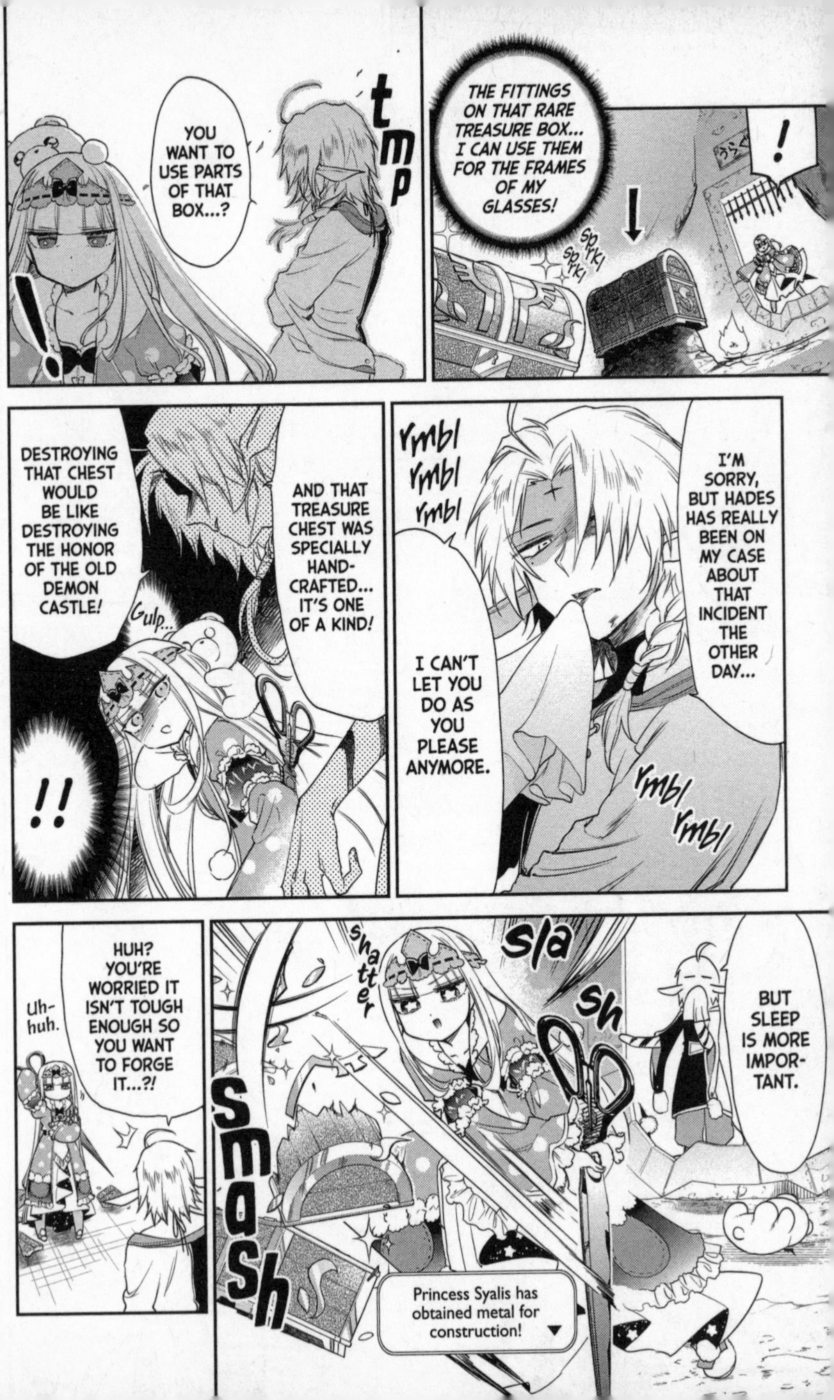
THE FITTINGS ON THAT RARE TREASURE BOX... I CAN USE THEM FOR THE FRAMES OF MY GLASSES!
!
sprkl sprkl
tmp
YOU WANT TO USE PARTS OF THAT BOX...?
!
rmbl rmbl rmbl
I'M SORRY, BUT HADES HAS REALLY BEEN ON MY CASE ABOUT THAT INCIDENT THE OTHER DAY...
I CAN'T LET YOU DO AS YOU PLEASE ANYMORE.
rmbl rmbl
AND THAT TREASURE CHEST WAS SPECIALLY HAND-CRAFTED... IT'S ONE OF A KIND!
DESTROYING THAT CHEST WOULD BE LIKE DESTROYING THE HONOR OF THE OLD DEMON CASTLE!
Gulp...
!!
BUT SLEEP IS MORE IMPOR-TANT.
sla
sh
shatter
smash
Princess Syalis has obtained metal for construction!
HUH? YOU'RE WORRIED IT ISN'T TOUGH ENOUGH SO YOU WANT TO FORGE IT...?!
Uh-huh.

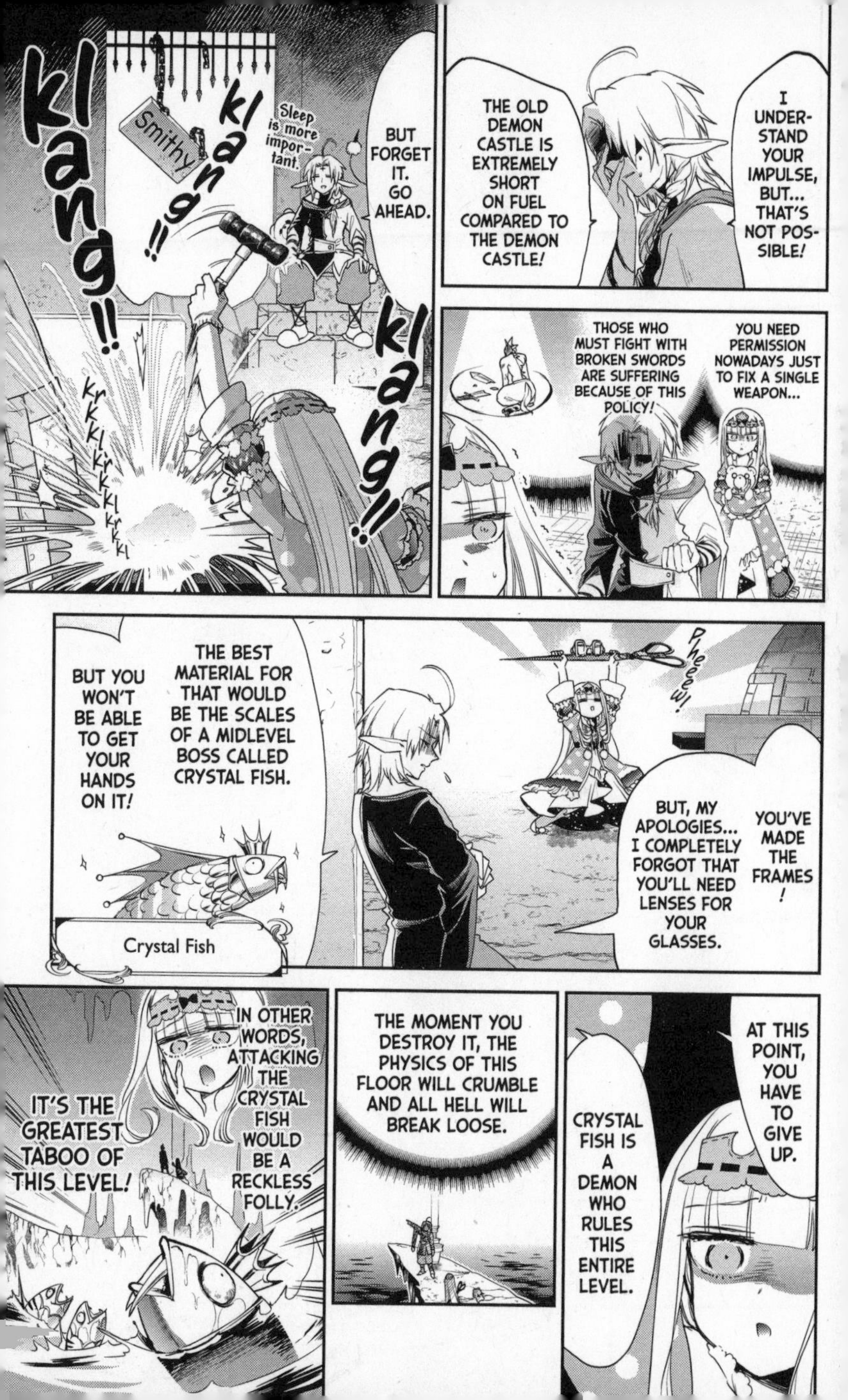
I UNDERSTAND YOUR IMPULSE, BUT... THAT'S NOT POSSIBLE!
THE OLD DEMON CASTLE IS EXTREMELY SHORT ON FUEL COMPARED TO THE DEMON CASTLE!
YOU NEED PERMISSION NOWADAYS JUST TO FIX A SINGLE WEAPON...
THOSE WHO MUST FIGHT WITH BROKEN SWORDS ARE SUFFERING BECAUSE OF THIS POLICY!
BUT FORGET IT. GO AHEAD.
Sleep is more important.
Smithy
klang!!
klang!!
klang!!
krkkl krkkl krkkl
Pheeew!
YOU'VE MADE THE FRAMES!
BUT, MY APOLOGIES... I COMPLETELY FORGOT THAT YOU'LL NEED LENSES FOR YOUR GLASSES.
THE BEST MATERIAL FOR THAT WOULD BE THE SCALES OF A MIDLEVEL BOSS CALLED CRYSTAL FISH.
BUT YOU WON'T BE ABLE TO GET YOUR HANDS ON IT!
Crystal Fish
AT THIS POINT, YOU HAVE TO GIVE UP.
CRYSTAL FISH IS A DEMON WHO RULES THIS ENTIRE LEVEL.
THE MOMENT YOU DESTROY IT, THE PHYSICS OF THIS FLOOR WILL CRUMBLE AND ALL HELL WILL BREAK LOOSE.
IN OTHER WORDS, ATTACKING THE CRYSTAL FISH WOULD BE A RECKLESS FOLLY.
IT'S THE GREATEST TABOO OF THIS LEVEL!

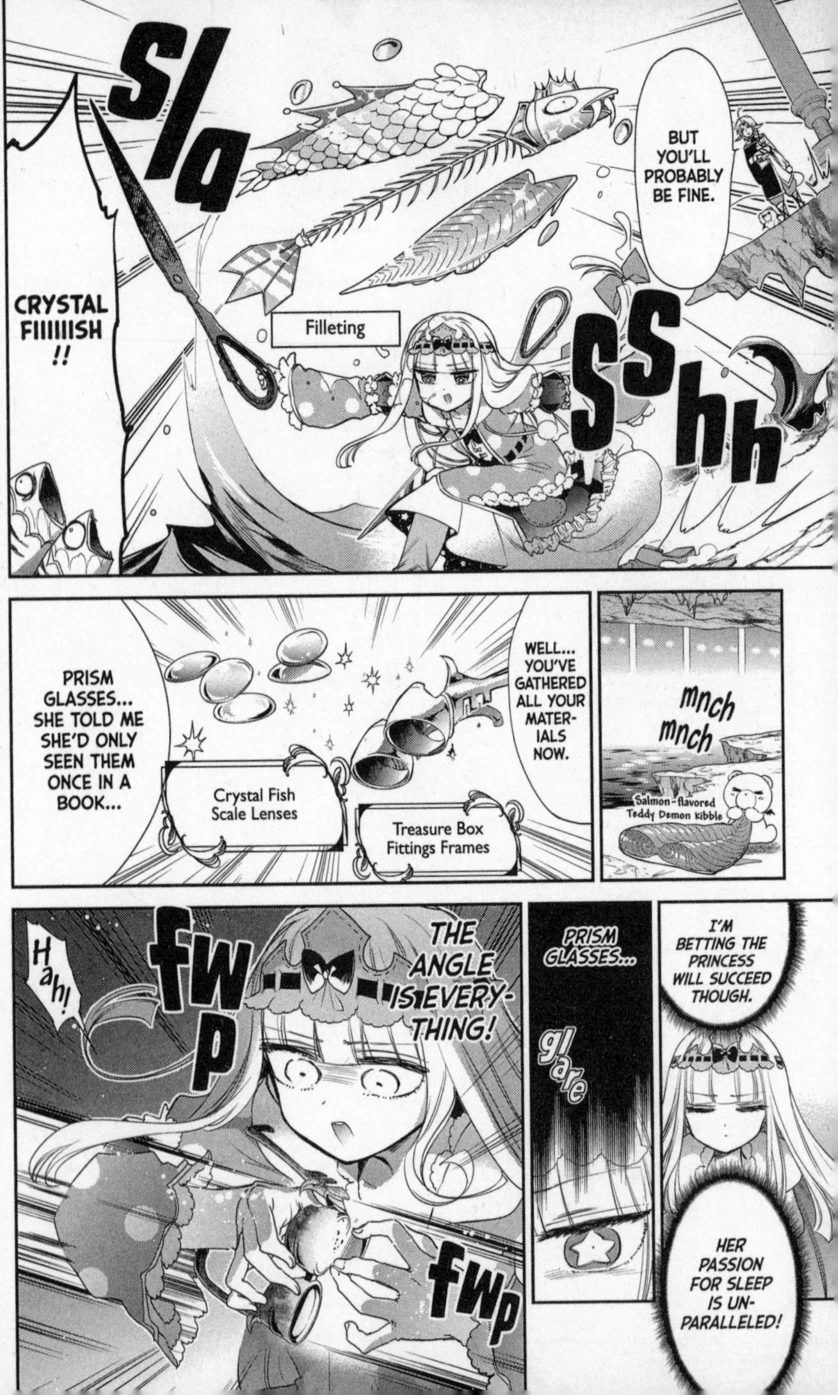
BUT YOU'LL PROBABLY BE FINE.
Sla
SShh
Filleting
CRYSTAL FIIIIIISH !!
mnch mnch
Salmon-flavored Teddy Demon kibble
WELL... YOU'VE GATHERED ALL YOUR MATER-IALS NOW.
Treasure Box Fittings Frames
Crystal Fish Scale Lenses
PRISM GLASSES... SHE TOLD ME SHE'D ONLY SEEN THEM ONCE IN A BOOK...
I'M BETTING THE PRINCESS WILL SUCCEED THOUGH.
HER PASSION FOR SLEEP IS UN-PARALLELED!
PRISM GLASSES...
glare
THE ANGLE IS EVERY-THING!
fwp
Hah!
fwp

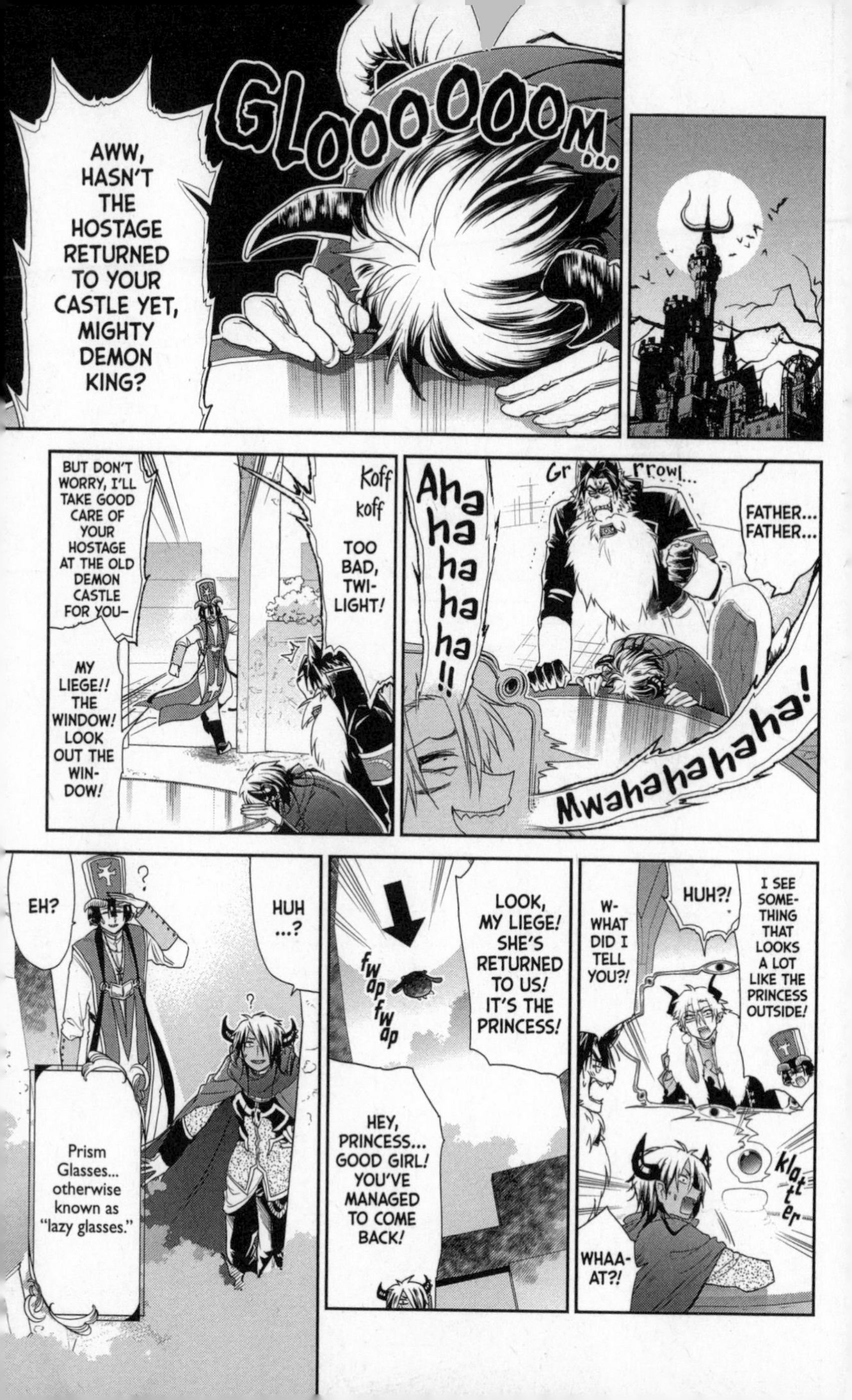
GLOOOOOOM...
AWW, HASN'T THE HOSTAGE RETURNED TO YOUR CASTLE YET, MIGHTY DEMON KING?
FATHER... FATHER...
Grrrowl...
Ahahahahaha!!
Mwahahahahaha!
Koff koff
TOO BAD, TWI-LIGHT!
BUT DON'T WORRY, I'LL TAKE GOOD CARE OF YOUR HOSTAGE AT THE OLD DEMON CASTLE FOR YOU—
MY LIEGE!! THE WINDOW! LOOK OUT THE WIN-DOW!
I SEE SOME-THING THAT LOOKS A LOT LIKE THE PRINCESS OUTSIDE!
HUH?!
W-WHAT DID I TELL YOU?!
klatter
WHAA-AT?!
LOOK, MY LIEGE! SHE'S RETURNED TO US! IT'S THE PRINCESS!
fwap fwap
HEY, PRINCESS... GOOD GIRL! YOU'VE MANAGED TO COME BACK!
HUH ...?
EH?
Prism Glasses... otherwise known as "lazy glasses."

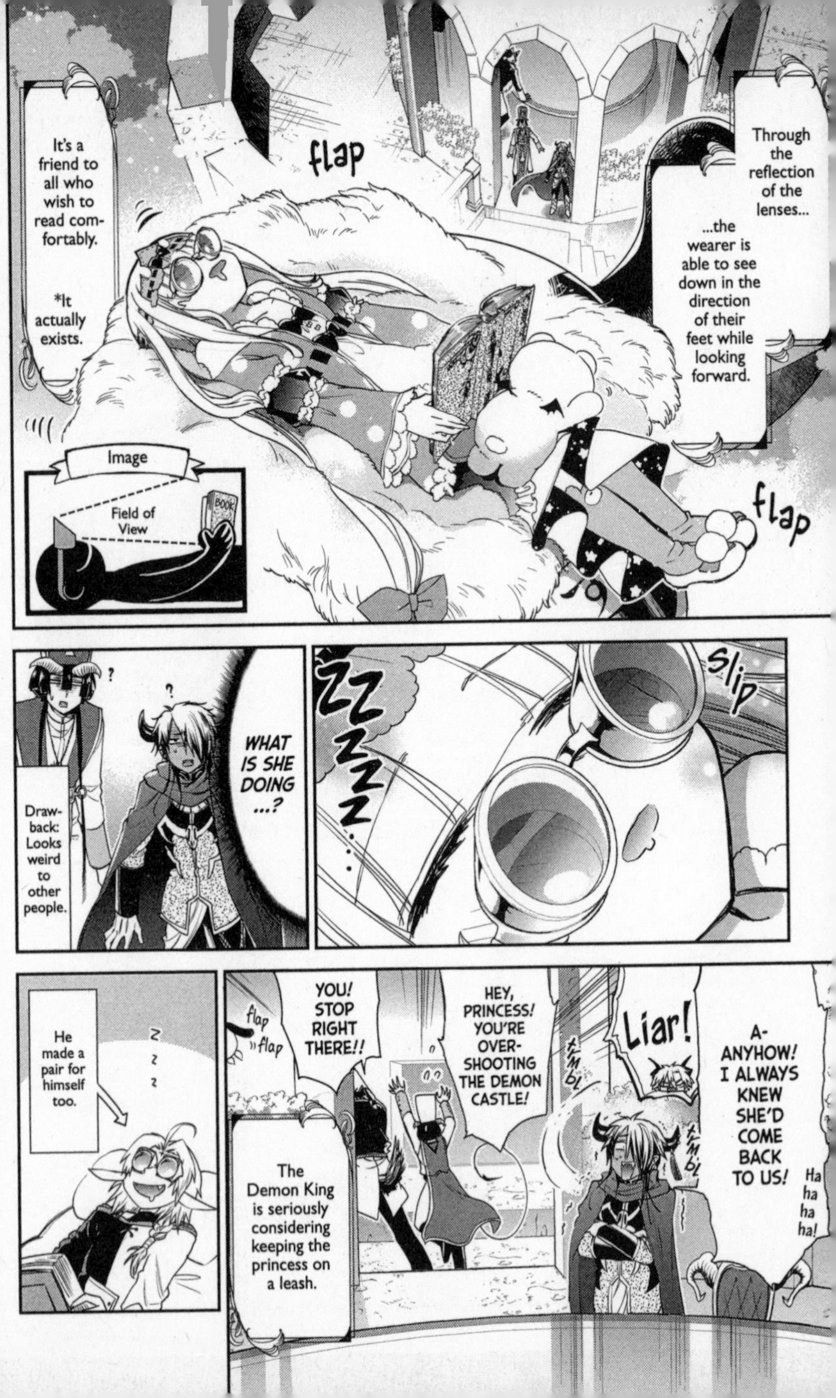
Through the reflection of the lenses...
...the wearer is able to see down in the direction of their feet while looking forward.
flap
It's a friend to all who wish to read comfortably.
*It actually exists.
flap
Image
Field of View
BOOK
Slip
ZZZ...
WHAT IS SHE DOING...?
Draw-back: Looks weird to other people.
A-ANYHOW! I ALWAYS KNEW SHE'D COME BACK TO US!
Ha ha ha ha!
Liar!
HEY, PRINCESS! YOU'RE OVER-SHOOTING THE DEMON CASTLE!
YOU! STOP RIGHT THERE!!
flap flap
The Demon King is seriously considering keeping the princess on a leash.
He made a pair for himself too.
z z z

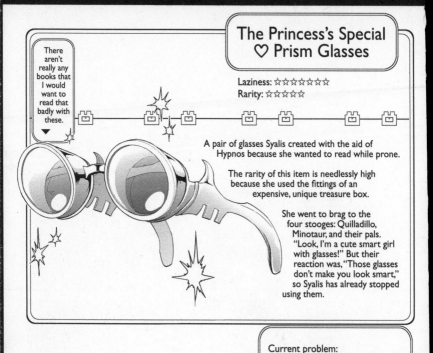

The Princess's Special ♡ Prism Glasses

Laziness: ☆☆☆☆☆☆☆
Rarity: ☆☆☆☆☆

There aren't really any books that I would want to read that badly with these.
▼

A pair of glasses Syalis created with the aid of Hypnos because she wanted to read while prone.

The rarity of this item is needlessly high because she used the fittings of an expensive, unique treasure box.

She went to brag to the four stooges: Quilladillo, Minotaur, and their pals. "Look, I'm a cute smart girl with glasses!" But their reaction was, "Those glasses don't make you look smart," so Syalis has already stopped using them.

Current problem:
"I've been trying to come up with a way to make them more compact, but it seems my master wants them more rugged, like a pair of goggles."
▼

...FLAVOR. ♡

IT'S SALMON...

...

OH, I SEE... ♡

Smug

...SALMON FLAVORED.

CRYSTAL FISH IS...

WHAT KIND OF FLAVOR IS SALMON FLAVOR? (Teasing)

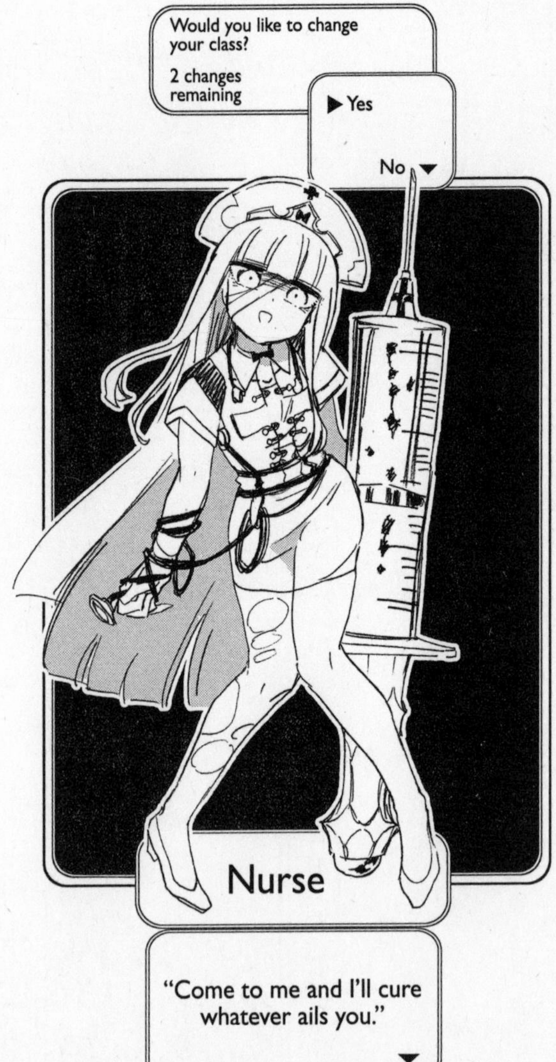
Would you like to change your class?
2 changes remaining
▶Yes
No
Nurse
"Come to me and I'll cure whatever ails you."

50th Night: The Princess Doesn't Only Dance at Meetings

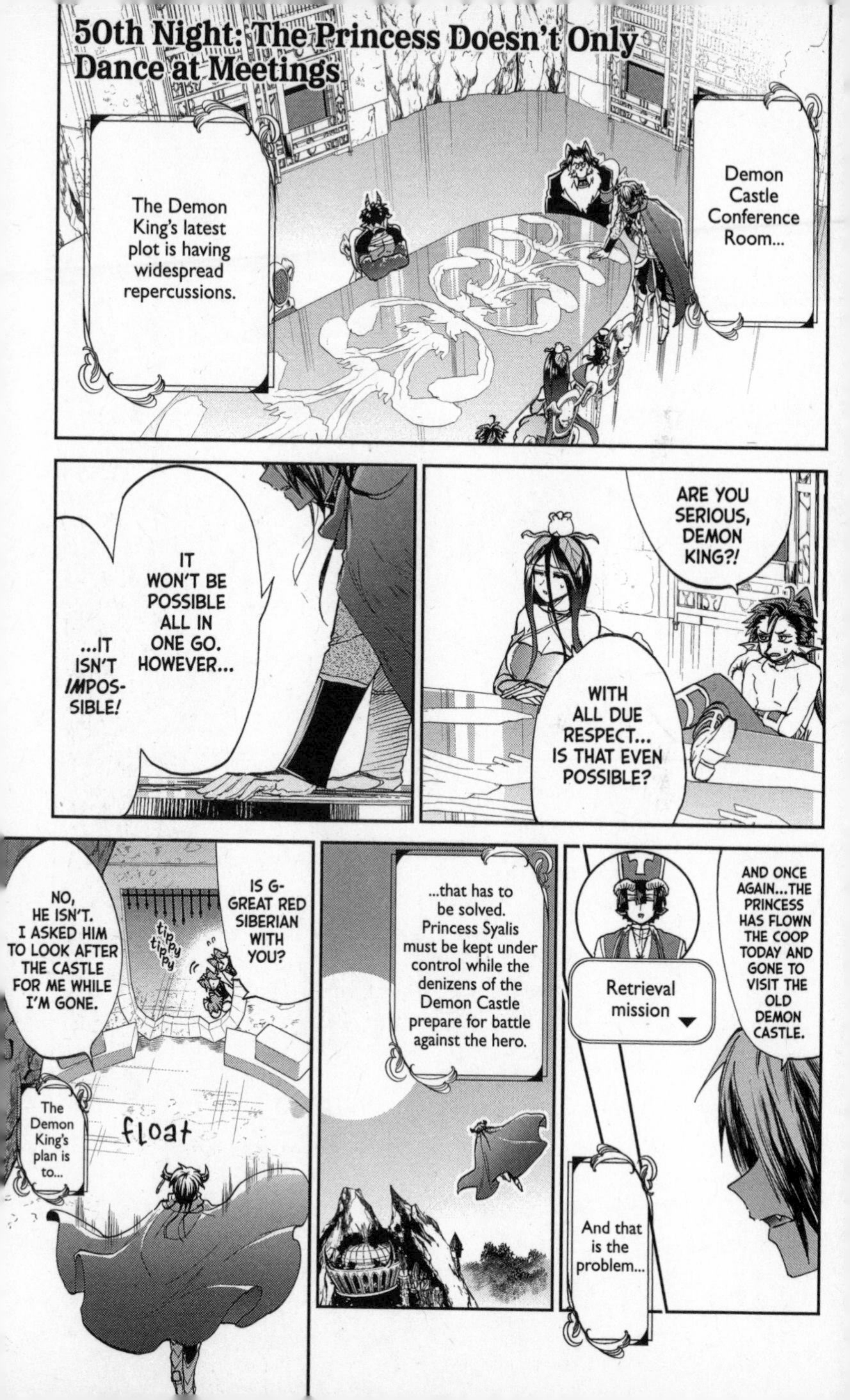
Demon Castle Conference Room...
The Demon King's latest plot is having widespread repercussions.
ARE YOU SERIOUS, DEMON KING?!
WITH ALL DUE RESPECT... IS THAT EVEN POSSIBLE?
IT WON'T BE POSSIBLE ALL IN ONE GO. HOWEVER...
...IT ISN'T *IMPOS*SIBLE!
AND ONCE AGAIN...THE PRINCESS HAS FLOWN THE COOP TODAY AND GONE TO VISIT THE OLD DEMON CASTLE.
Retrieval mission
And that is the problem...
...that has to be solved. Princess Syalis must be kept under control while the denizens of the Demon Castle prepare for battle against the hero.
IS G-GREAT RED SIBERIAN WITH YOU?
NO, HE ISN'T. I ASKED HIM TO LOOK AFTER THE CASTLE FOR ME WHILE I'M GONE.
tippy tippy
The Demon King's plan is to...
float

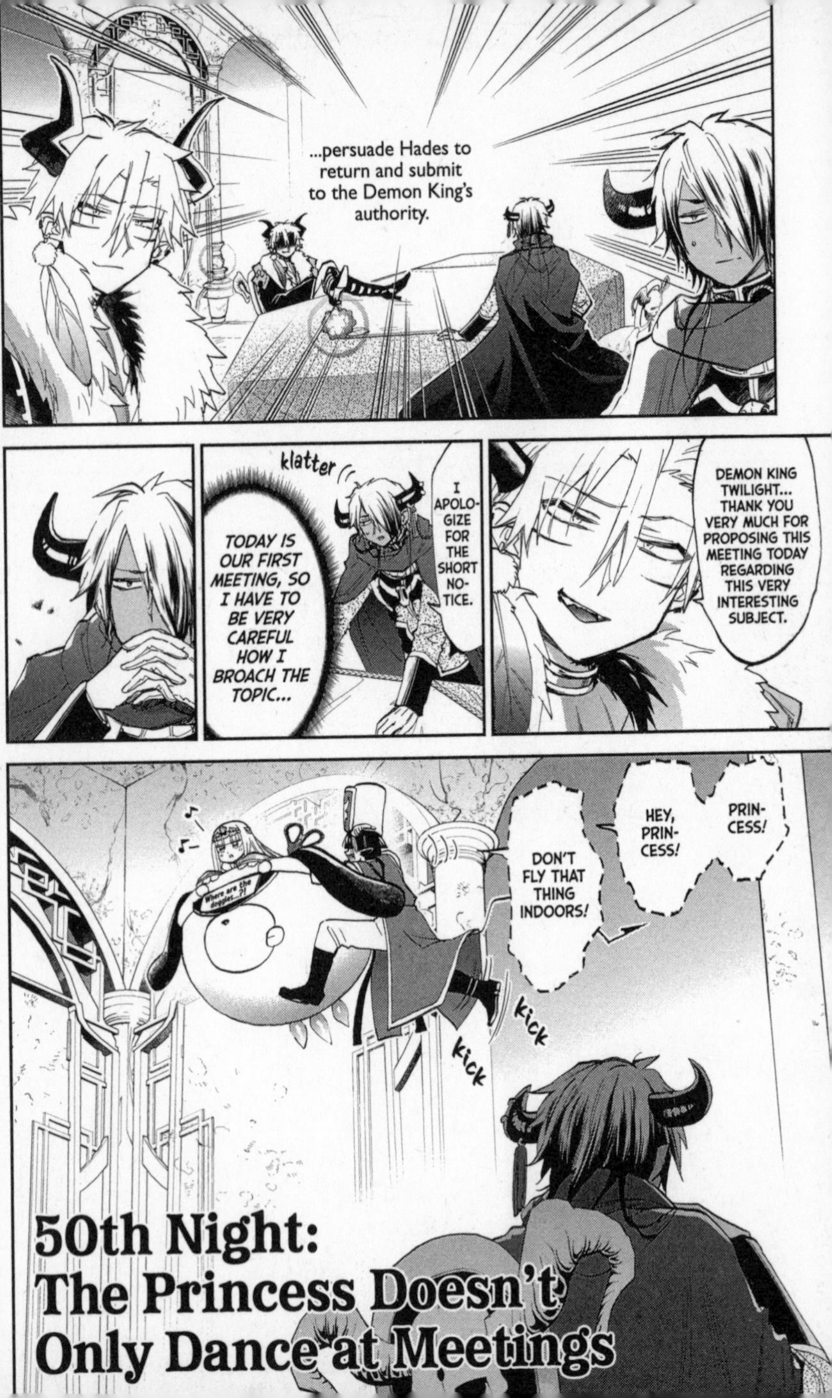
...persuade Hades to return and submit to the Demon King's authority.
DEMON KING TWILIGHT... THANK YOU VERY MUCH FOR PROPOSING THIS MEETING TODAY REGARDING THIS VERY INTERESTING SUBJECT.
I APOLOGIZE FOR THE SHORT NOTICE.
klatter
TODAY IS OUR FIRST MEETING, SO I HAVE TO BE VERY CAREFUL HOW I BROACH THE TOPIC...
PRINCESS!
HEY, PRINCESS!
DON'T FLY THAT THING INDOORS!
Where are the doggies...?!
kick
kick
50th Night: The Princess Doesn't Only Dance at Meetings

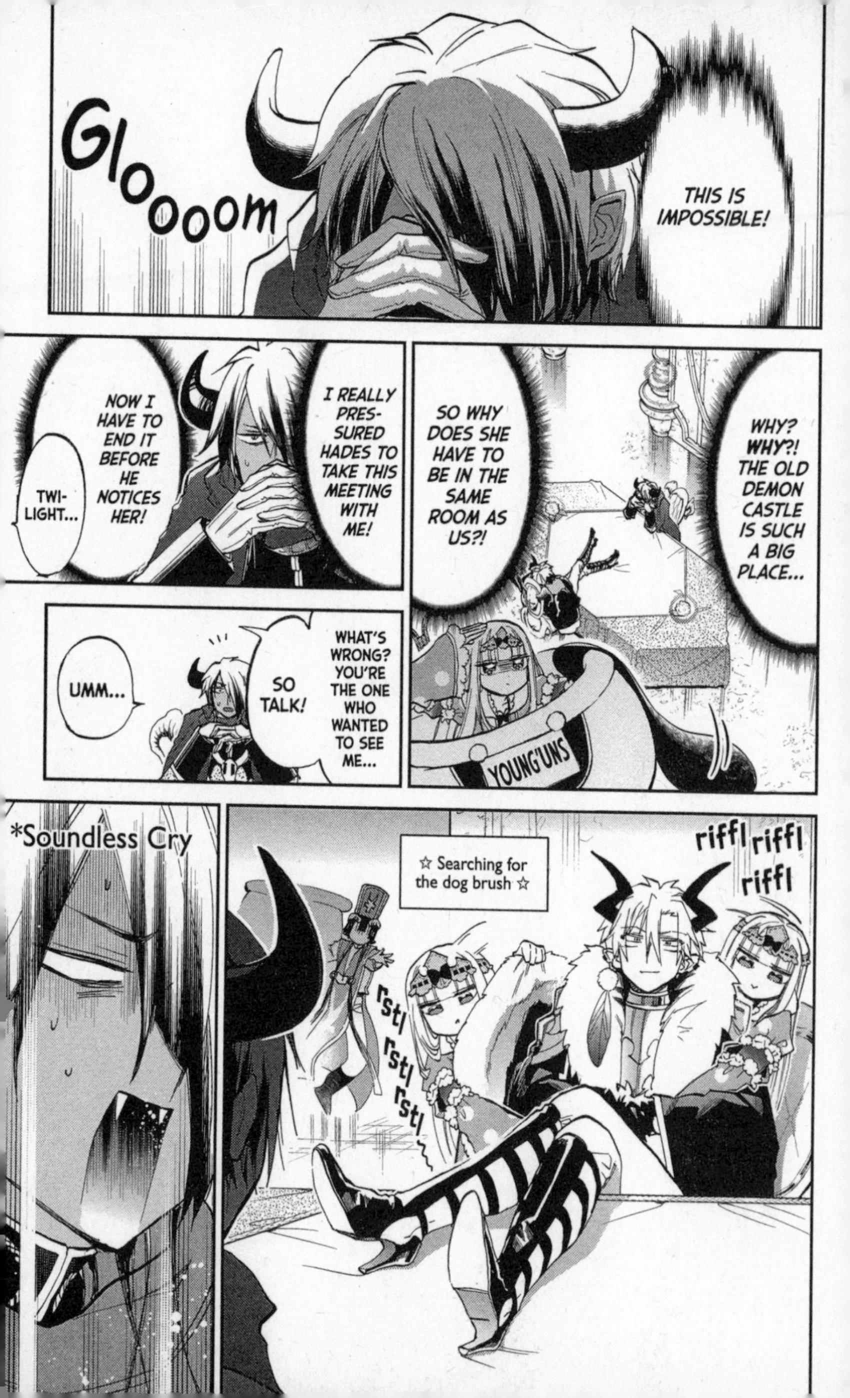
THIS IS IMPOSSIBLE!
Gloooom
WHY? WHY?! THE OLD DEMON CASTLE IS SUCH A BIG PLACE...
SO WHY DOES SHE HAVE TO BE IN THE SAME ROOM AS US?!
YOUNG'UNS
I REALLY PRES-SURED HADES TO TAKE THIS MEETING WITH ME!
NOW I HAVE TO END IT BEFORE HE NOTICES HER!
TWI-LIGHT...
WHAT'S WRONG? YOU'RE THE ONE WHO WANTED TO SEE ME...
SO TALK!
UMM...
riffl riffl riffl
☆ Searching for the dog brush ☆
rstl rstl rstl
*Soundless Cry

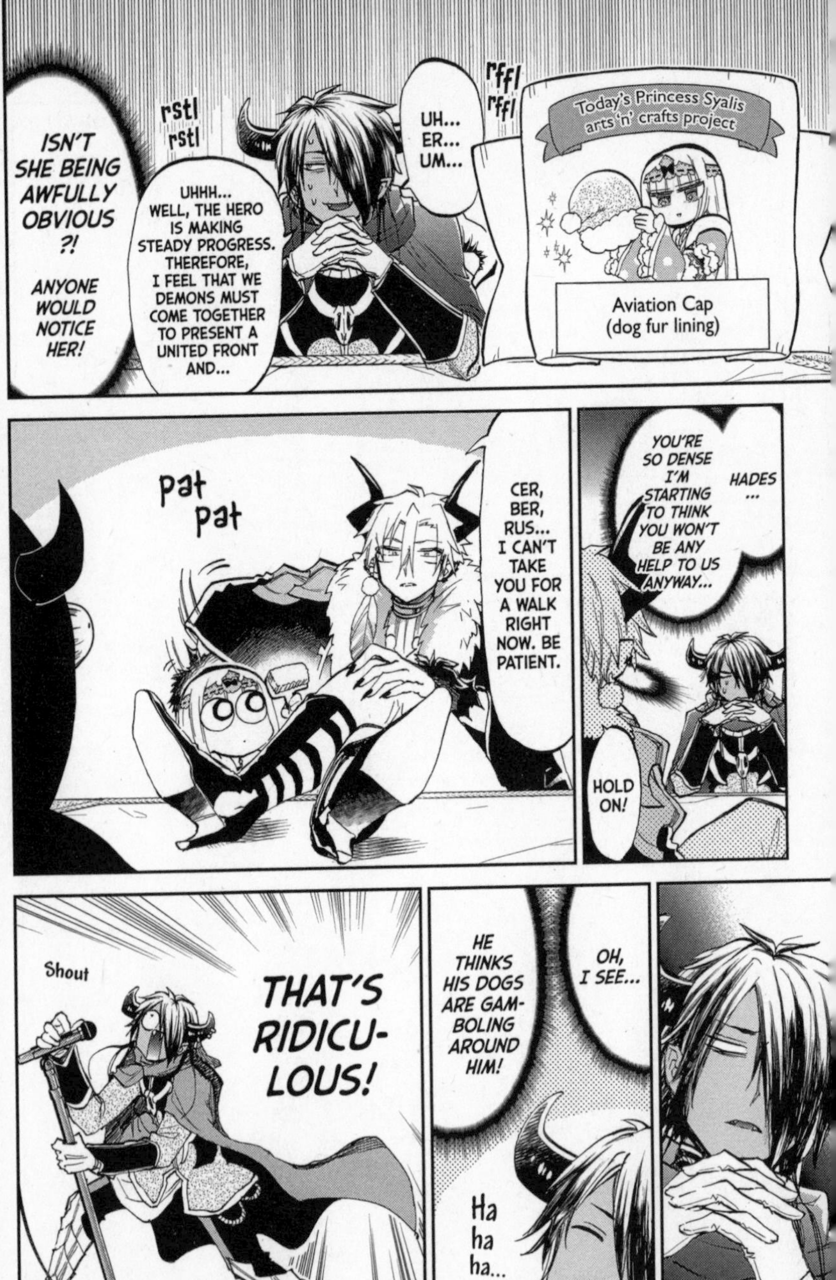
Today's Princess Syalis arts 'n' crafts project
Aviation Cap (dog fur lining)
rffl rffl
UH... ER... UM...
rstl rstl
UHHH... WELL, THE HERO IS MAKING STEADY PROGRESS. THEREFORE, I FEEL THAT WE DEMONS MUST COME TOGETHER TO PRESENT A UNITED FRONT AND...
ISN'T SHE BEING AWFULLY OBVIOUS?!
ANYONE WOULD NOTICE HER!
HADES ...
YOU'RE SO DENSE I'M STARTING TO THINK YOU WON'T BE ANY HELP TO US ANYWAY...
HOLD ON!
CER, BER, RUS... I CAN'T TAKE YOU FOR A WALK RIGHT NOW. BE PATIENT.
pat pat
OH, I SEE...
HE THINKS HIS DOGS ARE GAM-BOLING AROUND HIM!
Ha ha ha...
THAT'S RIDICU-LOUS!
Shout

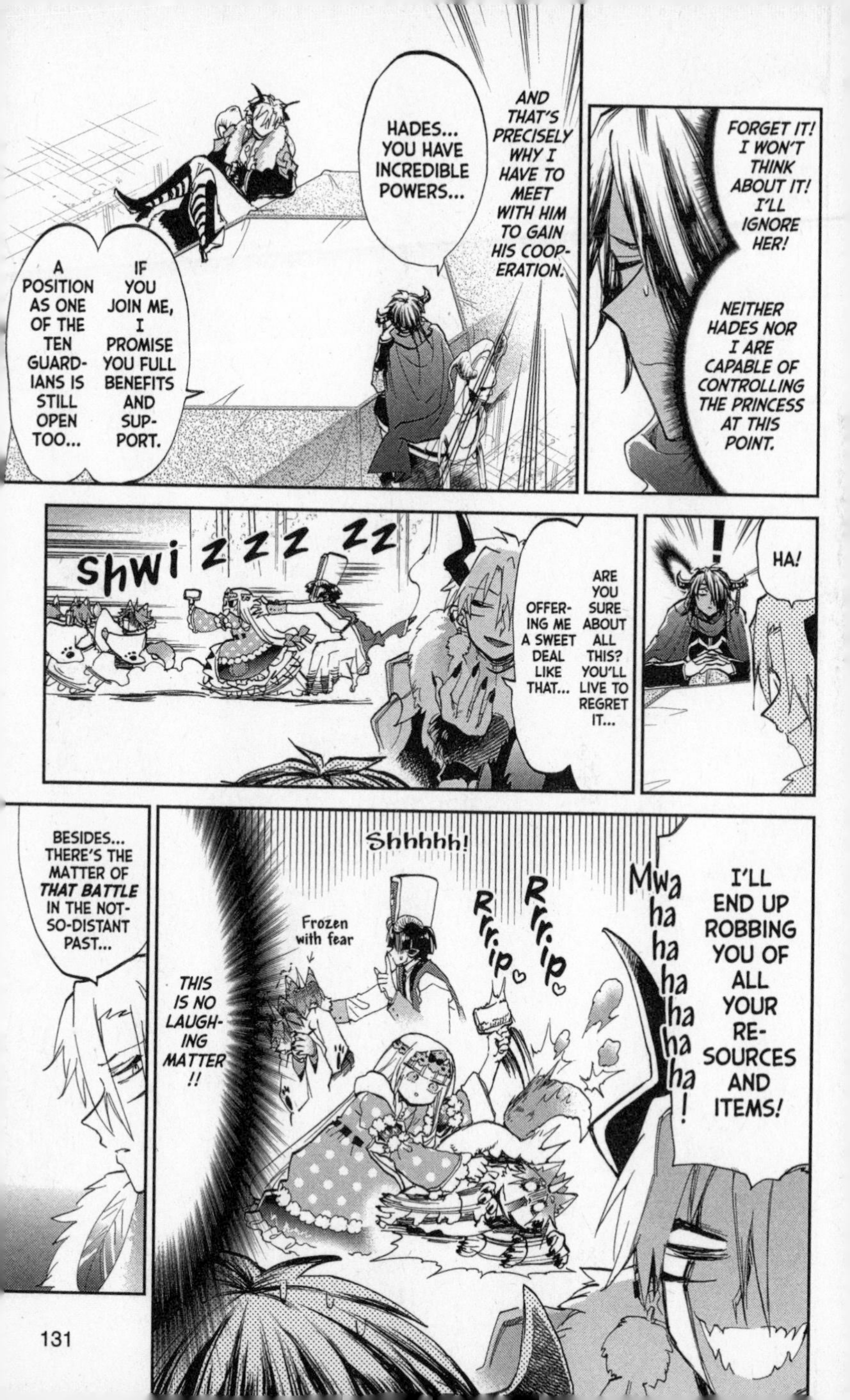

FORGET IT! I WON'T THINK ABOUT IT! I'LL IGNORE HER!
NEITHER HADES NOR I ARE CAPABLE OF CONTROLLING THE PRINCESS AT THIS POINT.
AND THAT'S PRECISELY WHY I HAVE TO MEET WITH HIM TO GAIN HIS COOPERATION.
HADES... YOU HAVE INCREDIBLE POWERS...
IF YOU JOIN ME, I PROMISE YOU FULL BENEFITS AND SUPPORT.
A POSITION AS ONE OF THE TEN GUARDIANS IS STILL OPEN TOO...
!
HA!
ARE YOU SURE ABOUT ALL THIS? YOU'LL LIVE TO REGRET IT...
OFFERING ME A SWEET DEAL LIKE THAT...
Shwi zzz zz
I'LL END UP ROBBING YOU OF ALL YOUR RESOURCES AND ITEMS!
Mwahahahahahaha!
Rrrip♡
Rrrip♡
Shhhhh!
Frozen with fear
THIS IS NO LAUGHING MATTER!!
BESIDES... THERE'S THE MATTER OF *THAT BATTLE* IN THE NOT-SO-DISTANT PAST...

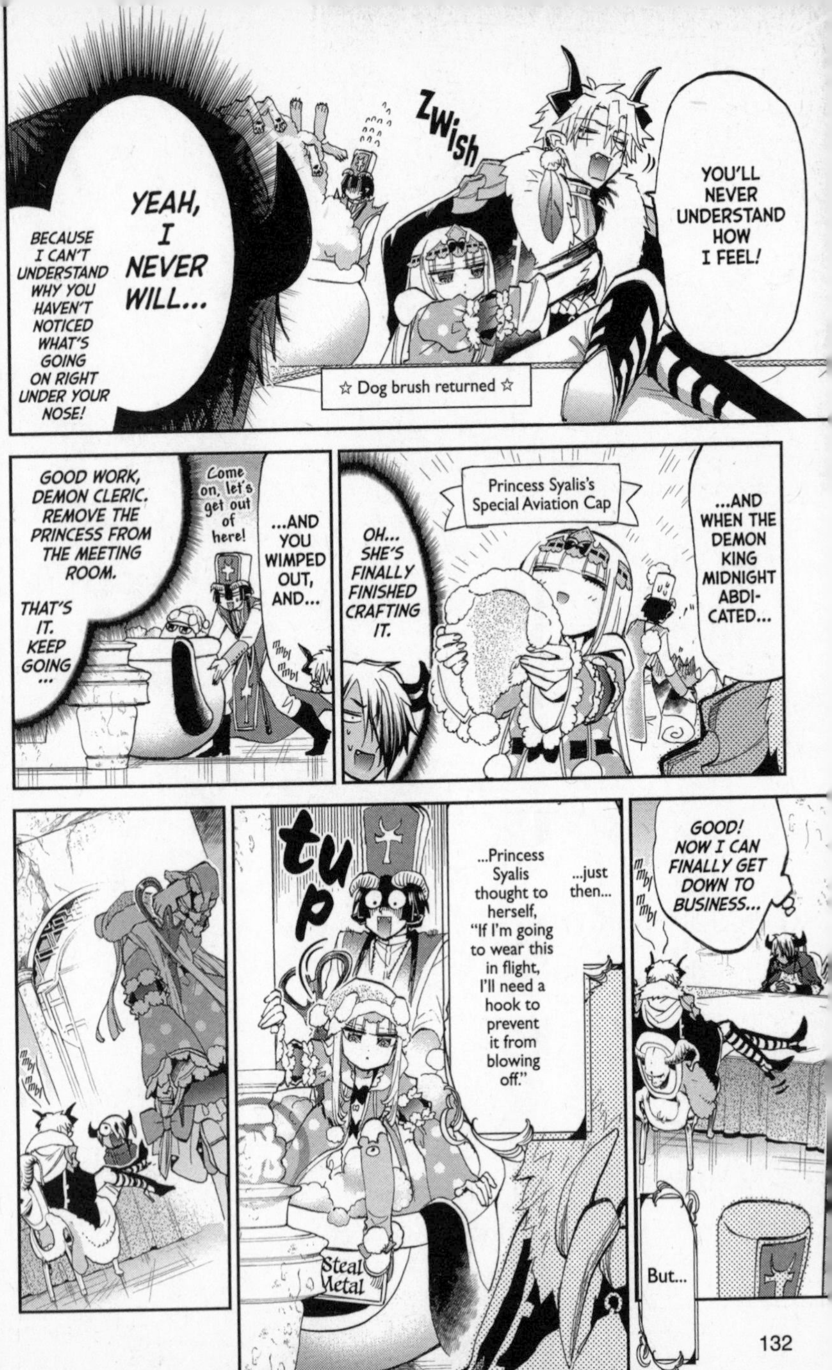
YOU'LL NEVER UNDERSTAND HOW I FEEL!
ZWish
YEAH, I NEVER WILL...
BECAUSE I CAN'T UNDERSTAND WHY YOU HAVEN'T NOTICED WHAT'S GOING ON RIGHT UNDER YOUR NOSE!
☆ Dog brush returned ☆
...AND WHEN THE DEMON KING MIDNIGHT ABDI-CATED...
Princess Syalis's Special Aviation Cap
OH... SHE'S FINALLY FINISHED CRAFTING IT.
mmbl mmbl
...AND YOU WIMPED OUT, AND...
Come on, let's get out of here!
GOOD WORK, DEMON CLERIC. REMOVE THE PRINCESS FROM THE MEETING ROOM.
THAT'S IT. KEEP GOING...
GOOD! NOW I CAN FINALLY GET DOWN TO BUSINESS...
mmbl mmbl mmbl
But...
...just then...
...Princess Syalis thought to herself, "If I'm going to wear this in flight, I'll need a hook to prevent it from blowing off."
tup
Steal Metal
mmbl mmbl

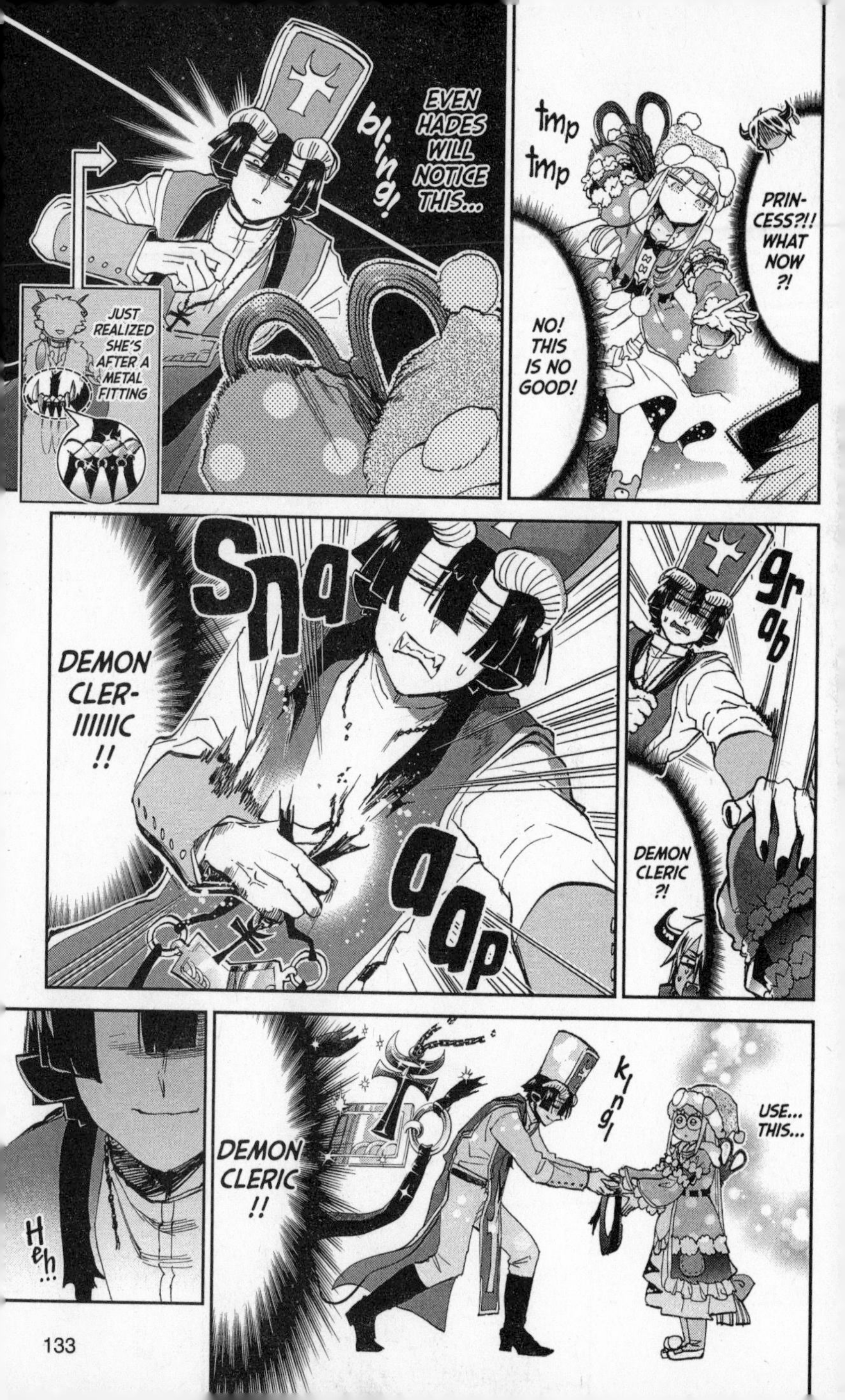
tmp
tmp
PRIN-CESS?!! WHAT NOW?!
NO! THIS IS NO GOOD!
EVEN HADES WILL NOTICE THIS...
bling!
JUST REALIZED SHE'S AFTER A METAL FITTING
grab
DEMON CLERIC?!
Snaaaap
DEMON CLER-IIIIIIC!!
USE... THIS...
kling!
DEMON CLERIC!!
Heh...

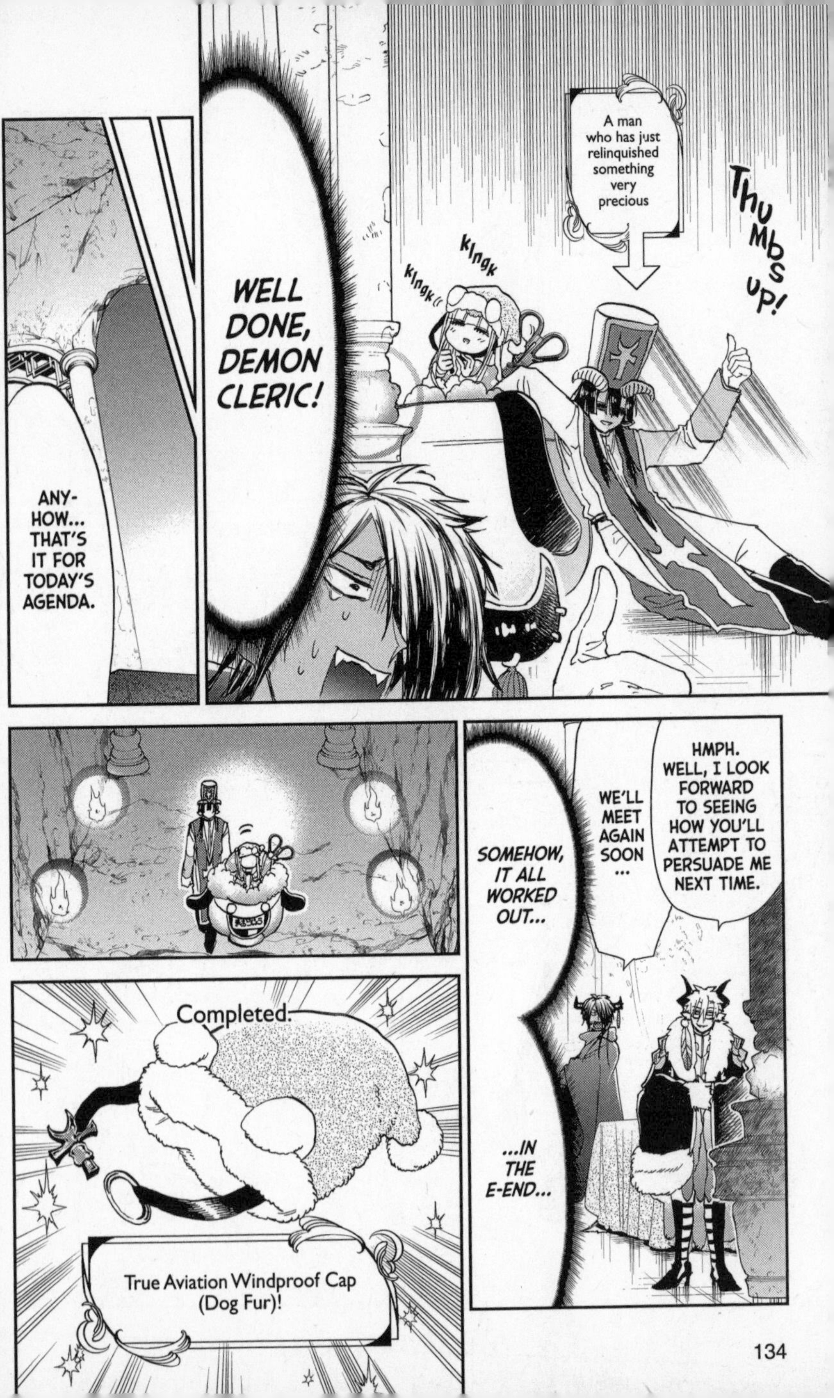
A man who has just relinquished something very precious
THUMBS UP!
klngk
klngk
WELL DONE, DEMON CLERIC!
ANY-HOW... THAT'S IT FOR TODAY'S AGENDA.
HMPH. WELL, I LOOK FORWARD TO SEEING HOW YOU'LL ATTEMPT TO PERSUADE ME NEXT TIME.
WE'LL MEET AGAIN SOON ...
SOMEHOW, IT ALL WORKED OUT...
...IN THE E-END...
Completed.
True Aviation Windproof Cap (Dog Fur)!

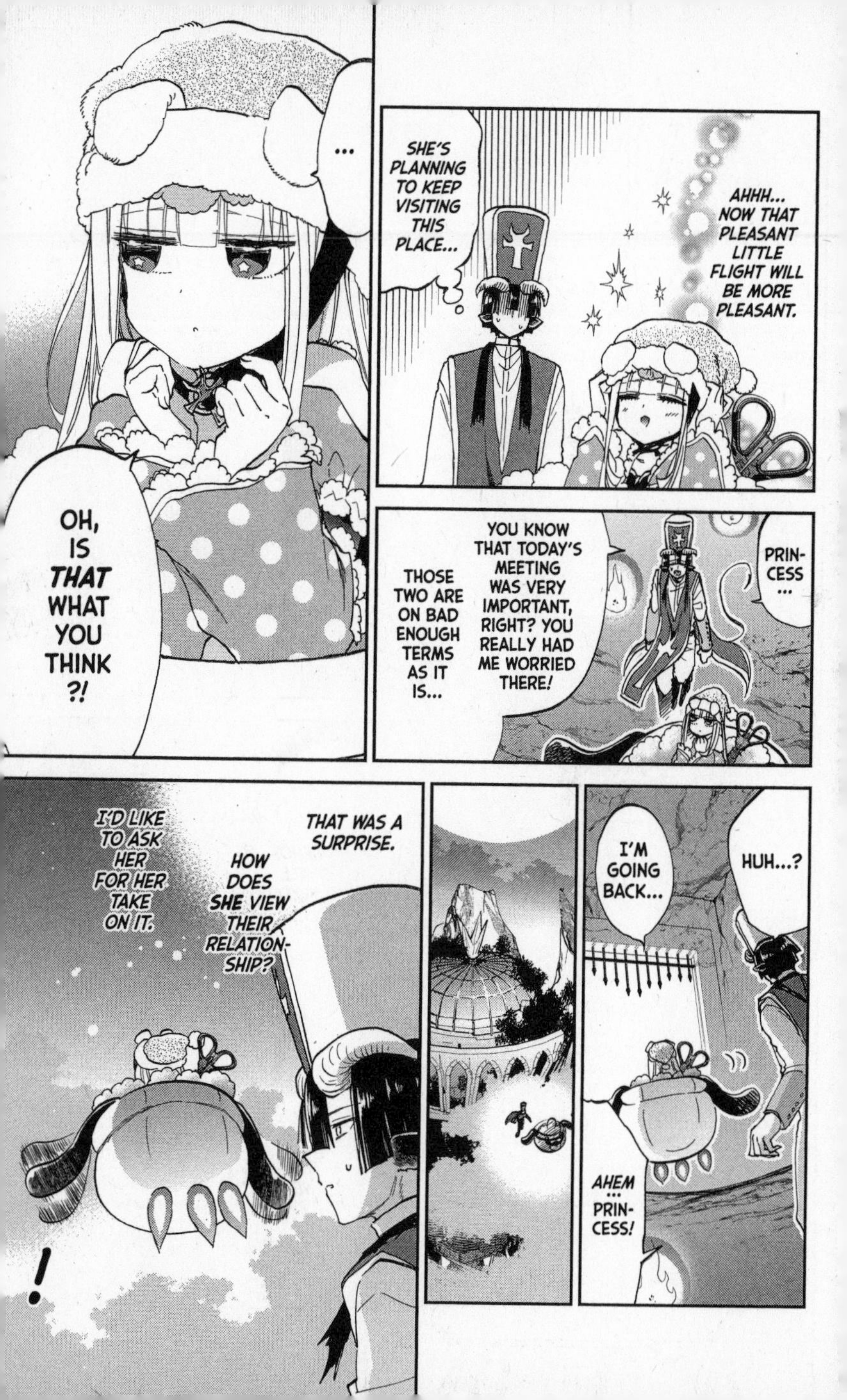
AHHH... NOW THAT PLEASANT LITTLE FLIGHT WILL BE MORE PLEASANT.
SHE'S PLANNING TO KEEP VISITING THIS PLACE...
PRIN-CESS...
YOU KNOW THAT TODAY'S MEETING WAS VERY IMPORTANT, RIGHT? YOU REALLY HAD ME WORRIED THERE!
THOSE TWO ARE ON BAD ENOUGH TERMS AS IT IS...
...
OH, IS THAT WHAT YOU THINK?!
HUH...?
I'M GOING BACK...
AHEM... PRIN-CESS!
THAT WAS A SURPRISE.
HOW DOES SHE VIEW THEIR RELATION-SHIP?
I'D LIKE TO ASK HER FOR HER TAKE ON IT.
!

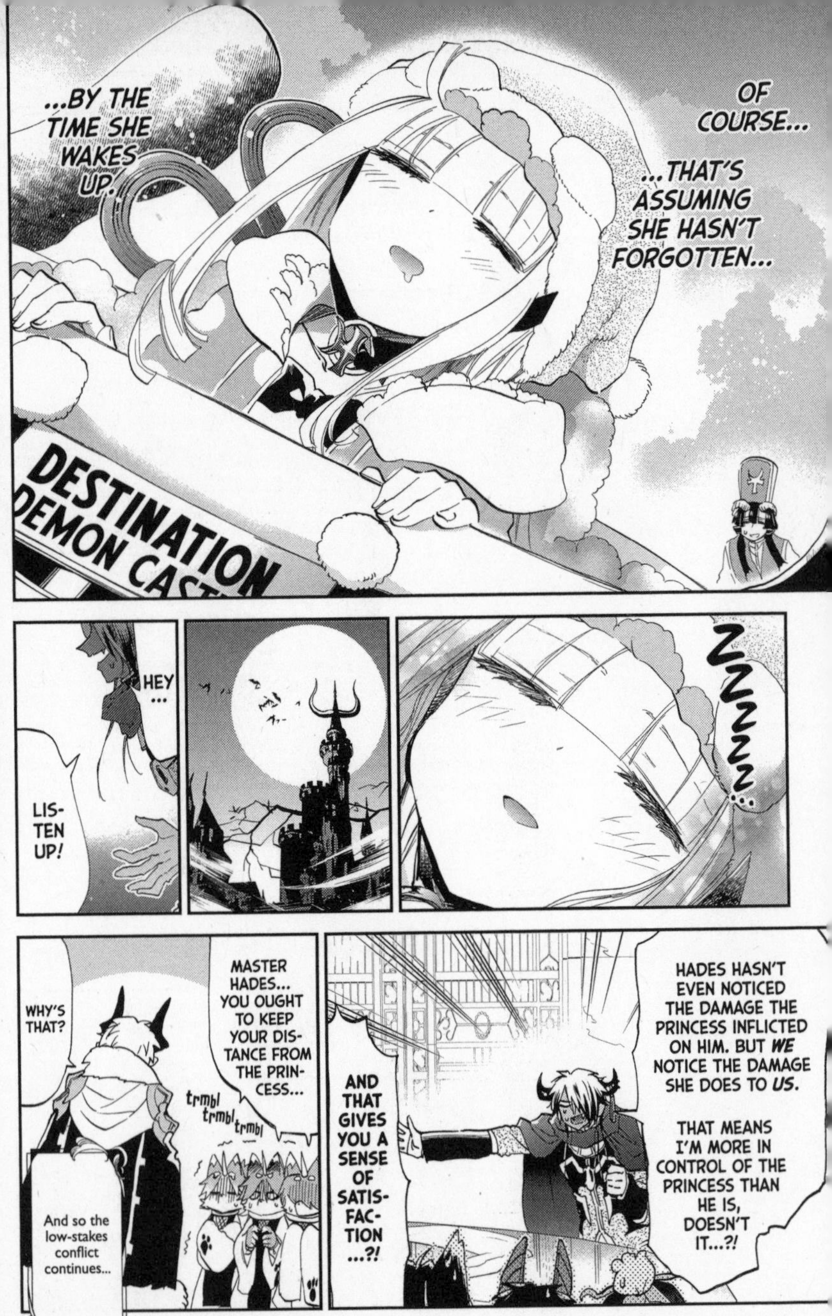
...BY THE TIME SHE WAKES UP.
OF COURSE...
...THAT'S ASSUMING SHE HASN'T FORGOTTEN...
DESTINATION DEMON CAST
ZZZZZ...
HEY...
LISTEN UP!
HADES HASN'T EVEN NOTICED THE DAMAGE THE PRINCESS INFLICTED ON HIM. BUT *WE* NOTICE THE DAMAGE SHE DOES TO *US*.
THAT MEANS I'M MORE IN CONTROL OF THE PRINCESS THAN HE IS, DOESN'T IT...?!
AND THAT GIVES YOU A SENSE OF SATISFACTION...?!
MASTER HADES... YOU OUGHT TO KEEP YOUR DISTANCE FROM THE PRINCESS...
trmbl trmbl trmbl
WHY'S THAT?
And so the low-stakes conflict continues...

Puppy Pod

A dog who swims across the night sky.

Canine Appropriateness: ☆☆☆☆☆☆☆☆☆
Difficulty of Handling: ☆

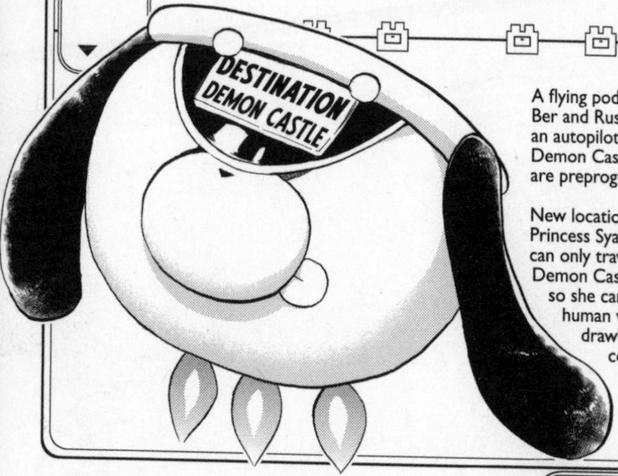

DESTINATION DEMON CASTLE

A flying pod that Hades invented for Cer, Ber and Rus because they can't fly. It has an autopilot function, and the locations Demon Castle and Old Demon Castle are preprogrammed into it.

New locations are being added by Princess Syalis. However, the Puppy Pod can only travel within the bounds of the Demon Castle and the Old Demon Castle, so she can't use it to fly back to the human world. Regardless of this drawback, it's still quite a convenience.

Former problem:
"But, Master Hades, we're afraid of heights!"

Current problem:
"Master Hades, we don't have the pod anymore, so please carry us!"

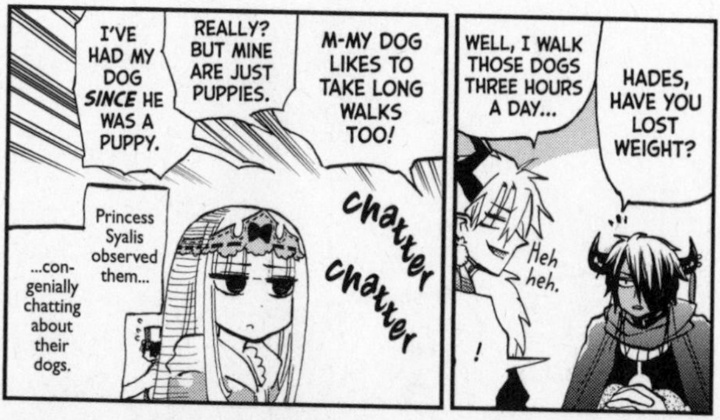

HADES, HAVE YOU LOST WEIGHT?
WELL, I WALK THOSE DOGS THREE HOURS A DAY...
Heh heh.
!
M-MY DOG LIKES TO TAKE LONG WALKS TOO!
REALLY? BUT MINE ARE JUST PUPPIES.
I'VE HAD MY DOG *SINCE* HE WAS A PUPPY.
Chatter chatter
Princess Syalis observed them...
...congenially chatting about their dogs.

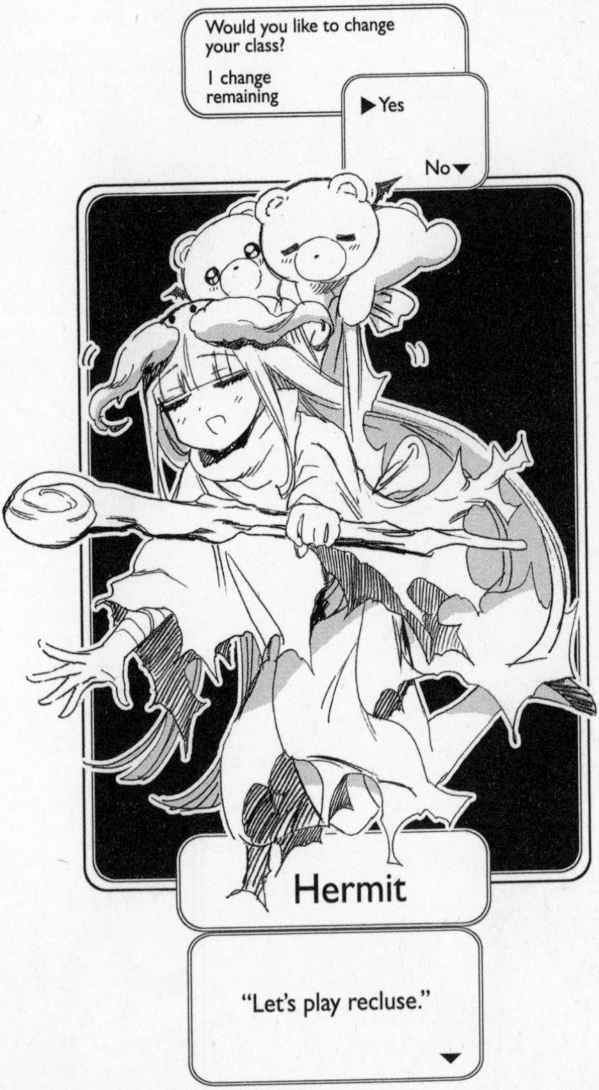
Would you like to change your class?
1 change remaining
▶Yes
No
Hermit
"Let's play recluse."

51st Night: Pollenella

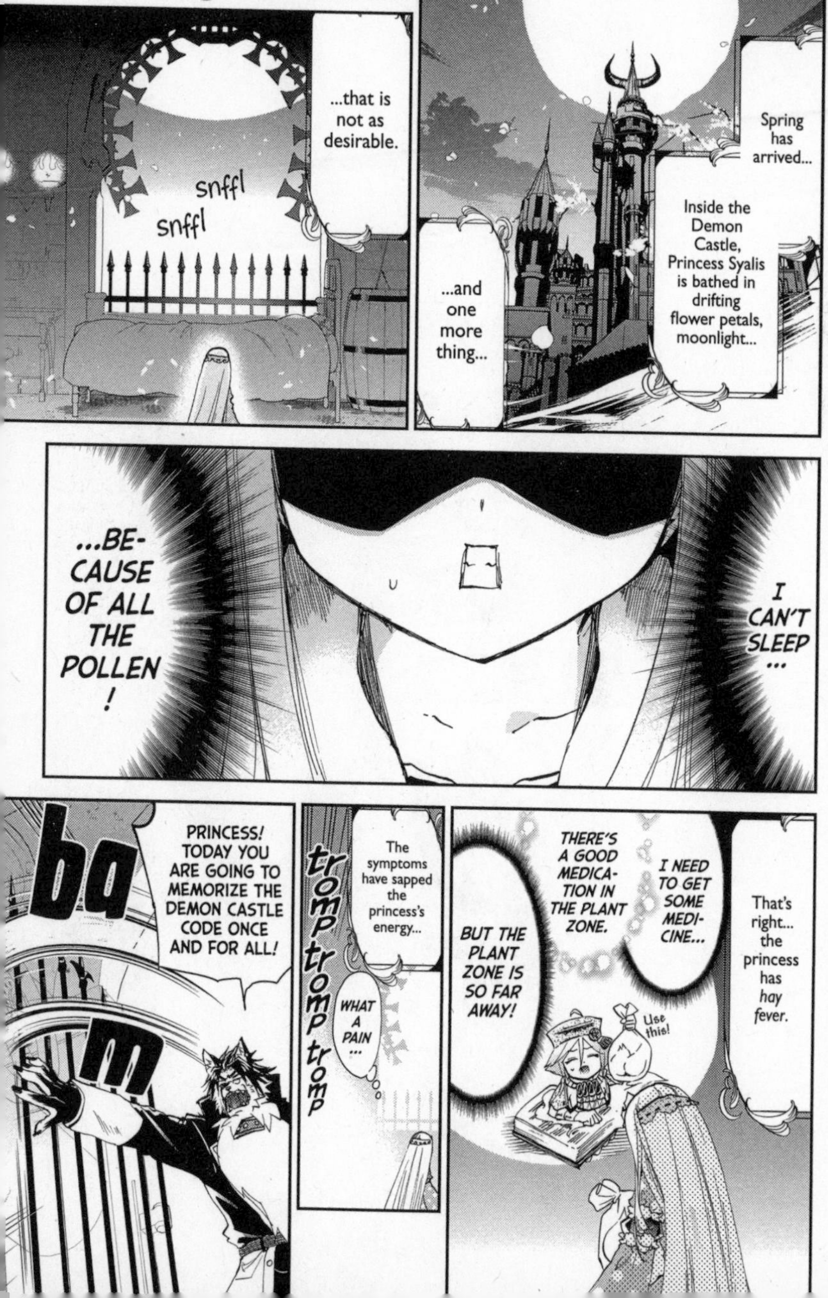
Spring has arrived...
Inside the Demon Castle, Princess Syalis is bathed in drifting flower petals, moonlight...
...and one more thing...
...that is not as desirable.
snffl
snffl
I CAN'T SLEEP...
...BE-CAUSE OF ALL THE POLLEN!
That's right... the princess has *hay fever.*
I NEED TO GET SOME MEDI-CINE...
THERE'S A GOOD MEDICA-TION IN THE PLANT ZONE.
BUT THE PLANT ZONE IS SO FAR AWAY!
Use this!
The symptoms have sapped the princess's energy...
tromp tromp tromp tromp
WHAT A PAIN...
PRINCESS! TODAY YOU ARE GOING TO MEMORIZE THE DEMON CASTLE CODE ONCE AND FOR ALL!
bam

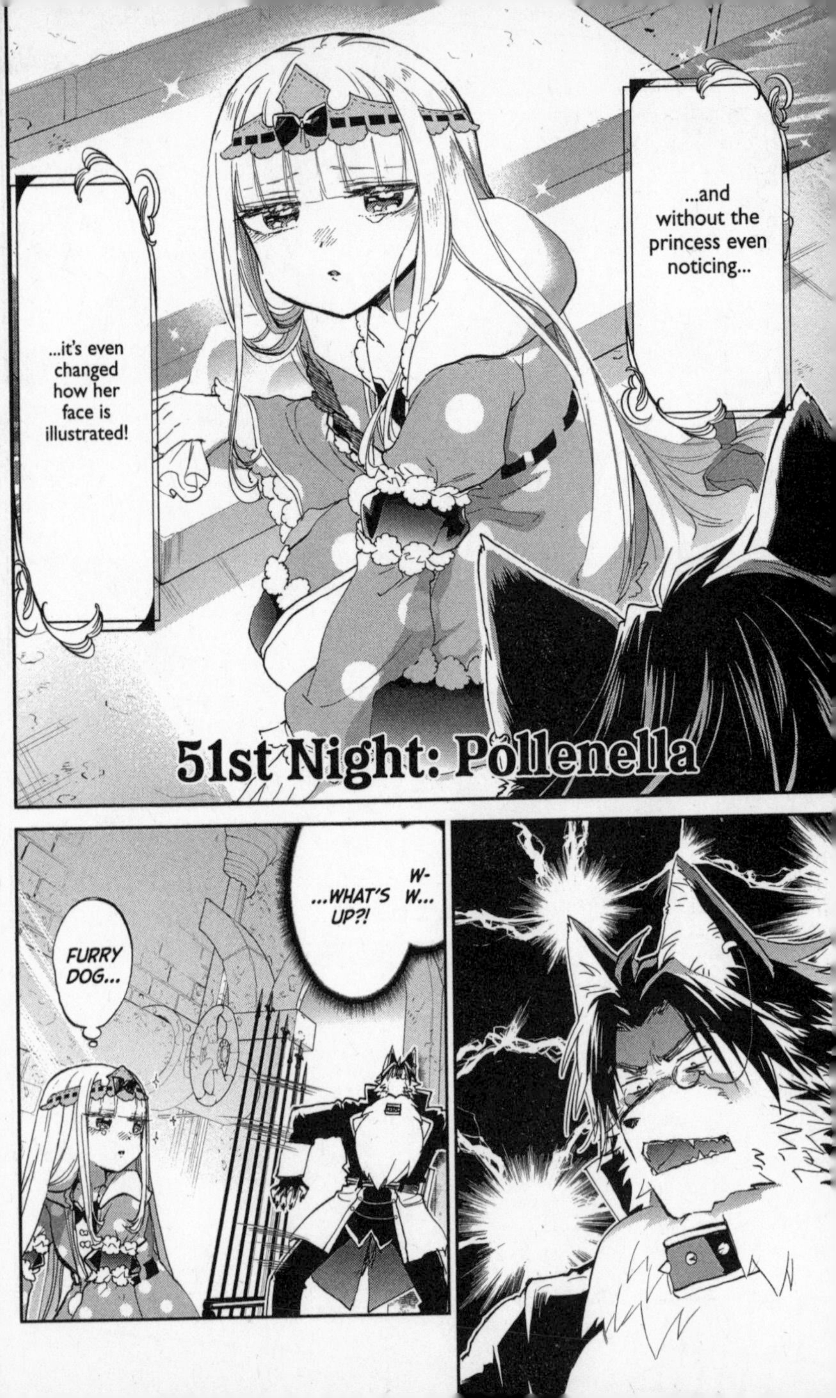
...and without the princess even noticing...
...it's even changed how her face is illustrated!
51st Night: Pollenella
W- W... ...WHAT'S UP?!
FURRY DOG...

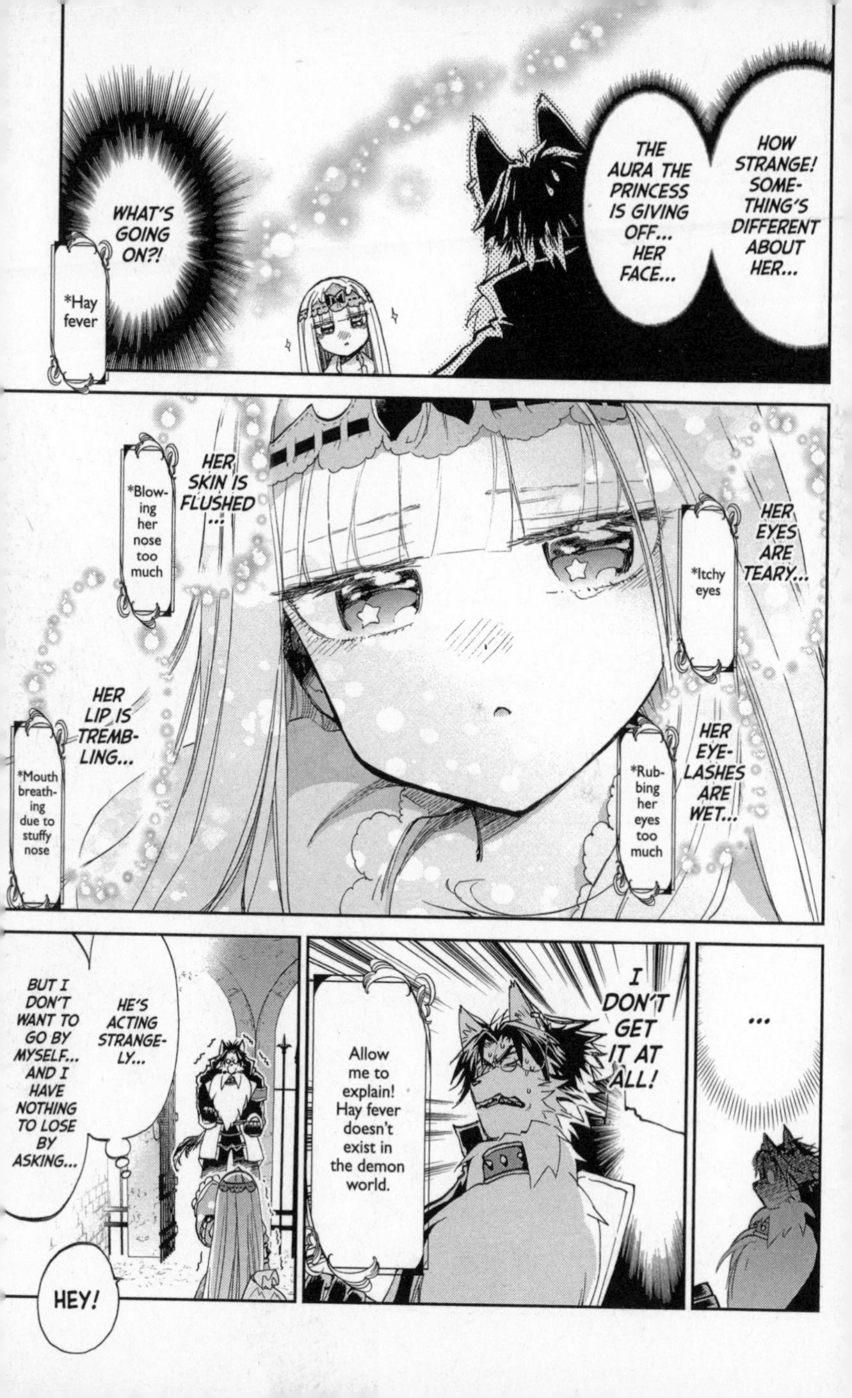
HOW STRANGE! SOMETHING'S DIFFERENT ABOUT HER...
THE AURA THE PRINCESS IS GIVING OFF... HER FACE...
WHAT'S GOING ON?!
*Hay fever
HER EYES ARE TEARY...
*Itchy eyes
HER EYELASHES ARE WET...
*Rubbing her eyes too much
HER SKIN IS FLUSHED...
*Blowing her nose too much
HER LIP IS TREMBLING...
*Mouth breathing due to stuffy nose
...
I DON'T GET IT AT ALL!
Allow me to explain! Hay fever doesn't exist in the demon world.
HE'S ACTING STRANGELY...
BUT I DON'T WANT TO GO BY MYSELF... AND I HAVE NOTHING TO LOSE BY ASKING...
HEY!

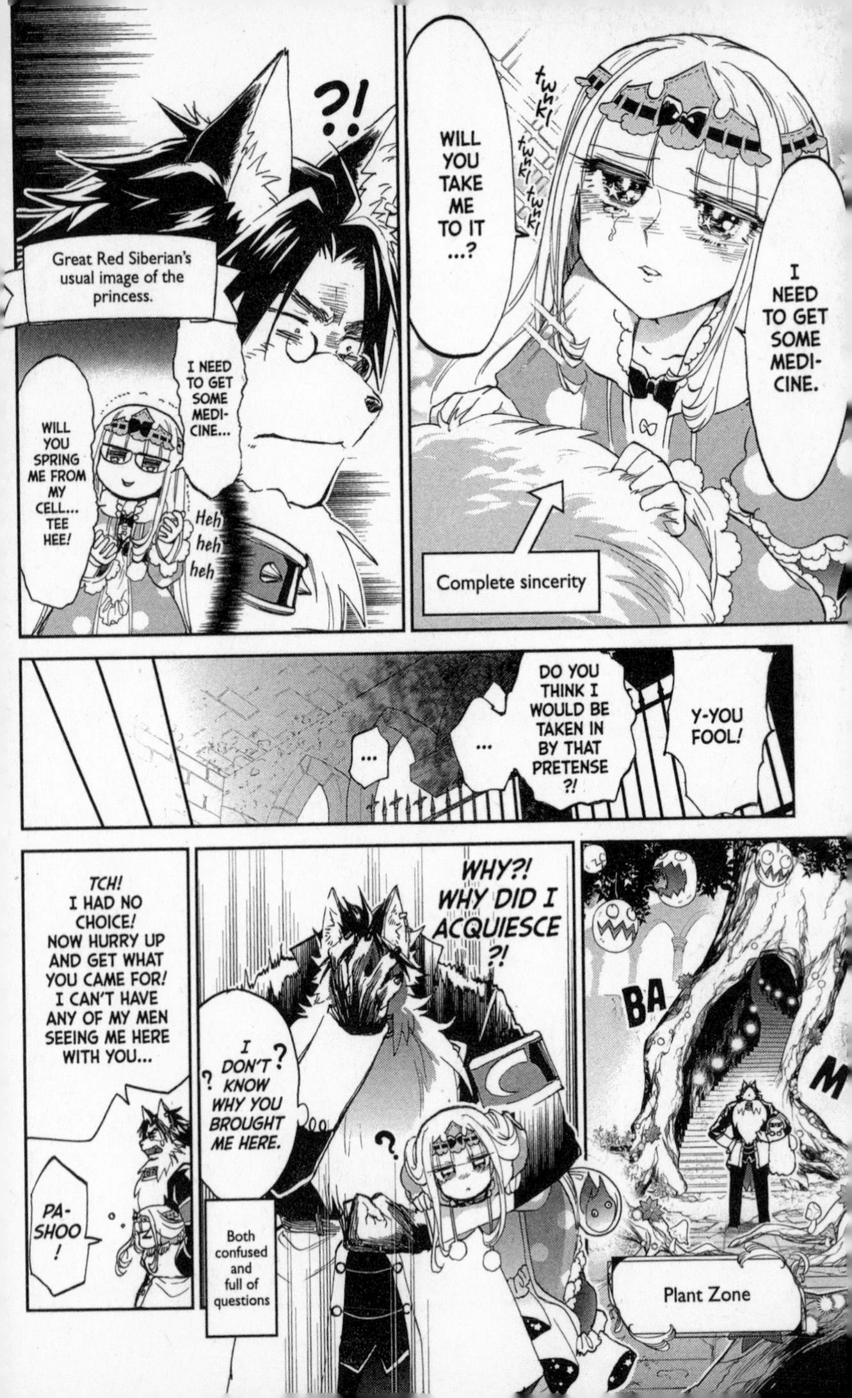
I NEED TO GET SOME MEDICINE.
WILL YOU TAKE ME TO IT ...?
Complete sincerity
?!
Great Red Siberian's usual image of the princess.
I NEED TO GET SOME MEDICINE...
WILL YOU SPRING ME FROM MY CELL... TEE HEE!
Heh heh heh
Y-YOU FOOL!
DO YOU THINK I WOULD BE TAKEN IN BY THAT PRETENSE ?!
...
...
BA
M
Plant Zone
WHY?! WHY DID I ACQUIESCE ?!
I DON'T KNOW WHY YOU BROUGHT ME HERE.
Both confused and full of questions
TCH! I HAD NO CHOICE! NOW HURRY UP AND GET WHAT YOU CAME FOR! I CAN'T HAVE ANY OF MY MEN SEEING ME HERE WITH YOU...
PA-SHOO!

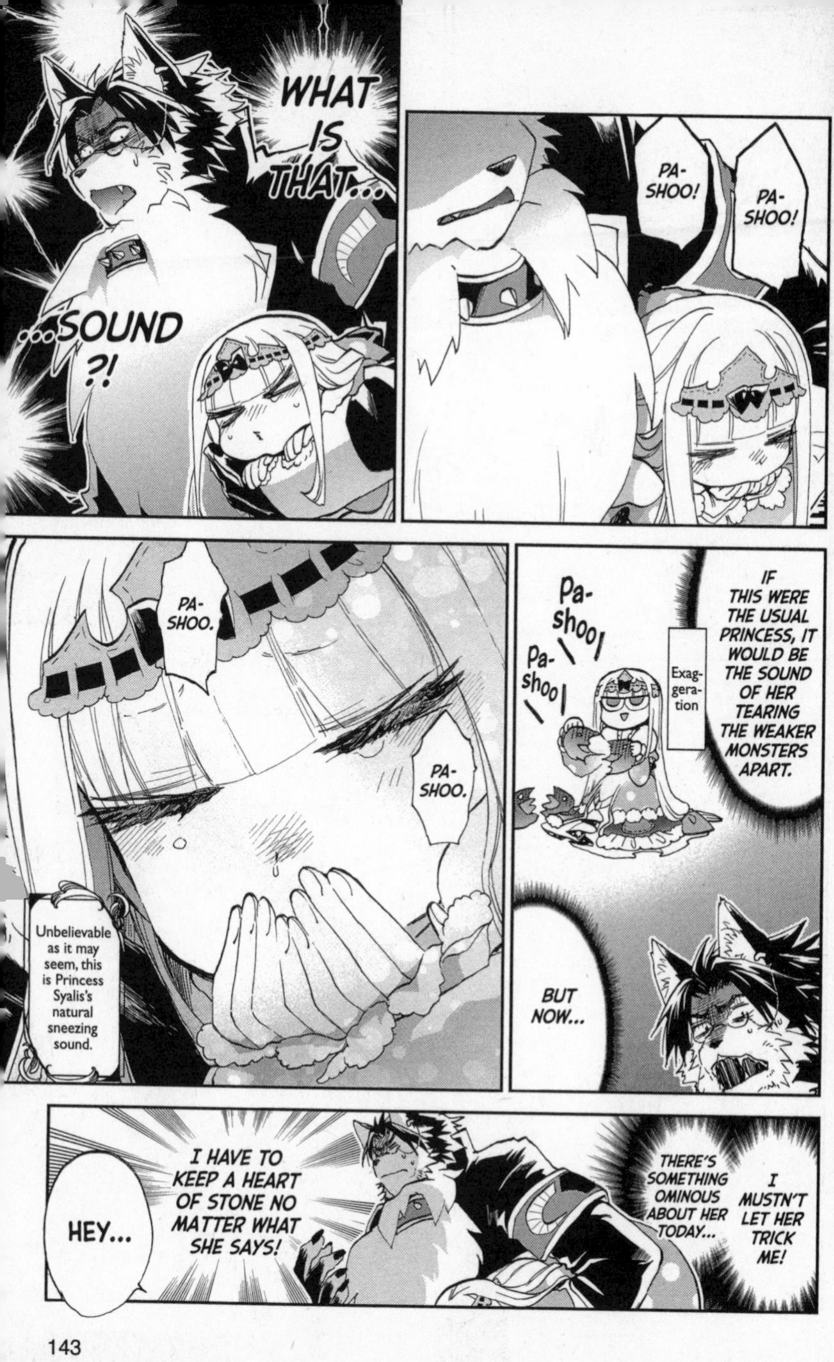
PA-SHOO!
PA-SHOO!
WHAT IS THAT...
...SOUND?!
IF THIS WERE THE USUAL PRINCESS, IT WOULD BE THE SOUND OF HER TEARING THE WEAKER MONSTERS APART.
Exaggeration
Pa-shoo!
Pa-shoo!
BUT NOW...
PA-SHOO.
PA-SHOO.
Unbelievable as it may seem, this is Princess Syalis's natural sneezing sound.
I MUSTN'T LET HER TRICK ME!
THERE'S SOMETHING OMINOUS ABOUT HER TODAY...
I HAVE TO KEEP A HEART OF STONE NO MATTER WHAT SHE SAYS!
HEY...

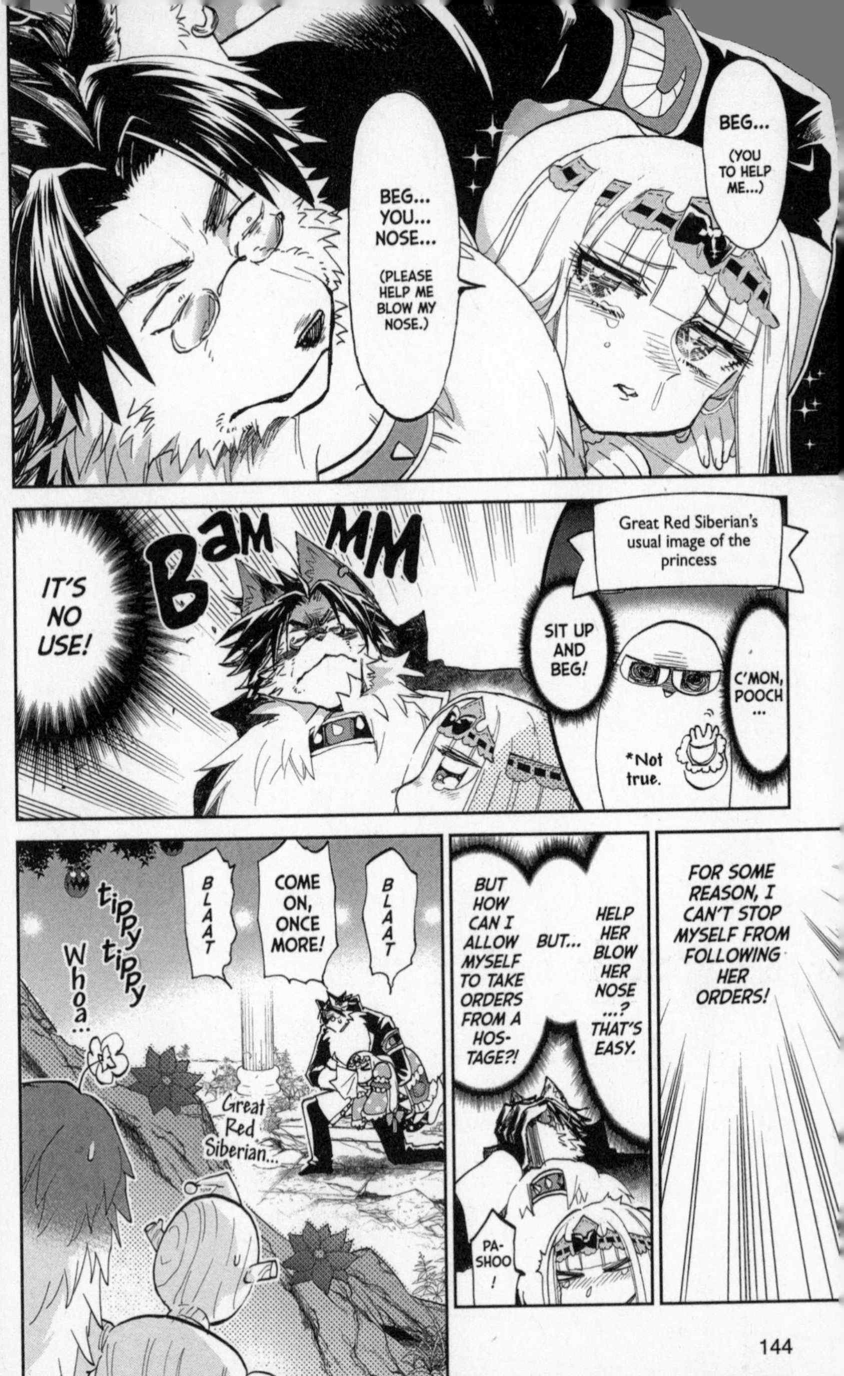
BEG...
(YOU TO HELP ME...)
BEG... YOU... NOSE...
(PLEASE HELP ME BLOW MY NOSE.)
Great Red Siberian's usual image of the princess
C'MON, POOCH ...
SIT UP AND BEG!
*Not true.
BAMMM
IT'S NO USE!
FOR SOME REASON, I CAN'T STOP MYSELF FROM FOLLOWING HER ORDERS!
HELP HER BLOW HER NOSE ...? THAT'S EASY.
BUT...
BUT HOW CAN I ALLOW MYSELF TO TAKE ORDERS FROM A HOS-TAGE?!
PA-SHOO!
BLAAT
COME ON, ONCE MORE!
BLAAT
tippy tippy
Whoa...
Great Red Siberian...

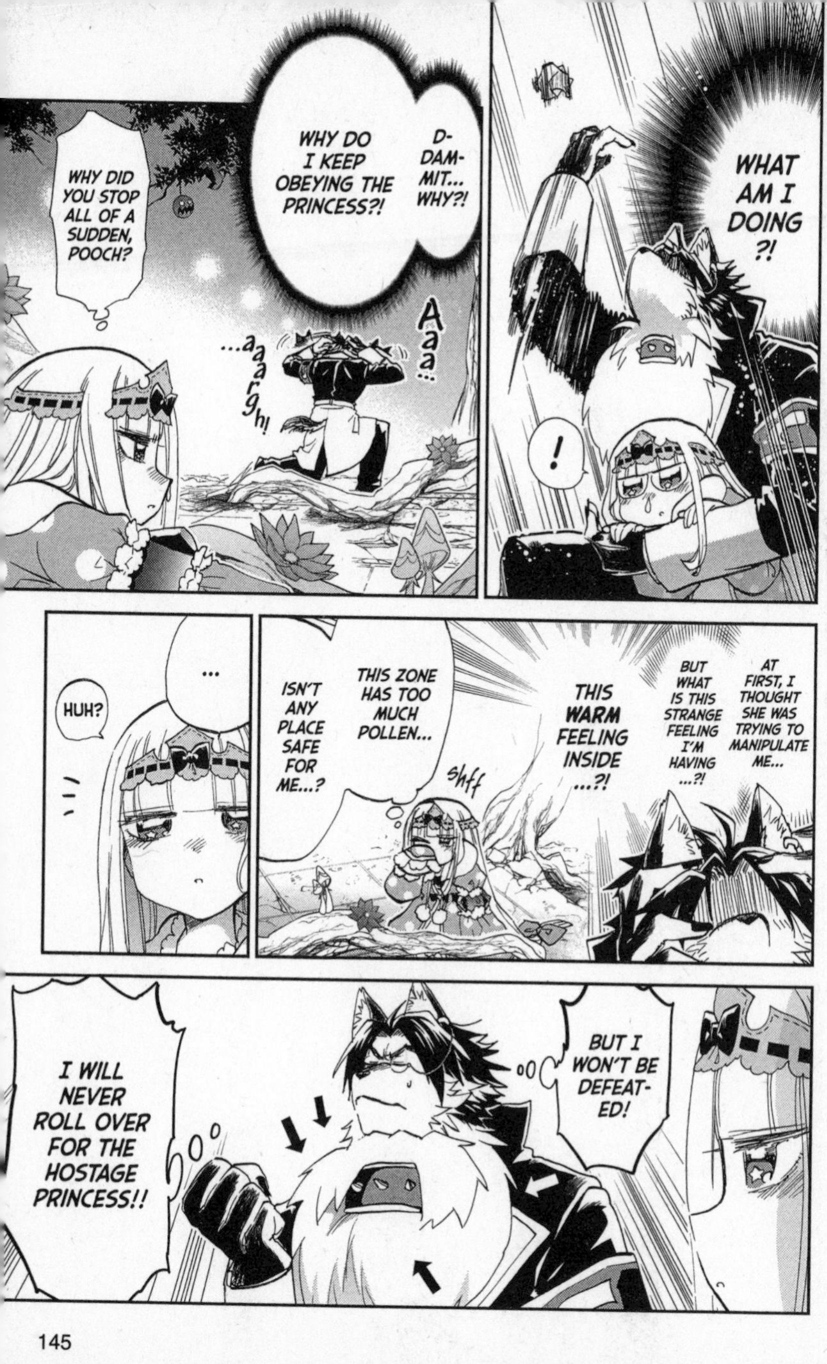
WHAT AM I DOING?!
!
D-DAMMIT... WHY?!
WHY DO I KEEP OBEYING THE PRINCESS?!
Aaa...aaargh!
WHY DID YOU STOP ALL OF A SUDDEN, POOCH?
AT FIRST, I THOUGHT SHE WAS TRYING TO MANIPULATE ME...
BUT WHAT IS THIS STRANGE FEELING I'M HAVING...?!
THIS **WARM** FEELING INSIDE...?!
shff
THIS ZONE HAS TOO MUCH POLLEN...
ISN'T ANY PLACE SAFE FOR ME...?
...
HUH?
BUT I WON'T BE DEFEATED!
I WILL NEVER ROLL OVER FOR THE HOSTAGE PRINCESS!!

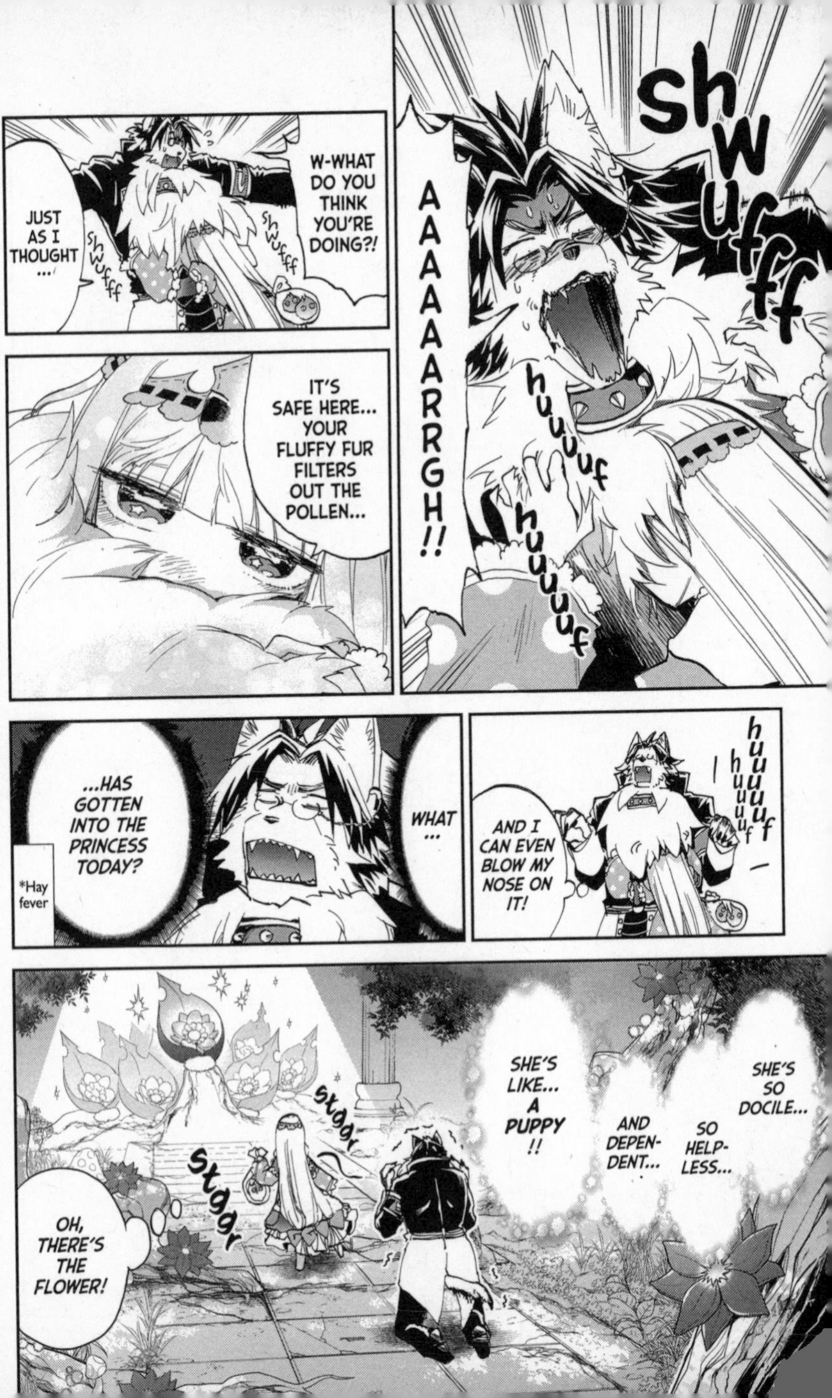
Shwufff
AAAAAAARRGH!!
huuuuf
huuuuuuf
W-WHAT DO YOU THINK YOU'RE DOING?!
shwufff
shwufff
JUST AS I THOUGHT...
IT'S SAFE HERE... YOUR FLUFFY FUR FILTERS OUT THE POLLEN...
huuuuuf
huuuuuf
AND I CAN EVEN BLOW MY NOSE ON IT!
WHAT...
...HAS GOTTEN INTO THE PRINCESS TODAY?
*Hay fever
SHE'S SO DOCILE...
SO HELP-LESS...
AND DEPEN-DENT...
SHE'S LIKE... A PUPPY!!
stggr
stggr
OH, THERE'S THE FLOWER!

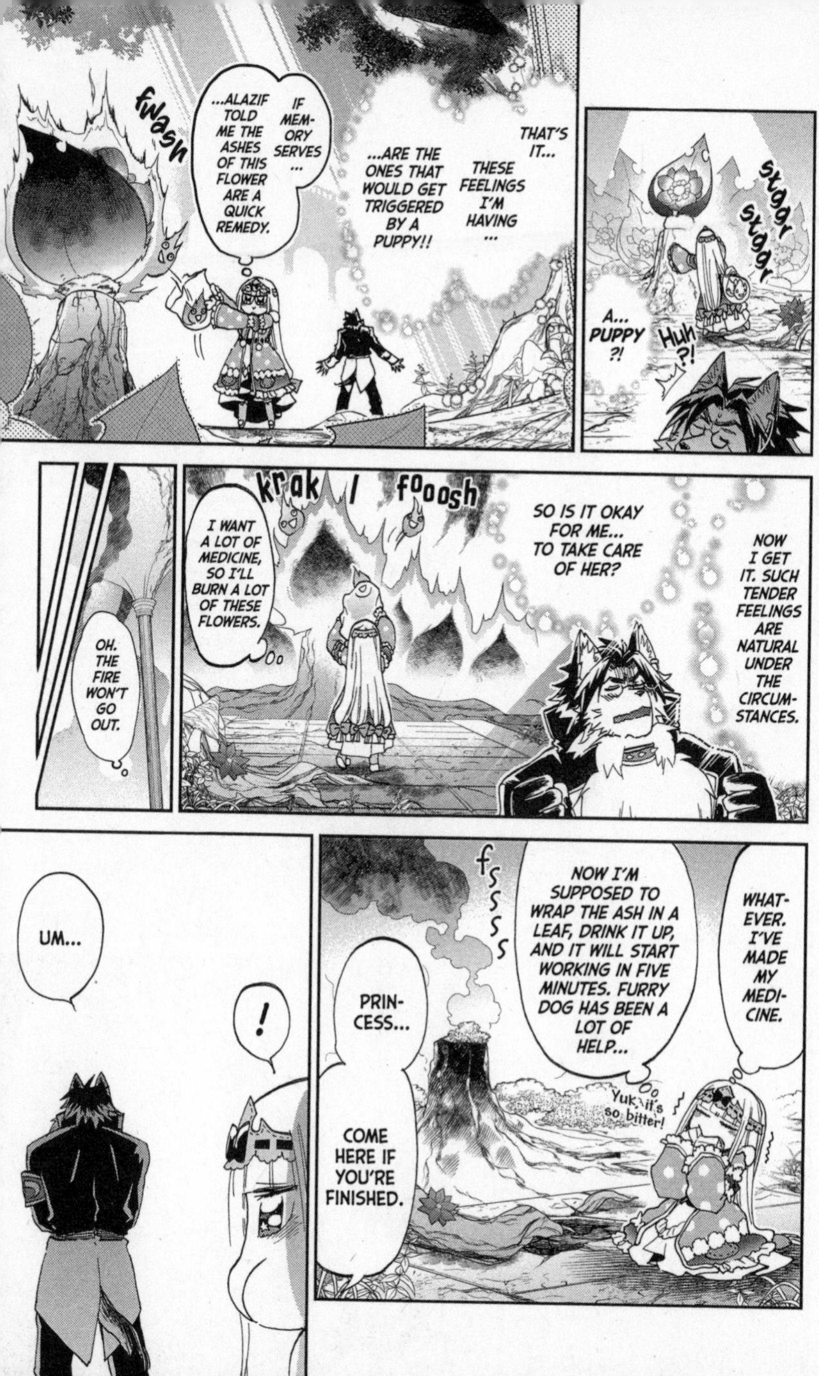
stggr stggr
Huh?!
A... PUPPY?!
fwash
IF MEMORY SERVES...
...ALAZIF TOLD ME THE ASHES OF THIS FLOWER ARE A QUICK REMEDY.
THAT'S IT... THESE FEELINGS I'M HAVING...
...ARE THE ONES THAT WOULD GET TRIGGERED BY A PUPPY!!
NOW I GET IT. SUCH TENDER FEELINGS ARE NATURAL UNDER THE CIRCUMSTANCES.
SO IS IT OKAY FOR ME... TO TAKE CARE OF HER?
foooosh
krak
I WANT A LOT OF MEDICINE, SO I'LL BURN A LOT OF THESE FLOWERS.
OH. THE FIRE WON'T GO OUT.
WHATEVER. I'VE MADE MY MEDICINE.
Yuk, it's so bitter!
NOW I'M SUPPOSED TO WRAP THE ASH IN A LEAF, DRINK IT UP, AND IT WILL START WORKING IN FIVE MINUTES. FURRY DOG HAS BEEN A LOT OF HELP...
fssss
PRINCESS...
COME HERE IF YOU'RE FINISHED.
!
UM...

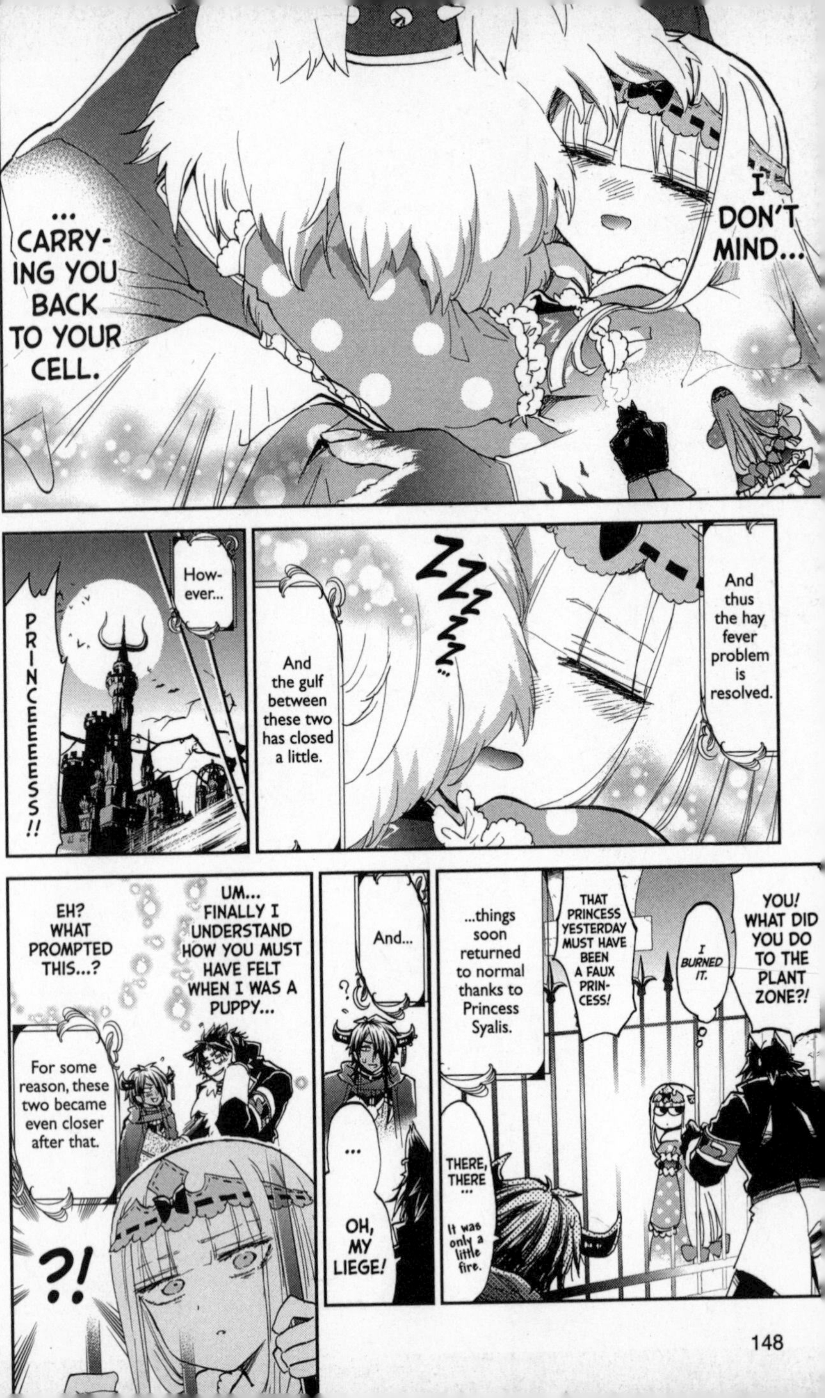
I DON'T MIND...
... CARRYING YOU BACK TO YOUR CELL.
And thus the hay fever problem is resolved.
ZZZZZ...
And the gulf between these two has closed a little.
However...
PRINCEEEEESS!!
YOU! WHAT DID YOU DO TO THE PLANT ZONE?!
I BURNED IT.
THAT PRINCESS YESTERDAY MUST HAVE BEEN A FAUX PRINCESS!
...things soon returned to normal thanks to Princess Syalis.
THERE, THERE ...
It was only a little fire.
And...
...
OH, MY LIEGE!
UM... FINALLY I UNDERSTAND HOW YOU MUST HAVE FELT WHEN I WAS A PUPPY...
EH? WHAT PROMPTED THIS...?
For some reason, these two became even closer after that.
?!

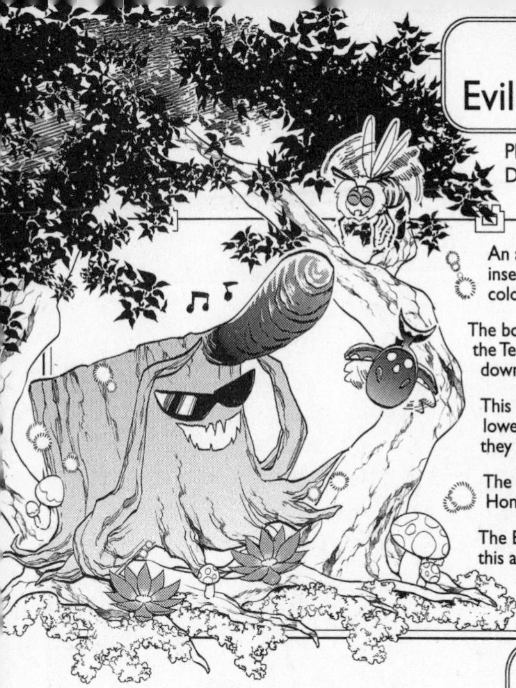

♫ ♪

Plant Zone
Evil Flower Garden

Pleasing Scent: ☆☆☆☆☆☆☆☆
Deadliness: ☆☆☆☆☆☆☆☆☆☆

An area for the plant species and demon insect species with flower beds varying in color from gold to white.

The boss of this zone is Neo Alraune, one of the Ten Guardians. She has decided to tone down the creepy vibe of the area.

This is the type of level where people lower their guard and end up dead before they know it.

The specialty item here is High-Quality Honey.

The Bee-Bee Worker demons live here, so this area has suffered the greatest number of casualties thanks to the princess.

Predominant Plant Zone Demon

Neo Alraune
Evil Wooden Man
Bee-Bee Worker
Massacre Rhinoceros Beetle
And others

▼

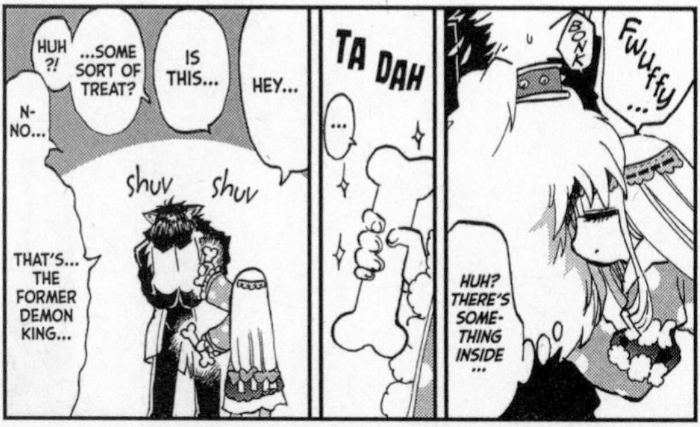

Fwuffy...
BONK
HUH? THERE'S SOME-THING INSIDE...
TA DAH
...
HEY...
IS THIS...
...SOME SORT OF TREAT?
HUH ?!
N-NO...
shuv shuv
THAT'S... THE FORMER DEMON KING...

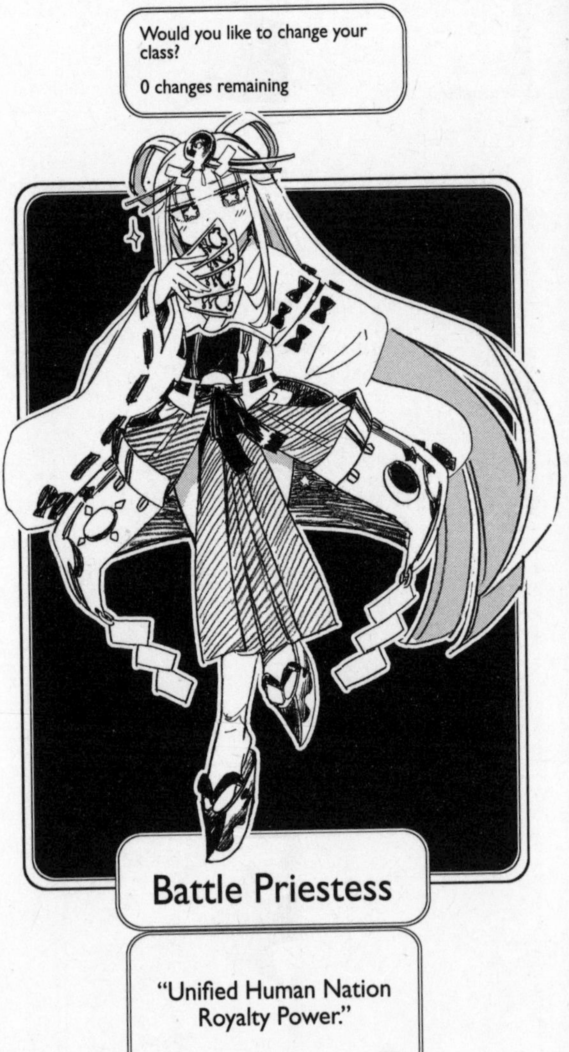
Would you like to change your class?
0 changes remaining
Battle Priestess
"Unified Human Nation Royalty Power."

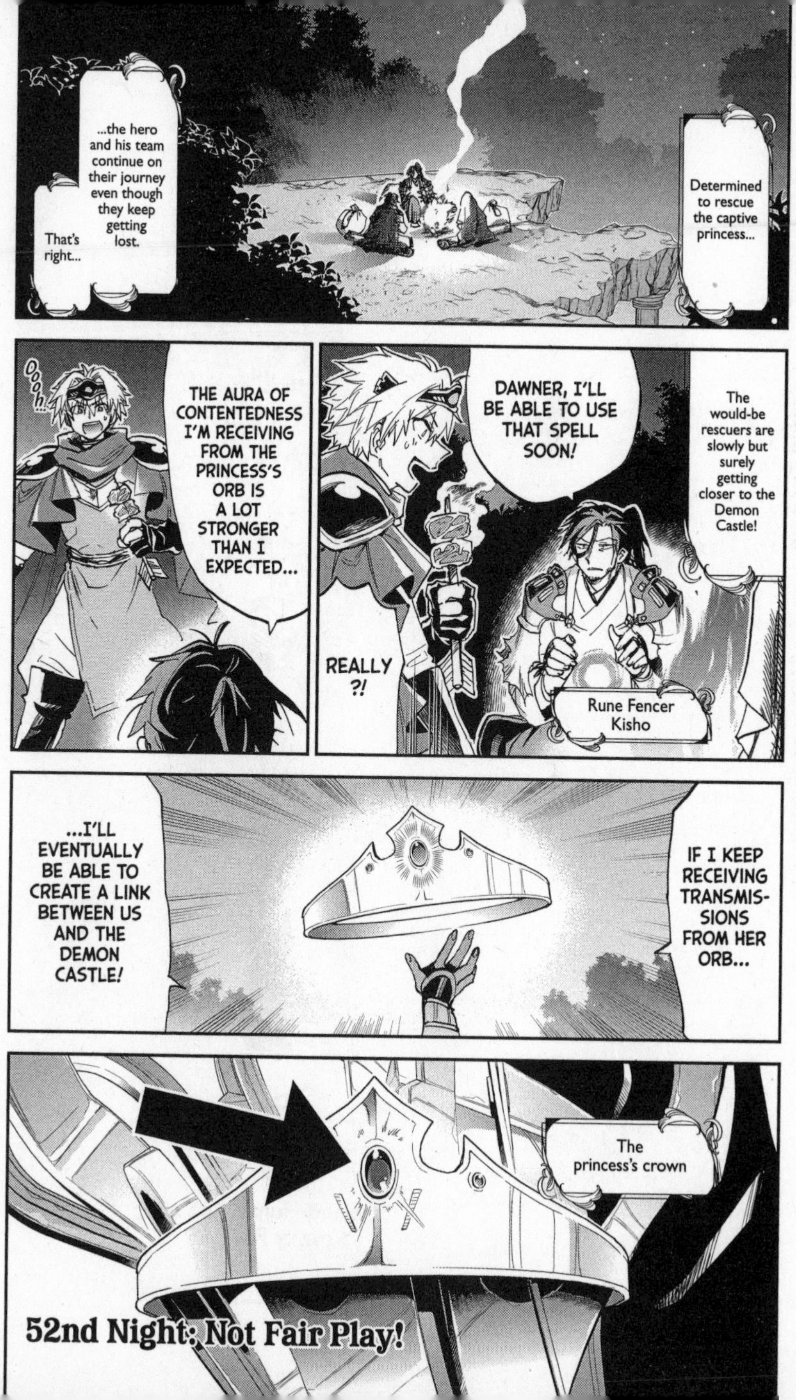
Determined to rescue the captive princess...
That's right...
...the hero and his team continue on their journey even though they keep getting lost.
The would-be rescuers are slowly but surely getting closer to the Demon Castle!
DAWNER, I'LL BE ABLE TO USE THAT SPELL SOON!
REALLY ?!
Rune Fencer Kisho
Oooh...
THE AURA OF CONTENTEDNESS I'M RECEIVING FROM THE PRINCESS'S ORB IS A LOT STRONGER THAN I EXPECTED...
IF I KEEP RECEIVING TRANSMIS-SIONS FROM HER ORB...
...I'LL EVENTUALLY BE ABLE TO CREATE A LINK BETWEEN US AND THE DEMON CASTLE!
The princess's crown
52nd Night: Not Fair Play!

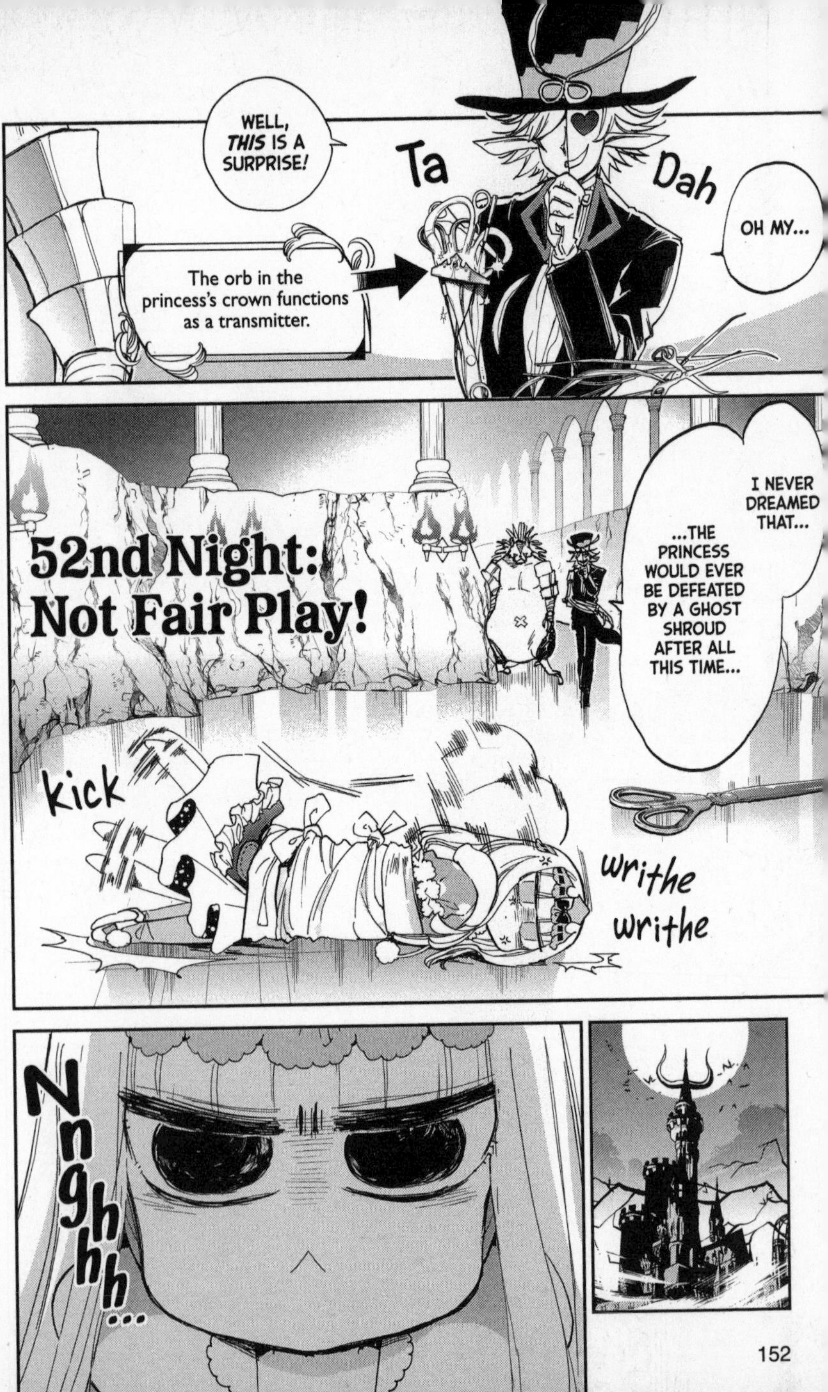
WELL, *THIS* IS A SURPRISE!
Ta
Dah
OH MY...
The orb in the princess's crown functions as a transmitter.
I NEVER DREAMED THAT...
...THE PRINCESS WOULD EVER BE DEFEATED BY A GHOST SHROUD AFTER ALL THIS TIME...
52nd Night: Not Fair Play!
writhe
writhe
kick
Nnghhh...

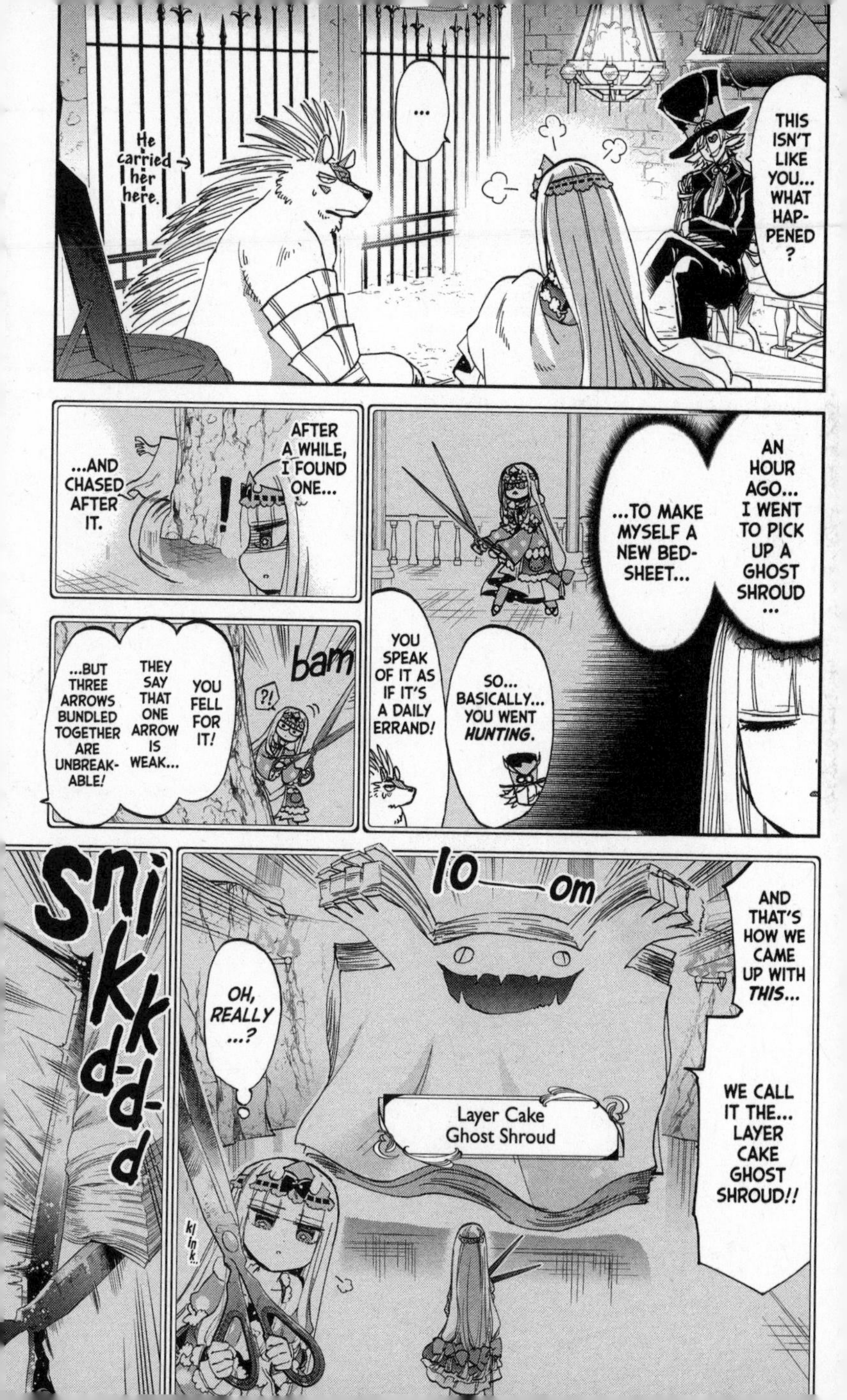
THIS ISN'T LIKE YOU... WHAT HAPPENED?
...
He carried her here.
AN HOUR AGO... I WENT TO PICK UP A GHOST SHROUD...
...TO MAKE MYSELF A NEW BEDSHEET...
AFTER A WHILE, I FOUND ONE...
...AND CHASED AFTER IT.
SO... BASICALLY... YOU WENT HUNTING.
YOU SPEAK OF IT AS IF IT'S A DAILY ERRAND!
bam
?!
YOU FELL FOR IT!
THEY SAY THAT ONE ARROW IS WEAK...
...BUT THREE ARROWS BUNDLED TOGETHER ARE UNBREAKABLE!
lo—om
AND THAT'S HOW WE CAME UP WITH THIS...
WE CALL IT THE... LAYER CAKE GHOST SHROUD!!
Layer Cake Ghost Shroud
OH, REALLY...?
klink...
Snikkd-d-d

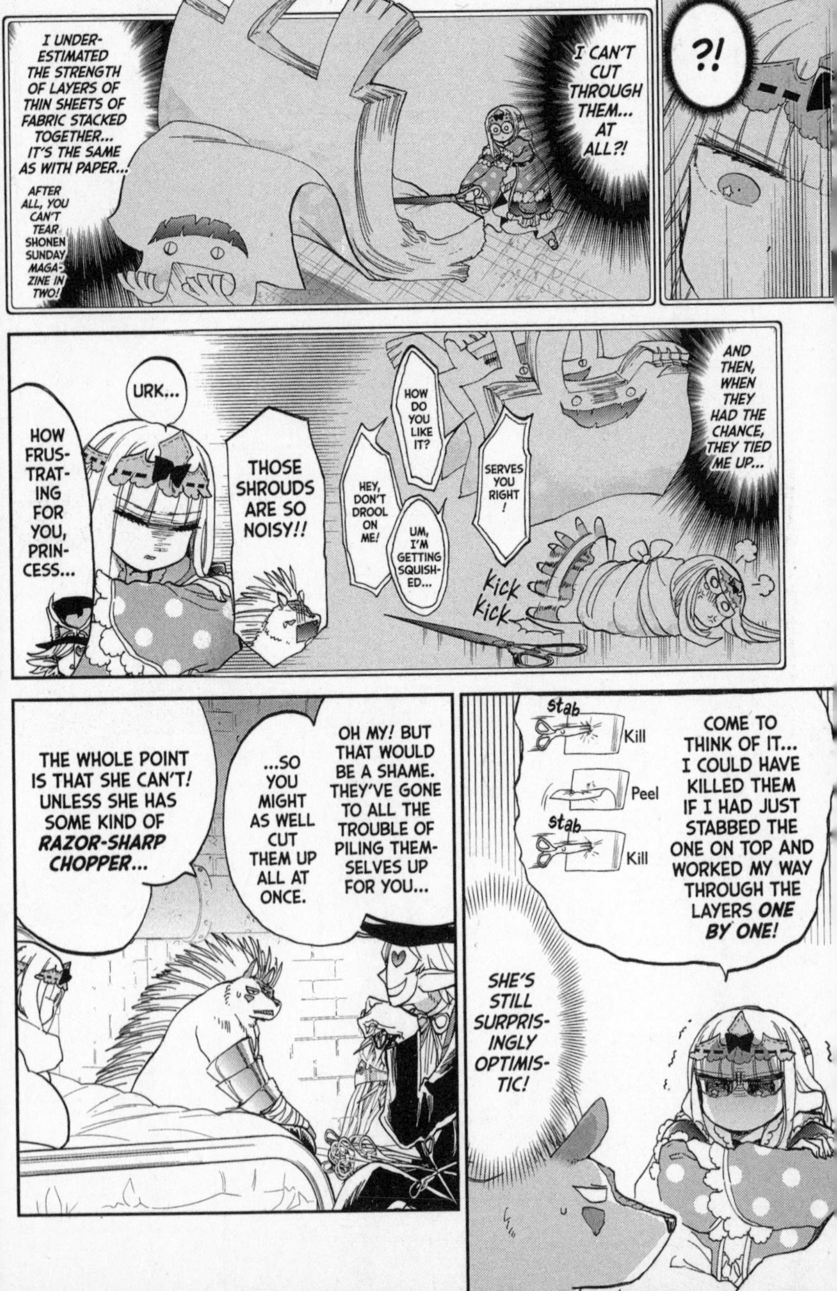
?!
I CAN'T CUT THROUGH THEM... AT ALL?!
I UNDERESTIMATED THE STRENGTH OF LAYERS OF THIN SHEETS OF FABRIC STACKED TOGETHER... IT'S THE SAME AS WITH PAPER...
AFTER ALL, YOU CAN'T TEAR SHONEN SUNDAY MAGAZINE IN TWO!
AND THEN, WHEN THEY HAD THE CHANCE, THEY TIED ME UP...
SERVES YOU RIGHT!
HOW DO YOU LIKE IT?
UM, I'M GETTING SQUISHED...
HEY, DON'T DROOL ON ME!
KICK KICK
THOSE SHROUDS ARE SO NOISY!!
URK...
HOW FRUSTRATING FOR YOU, PRINCESS...
COME TO THINK OF IT... I COULD HAVE KILLED THEM IF I HAD JUST STABBED THE ONE ON TOP AND WORKED MY WAY THROUGH THE LAYERS ONE BY ONE!
stab
Kill
Peel
stab
Kill
SHE'S STILL SURPRISINGLY OPTIMISTIC!
OH MY! BUT THAT WOULD BE A SHAME. THEY'VE GONE TO ALL THE TROUBLE OF PILING THEMSELVES UP FOR YOU...
...SO YOU MIGHT AS WELL CUT THEM UP ALL AT ONCE.
THE WHOLE POINT IS THAT SHE CAN'T! UNLESS SHE HAS SOME KIND OF RAZOR-SHARP CHOPPER...

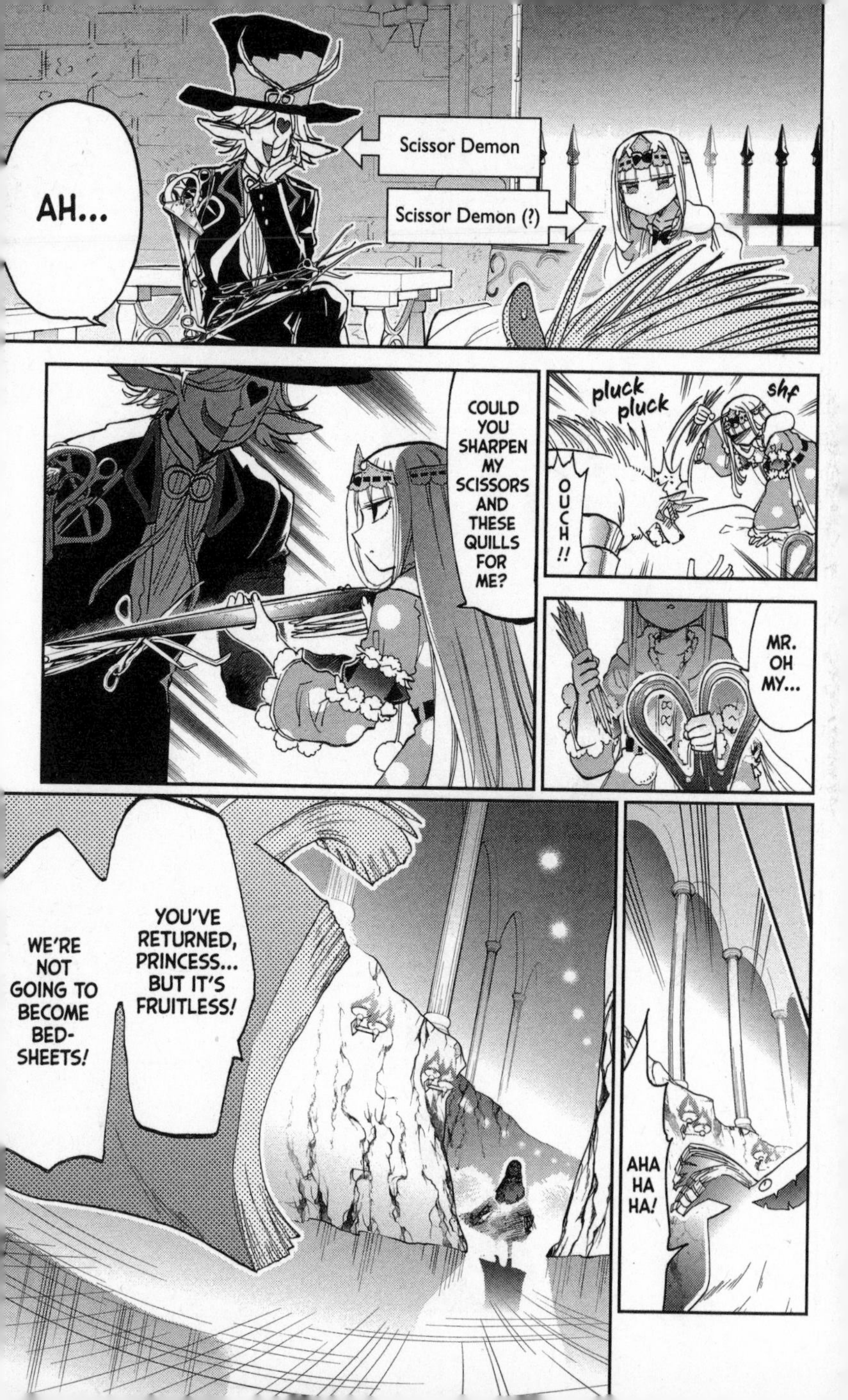
Scissor Demon
Scissor Demon (?)
AH...
shf
pluck pluck
OUCH!!
MR. OH MY...
COULD YOU SHARPEN MY SCISSORS AND THESE QUILLS FOR ME?
AHA HA HA!
YOU'VE RETURNED, PRINCESS... BUT IT'S FRUITLESS!
WE'RE NOT GOING TO BECOME BED-SHEETS!

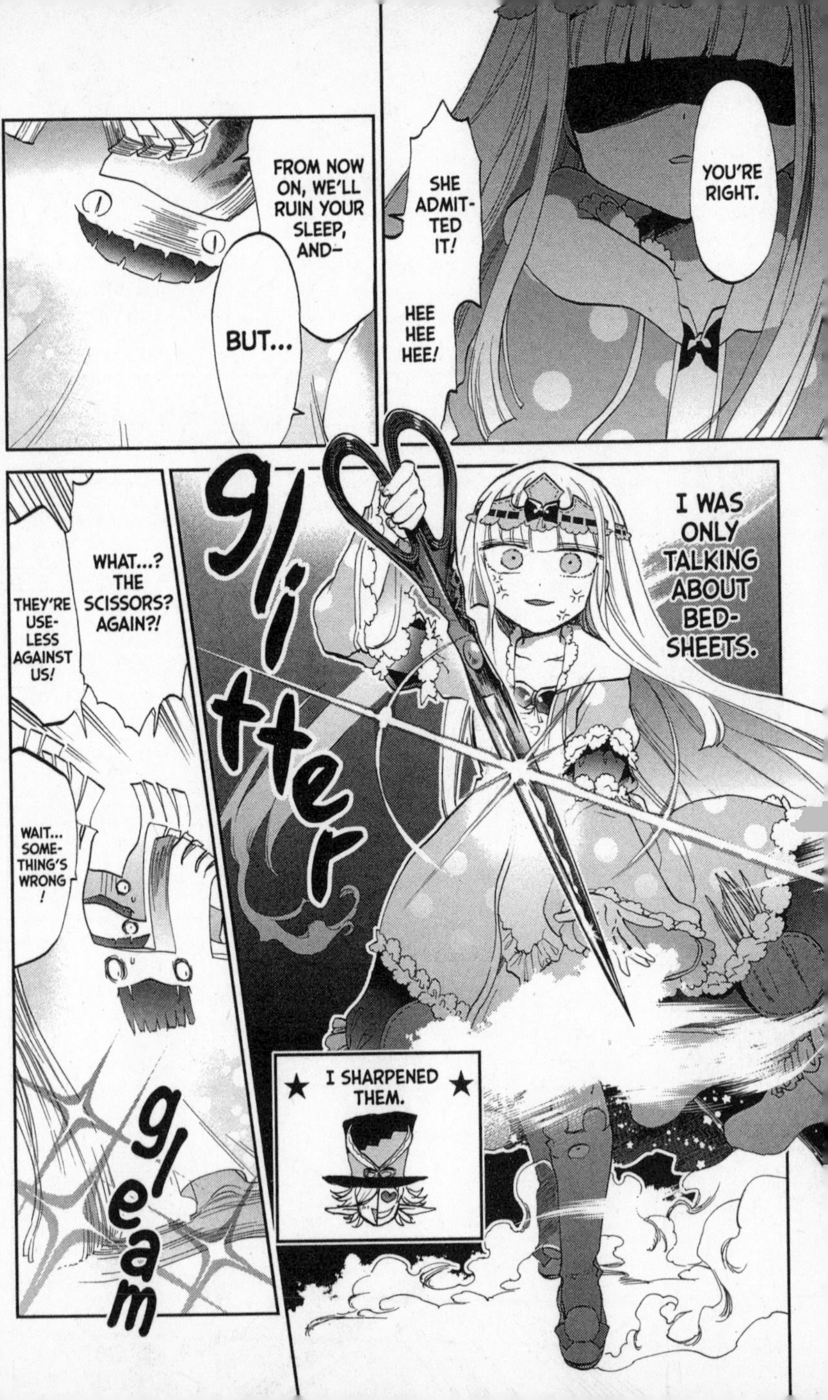
YOU'RE RIGHT.
SHE ADMIT-TED IT!
HEE HEE HEE!
FROM NOW ON, WE'LL RUIN YOUR SLEEP, AND–
BUT...
I WAS ONLY TALKING ABOUT BED-SHEETS.
glitter
WHAT...? THE SCISSORS? AGAIN?!
THEY'RE USE-LESS AGAINST US!
WAIT... SOME-THING'S WRONG!
gleam
★ I SHARPENED THEM. ★

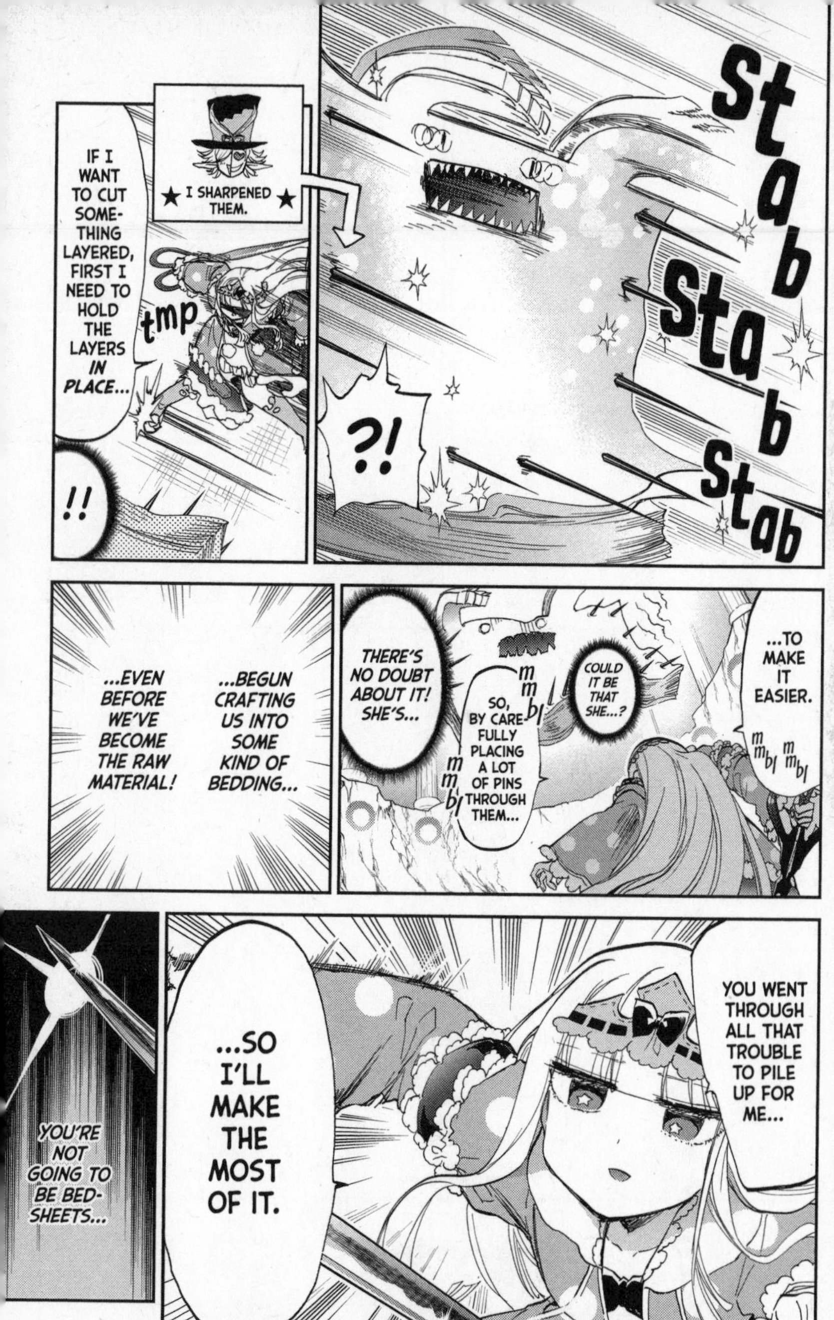
Stab
Stab
Stab
Stab
?!
IF I WANT TO CUT SOME-THING LAYERED, FIRST I NEED TO HOLD THE LAYERS *IN PLACE...*
★ I SHARPENED THEM. ★
tmp
!!
...TO MAKE IT EASIER.
mmbl mmbl
COULD IT BE THAT SHE...?
mmbl
SO, BY CARE-FULLY PLACING A LOT OF PINS THROUGH THEM...
mmbl
THERE'S NO DOUBT ABOUT IT! SHE'S...
...BEGUN CRAFTING US INTO SOME KIND OF BEDDING...
...EVEN BEFORE WE'VE BECOME THE RAW MATERIAL!
YOU WENT THROUGH ALL THAT TROUBLE TO PILE UP FOR ME...
...SO I'LL MAKE THE MOST OF IT.
YOU'RE NOT GOING TO BE BED-SHEETS...

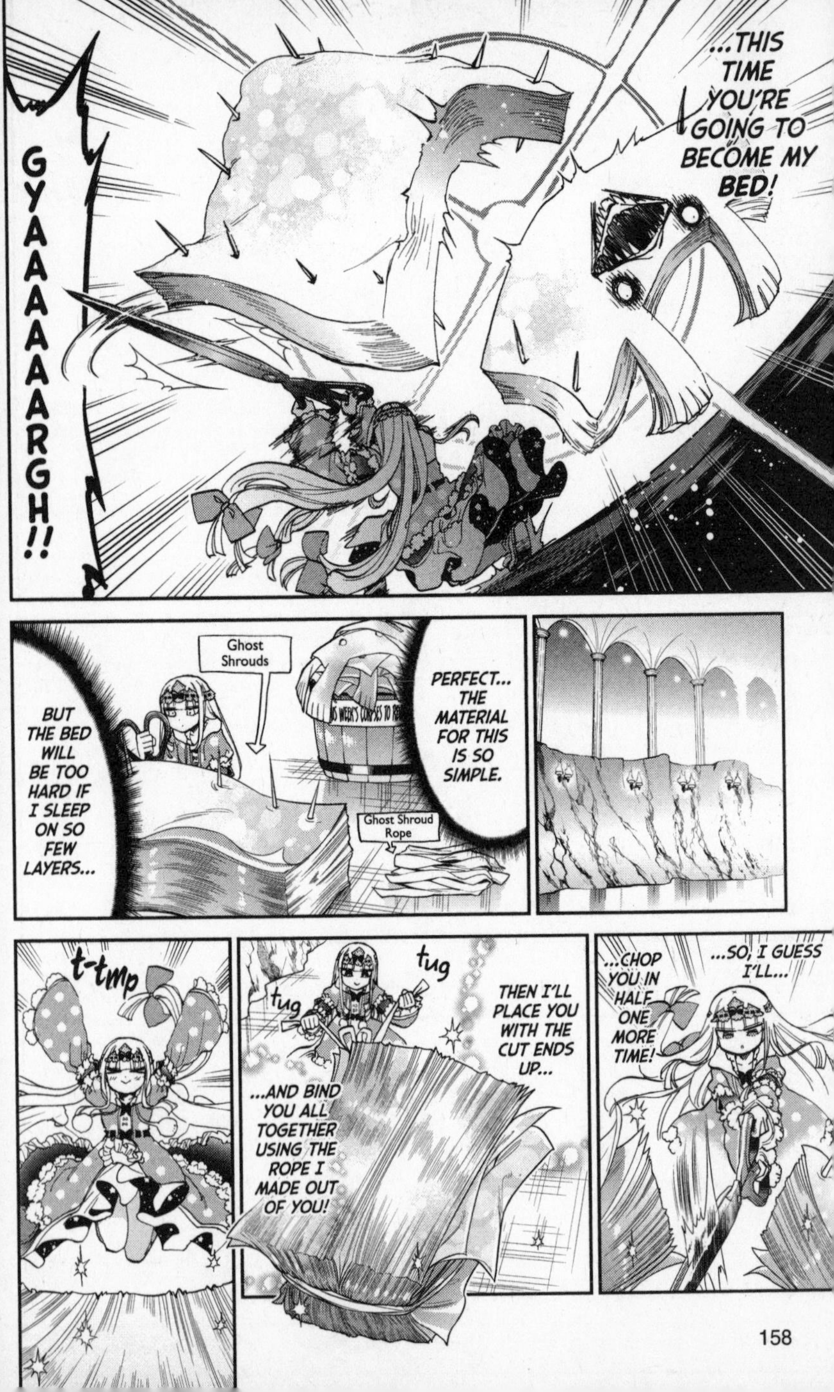
...THIS TIME YOU'RE GOING TO BECOME MY BED!
GYAAAAAAARGH!!
PERFECT... THE MATERIAL FOR THIS IS SO SIMPLE.
Ghost Shrouds
BUT THE BED WILL BE TOO HARD IF I SLEEP ON SO FEW LAYERS...
Ghost Shroud Rope
...SO, I GUESS I'LL...
...CHOP YOU IN HALF ONE MORE TIME!
THEN I'LL PLACE YOU WITH THE CUT ENDS UP...
tug
tug
...AND BIND YOU ALL TOGETHER USING THE ROPE I MADE OUT OF YOU!
t-tmp

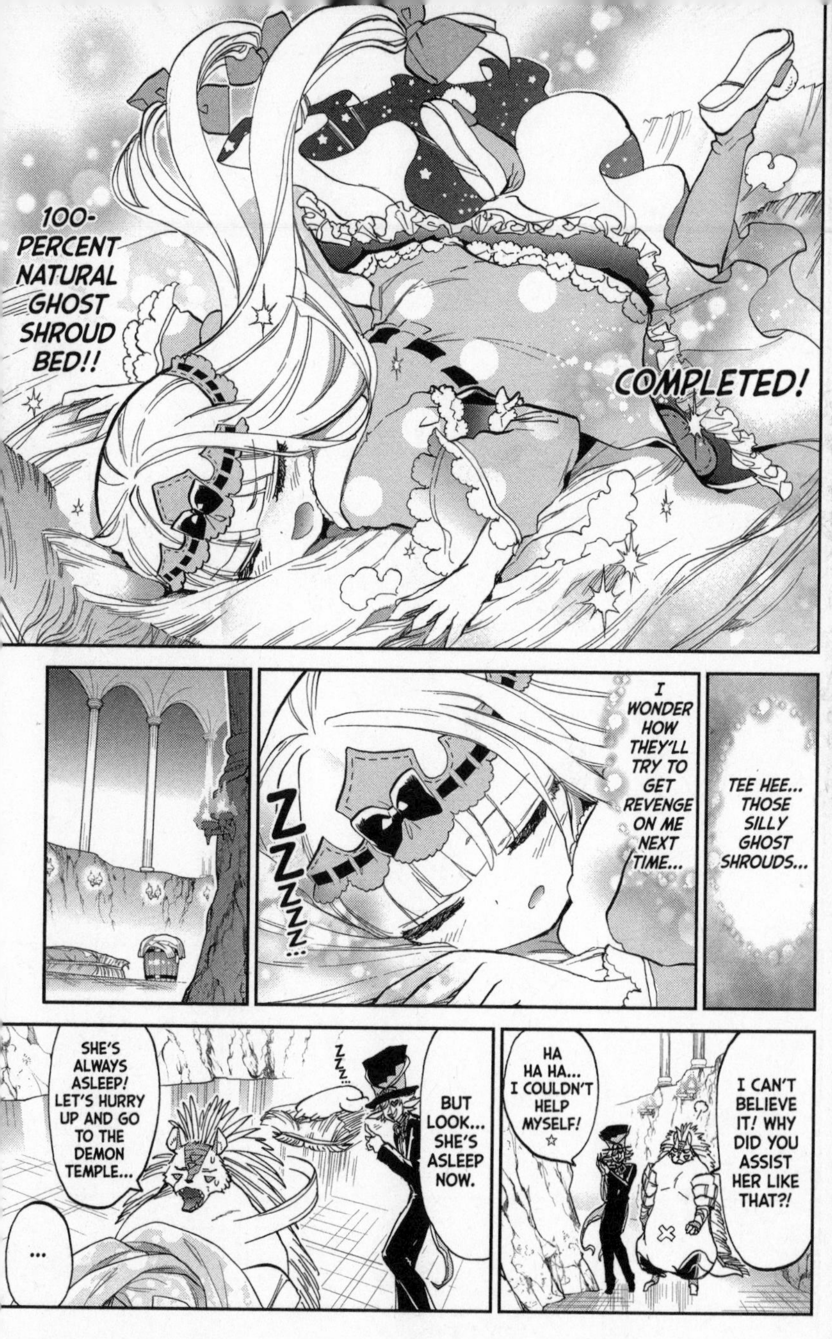
100-PERCENT NATURAL GHOST SHROUD BED!!
COMPLETED!
TEE HEE... THOSE SILLY GHOST SHROUDS...
I WONDER HOW THEY'LL TRY TO GET REVENGE ON ME NEXT TIME...
ZZZZZ...
I CAN'T BELIEVE IT! WHY DID YOU ASSIST HER LIKE THAT?!
HA HA HA... I COULDN'T HELP MYSELF! ☆
BUT LOOK... SHE'S ASLEEP NOW.
ZZZ...
SHE'S ALWAYS ASLEEP! LET'S HURRY UP AND GO TO THE DEMON TEMPLE...
...

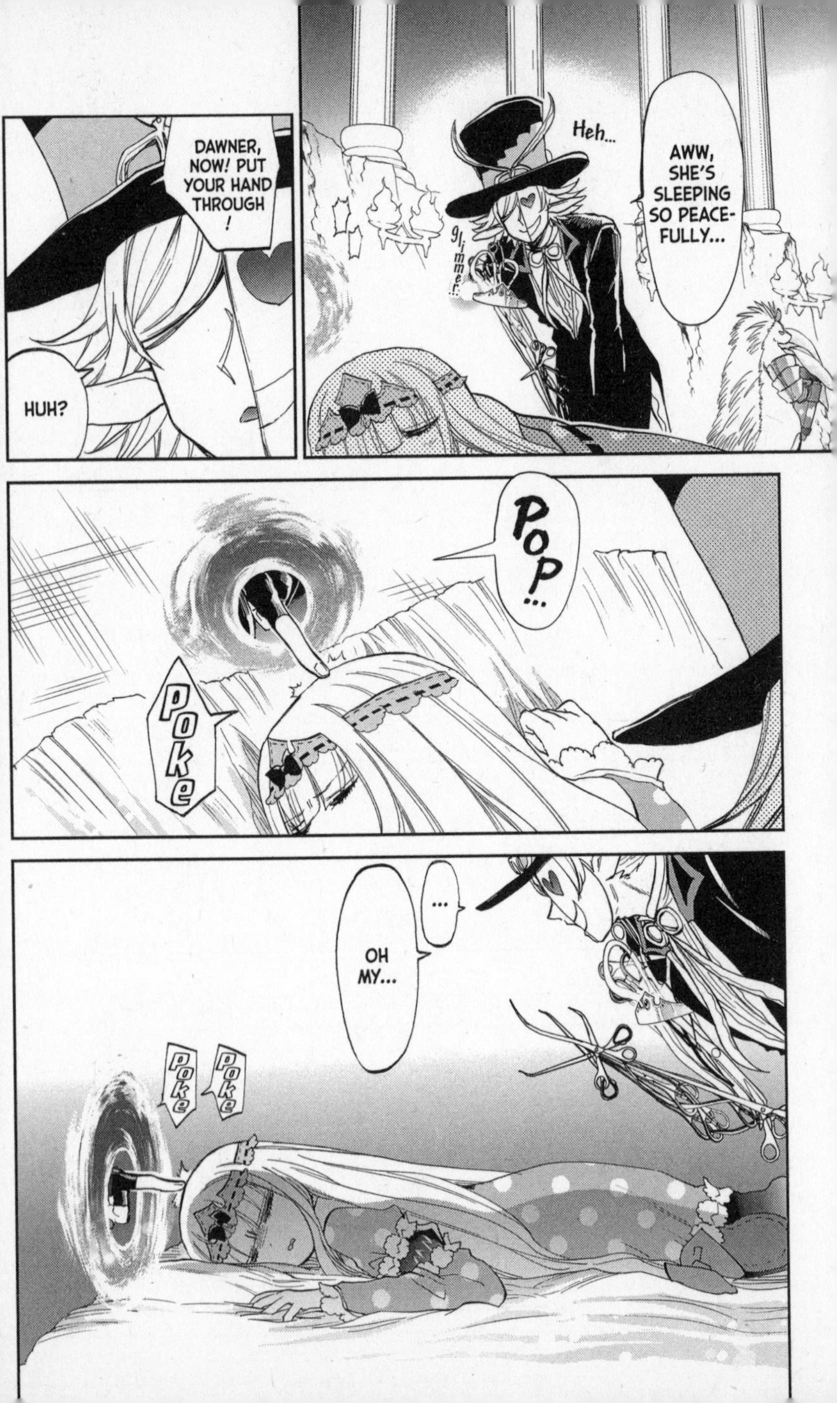

AWW, SHE'S SLEEPING SO PEACE-FULLY...
Heh...
glimmer
DAWNER, NOW! PUT YOUR HAND THROUGH!
HUH?
POP...
Poke
...
OH MY...
Poke
Poke

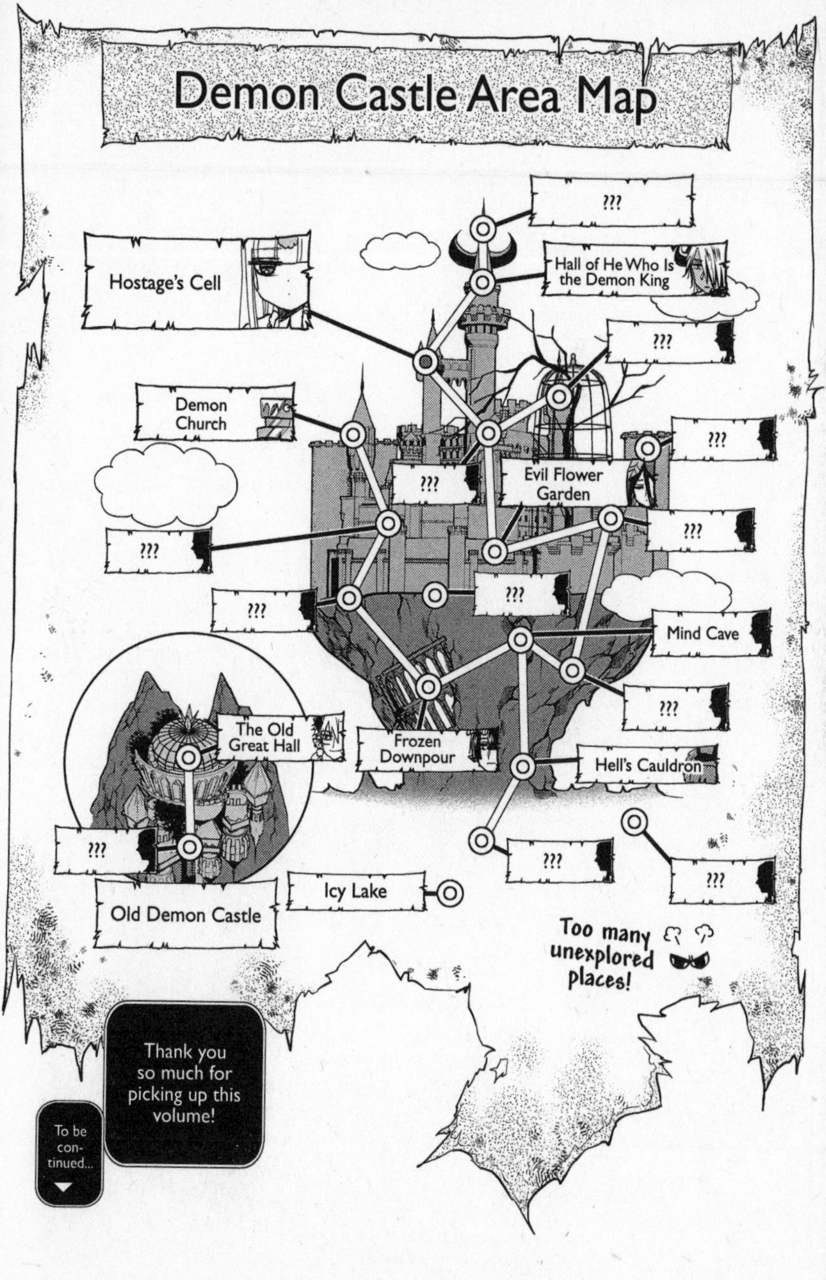
Demon Castle Area Map
???
Hall of He Who Is the Demon King
Hostage's Cell
???
Demon Church
???
Evil Flower Garden
???
???
???
???
???
Mind Cave
???
The Old Great Hall
Frozen Downpour
Hell's Cauldron
???
???
???
Icy Lake
Old Demon Castle
Too many unexplored places!
Thank you so much for picking up this volume!
To be con-tinued...

The following appears to be a bonus manga.
Will you continue?

▶ Yes
No

Two popular series in *Weekly Shonen Sunday* magazine!

Komi Can't Communicate × Sleepy Princess in the Demon Castle

A meeting of two characters who would never be expected to meet...?! It's a *Shonen Sunday* heroine collaboration manga!

Sleepy Princess in Komi's House
(Originally printed in *Weekly Shonen Sunday* Super Extra Issue, March 2017)

▶ Page 163

From (KYUNPAD),
a recipe site that provides instructions on how to gift Valentine's Day chocolate!!

It's hard to believe that Princess Syalis would give anyone chocolate for free...

Not Everything That Looks Tasty Is...

▶ Page 167

Bonus Chapter: Sleepy Princess in Komi's House

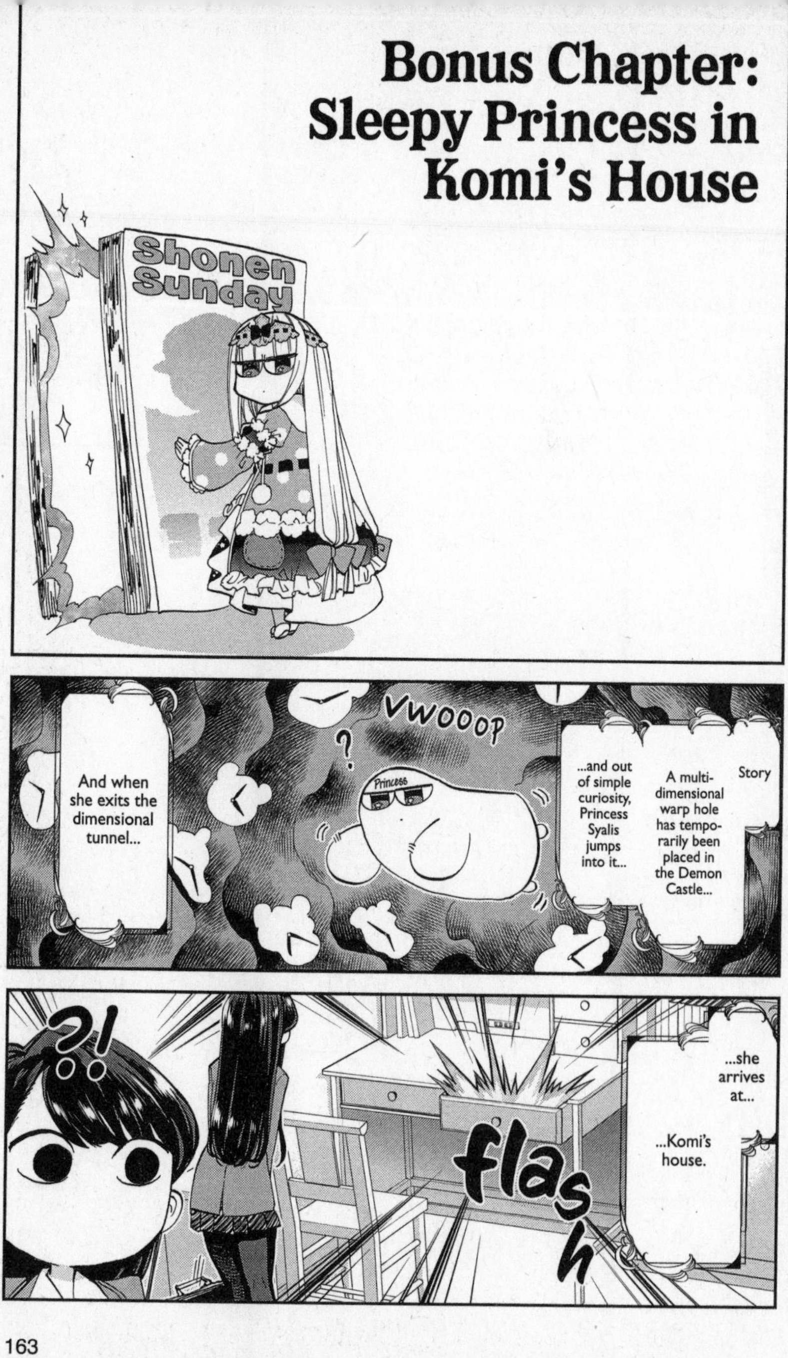

Shonen Sunday
Story
A multi-dimensional warp hole has temporarily been placed in the Demon Castle...
...and out of simple curiosity, Princess Syalis jumps into it...
VWOOOP
Princess
?
And when she exits the dimensional tunnel...
...she arrives at...
...Komi's house.
flash
?!

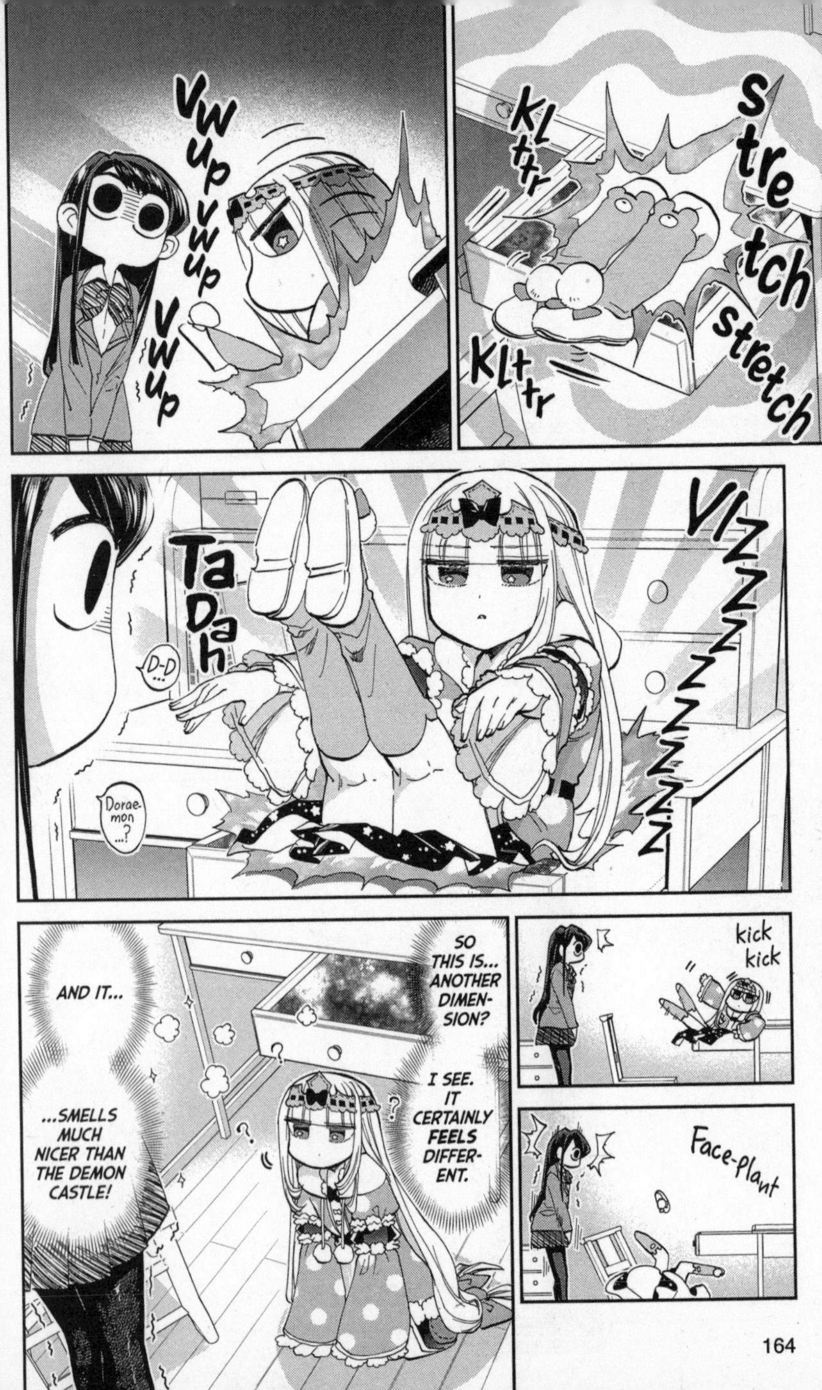
stretch
stretch
KLttr
KLttr
VWup
VWup
VWup
VIZZZZZZZZZZ
TaDah
D-D...
Doraemon...?
kick kick
Face-plant
SO THIS IS... ANOTHER DIMENSION?
I SEE. IT CERTAINLY FEELS DIFFERENT.
AND IT...
...SMELLS MUCH NICER THAN THE DEMON CASTLE!

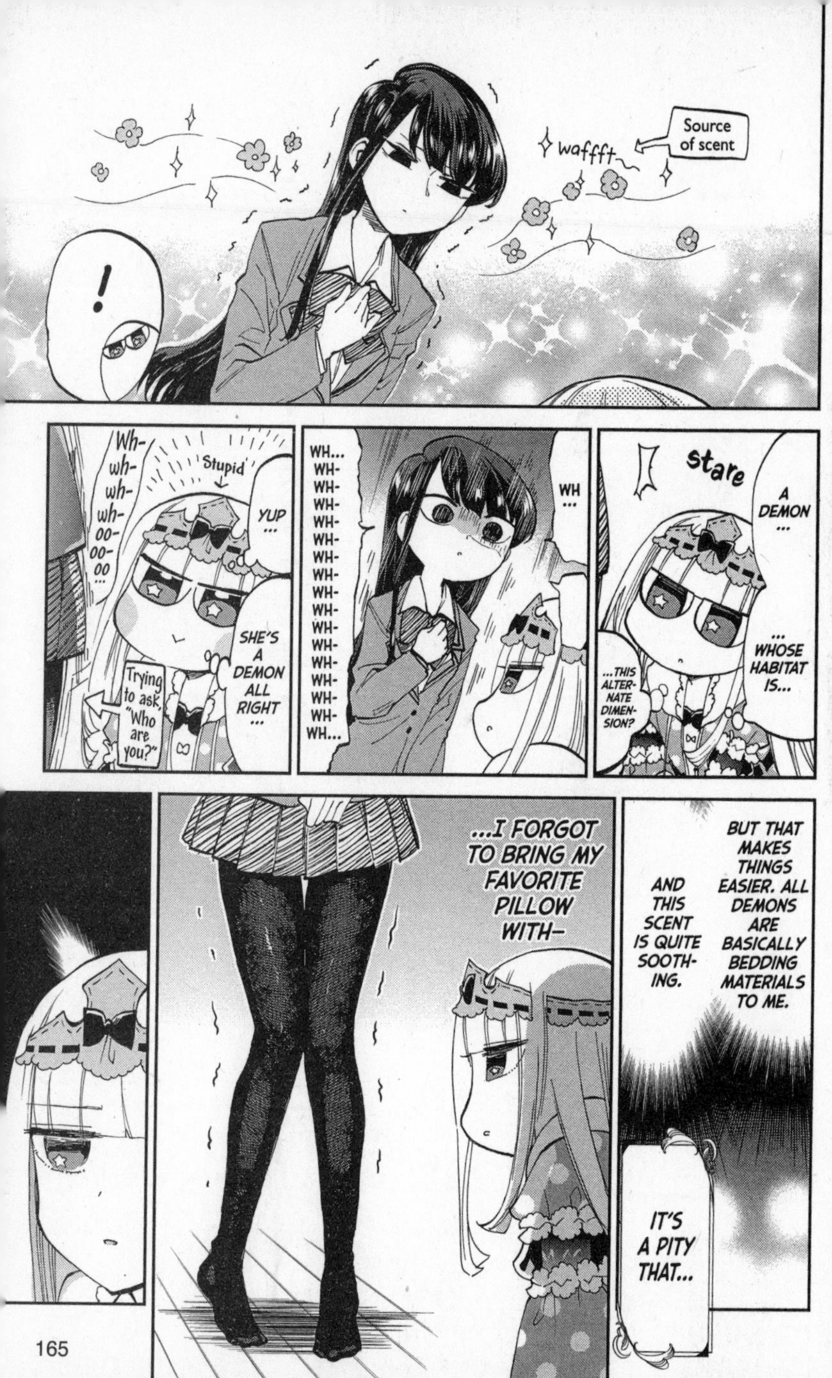

Source of scent
waffft
!
A DEMON...
stare
... WHOSE HABITAT IS...
...THIS ALTERNATE DIMENSION?
WH...
WH... WH- WH- WH- WH- WH- WH- WH- WH- WH- WH- WH- WH- WH- WH- WH- WH- WH- WH...
Wh- wh- wh- wh- oo- oo- oo...
Stupid
YUP...
SHE'S A DEMON ALL RIGHT...
Trying to ask, "Who are you?"
BUT THAT MAKES THINGS EASIER. ALL DEMONS ARE BASICALLY BEDDING MATERIALS TO ME.
AND THIS SCENT IS QUITE SOOTHING.
IT'S A PITY THAT...
...I FORGOT TO BRING MY FAVORITE PILLOW WITH–

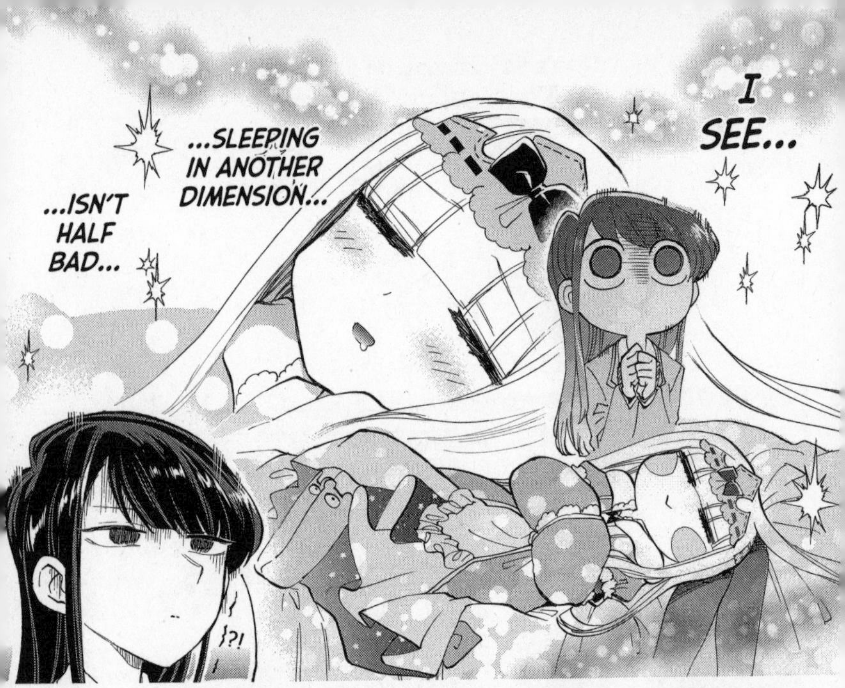
I SEE...
...SLEEPING IN ANOTHER DIMENSION...
...ISN'T HALF BAD...
?!

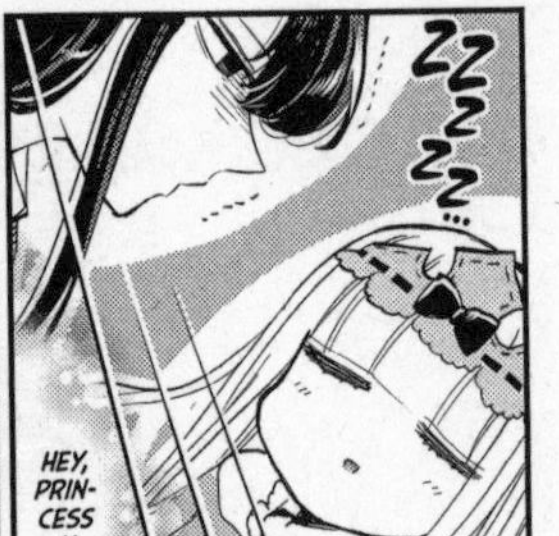
ZZZZZ...
HEY, PRINCESS!!

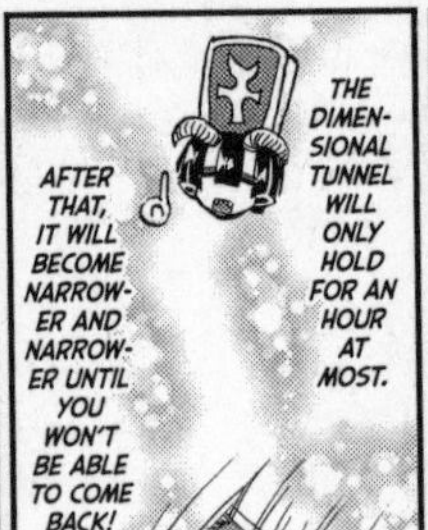
THE DIMENSIONAL TUNNEL WILL ONLY HOLD FOR AN HOUR AT MOST.
AFTER THAT, IT WILL BECOME NARROWER AND NARROWER UNTIL YOU WON'T BE ABLE TO COME BACK!

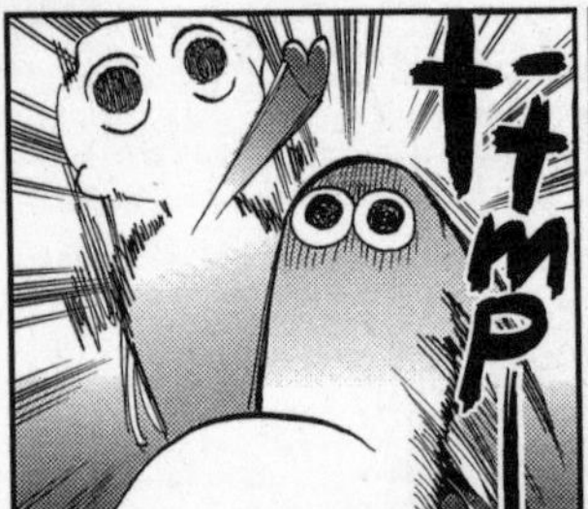
ttmp

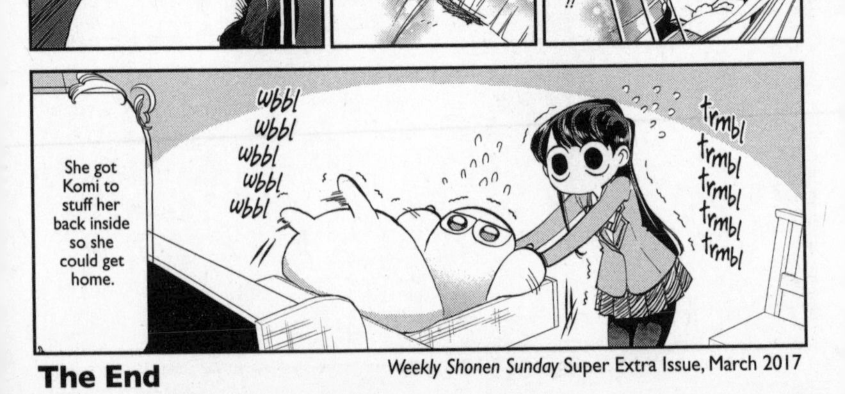
trmbl trmbl trmbl trmbl trmbl
wbbl wbbl wbbl wbbl wbbl
She got Komi to stuff her back inside so she could get home.

The End

Weekly Shonen Sunday Super Extra Issue, March 2017

How to Gift Valentine's Day Chocolate: Syalis Edition

Not Everything That Looks Tasty Is...

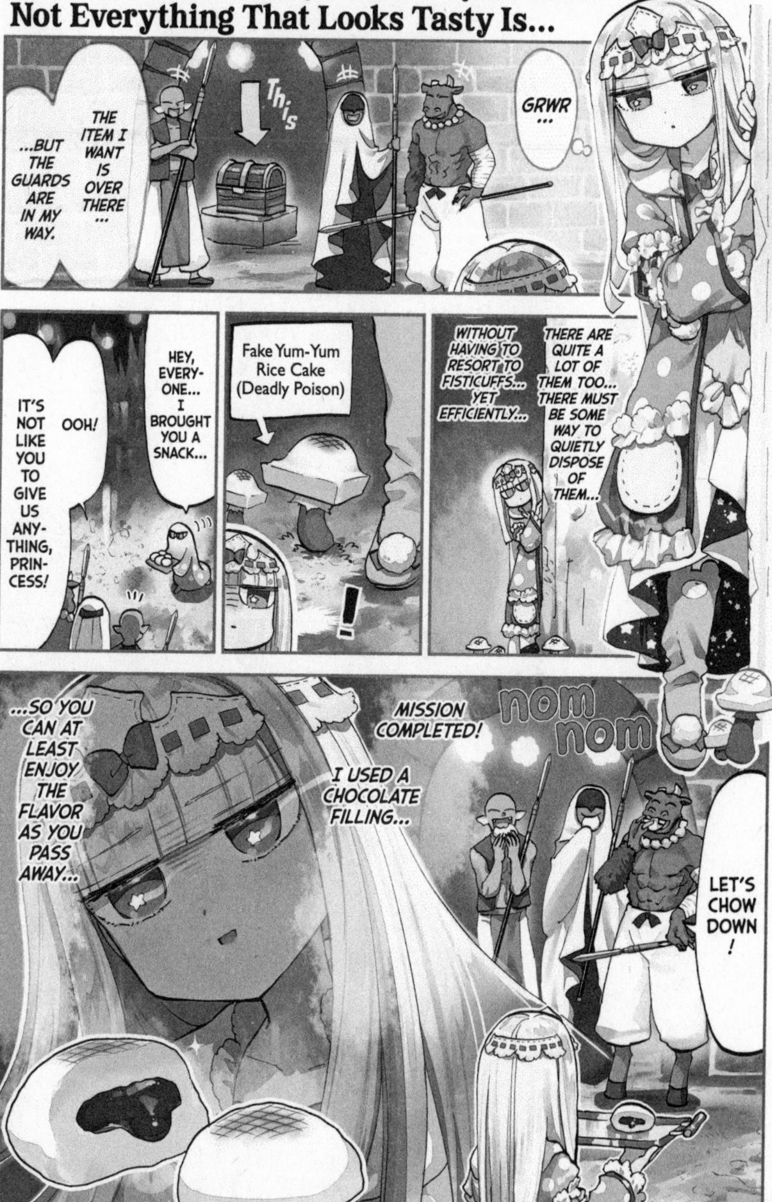
GRWR...
THE ITEM I WANT IS OVER THERE...
...BUT THE GUARDS ARE IN MY WAY.
This
THERE ARE QUITE A LOT OF THEM TOO... THERE MUST BE SOME WAY TO QUIETLY DISPOSE OF THEM...
WITHOUT HAVING TO RESORT TO FISTICUFFS... YET EFFICIENTLY...
Fake Yum-Yum Rice Cake (Deadly Poison)
HEY, EVERYONE... I BROUGHT YOU A SNACK...
OOH!
IT'S NOT LIKE YOU TO GIVE US ANYTHING, PRINCESS!
LET'S CHOW DOWN!
nom nom
MISSION COMPLETED!
I USED A CHOCOLATE FILLING...
...SO YOU CAN AT LEAST ENJOY THE FLAVOR AS YOU PASS AWAY...

From (KYUNPAD), a recipe site that provides instructions on how to gift Valentine's Day chocolate

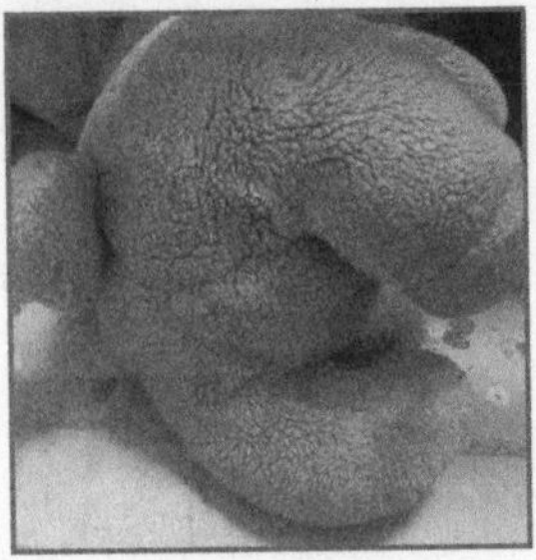

Hello, I'm Kumanomata. This is volume 4.
No matter how many times I look at them,
teddy bear butts are cute.

– KAGIJI KUMANOMATA

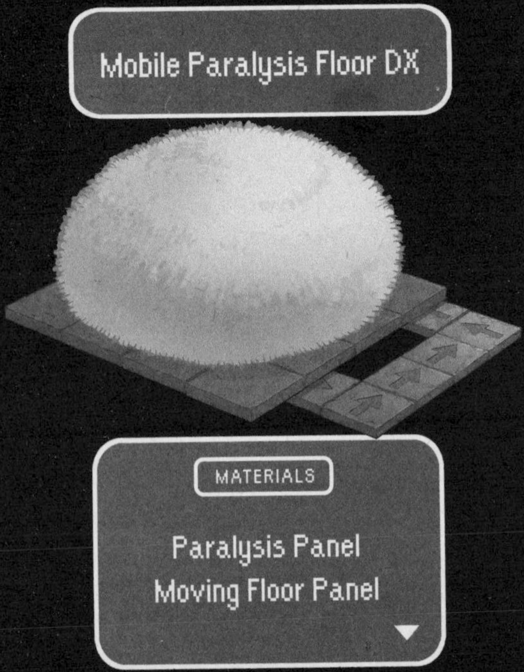
Mobile Paralysis Floor DX
MATERIALS
Paralysis Panel
Moving Floor Panel

Those who lurk beneath the cover...

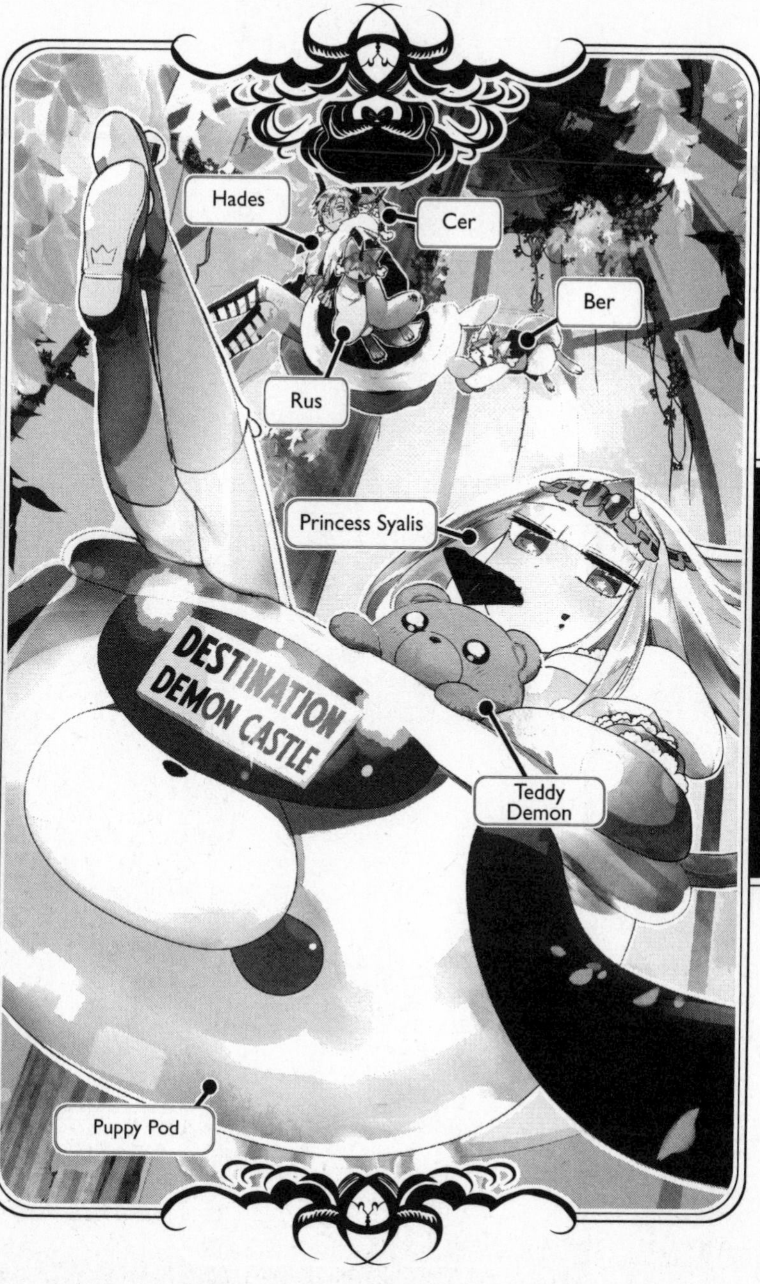
Hades
Cer
Ber
Rus
Princess Syalis
DESTINATION
DEMON CASTLE
Teddy
Demon
Puppy Pod

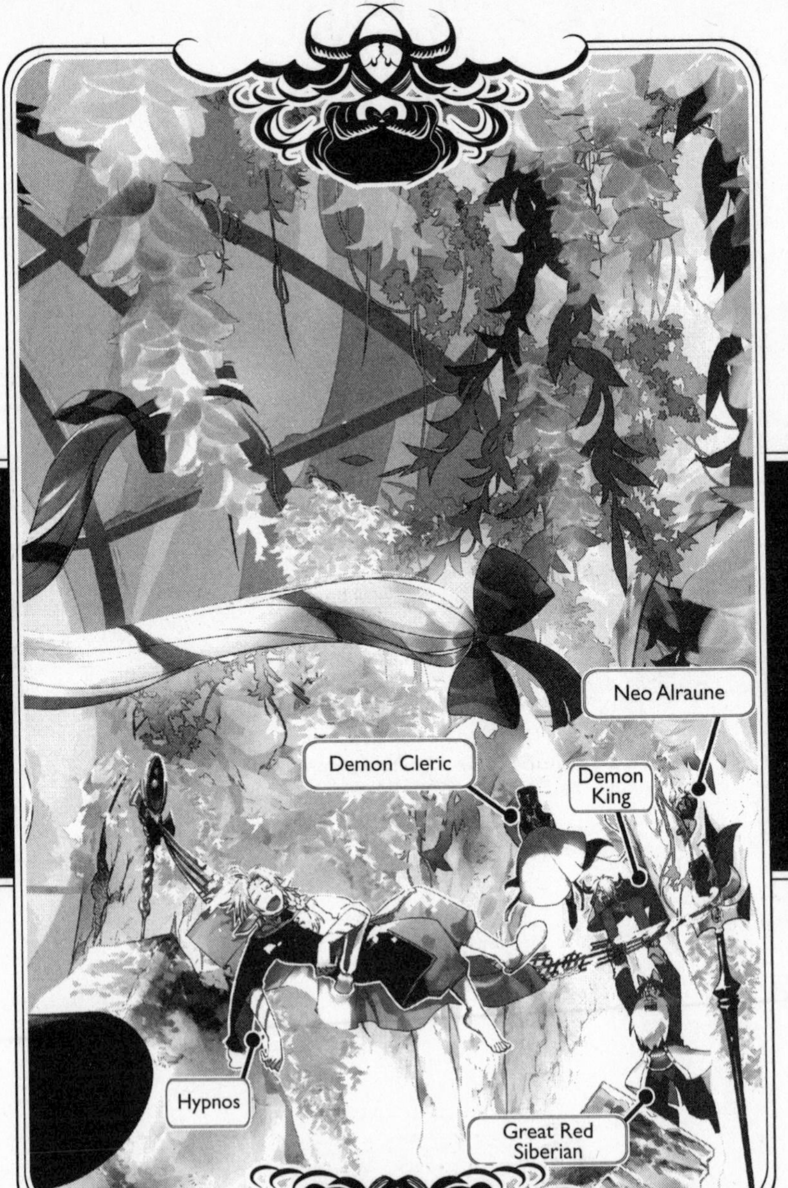
Neo Alraune
Demon Cleric
Demon King
Hypnos
Great Red Siberian

SLEEPY PRINCESS IN THE DEMON CASTLE

4

Shonen Sunday Edition

STORY AND ART BY

KAGIJI KUMANOMATA

MAOUJO DE OYASUMI Vol. 4
by Kagiji KUMANOMATA
© 2016 Kagiji KUMANOMATA
All rights reserved.
Original Japanese edition published by SHOGAKUKAN.
English translation rights in the United States of America, Canada,
the United Kingdom, Ireland, Australia and New Zealand arranged
with SHOGAKUKAN.

TRANSLATION **TETSUICHIRO MIYAKI**

ENGLISH ADAPTATION **ANNETTE ROMAN**

TOUCH-UP ART & LETTERING **SUSAN DAIGLE-LEACH**

COVER & INTERIOR DESIGN **ALICE LEWIS**

EDITOR **ANNETTE ROMAN**

Printed in the U.S.A.

Published by VIZ Media, LLC
P.O. Box 77010
San Francisco, CA 94107

10 9 8 7 6 5 4 3 2 1
First printing, December 2018

viz.com   shonensunday.com

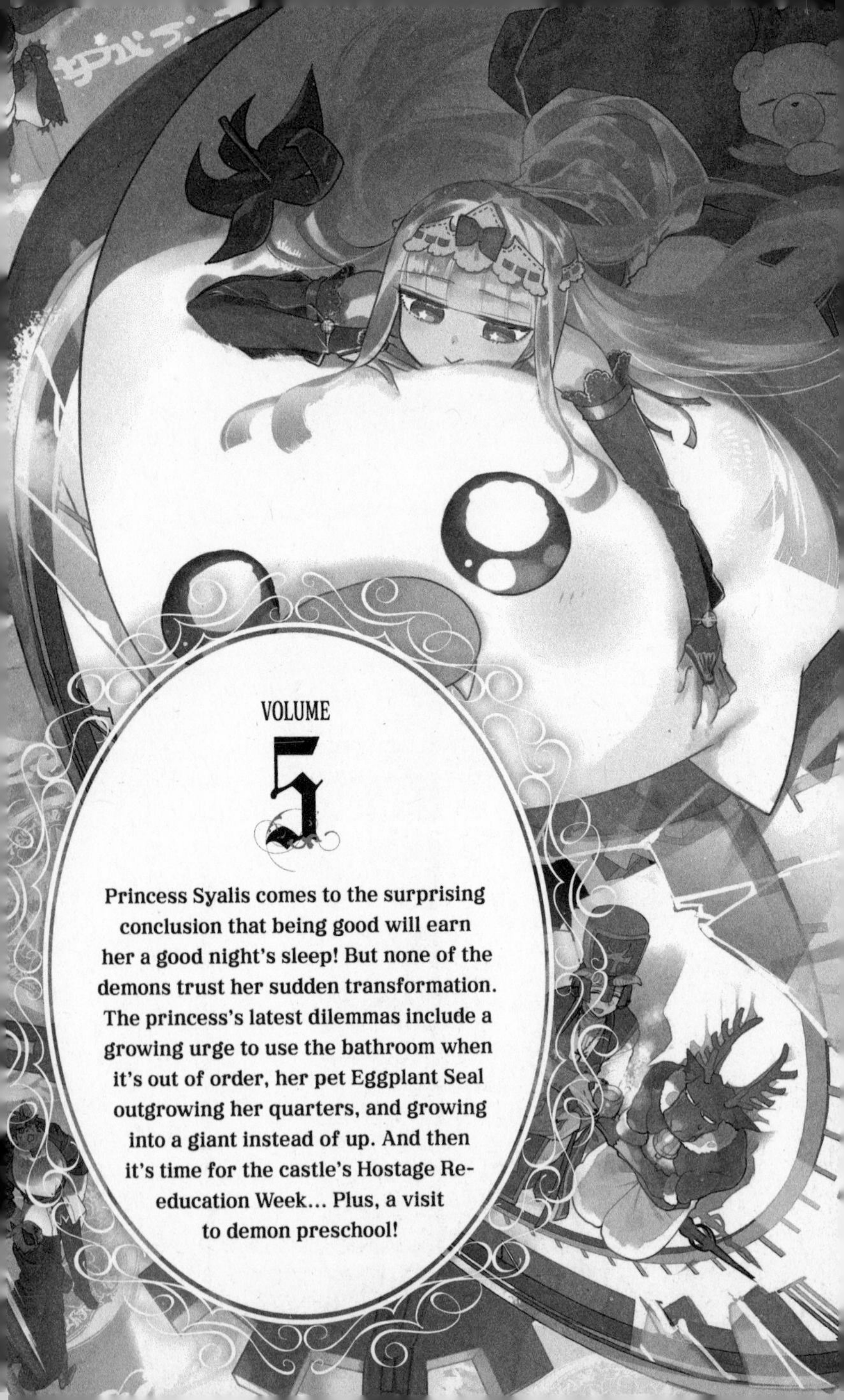
VOLUME
5
Princess Syalis comes to the surprising conclusion that being good will earn her a good night's sleep! But none of the demons trust her sudden transformation. The princess's latest dilemmas include a growing urge to use the bathroom when it's out of order, her pet Eggplant Seal outgrowing her quarters, and growing into a giant instead of up. And then it's time for the castle's Hostage Re-education Week... Plus, a visit to demon preschool!

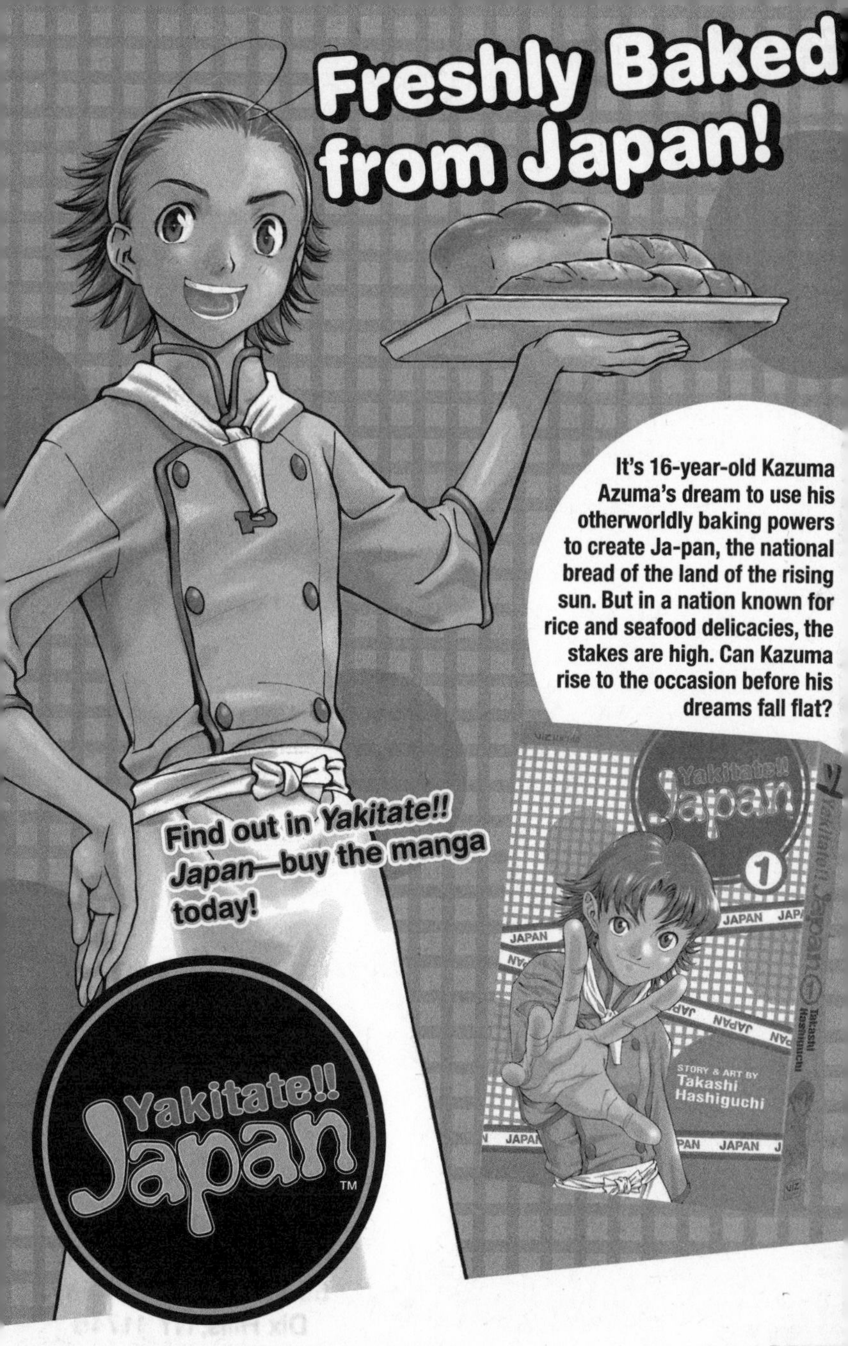
Freshly Baked from Japan!
It's 16-year-old Kazuma Azuma's dream to use his otherworldly baking powers to create Ja-pan, the national bread of the land of the rising sun. But in a nation known for rice and seafood delicacies, the stakes are high. Can Kazuma rise to the occasion before his dreams fall flat?
Find out in Yakitate!! Japan—buy the manga today!
Yakitate!! Japan
1
JAPAN
STORY & ART BY
Takashi Hashiguchi
Yakitate!! Japan™
VIZ

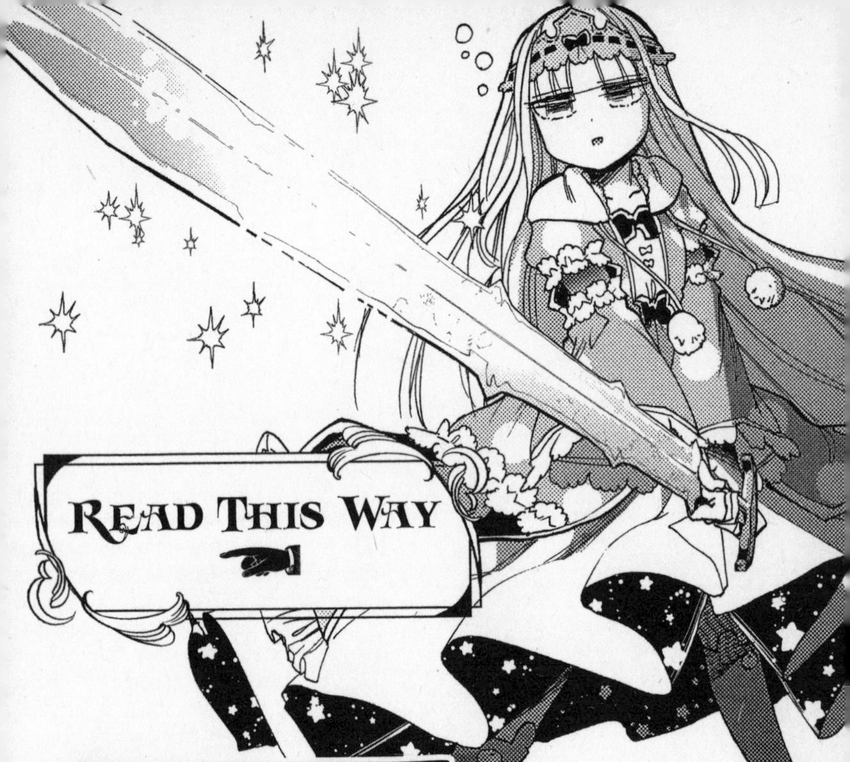
READ THIS WAY

STOP!

You may be reading the wrong way!

In keeping with the original Japanese comic format, this book reads from right to left—so action, sound effects and word balloons are completely reversed to preserve the orientation of the original artwork.

Check out the diagram shown here to get the hang of things, and then turn to the other side of the book to get started!

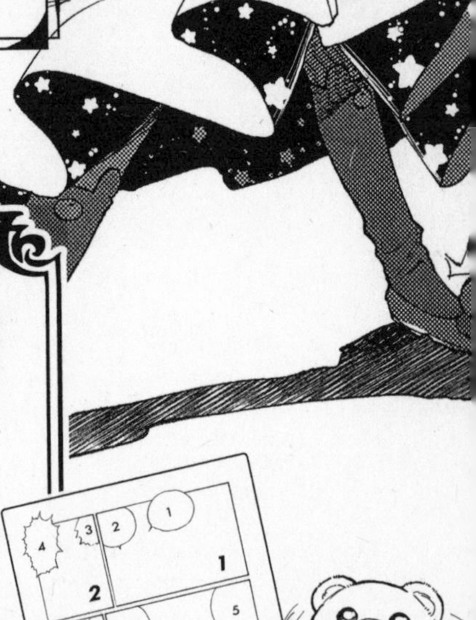

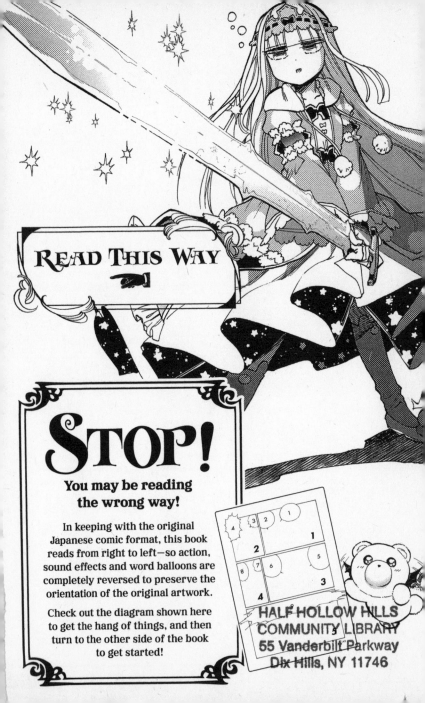